"The book by Maria Pierri, a passionate and recognized connoisseur of 'coincidences', can be read as an engrossing detective novel of historical reconstruction as it unfolds towards its resolution, elegantly written and full of surprises, and opening up unexpected new fields of thought. Which is not to say that it actually is a novel: rather, it is real History with a capital H, thoroughly documented with a precise investigative method which revisits one of the most mysterious and controversial areas of Freudian research, that of telepathy."

– **Stefano Bolognini**, *past president of the IPA and the Italian Psychoanalytic Society*

"With rigorous documentation, including previously unpublished material, and elegant writing, Maria Pierri conducts a passionate investigation of hypnosis, occultism, suggestion, 'coincidences and misunderstandings', studied by Freud, who applied his scientific mentality to them. The secrets and enigmas around the origins of psychoanalysis, the deep ties and conflicts between the pioneers 'who made the venture' with Freud will emerge from the courageous search for that 'elsewhere' of human thoughts we call unconscious, with which we are confronted daily in clinical practice and theory."

– **Paola Golinelli**, *training analyst, Italian Psychoanalytic Society. Author of Psychoanalytic Reflection on Writing, Cinema and the Arts. Routledge, 2021*

"Maria Pierri's work is not only an excellent example of historical and archival research into the interest of emergent psychoanalysis in telepathic events, but a radical demonstration – thanks to the 'work as a double' performed by thought-transmission – of how unsustainable it is to maintain that Freud was a monist. In this way, through the wealth of phenomena being observed, the author opens up a new direction for study and theoretical enquiry that will send us back to Freud, *differently* every time, and to his very early intuition of a *psychic field* that is created in the analytic relationship."

– **Maurizio Balsamo**, *training analyst, Italian Psychoanalytic Society. Maître de Conférences et Directeur de Recherche, UFR Études Psychanalytiques, Université Paris – Diderot*

Sigmund Freud and The Forsyth Case

Sigmund Freud and The Forsyth Case uses newly discovered primary sources to investigate one of Sigmund Freud's most mysterious clinical experiences, the Forsyth case. The book details Pierri's attempts to recover the lost original case notes, which are published here for the first time, to identify the patient involved and to set the case into the broader frame of Freud's work.

Maria Pierri begins with a preliminary illustration of the case, its historical context, and how it connects to Freud's interests in "thought-transmission," or telepathy. The author illustrates the possibility of a psychoanalytic interpretation of the transference and countertransference elements potentially conveyed by certain "magical" coincidences during the analysis, introducing the reader to a psychopathology of everyday life of the setting. The book also explores Freud's further investigations into thought transmission, focusing on a meeting of the Secret Committee in October 1919 and his clinical work with his own daughter Anna.

Sigmund Freud and The Forsyth Case features supplementary historical materials, adding valuable insight to the context and meaning of the case. It will be essential reading for psychoanalysts in practice and in training, as well as academics and scholars of psychoanalytic studies, spirituality, and the history of psychology. It is complemented by *Occultism and the Origins of Psychoanalysis: Freud, Ferenczi and the Challenge of Thought Transference.*

Maria Pierri is a psychiatrist and child neuropsychiatrist, formerly researcher and adjunct professor at the Psychiatric Clinic, Medical School, University of Padua. She is a training analyst of the Italian Psychoanalytical Society and International Psychoanalytical Association and member of the editorial board of the *Rivista di Psicoanalisi.*

History of Psychoanalysis

Series Editor Peter L. Rudnytsky

This series seeks to present outstanding new books that illuminate any aspect of the history of psychoanalysis from its earliest days to the present, and to reintroduce classic texts to contemporary readers.

Other titles in the series

A Forgotten Freudian
The Passion of Karl Stern
Daniel Burston

The Skin-Ego
A New Translation by Naomi Segal
Didier Anzieu

Karl Abraham
Life and Work, a Biography
Anna Bentinck van Schoonheten

The Freudian Orient
Early Psychoanalysis, Anti-Semitic Challenge, and the Vicissitudes of Orientalist Discourse
Frank F. Scherer

Occultism and the Origins of Psychoanalysis
Freud, Ferenczi and the Challenge of Thought Transference
Maria Pierri, Translated by Adam Elgar

Sigmund Freud and the Forsyth Case
Coincidences and Thought-Transmission in Psychoanalysis
Maria Pierri, Translated by Adam Elgar

For further information about this series please visit www.routledge.com/The-History-of-Psychoanalysis-Series/book-series/KARNHIPSY

Sigmund Freud and The Forsyth Case

Coincidences and Thought-Transmission in Psychoanalysis

Maria Pierri

Translated by Adam Elgar

LONDON AND NEW YORK

Cover image: © Getty Images

First published in English 2023
by Routledge
4 Park Square, Milton Park, Abingdon, Oxon OX14 4RN

and by Routledge
605 Third Avenue, New York, NY 10158

Routledge is an imprint of the Taylor & Francis Group, an informa business

Translated by Adam Elgar

Published in Italian as Un Enigma per il dottor Freud. La sfida della telepatia by Franco Angeli 2018

British Library Cataloguing-in-Publication Data
A catalogue record for this book is available from the British Library

ISBN: 978-1-032-15957-7 (hbk)
ISBN: 978-1-032-15958-4 (pbk)
ISBN: 978-1-003-24648-0 (ebk)

DOI: 10.4324/9781003246480

Typeset in Times New Roman
by Apex CoVantage, LLC

Contents

Prologue

Telepathy, superstitions, and mushrooms

In the Fifties, Ernest Jones was working on the draft of *Sigmund Freud Life and Work*. His wife Katherine Jokl helped him collect and organise all the documentary material – letters, manuscripts, notes – that he would bring back after his visits to Maresfield Gardens, the London house where Sigmund Freud lived in the last few months of his life. Kitty would type the Gothic manuscript, and she was also in charge of reviewing and editing the drafts.

Anna Freud would receive them as soon as they were ready.

After reading chapter XIV, "Occultism," Anna wrote Jones a letter quite clearly expressing her regret, showing she was not entirely satisfied with the way he had treated the subject, for his complete lack of comprehension of a topic her father had been so passionate about.[1]

Dear Ernest,

I spent several nights with all the interesting things which you given me to read. First your two chapters.

I was delighted with chapter XV on ART. It was refreshing to see you cut right through the arguments which had collected around this subject and which had always left me dissatisfied.

No one could have caught more explicitly than you have done here what my father felt and knew about the subject and from what he remained remote. It is most convincing and satisfying.

It is perhaps very natural that I did not feel quite the same about chapter XIV on OCCULTISM. It gave me the feeling that here you remained an outside critic instead of seeing it with my father's eyes as you had done with "art." This may be inevitable on the basis of your intellectual disagreement with him on this point. But I am not so sure. I have an idea that you would not have disagreed if you could have felt his feelings about the matter more fully.

Perhaps I can refer back in this respect to our lunch conversation last week. You remember what I told you about the "superstitions" acted out in our mushroom hunts. It was all such nonsense but such good fun at the same time as if we were playing to be people who believe in things of this kind. There must have been

DOI: 10.4324/9781003246480-1

other pretend games which he played with us and which I cannot remember at the moment. But the whole spirit of acting seems such a familiar one as if it had appeared in many respects, not only this one. I believe what interested him in superstitious attitudes was no more than findings the remnants of it even in highly rational people and making fun of it.

This, of course, does not extend to the question of thought transference. There, I believe, he was trying to be "fair," i.e. not to treat it as other people had treated psycho-analysis. I never could see that he himself believed in more than the possibility of two unconscious minds communicating with each other without the help of a conscious bridge. In all other cases he really tried to disprove the occurrence. I remember very vividly discussing one or two instances of this kind with him when I had had dreams which coincided in a surprising way with occurrences in other people's minds. What he looked for was always the unconscious identification with the consequent heightening of perceptiveness for the other person's thought and feeling processes.

Of course, I agree with your argumentation that the subject must have fascinated him, as well as repelled him. Only I fear that the reader of your chapter will be impressed more by evidence of the former than the latter.

Will people after reading this say exactly what my father always feared they would say if psycho-analysis and occultism came to near each other? By the way, Ferenczi also did this thought reading experiment with me and he gave me the same distressing impression of expecting results. Once there really was a parallel between his thoughts and mine and he felt overjoyed.

Forgive this long dissertation. . . .

Love
Anna

Anna Freud never wrote on the transmission of thought. With Paul Roazen, one of the first historians who had become interested in Sigmund Freud and the psychoanalytic movement in the Sixties, she denied ever taking part in telepathic experiments. A few years later, she mentioned it to Christian Moreau, a psychiatrist with a psychoanalytic background, who was interested in understanding "paranormal" phenomena. With him, she recalled the "telepathy" experiments (guessing the topic the other person was intensely thinking about) conducted with her father and Sàndor Ferenczi in the spring of 1925: according to Freud, they would turn out well enough, especially when he himself played the medium and then analysed his associations.[2] In any case, she treated them as summer pastimes.

By contrast, with Lou Andreas Salomé she would more enthusiastically recall her father's so-called "superstitions" and his magic tricks:

> Listening to Anna talking about her father; about picking mushrooms when they were children. When they went collecting mushrooms he always told them to go into the wood quietly and he still does this; there must be no chattering and they must roll up the bags they have brought under their arms, so

> that the mushrooms shall not notice; when their father found one he would cover it quickly with his hat, as though it were a butterfly. The little children – and now his grandchildren – used to believe what he said, while the bigger ones smiled at their credulity; even Anna did this, when he told her to put fresh flowers every day at the shrine of the Virgin which was near the wood, so that it might help them in their search. The children were paid in pennies for the mushrooms they had found, while the best mushroom of all (it was always Ernst who found it) got a florin. It was the quality and not the quantity of the mushrooms that mattered.
>
> (Andreas-Salomé, 1921)[3]

Jean Martin Freud, too, when he collected his memories of his father and family life, recalled these playful aspects of his childhood: the walks in the woods that had the flavour of a marvellous story, with an exciting plot full of emotions, but also the walks around Vienna, pacing like the Italian *Bersaglieri*. His father, when crossing the *Franzjosefkai* crenelated with chimney-pots and other adornments jutting up, would tell a favourite joke about "the coffee-party of the devil's grandmother," who, flying over the town with her best coffee service's enormous tray, distributed on the roofs a large quantity of pots, jugs, and cups and saucers, where they were still stuck.[4]

Unlike Anna's, the memories of Freud's first-born feature a degree of bitterness for that mythical father. Martin doesn't hide his childhood fear of those mushrooms that could have been poisonous: "few summers passed without visitors suffering from acute food poisoning, occasionally fatal," but he claims, "We had no fear. Father had taught us much about fungi." And he remembers how the very presence of the alarming red mushrooms with white spots, during the exploration phase, was helpful in identifying the area which contained *porcino* mushrooms:

> Once the area had been found, father was ready to lead his small band of troops, each young soldier taking up a position and beginning the skirmish at proper intervals, like a well-trained infantry platoon attacking through a forest. We played that we were chasing some flighty and elusive game, and there was always a competition to decide on the best hunter. Father always won. . . . When father had spotted a really perfect fungi specimen, he would run to it and flung his hat over it before giving a shrill signal on the flat silver whistle he carried in his waistcoat pocket to summon his platoon. We would all rush towards the sound of the whistle, and only when the concentration was complete would father remove the hat and allow us to inspect and admire the spoil.
>
> (1957, pp. 58–59)

For Anna, the youngest, captivated by her father, and who managed to inherit exclusively his magnificent "spoil," psychoanalysis was also a way to continue experiencing those excursions with him, in the troubles and exciting illusions of her childhood. She never talked to anyone about her analysis. Martin himself, back from the war, discovered it only when he asked what his sister did when she went to their father's consulting room in the evening. Lou Salomé knew about it, and she kept the secret of that consulting room's magic circle:

> These mushrooms which give away their presence by springing up out of the soil seem to me to be a living parallel on the fairy-story plane of Freud's archaeological discoveries. As a teacher Freud took the fairy-story half in earnest, half in jest. When one of the children's balls came in again through his window after he had threatened to confiscate it, the ball disappeared, never to return, and even today he apparently does not know what has happened to it.
>
> (Andreas-Salomé, 1921)[5]

Notes

1 Unpublished letter by A. Freud to E. Jones, 24/11/1955, Ernest Jones collection, P04-C-C-06. The Archives of the British Psychoanalytical Society have granted us kind permission to reproduce this letter. Copyright @ the Estate of Anna Freud. Published by arrangement with the Marsh Agency Ltd; Courtesy of Jackie Jones copyright.
2 Freud, circular letter 15/3/1925, in Jones *III*.
3 In Pfeiffer, 1972.
4 M. Freud, 1957, p. 27.
5 In Pfeiffer, 1972.

Chapter 1

Coincidences of the psychoanalytic setting

A strange home visit

M. de Fortgibu and his plum-pudding

In his encyclopaedic collection of testimonies, *L'Inconnu et les problèmes psychiques* (1900), Camille Flammarion reports an anecdote told by the poet Emil Deschamps which, if not true, was certainly well constructed:

> In his childhood, being at a boarding-school at Orleans, he chanced to find himself on a certain day at table with a M. de Fortgibu, an émigré recently returned from England, who made him taste a plum-pudding, a dish almost unknown at that time in France. The remembrance of that feast had by degrees faded from his memory, when, ten years later, passing by a restaurant on the Boulevard Poissonière, he perceived inside it a plum-pudding of most excellent appearance. He went in and asked for a slice of it, but was informed that the whole had been ordered by another customer. "M. de Fortgibu," cried the dame du comptoir, seeing that Deschamps looked disappointed, would you have the goodness to share your plum-pudding with this gentleman?" Deschamps had some difficulty in recognizing M. de Fortgibu in an elderly man, with powdered hair, dressed in a colonel's uniform, who was taking his dinner at one of the tables. The officer said it would give him pleasure to offer part of his plum-pudding to the gentleman.
>
> Long years had passed since Deschamps had even thought of plum-pudding, or of M. de Fortgibu. One day he was invited to a dinner where there was to be a real English plum-pudding. He accepted the invitation, but told the lady of the house, as a joke, that he knew M. de Fortgibu would be of the party, and he caused much amusement by giving the reason. The day came, and he went to the house. Ten guests occupied the ten places at table and a magnificent plum-pudding was served. They were beginning to laugh at Deschamps about his M. de Fortgibu, when the door opened and a servant announced: "M. de Fortgibu." An old man entered, walking feebly, with the help of a servant. He went slowly, greatly disconcerted. Was it a vision? Or was it a joke? It was the time of the Carnival, and Deschamps was sure it was a trick. But as the old man approached him he was forced to recognize M. de

DOI: 10.4324/9781003246480-2

> Fortgibu in person. "My hair stood up on my head," he said. "Don Juan, in the chef d'oeuvre of Mozart, was not more terrified by his guest of stone." All was soon explained. M. di Fortgibu had been asked to dinner by a friend who lived in the same house, but had mistaken the door of his apartment.
>
> (p. 194–195)

The curious series of coincidences, a kind of game played by chance, well conveys the gratuitousness and also the frivolity of certain insignificant events that have no meaning and do not require one, which accompany the circumstances of our daily life, surprising us and making us construct the plot of a story that we can tell. M. de Fortgibu with his plum pudding could be the protagonist of a nonsense poem, a limerick, or one of those nursery rhymes with no more meaning than the music of the rhymes themselves, the rhythm of the refrain, their formal distinctiveness.

If we had any further information about the relationship between Emil Deschamps and that M de Fortgibu who pops up like a double, an elder brother, ready to share his plum pudding, we could expatiate on the deeply evocative significance of the rapport between these two men and also metaphorically summon up the passing of time which seems to move cyclically at the different ages of life, the encounter with our origins and with that precious maternal breast which the father presents for the new-born infant to taste.

In any case, we can reflect on the apparently anodyne anecdote: let's observe how, in its repetition, the scene of the encounter changes and evolves, the two characters are transformed, modify their relationship by becoming rivals, grow old, and finally exchange roles, so that on the third occasion, it is Deschamps who could invite M. di Fortgibu to his own table this time and offer him the plum pudding, which now belongs to him.

At the same time that Flammarion was publishing *L'Inconnu*, Théodore Flournoy, in *From India to the Planet Mars: A Study of a Case of Somnambulism with Glossolalia* (1899), was wondering what imponderable influences might connect organisms and what unknown waves might give rise to the phenomenon of telepathy. Criticising mystics and occultists for only giving consideration to spiritual communication regardless of the subject, he wrote:

> innumerable waves . . . coming from all other living beings, shock at every moment a given brain: their efforts are counterbalanced, or their resultant too slight to be perceived. But they exist none the less in reality, and I confess I do not understand those who reproach telepathy with being strange, mystical, occult, supernormal, etc.
>
> (p. 387–388)

In 1929, seeking a guiding thread in the chaos of existence, Frigyes Karinthy, an eccentric Hungarian thinker with a passion for finding connections between small things, formulated the theory of six degrees of separation based on the assumption of a world that had become so small that – he maintained – using a chain of only interpersonal acquaintances, he could contact anyone by passing through no more than five individuals (1929).

The "small-world phenomenon" was confirmed in 1967 through a study by Stanley Milgram, but today, even though the internet has reduced the degrees of separation,[1] the deep fabric that unites people and objects is still a subject of investigation.

Rather like Flammarion, Paul Auster made a collection of true anecdotes, personally experienced or reported by friends and acquaintances. Not content with this, by means of a radio broadcast, over the course of a year, he was able to collect over 4000 accounts, "dispatches, reports from the front lines of personal experience." *The Red Notebook* (1992) and *True Tales of American Life* (2001) are anthologies of true stories which seem to have been invented to challenge every expectation and reveal the mysterious and impenetrable forces at work in our lives. Misunderstandings, coincidences, near-death experiences, improbable encounters and premonitions, but also telepathic dreams . . . all of these seem to affirm the lack of an adequate definition of reality.

Everyday existence seems impregnated with creativity.

In the entanglements scattered through our existence, the countless possibilities of chance open up unexpected choices, unknown paths ready to be filled with meaning. Certain coincidences, diabolical or providential, evoking wonder and fear, make us think of a dream becoming reality, a novel that turns into real life, as if the will of chance and its unpredictable links were meeting the needs of that story which everyone alive is trying to construct. Like slips or mistakes, they involve those characteristics of surprise, revelation, proximity – familiar and estranging – which accompany insight into the manifestation of that unknown power that is the unconscious.

The maternal in the circumstances of the setting: the psychoanalytic clock

At the start of the century, when Sigmund Freud began to investigate the psychic meaning to be attributed to certain everyday phenomena – errors, forgetting, carelessness, and bungled actions that only apparently seemed unintentional and that were usually explained as inattention or pure chance – he was able to demonstrate that, like the representations of dreaming and so-called "free" associations, when subjected to analytic investigation, these actions revealed themselves to be precisely determined by unconscious processes. It is just the same with insignificant decisions of little importance, when "we would like to claim that we could just as well have acted otherwise: that we have acted of our free – and unmotivated – will":[2] for example, in thinking of a number or a name at random or in choosing favourite numbers. Freud highlighted the presence of highly complex motivations and ideational sequences outside the range of consciousness.

To confirm his theory of internal psychic causality, in the final chapter of *The Psychopathology of Everyday Life*,[3] he provided examples of paranoid delusion and superstition which equally, in their different ways, disregard the category of the accidental in external reality. He explained how both are sustained by the unconscious awareness of their internal motivations, denied and displaced into the external world: in paranoia, the behaviour of others is interpreted in minute detail so as to draw extensive self-referential conclusions from it; in superstition, certain real events appear suffused with omens.

In order to differentiate the interpretative mode of psychoanalysis from the superstitious outlook, Freud introduced an anecdote taken from his habitual experience with an elderly patient, the often-cited "very old lady"[4] who had been a secure source of financial support in the early years of his professional life. For many years he had performed the same professional services for her twice every day: applying some drops of collyrium to her eye and giving her a morphine injection. Freud explained that, owing to the uniformity of the circumstances, unconscious thoughts very often managed to find expression while he was on his way to the patient and while he was treating her. Errors and inattention that were by no means a matter of chance crept in because of these automatic actions, and Freud was able to interpret their meaning in detail: going to the wrong floor, often the floor above (an expression of his frustrated ambition)[5] or pouring some drops of morphine into the eye instead of collyrium (associated with the unconscious idea of doing "violence to the old woman" and having "sexual intercourse with his own mother").[6]

These same thoughts had also played a part in a dream where, half dressed, he was climbing a poorly lit flight of stairs and passed her maid coming down: analysing this, he confronted his feelings of ambition, scorn, and shame but also his anxieties about death.[7]

In September 1900, after the summer break, a mistake occurred for which one of his two usual cab-drivers was responsible. Freud tells the story:

> On my return from my holidays my thoughts immediately turned to the patients who were to claim my attention in the year's work that was just beginning. My first visit was to a very old lady for whom I had for many years performed the same professional services twice every day. . . . She is over ninety years old; it is therefore natural to ask oneself at the beginning of each year's treatment how much longer she is likely to live. On the day I am speaking about I was in a hurry and called a cab to take me to her house. Every cabman on the rank in front of my house knew the old lady's address, as they had all often taken me there. But on this day it happened that the cabman did not draw up in front of her house but in front of a house with the same number in a nearby street which ran parallel and was in fact of a similar appearance. I noticed the error and reproached the cabman with it, and he apologized. Now is it of any significance that I was driven to a house where the old lady was not to be found?
>
> (1901, pp. 256–257)

Freud rejects the superstitious interpretation – the foretelling of the patient's imminent demise, which had suddenly flashed into his mind – and uses the episode as an example of "an accident without any further meaning," occurring with no involvement of his psychic life. As he makes clear:

> The case would have been quite different if I had made the journey on foot, and while "deep in thought," or through "absent-mindedness" had come to the house in the parallel street instead of the right one. This I should not explain as an accident but as an action that had an unconscious aim and required interpretation. My interpretation of "going astray" like this would probably have had to be that I did not expect to see the old lady for much longer.
>
> (*ibid.*)[8]

Freud takes no account of the unconscious collaboration on the part of the cabman, that double who accompanies him and, perhaps infected by his haste and his resistance to resuming work with the patient after the interruption, in erring/losing his way makes Freud face his anxiety about loss. But today we wonder what to think when certain happenings, mistakes, or coincidences occur in the course of analysis, within the automatic actions of mutual habit, in the to-and-fro rhythm which composes the texture and junctions of the relationship in a deep and invisible entanglement.

Where can certain visits to the patient's home take us? Who accompanies us and who is really driving the cab on the analytic journey?

Continuing with the metaphor, wasn't the same horse summoned by Freud in the representation of the Id, even giving the example of situations in which the rider, the Ego, "who has to hold in check the superior strength of the horse . . . is obliged to guide it where it wants to go"?[9]

In Freud's anecdote we notice an image that is far from anodyne: the coachman. He is an important character; just think of the charioteer of the ancient representation of the human soul in the Platonic allegory of the winged chariot (Plato, *Phaedrus*).

But let's go on: without realising it, in the example of caring for the very old lady, Freud is talking about his first experiment with that setting which will later become unique to psychoanalytic treatment and is still considered one of its distinctive elements: the set-up characterised by the rhythmic spatiotemporal stability of the sessions which take place almost daily, by the patient's "leasing" of a certain working hour, and by the fact that the journey has no predetermined conclusion. It is an entirely unique feature that Freud will try to introduce, repeating the therapeutic arrangement of Breuer at Anna O's bedside: for his part, Freud is motivated by the difficulties of making inroads into the neuroses on the one hand and the analyst's own need for survival on the other.[10]

It's actually an ingenious invention.

What entirely unexpected elements can be stirred up and highlighted in the two people involved by the establishment of a routine structured in this way? What psychic potentialities can develop and emerge in the encounter, in its daily repetitions or in its spontaneous variations after such a synchronising of rhythms? It is not by chance that Fachinelli would call the psychoanalytic setting the "telepathic clock."[11]

Let's ask ourselves once again: what did Freud experience during the six years of attending that lady who was important enough to feature in the composition of the dream about Irma and capable of evoking his old nurse and his mother? Moreover, what might he have unconsciously introduced into the structuring of the analytic setting from that rhythmic and automatic pattern of care?

On 9 June 1901, near the start of the summer vacation, he wrote to Fliess

> My ancient lady, whom I have been visiting twice a day regularly, was taken to the country yesterday, and I am looking at the clock every fifteen minutes to see whether I am not keeping her waiting too long for her injection. Thus we still feel our shackles even after they have been removed and do not really know how to enjoy our freedom.

Perhaps Freud had discovered that the stability of the tie, this unwritten contract, these "shackles" could also offer containment for the anxieties of waiting and the hungry intensity of his passionate nature, being someone who on certain occasions showed that he could experience even a small variation on a repeated theme as potentially dangerous: arriving in a street that is not his own but a parallel one leaves him faced with an empty house, with loss, and seems also to introduce him to a parallel universe of his own.

"All things are chained, knotted, in love . . . "

Coincidence – from "*cum incidere*: "to fall upon together," onto the same point – makes us think of an idea that "falls in" (*einfallen*) two individuals simultaneously. It is perhaps a "free" association "*à deux*," in the specific sense of being psychically determined by the encounter.[12] It certainly has something to do with the transference, with obstacles and mistakes, when coincidences throng the process of "falling" in love just as they do at the start of analysis:

> She was in her room, kneeling on the floor with her head buried in a chair and sobbing in passionate longing for her friend and helper the barrister, when at that very moment the door opened and in he came to visit her . . . accidents which seem preconcerted like this are to be found in every love story.
>
> (Freud, 1899 [1941], p. 624)[13]

It is sometimes a matter of subtle details, similarities, or cruxes on which the unconscious transferential texture is woven and supported: a name, a date, a circumstance, a place, a physical feature of the analyst, and so on. A closeness and kinship can be built up from "slight resemblances,"[14] offering initial reassurance about the strangeness of the encounter, its absolute lack of familiarity, like something predestined: the analyst is hard of hearing, like the patient's father; he lives in the district where the patient grew up; she has the same name as the patient's sister who died in infancy or the mother he never knew; she comes from the same country as his parents . . .[15]

There can be the surprise of more elaborate and unexpected convergences: what are we to think of certain correspondences at the start of treatment?

An analyst unwittingly decides to start the analysis on the patient's birthday and then discovers that it is also the date of his wedding anniversary, a marriage never consummated: this speaks of the patient's tireless search for that primal relationship with the mother which was never consummated and which the patient repeatedly tries to resume in his love life. A patient asks for help because she is looking for a twin soul after breaking up with a boyfriend who was born on the same day as she was, and the analyst is surprised to hear that this is his own birthday: is it perhaps the expression of a desire to rediscover a part of oneself, a double or a counterpart, from whom the patient felt prematurely divided?[16]

A seriously ill patient who has recently started treatment surprises her analyst by telling her that she is going on holiday to the same island as the analyst, as if wanting to reassure her about a possible shared absence.[17]

Enquiries among our colleagues teach us how common such coincidences are, even though they are rarely reported in the literature, or else with a certain embarrassment. They are joint constructions of such sensory vitality that they bring with them a sensation of omnipotence, an illusion that could make us think of hallucination or delusion: as in the example of a patient who, as soon as she has lain down on the couch, points to a painting in front of her and says, "That's my house." Or the patient who, after a first negative experience, decides to begin a new treatment and discovers that the second analyst has a consulting room in the same building as the first. Could there be a worse start – or a better one?[18]

These incidents, which could be attributed to mistakes or the whim of chance, entail a remarkable and "ultra-clear" way of remembering and reconstructing.[19] They answer the patient's need to "return to the scene of the crime,"[20] the need for that automatic pilot to guide him in his tenacious and subterranean search for a real event which, in the concrete and tangible reality of the analytic setting, might recreate the original circumstances of his *own beginning*, with the "basic faults"[21] from which to begin again, and elicit the analyst's inclination to accompany the patient, to adapt as requested to his forms as a particular mode of "erring" or mistaking, and also, in his own specific and personal environmental function, reactivating the failures of the context.[22]

There are creative modes of communication in play here which we could consider as belonging to a primitive stage of unconscious identification: a correspondence, convergence, confluence of two into one.[23] From the newborn's first experience with the nipple to later romantic encounters, a multi-determined aura of aggregation seems to condense around chance points of coincidence, becoming the matrix for the process of illusion-disillusion.

How will these convergences develop in analytic treatment?

Granoff and Rey write that certain facts are never "pure" and "continually mobilize beliefs, superstitions, forms of faith, or fragments of desire."[24] We can imagine them silently becoming part of the relationship's heritage, emphasising alliance and good understanding, mutual satisfaction and familiarity in distinction, as in the relationship of couples when they have the same thought at the same moment.

Coincidences become fundamental elements in the initial establishment of the setting: "mute" junctions with the potential for "speech" that come to the fore in states of impasse and reversals of perspective when, as Bleger claims,[25] the process is located in the framing.

And we can also think that the setting, representing the dimension in which coinciding but not conscious parts of the patient's Self and the analyst's are progressively deposited and gradually organised through the rhythmicality, uniformity, and automatic activity of habit, possesses its own dynamic capable of developing in parallel to the dynamic of the analytic dialogue to which it forms a background and a frame. Through the events of the setting (the not always fully appreciated interruptions, variations, etc.), a potential for expression comes into being, which instantly seems to construct and make visible the reciprocity and the threatened automatic interconnection, a potential for thought and speech able to configure an "everyday psychopathology of the setting."[26]

How, for example, should we interpret the return and emergence of unexpected and almost irritating coincidences in phases of impasse during treatment?[27]

These are often the conditions in which dreams or associations arise, bringing with them a strange telepathic effect in the analyst. The co-incident may remain unknown or risk being freighted with an excess of meaning. Considering these phenomena as belonging to areas of extrasensory, occult communication, or relegating them forever to inexplicable and meaningless chance can lead to mysticism, to an interpretive frenzy, or, conversely, to exclusion of the psychosensory, to the mortification of a potentially valuable area that we can instead occasionally find useful. In certain hidden convergences of the preconscious, we can recognise once again the deterministic action of the oneiric at work, in which "*automatic activities*" characterised by correctness and reliability work with the "dexterity of a conjurer."[28]

Recognising in these combinations "a specific construction that could only have been generated in precisely the way that it was by means of an interaction between this therapist and this patient at this moment in the therapy"[29] may lead us to identify them early on both as a possible meeting place for a symptomatic collusion between analyst and patient – a collusion that then works as resistance and blocks the realisation of the experience in a pathological shared misunderstanding – and as a starting point for the desire to reconstruct, from the "co-incidental" event which reveals the entanglement towards a distinction in dreams and representations.

Because of the unconscious origin of the countertransference, these *occult convergences* possess the same informative potential as a dream or a mistake[30] and form part of a flow of free associations *à deux*. In my opinion, they are slips *à deux*, and they go on to conclude the final chapter of *The Psychopathology of Everyday Life* on which Freud continued to work throughout his life.

The reading of authoritative examples provided by the psychoanalytic literature has encouraged me to give these incidents credit and to look for their potential meaning, which, in the case of slips, can be traced back to "incompletely suppressed psychical material, which, although pushed away by consciousness, has nevertheless not been robbed of all capacity for expressing itself."[31]

Coincidences in analysis: sites of memory

All my research has started out from the appreciation of certain coincidences in analytic work. Naturally what had motivated me initially was the direct and personal experience I had gained in clinical practice,[32] but I found myself noting the presence of coincidences in the psychoanalytic literature, in particular when it revealed certain strange correspondences of events and circumstances reported in case histories, which all recounted a serious impasse in the treatment and in theorising about it.

I came up with the idea that they constituted a strange type of enactment and started to think they might contain an important potential for actually explaining the analytic impasse. What struck me most was the occurrence of these significant events in close connection to a change of rhythm, a variation or interruption of the setting which introduced a novelty into the shared habit.

Once the characteristics of the setting were firmly established on the basis of four sessions a week, every analyst in practice after the Second World War was accustomed to interpreting the patient's turbulences or the worsening of the defensive armour-plating in the Monday session after the weekend break, and even more so after longer breaks for holidays, just as they learned to recognise the resistances activated by variations of the setting introduced by the patients themselves: for example, being late, asking for a change of time, or missing a session.

This is not to say that we are equally prepared to recognise what happens to the analyst in these circumstances, not only in threshold moments such as the beginning and end of analysis but in all those situations where the patient is not there, and making us wait or missing a session introduces something unforeseen, a threat in the countertransference.

This would mean experiencing a very particular kind of mourning. In my opinion, the unconscious identifications located in the setting would be mobilised by any interruption of the rhythm that introduces the sense of reality and provokes us into coming out of the illusion:[33] in this way, depending on the context, traumatic experiences connected to early, sudden, unexpected, and especially unforeseeable modifications of the first relationship with the mother can be reactivated in the patient and the analyst.

There are those who, though uncertain whether to consider these "fortuitous breaks of the setting"[34] errors or entirely chance events, recognise them as having a strange, positive aspect in some cases: while, by contrast, others are strongly inclined to appreciate the circumstances of the encounter as places from which traumatic childhood memories can emerge, having previously been left anchored to the environment.[35]

Variation is a fertile and dangerous moment when something crumbles:[36] it is the unforeseen event which, interrupting habit, reawakens the involuntary memory that had been imprisoned there.[37]

My hypothesis is that in these incidents, the occurrence of strange coincidences that may remain unrecognised and unrecorded or arouse the telepathic effect in the analyst's countertransference, may be the precious signal that something is coming to light which had been shared by the couple through the "secret language" of automatic actions: a coincidental inter-transferential experience, a jointly constructed fantasy would be coming to the fore through this breach.

Notable examples

From Carl G Jung

For Jung, coincidences were to be included among the phenomena of "synchronicity" in the special sense of "a coincidence in time of two or more causally unrelated events which have the same or a similar meaning in contrast to 'synchronism', which simply means the simultaneous occurrence of two events."[38] He gives them an interpretation, outside the causality of the transference, in the universal perspective of a collective unconscious, bearer of a disembodied knowledge that predates all consciousness. His own existence was characterised by the pervasive presence of strange correspondences. For Freud, such unconscious appointments (in which we meet the person we had dreamed or thought of) were constructions created by the consummate ability of oneiric work, but for Jung they constituted typical manifestations of a religious order, an immense fabric of potential meanings infusing nature and transcending space and time, and the internal and external events that were produced formed part of it.[39]

> A young woman I was treating had, at a critical moment, a dream in which she was given a golden scarab. While she was telling me this dream, I sat with my back to the closed window. Suddenly I heard a noise behind me, like a gentle tapping. I turned round and saw a flying insect knocking against the window-pane from the outside. I opened the window and caught the creature in the air as it flew in. It was the nearest analogy to a golden scarab one finds in our latitudes, a scarabaeid beetle, the common rose-chafer (*Cetonia aurata*), which, contrary to its usual habits had evidently felt the urge to get into a dark room at this particular moment.
>
> (1952, pp. 22–24)

In this first famous example that he reports, it is the endorsement of coincidence in analysis, rather than any pre-existing and mystical meaning it might have, which allows Jung to offer the scarab to the patient and take the golden opportunity to overcome a serious relational impasse with a first possibility of understanding.

From Eugenio Gaddini

Gaddini used to claim that anyone familiar with analysis knows from experience how little of what passes between doctor and patient in the analytic situation is attributable to chance coincidences (1962). He provides us with an example that may explain the connection between phenomena of so-called ESP and the countertransference: he refers to a very brief, "limited and unimportant episode" that happened at the start of an analytic session, or "seemed to have occurred even before the session began, from the moment the patient rang the bell." The whole event only struck the analyst as being important when the patient, a 30-year-old man "suffering from neurosis of character and serious disorders of potency," began the session with words that could not be mere coincidence:

> I don't know why, but it occurs to me that you are neurotic, or that you need to seek treatment; something like that.
>
> (1962, p. 106)

The idea had appeared in his mind little by little, "without his knowing how," and he had immediately moved on to talk about something quite different.

In providing further information to explain the strangeness of the episode, Gaddini also reveals that there had previously been a change in the rhythm of the analysis, an interruption of the setting proposed by the patient and accepted by the analyst. And so he moves on to make clear the dynamic of the event:

> A few days earlier the patient had asked to change the time of his session and, overcoming a certain reluctance, the analyst had agreed to move it from morning to afternoon. The reluctance was due to the fact that, where possible, the analyst used to keep that afternoon of the week free from commitments with patients. At the appointed time, however, the analyst found himself forgetting the agreement of a few days before. It was only when he had heard the doorbell of the front door ring that the commitment he had made came back to him in a flash. A minute later, however, he was in the consulting room with his patient. Apparently nothing different from usual had happened. The maid, completely unaware, had gone to open the door and, recognizing the patient, had introduced him, as usual, into the study where the analyst was waiting for him. After greeting him, the young man stretched out on the couch, remained silent for a few seconds and finally began with the words we know.
>
> We must assume that the analyst reacted to the doorbell signal as a sudden irruption of his super-ego into the fragile defensive equilibrium that had led him to ignore the commitment of the session. Awoken, he immediately had

> to attune himself to what the situation required, without being able to pause with an active intervention of consciousness to consider what had happened.

And so he concludes:

> One can understand how the beginning of the session surprised him and how, above all, it forced him to reflect. Through the mouth of the patient – who had unconsciously become the object of an unconscious projection – it had come back to him as a rebound, the severe and mocking reproach of his super-ego, which he had tried not to listen to.
>
> (1962, p. 107)

From José Bleger

While illustrating the topic of ambiguity, Bleger encounters a coincidence in the very clinical vignette that he is using to make clear how the ambiguous personality is "furtive," capable of causing an impasse in treatment with its permeability and mimetism: it "characteristically does not assume responsibility, but avoids or does not commit to or take responsibility for a situation, its meaning, motivations or consequences" (1967b, p. 167).

He is referring to a patient who had recently gone through some very traumatic situations, as a result of which he "coincidentally" began his analysis in a condition of extreme dependence on the analyst and total submission to him. He showed undisputed acceptance of everything that was said or interpreted to him, although the sessions always transpired with an intense ambiguity.

Bleger writes:

> In one session he [L.L.] announces that the following day he will not be able to come because he will have to go on a trip. I interpret his attempt to draw apart from everything that he perceives as disturbing in the relation with me.
>
> The following morning, during the course of his hour, I was reading in a place where I can hear the doorbell, but as I learned afterwards, it was ringing much more softly than usual that day.
>
> He comes to the next session and says that he did not go away and explains the reasons in detail. At one moment, I point out that he is explaining why he did not go away, but is not saying that yesterday he missed his session and that this omission must have some meaning, since although he did not go away as planned, he didn't come to the session either. At that moment, he tells me that he came to the session, rang the bell, waited a few minutes and, since nobody answered the door, returned home.
>
> (1967b, p. 168)

Bleger does not dwell on an interpretation of the coincidence and the experience of swapping roles: the patient's attempt to keep his distance and be refractory has infected the analyst. He does not analyse the fact that he was not expecting to be listened to (that the patient might change his plans after his interpretation), nor does he take responsibility for his own deafness at the time when the session was due to start. Bleger concentrates on the patient's ambiguity, on how he does not tell his analyst about the missed session in order to maintain a situation of "*non-conflict*," "*as if nothing had happened or were happening now*," but he himself seems to avoid revealing his own countertransference and integrating the contradictions.

From Joyce McDougall

Exploring the limit of analysability of certain psychosomatic patients, Joyce McDougall comes to identify a hidden symptomatology, different from neurosis, based on a mechanism that she calls *désaffectation* (1989): these patients would use an armour of detachment and alienation from their own emotions, and their own inner world, in order to protect themselves from a traumatic situation characterised by their having been unable to contain an excess of affective experience. In her opinion, this primitive, pre-neurotic defensive mode would show itself more in second analyses, which the patient would bring to an impasse with attacks connected to the disappointment suffered at the conclusion of the previous treatment. As an example, she presents the case of a man she calls Jack:

> Prior to coming to see me Jack had had 12 years of analysis with two different male analysts. During our first two interviews, he expressed his conviction that I would be unable to understand him and therefore incompetent to help him.
>
> (1989, p. 107)

She adds:

> Jack . . . brought to his first interview, as though offering me a gift that would entitle him to treatment, two "good" neurotic symptoms . . . having a psychosomatic dimension . . . a certain form of sexual impotence as well as recalcitrant insomnia.
>
> (p. 110)

But she explains that Jack's fundamental problem was of a pre-neurotic order.

She reports that in the first three years of analysis, the impotence and insomnia had disappeared, but the patient was by no means happy about these changes, didn't know "how to live," and continually attacked analysis while not considering it possible to give it up. For example, Jack usually arrived, as he put it, "deliberately 15 minutes late," but he hadn't missed a single session in eight years (p. 107).

At this point, McDougall offers a clinical fragment with the single aim of illustrating the nature and origin of his particular defensive mode. In this case, too, the account has its starting point in a coincidence, a convergence of events and circumstances that sees the analyst singularly identified with the patient and his symptom:

> Jack usually arrived from 10 to 15 minutes late, proclaiming that, in any case, he was better off in the waiting room than on the couch. As a result of my drawing attention to this acting-out on numerous occasions, he eventually became curious, during the fifth year of our work, about the unconscious meaning of his unpunctual behaviour and told me that he intended to come right on time to the next session. Apparently he came 10 minutes early. Due to *unforeseen and unavoidable circumstances* I myself was 10 minutes late. Given the context I found this most unfortunate, and I told him so.
>
> (p. 112, my italics)

McDougall analyses the fantasies and thoughts then expressed by the patient in relation to his having waited for her, emphasising his difficulty in recognising and naming the conflicting feelings about the analyst. However, she does not interpret the coincidence of her own lateness or use it to comprehend the impasse which, according to the associations she reports, could plausibly have something to do with the countertransferential difficulty in working through the patient's constant threat to "not be there" and break off that analysis, as had happened with the previous ones. She seems to have little contact with her own action, not being prepared to interpret it but ready to consider it as having no meaning.

Telepathy, an *enlightening* mistake

When the sense of guilt, surprise, or fear of being caught out in a mistake does not repress the analyst's capacity for listening, it becomes possible to grasp the potential significance of certain predictable unpredictabilities. Far from regarding such occurrences as an accident, an unfortunate mistake, or a failure for which we must apologise, I think we can take them as opportunities to be seized in order to understand the symptom that the patient makes us act out, entrusting it to the analyst in a sort of contagion, and the unconscious fantasy that becomes shared: perhaps the fear of that risky excess of uncontainable affect associated with coming to the appointment together at the right moment is at the base of the original "failure situation" which could be unfrozen and relived in analysis.

From this perspective, the "error" shows its richness and its capacity for guiding us towards the primal truth.

In order to understand the specific psychological and interpersonal meaning which can be conveyed by certain incidents in the setting, and to avoid considering them chance events or errors to be eliminated or rectified, analysts need to know how to face their personal embarrassment, the pain of acknowledging that they have been drawn by the patient into an enactment.[40] Both Bleger and McDougall refer to situations of impasse in which the unconscious fantasy of maintaining a condition of primitive undifferentiation is activated, an indissoluble bond between mother and nursing infant. *Désaffectation* and ambiguity manifest their roots in relation to an object responsible for unreliable early care, which gives the illusion of care but then presents a closed door and does not nurture the indispensable basic reciprocity. They reveal strategies dictated by the fear of expressing an aggressiveness that is too destructive for the link and by the need to make the object survive so as to put it once again to the test. These strategies seem to fix a stable relational distance, one of safety in a state of constant conjunction: if one advances, the other retreats, and vice versa.

In defining the characteristics of *désaffectation* and ambiguity, both writers inadvertently choose highly significant illustrations of the trauma being re-actualised in analysis: when, after really accepting the interpretation at a deep level and believing it, the patient gives up his own defensive strategies and challenges fate, he finds himself once again a victim of his destiny: the object is not waiting for him.

Coincidence contains the enacting of a memory in the relationship but also a potential innovation since it brings to light the significance of the impasse as a challenge to the analyst's credibility and an unconscious proposal to engage in role reversal: it could open the way to a comprehension of the traumatic scene and give it a new ending.

In analysis, coincidences occasionally offer time for the special event which the Greeks called *Kairòs*, "the mythic time of both repetitive tragedies and new beginnings,"[41] a propitious occasion which they represented as a young man running, with his long hair tied back, since the moment can only be seized as it arrives, not when it has passed us by.[42]

Chance convergences of events and circumstances can act as points of attachment between analyst and patient, for that shared umbilical intertwining which connects to the unknowable, to the meaningless world of chance, of that which makes no sense, but also with what may finally be invested with sense and be thought about. They could be regarded as sites of memory.

Freud and the "Forsyth case"

As I continued my research into coincidences in analysis, I came across Freud's enchanting clinical study, the "Forsyth case," a session in which he had been able to observe some phenomena of thought transference (1933).

Among his own associations during the treatment, Freud refers to a remarkable coincidence of the setting which seemed to me to prepare the way for the later, extraordinary "telepathic" construction and to give advance notice of it: when the patient, Mr P, missed a session, the analyst had reacted as if trying to find him at his home.

He writes:

> Firstly: One day of the previous week I had waited in vain for Herr P at eleven o'clock, and had then gone out to visit Dr Anton von Freund in his pension. I

> was surprised to find that Herr P lived on another floor of the same building in which the pension was located. In connection with this I had later told P. that I had in a sense paid him a visit in his house.
>
> (p. 49)

Freud reveals the irony of having "paid him a visit in his house" but does not use the incident as a guide to bring the treatment out of its impasse. He does not seem to notice those elements of identification and unconscious communication already present, which he had himself experienced and were in play in the relationship only a few days before, revealing them in the patient as the telepathic ability to read his analyst's thoughts. The circumstances of the coincidence had also struck me because they presented a certain similarity with other previous disturbing or conflicted situations that Freud had faced, all connected with a misunderstanding, a meeting wished for and yet disregarded, finding himself in front of the wrong door or on the wrong floor (see the visit to the "very old lady's" home).

Also in the example reported by Freud, it is the patient who highlights what the analyst has just unconsciously experienced first hand, and, precisely because of the unconscious origin of the countertransference, he will find himself bringing just that clinical case to his colleagues' attention as they discuss and construct theory.[43]

In psychoanalytic writing, especially when we set ourselves the problem of addressing a clinical and technical impasse, exploring new territories and building concepts, the analyst talks and writes about that part of himself which, being countertransferentially repressed, he has not been able to reach and will never be able to reach completely and which needs to find acceptance in relationship, to be brought back into play in the dialogue with the group, with a supervisor, or in any case with another person.[44] According to Faimberg (2000), responding to another analyst's clinical material by saying "I would have proceeded differently," since it presents a problem in the session, is a further way of posing the question of how to use obstacles and even mistakes in analysis.

While it is not always possible to catch the sense of the relational moment that is achieved, this sense does not fall into the void and must not be lost.

For this reason, the clinical examples of the masters – not so much stories as oneiric reconstructions of the session – and the collusive entanglement they are able to risk with their authoritative ability to fall towards and with the patient, are capable of continuing to speak with the same richness as dreams, and at each rereading, they offer new nuances to their interpretations.

To my surprise, in attempting a more detailed understanding of such coincidences in the setting and starting out from the strange case described in *Lecture XXX*, I have found myself encountering a historic, theoretical, and affective moment of great importance for Freud and for the history of the psychoanalytic movement.[45]

Notes

1 Backstrom et al., 2011.
2 Freud, 1901, p. 254.
3 "Determinism, Belief in Chance and Superstition – Some Points of View."
4 1901, p. 177.
5 *ibid.*, pp. 164–165.
6 *ibid.*, pp. 177–178.
7 1900, p. 238.
8 He will mention the actual death again to Fliess: "my nice old lady, who was a small but sure source of income, died during the vacation" (7/08/1901).
9 Freud 1923, p. 25, 1933, p. 77.
10 "Nothing brings home to one so strongly the significance of the psychogenic factor in the daily life of men, the frequency of malingering and the non-existence of chance, as a few years' practice of psycho-analysis on the strict principle of leasing by the hour" (1913a, p. 127).
11 1983.
12 See Pierri, 2010.
13 In Freud, 1900.
14 Ferenczi, 1909, p. 42.
15 See Pierri, 1997a.
16 Pierri, 1994, 1997b.
17 De Toffoli, 1996.
18 Pierri, 2016b.
19 Freud, 1937, p. 266.
20 Pierri, 1994, p. 138.
21 Balint, 1968.
22 Ferenczi, 1932; Winnicott, 1956; Martin-Cabré, 1999.
23 Ferenczi writes about "mutual flux" (*Clinical Diary*, 17/01/1932); Tustin "flowing-over-at-oneness" (1981); H Rosenfeld "osmosis" (1987): on this, see Hidas, 1993.
24 1983, p. 11.
25 1967a, 1967b.
26 Pierri, 2010, 2014.
27 Pierri, 1998.
28 Freud, 1901, pp. 273 and 176.
29 Ogden's perspective on the subject of projective identification (1993, p. 6.).
30 Like "the analyst's mistakes," Chused and Raphling, 1992.
31 Freud, 1901, p. 279.
32 Pierri, 1994, 1997a, 1997b, 1998, 2001a, 2002, 2006, 2008.
33 See Ferenczi, 1913.
34 Berti Ceroni, 1995.
35 Bordi, 2001.
36 Habit can function as a container and "ghost catcher," Bruni (1991).
37 So Beckett comments, re-reading Proust, 1931.
38 1952, p. 25. Jung began to theorise about it as early as 1928.
39 See Aziz, 1990, Miller, 2009.
40 Ogden, 1993.
41 Modell, 1990, p. 75.
42 Pierri, 1997b, 2006, 2008.
43 Kluzer Usuelli, 1999.
44 McDougall, 1989; Balsamo and Napolitano, 1998.
45 See Pierri, 2010.

Chapter 2

Dr Forsyth arrives in Vienna to undertake a seven-week analysis with Prof Freud

The decline of the West

Our story begins in Vienna on an October day in 1919 shortly after the end of the war. We do not know if it was a fine day, but that autumn was remembered as being particularly mild. However, only the weather was gentle with Austria during that season. Those who managed to return after surviving battles, imprisonment, or exile, finding themselves back in their homeland after the disaster of the Great War, after the exaltation, the horrors, and the despair of that slaughter and defeat, had to face the collapse of the Empire and the loss of the world they had lived in and regarded as certain.

These were the days when Lieutenant Robert Musil, recently returned from the Italian front, was devoting himself to the book he would be working on for the rest of his life and which would remain unfinished. *The Man Without Qualities* begins by conjuring up Vienna in its final summer of peace:

> A barometric low hung over the Atlantic. It moved eastward toward a high-pressure area over Russia without as yet showing any inclination to bypass this high in a northerly direction. The isotherms and isotheres were functioning as they should. . . . In a word that characterizes the facts fairly accurately, even if it is a bit old-fashioned: it was a fine day in August 1913.
>
> (1921–43, incipit)

The contortions to which Musil subjects his prose are symptoms of the desire to look away from the political ruin of the *finis Austriae* and to reconstruct, with eyes closed, the qualities of its sounds, the animation and familiar racket of his *Kaiserlich-Königlich* Vienna before the storm, "a fine day in August 1913." But "the times had changed, like a day that begins radiantly blue and then by degrees clouds over."[1]

Only a few years had passed, and the sumptuous palaces and broad, animated streets had become the empty scenery stage sets of a now voiceless world. The foreigner arriving for the first time in the capital on that day would have struggled to imagine its previous splendour when Vienna, Europe's third city with over two

DOI: 10.4324/9781003246480-3

million inhabitants, was the beating heart of a multi-ethnic culture containing more than 15 languages and five religions, an Empire which, without passports or customs controls, had stretched all the way the Near East.

The catastrophe had come without warning: the fortifications which had defended the city from the Turks in 1683 had now given way to the broad avenues and parks of the Ringstrasse, embellished with buildings and monuments in the most varied styles. The neoclassical Parliament building beside the Gothic fantasy of the *Rathaus* and the Renaissance University opposite the baroque *Burgtheater* had only just been the triumphal setting for the celebrations of the 60th anniversary of Emperor Franz Josef's ascent to the throne. On 12 July 1908, 60,000 spectators in grandstands and on the pavements of the Ring had attended the great procession led by the costumed aristocrats – with Radetsky's great-grandson in his ancestor's uniform welcomed by ovations to the sound of Johann Strauss's march – followed by delegations arriving from every nation to celebrate the sovereign unity of the Empire. And on 2 December, at the conclusion of the jubilee, the city had been lit up by fireworks and the newly installed electric lights accompanied by peals from all the city's bells.[2]

The Habsburg *Securität* seemed to be in its golden age. With the second industrial revolution, faith in the miracles of science and technology had attained the force of a religion. "There was as little belief in the possibility of such barbaric declines as wars between the peoples of Europe as there was in witches and ghosts," Stefan Zweig[3] would bitterly recall 20 years later, when the same Ring would witness the great parade of the Third Reich as Hitler entered Vienna: troops and armoured cars with more than 400 planes performing acrobatics in the skies above Vienna while swastikas danced in the breeze.

At the peak of European civilisation, on 28 June 1914, the action of an 18-year-old in Sarajevo not only caused the death of the couple who had been intended to guarantee the continuity of the Austro-Hungarian throne – Archduke Franz Ferdinand and his wife Sophie – but provoked a wave of destruction which overturned the destiny of the West and all its illusions.

The atrocity of the First World War had sounded the funeral march of that world.

Introduction to psycho-analysis: the first 28 lectures

In this climate of great uncertainty, as a mystical and occultist tendency was growing, especially in the Anglo-Saxon countries, mediums and spiritualists had returned to nourish hope in the divinatory and telepathic capacities of the human mind, especially the belief in being able to communicate with the dead.

"How wild, anarchic and unreal were those years" – Zweig remembered:

> years in which, with the dwindling value of money, all other values in Austria and Germany began to slip! It was an epoch of high ecstasy and ugly

> scheming, a singular mixture of unrest and fanaticism. Every extravagant idea that was not subject to regulation reaped a golden harvest: theosophy, occultism, spiritualism, somnambulism, anthroposophy, palm reading, graphology, yoga and Paracelsism.
>
> (1942, p. 301)

Interest had been reignited not only in so-called "psychical research" but also in psychoanalysis.

Those theories were still unknown to the scientific world at the beginning of the century when they started, almost clandestinely, to do the rounds of cultivated Viennese salons in *The Interpretation of Dreams* (1900), arousing interest, prudery, and parodies – like *Reigen* (*Hands Around*), which Schnitzler had printed and distributed as a gift to his friends in the same year. The popularity achieved by *The Psychopathology of Everyday Life* (1901) later spread these theories through the cafés, where they were now gaining due recognition. After the manifestations of cruelty which everyone had personally witnessed or actively participated in, the horror, repugnance, and panic of that war conducted with bayonets and gas, with daggers and the first missiles, the conception of the *oedipal conflict* provided by Freud made itself indispensable for working through the atrocities and homicidal tendencies.[4] And that was not all: faced with the post-war neuroses, a traumatic pathology shared by all armies and filling the hospitals on both fronts, international medicine was also discovering psychoanalysis.

In the winter semesters of 1915 to 1917, Sigmund Freud had given three series of lectures at the Vienna Psychiatric Clinic. The lectures were open to all the faculties: even though most of the students were at the front, they had a substantial audience of doctors and lay people from both sexes (the university was beginning to admit women). His daughters Mathilde and Anna were also present. Freud had been a *Professor Extraordinarius* since 1902; he had recently turned 60 and, moved by the desire to sum up his life's work, he decided that these would be his final lectures. "Everything seemed to be closing down," comments Jones.[5] The 28 *Introductory Lectures* on dreaming, lapses, and the theory of the neuroses, collected and immediately published (1916–1917), would meet with instant success, bringing Freud and psychoanalysis worldwide fame.

The psychoanalytic movement had managed to survive the war but also the grave crisis within its ranks, caused by the theoretical and personal conflict between Freud and one of his most eminent students, the Swiss Carl Gustav Jung, his designated heir. A few months after the outbreak of war, Jung had embarrassingly resigned, as had been expected since the Munich Congress (1913).

The break with the Swiss could have had disastrous consequences for the survival of the young discipline and its recently formed international organisation. This is why, in order to reconstruct the Association and break the long stalemate caused by the war, psychoanalysts in the Empires of the Central Powers decided in the autumn of 1918 to move the 5th Psychoanalytic Congress to Budapest: the main scientific topic was naturally that of the traumatic neuroses, "shell shock," as it had begun to be called.[6]

Medicine had found itself powerless in the face of this phenomenon and its unprecedented scale, with the result that it was applying punitive and inhumane therapeutic techniques which, in the case of electrical treatment, were barely distinguishable from torture. Being sensitive to the ethical problems that were arising, psychoanalysts had been able to bring their experience to bear in proposing alternative and efficacious alternative psychological interventions.

The Congress elected Sándor Ferenczi as president and Anton von Freund as secretary, both Hungarians and close friends of the professor. In this way, the movement's centre of gravity was transferred from Zurich to Budapest, rewarding Ferenczi's commitment and leadership in building up a strong group of students. Among these was the wealthy von Freund, who had made a substantial donation to support the founding of a psychoanalytic publishing house, the *Internationaler Psychoanalytischer Verlag*, and the planning of a training institute in Budapest, which at first seemed achievable. But the Hungarian season was short lived, brought down by the defeat of the Central Powers and the political tensions of the early post-war period. And when the border with Austria was closed for much of 1919, the new president lost all contact with Freud and remained cut off for even longer from the rest of the Association.

Hunger in Vienna

In the autumn of 1919, the encirclement by the Allies, internal revolts, and shortages of food, raw materials, and coal had brought the Viennese population to its knees: outside the shops, the queues for flour, bread, and milk grew longer and longer; supplies quickly ran out and it became a struggle to buy food even on the black market. Money had no value.

An expository manuscript which Freud provided for a Hungarian journal earned him payment in the form of a precious sack of potatoes and was later famous as *Kartoffellschmarrn*.[7] And it took Martha, Minna, and Anna a whole day to remove the worms from a precious bag of peas brought back from leave by Ernst.[8] The worst distress was caused by the frost in Vienna, and during those years, it was not unusual to see people rummaging in the ash heaps by the roadside, searching for some leftover coal or waiting for hours for the trains laden with logs from the local woods. Those who could do so sought warmer climes. Tuberculosis was claiming victims among children above all, and the humanitarian organisations set up the famous *Kinderzüge* (children's trains), sometimes the only convoys that functioned regularly, to take the poorest children for treatment in the Netherlands and Switzerland.

After the signing of the armistice, the break-up of the Empire's territories, and the proclamation of the First Republic, the situation grew even worse. As events unfolded after the end of the war, the drama and disorientation of the defeat were followed by uprisings, rebellions, pillaging, civil unrest, and, in certain regions of the former Empire, after the rapid assimilation of the Eastern Jews (*Ostjuden*) in the second half of the nineteenth century, the renewed unleashing of antisemitism with *pogroms* already happening in Ukraine in 1917 and then the persecutions of 1919 in Hungary. Many Jews from eastern Europe, most of them originally from Russia, moved westwards, to England or the United States and South America. The Zionist movement, which had originated in Vienna during the early 1880s and had made the capital the centre of German-speaking Jewish nationalism, was starting to plan the constitution of a Jewish community in Palestine with its own self-governing agency, and some of the new wave of migrants went there.

In Austria, the revolution did not entail the wave of antisemitism which arose in Hungary, nor did it produce the same violence as in Germany, where the confrontation with the *Dolchstoss* ("stab in the back") of the defeat was more critical for the impoverished and unemployed veterans who could not easily be reinserted into the context of civic life: in January 1919, the vengeful nationalist, anti-communist, and antisemitic turn in Berlin that would lead to the constitution of the Weimar Republic created two illustrious victims in the Spartacists Rosa Luxemburg and Karl Liebknecht. The disturbances were less severe in Vienna, and yet, in June, when Freud was walking along Hörlgasse, near his home, with his eldest daughter Mathilde, they were caught up in a gunfight when the police killed six communist workers and had to run away to escape danger.[9]

The elections in May, in which women participated for the first time, including the young Anna Freud, brought the Social Democrats to power, and Red Vienna began to formulate a vast programme of reforms in town planning, social services, and education. However, it was the Weimar Republic which attained the international recognition that the old Habsburg capital had lost forever. And it was in post-war Berlin that many Viennese and Hungarian psychoanalysts would seek asylum and work.

Freud was also gripped by the desire to leave Austria and go to live in England, as he had dreamed of doing at the age of 20 when he had visited relations who lived there. These were his half-brothers Emanuel and Philip – children from Jacob Freud's first marriage – who in 1859 had decided to emigrate to Manchester, then one of the most flourishing industrial centres. That year, the entire family had had to leave Freiberg and Moravia and travel west because of the crisis in textile manufacturing and the revival of antisemitism: Jacob had stayed in central Europe with his third wife Amalia and his children Sigmund and Anna. After stopping first in Leipzig, they had moved on to Vienna, enduring a period of extreme precariousness and privation. At the age of three, Sigmund had had to abandon the safety of his hometown and was separated from his playmates John and Pauline, Emanuel's children.[10] Since then, England had represented for him not only a haven in a free, prosperous, and hospitable land (since 1858, it had recognised the civil rights of Jews, whereas the Austro-Hungarian Empire had only done so in 1867) but above all a reconnection with a happy part of his own childhood.

And yet, despite his ambivalence towards the city of Vienna and the miserable, uncertain conditions he was once again experiencing, Sigmund Freud felt he could not live anywhere else:

> Austria-Hungary is no more. I could not live anywhere else. Emigration is out of the question for me. I will continue to live with the trunk and imagine that it is the whole.
>
> (in Ellenberger, 1970, p. 829)

While before the closing of the border with Hungary, Ferenczi and von Freund, making use of their military rank, were still able to provide Freud with contraband flour, bread, and, when possible, some *Delikatessen*, at the end of 1918, it was clear that he would need to start receiving help from the West.

With the proclamation of the armistice, when the post begins to function again, he resumes his correspondence with Jones and, almost as a sign of surrender, gives up German for once, writing to him in English:

> I am sure you cannot conceive what our condition here really is. But you should come over as soon as you can, have a look upon what was Austria, and bring my daughter's boxes with you.
>
> (22/12/1918)

Shortly afterwards, he went into more detail:

> These last months are growing the worst we had to endure while this war lasted. . . . We are all of us slowly failing in health and bulk, not alone so in this town I assure you. Prospects are dark.
>
> (15/01/1919)

The mention of Anna's "boxes" refers to the journey his daughter, then 18 years old, had made to London in the summer of 1914 – as her father had done at the same age – and gone to visit their English relatives. Her stay had been cut short by the declaration of war. So as not to risk being stuck in England, Anna Freud entrusted her luggage to the faithful Jones and, with the assistance of his former common-law wife Loe Kann, had managed to get herself included in the entourage of the Austrian ambassador and returned home as soon as she could. With the war already being waged, the enterprising young woman had returned safe and sound to her homeland in the third week of August, after ten days at sea on a small overcrowded ship, meeting a storm near Cape Finisterre, a gunboat at Gibraltar, and, after disembarking, an escort of rather threatening soldiers during the 40-hour train journey through still-neutral Italy.

This was the luggage still being awaited in Vienna and, despite Anna's joke about the contents being suitable for an exhibition of pre-war fashions (her father called her *Schwarzer Teufel*[11] because of her impertinence), she was nevertheless glad to have them.[12]

The drama of the situation and the anxiety of parents are underlined by the fact that Felicitas von Arnim, 17-year-old daughter of the writer, Elizabeth, was unable to make the journey in the other direction: surprised by the start of war while in Germany, where she had gone to further her musical studies, she was unable to return to London and died at a hospital in Stuttgart on the morning of 8 August 1914 of acute double pneumonia contracted while she was trying unsuccessfully to cross the border.[13]

Parcels from England

1919 was certainly the most difficult year, but, despite the financial problems and terrible travelling conditions, Freud nevertheless decided not to give up his restorative summer holiday ahead of the winter cold. He spent the summer first at Bad Gastein and then at Badersee in the Bavarian Alps. In the general chaos, while the state printed all the money it could in an attempt to counter devaluation, and metal coinage had already vanished, he was certainly making a gesture of defiance.

And even though Freud borrowed 2000 marks in August from his student Max Eitingon – a rich Jew of Russian origin – so that he could go to Hamburg to stay with his daughter Sophie and his grandchildren, on his return home it became clear that his earnings were not keeping up with inflation. Realising that he would have to eat into his savings, he optimistically estimated that these would last another 18 months. But the situation was so out of control that – as Jones illustrates the state of things – the life insurance with which Freud had hoped to secure his wife's future was soon not enough to pay a cab fare.[14]

Max Schur, a medical student at the time (in 1928 he became Freud's personal physician, accompanying him to London in 1938, and was one of his first biographers), vividly recalled the enthusiastic welcome when special eating places for students received the cans of American corned beef and cocoa that he brought home to feed his family (1972).

In the meantime, Sigmund Freud was once again exchanging letters with his relatives in Manchester. His half-brother Emanuel had died during the war, and so it was in collaboration with his nephew Samuel – younger brother of John and Pauline, born after the move to England – that he made new arrangements for delivery of the most urgently needed items from the West. The food parcels, selected according to his detailed specifications, did not begin to arrive until 1920, and so the final months of 1919 were the most challenging of all. On 24 November, Freud wrote to Sam:

> Dear Sam. . . . The collection you sent in the parcel is very suitable to our wants. I will wire you as soon as it arrived. . . . Our condition has improved somewhat by gift not sent but brought by friends from Holland and

> Switzerland, friends and pupils I should say. . . . General conditions at Vienna are going from bad to worse.
>
> . . . It is one of the good things of these miserable times that connection between us has been reopened.[15]

The cases of food, clothing, and cigars which Eitingon was still sending the Freud family from Berlin were often rifled through,[16] and the most effective aid was now being delivered in person by Western civilians: Loe Kann was able to send some food parcels via her Dutch brother; Pastor Pfister personally brought supplies from Switzerland; and at Christmas a delivery of foodstuffs also arrived safely from Binswanger. When an American in Wilson's staff visited Berggasse, arriving with two full bags of food, in a unique piece of bartering, Freud presented him with copies of the *Introductory Lectures on Psycho-Analysis* and *The Psychopathology of Everyday Life*.[17]

From February 1920, Sam's long-awaited "special parcels" began to make the journey quite regularly, absorbing much of Freud's time and energy. The first consignment from England, a few weeks after Sophie's death, caught him in the full dismay at his loss and helped him to concentrate on the elemental demands of survival. Anna wrote to Sam:

> Dear cousin Sam,
>
> Parcel N. 1 arrived yesterday safe and sound in spite of its journey of more than two months. Its contents were received with great pleasure and are considered splendid. We're cooking with your margarine already and my mother declares, that the tea and cocoa (I've drunk one cup of it already) are quite extraordinarily good. We thank you heartily, all of us, and expect that parcel N. 2 and 3. . . . I wonder if it would be possible to send small quantities of sugar. That is one of the things most difficult to be got here. . . .
>
> I suppose that Papa wrote you about the sad event in our family. If you remember my sister Sophie, you will easily imagine how sad we all are and how hard it seems to bear? the thought of her being dead and of her poor motherless children whom we love very dearly. We are all of us very much shaken by this blow.[18]

Life in Berggasse had to pick up. Freud monitored the arrival of the parcels, individually numbered according to the letters reporting their departure, checked the contents and their condition, and confirmed receipt to his nephew. These deliveries had to conform to precise rules: in order to follow the preferred route of the "Food Organization," they could only contain basic necessities – fats, salted meat, sardines, cheese, cocoa, tea, biscuits, saccharine, Nestlé milk – which Freud assiduously listed in his letters. He occasionally reported some damage or problem with the packaging to Sam or suggested more reliable, less restricted routes, such as the British military mission or acquaintances who were due to make the journey. It was not permitted to send butter or sugar because these were luxury items – and obviously not tennis balls, which Anna, inserting herself into the correspondence, shamelessly asked for after her father had earned a bit of English money.[19]

As for his cigars, the famous *Trabucco*, Freud managed never to be without them, receiving them as gifts from friends and patients who knew how much he enjoyed them, but he also ended up bartering for them with his tobacconist in exchange for the needlework made by his wife and sister-in-law. He claimed that cigars were vital to his self-control, but Jones regretted that Freud had not made use of the opportunity to give up smoking, even though, as early as 1917, he had experienced a first painful swelling of the gums, paradoxically increasing in a period of abstinence.[20]

As time went by, Freud became able to afford a length of tweed for a suit or a good pair of shoes, and in his correspondence with Samuel, he was beginning to receive congratulations from his nephew on the increasingly frequent appearance of his name and references to his theory in the English press:

> Regarding yourself, we are always eagerly watching for your name on the papers we read. Somewhile last there was quite a discussion about you and your work on the *Daily News*. . . . Whilst passing the time in the waiting room of the dentist the other day, I went right through a copy of Punch and to my astonishment and delight, there was a poem in it about Freud and Jung. Also in a popular weekly, John Bull London, bought to read on a train journey, I came across an article concerning your writings, disfigured as I was sorry to see by a most atrocious portrait of yourself.[21]

His new-found fame and the arrival of "patients from the Allied Powers," his new British and American students, would enable the family to emerge from this time of crisis. It would be the West that sustained Freud: "But what will happen if Jones can't send me any more?" he was now mercilessly writing to Ferenczi, who could no longer help him.[22]

That autumn the professor foresightedly decided to take lessons to improve his English, the language he would find himself speaking in his consulting room for up to nine hours a day. From the start, he appreciated Forsyth's clear and intelligible pronunciation, whereas in 1920, he was much irritated by that of James Strachey. The Cambridge graduate who would become his official translator spoke such indistinct, strange English that paying attention to him was a torture.[23] The effort of listening and internal translation, an exhausting business,[24] made Freud's analytic work particularly arduous, but he got used to it. In December 1921, he reported to Sam he had worked with six Americans, three Britons, and one Swiss.[25] Postponing the treatment of a patient, he wrote to Weiss, "I was, however, not prepared for the extent to which I would be kept busy with a stream of students from abroad. Out of nine people, I now have only one patient."[26] And he complained to Anna that even his German writing style was now showing the visible effect of all those hours of English.[27]

Rich patients, made curious by his fame or referred for a consultation, soon arrived from abroad: sometimes they were actually too ill, like the Rothschild from London who refused his treatment in 1920 and tried not to pay the fee of ten guineas. In December the same year, Freud was highly annoyed by a request that he spend six months in New York, largely because of the meagre payment on offer: "At another time, no American would have dared to make me such offer. They are banking on our *dalles* [Yiddish for *misery*] and want to buy us cheaply," he lamented again to Anna.[28] Over time he started to ignore the demands of extravagant American billionaires taking advantage of his vacations in Bad Gastein to seek his opinion – like the copper magnate Mrs Carrie Guggenheim, relative of the famous Peggy – or trying to negotiate how much he would charge to move abroad for improbable consultations – as in the desperate case of a Dutch banker's sister-in-law who had been unsuccessfully treated for years in New York.[29] But sometimes, despite the irritation, he accommodated the Americans and treated them during his summer break. In the period when the economic crisis was spreading across Europe, the price of food, coal, and clothes rose to impossible levels and Vienna became a theatre of strikes, unrest, and looting, with beggars on the streets – Alix Strachey recalled how "a black coated man," a professional, had asked at a restaurant if he could have the rest of her pudding[30] – Freud, earning his *real* money in foreign currency, was in a position to turn down an offer of a second loan by Eitingon, paid his debts to his nephew, and even began to recover the losses he had suffered.

Perhaps it was then that the Vienna tax office questioned Prof Sigmund Freud's declaration of his income "since it is well known that your fame attracts patients who are able to pay high fees."[31] In the ironic vein that never left him, Freud considered this communication the first official recognition he had received from his city.

A passage to Austria

On that October morning, a Londoner had just arrived in the capital on one of the first trains that were beginning to come from Zurich after the borders were opened. This undertaking by Dr David Forsyth, paediatrician and psychoanalyst, founding member of the British Psychoanalytical Society, must have been far from straightforward.

"At that time a visit to Austria called for preparations similar to those for an Arctic expedition."[32] You had to travel with everything necessary for life and make sure you had thick, warm clothing to face the rigour of the coming winter: every item of clothing was irreplaceable, and it became essential to insure your luggage to the highest possible value since most baggage cars were looted. At the Swiss border, the overnight transfer from the immaculate, comfortable Swiss train to Austria's wrecked carriages must have dramatic for Dr Forsyth. The moment you got on board, you understood what had happened in Austria.

These skeleton cars, impregnated with the stench of lignite and the sharp smell of iodoform, a reminder of the sick and wounded who had been transported during the war, moved slowly, with swarms of people hanging outside on the footplates.

Getting off the train at Franz-Josef-Bahnhof, Dr Forsyth finally set eyes on Vienna. With his big leather suitcases, his travelling blanket, overcoat, and umbrella, he found himself in the middle of the noisy, heaving crowd around the station: groups of soldiers in transit, labourers looking for work, the unemployed, street-vendors, porters, and coachmen piling luggage onto the carts and carriages that were clattering in and out.

As far as we know, as soon as the carriage had brought him to the Hotel Regina on the northern edge of District 1 near the university quarter, he had already decided to set off without delay to the house of Professor Sigmund Freud. He must have been eager to meet him and start the seven weeks of psychoanalysis that he had decided to devote to his training. Our Dr Forsyth was the first of the new English-speaking trainees to arrive in Vienna for an analysis with Freud after the conflict had ended.

That Saturday morning, the foreigner could have been seen walking towards the Ring, leaving behind him the neogothic spires of the Votivkirche untouched by the desolation of the Empire: Franz Josef, who on that very spot in 1853 had been miraculously saved by a buckle from a Hungarian separatist's dagger, had not been spared by fate. He now lay at rest in the Capuchin Crypt, the last Emperor of Austria and "poor sinner" to be received there.

As he went along the broad Währingerstrasse, the doctor could pass unobserved in the flow of Viennese people: soldiers in the most varied uniforms, civilians, bearded Jews with curled hair, young ladies with boas and high heels, older ladies wearing huge hats and with their maids in attendance. . . . The haggard faces betrayed their privations, and many in the crowd were wearing clothes patched with bits of canvas or scraps from military tunics. The combatants returning from the East could be recognised by their worn-out uniforms – some even wore Russian ones – and hobnailed boots or the heavy knapsacks they were dragging behind them; the Galician refugees who had filled Leopoldstadt were identifiable by their black caftans and their wide-brimmed hats. Even so, some passers-by will have turned to look at that civilian with the foreign look about him, recognising him as an Englishman.

On his way to Freud's house, Dr Forsyth was already familiarising himself with the brief stretch of road of the Alsergrund which would become his regular route, with its distinctive and still unfamiliar cafés behind whose glass the Viennese, despite everything, still sat intently reading tarot cards, and the repertoire of waltzes and marches played on the beggar's barrel organ at the corner. He had some intense weeks ahead of him: the analysis would unfold with the rhythm of one session a day, six days a week. As he himself had explained in the courses he gave at the London Polyclinic, the method would use the patient's free associations and the technique of the interpretation of dreams. In his article "On

Psychoanalysis" – one of the first writings on the subject to appear in Britain – Forsyth had described the setup of the treatment in detail:

> The patient, when freely associating, should lie on a couch, his eyes closed, the better to keep his attention from being drawn elsewhere, while the physician takes up a position behind the head of the couch, where his presence is least likely to be obtrusive.
>
> (1913, p. 17)

The doctor was preparing himself to experience the very method he had taught and applied. Now Sigmund Freud no longer invited patients to close their eyes, nor did he apply pressure from his hands onto their foreheads, as he had in the beginning; his presence behind the couch would have had no small impact on the analysand from London, but fortunately Freud had agreed to conduct the analysis in English.

A piece of forgetfulness by Freud

The arrangements agreed to in their exchange of correspondence at the start of that summer involved Forsyth entering Austria as soon as the borders were open again, but after this, the professor had fallen silent. When he set off for Gastein, near Salzburg, where he usually spent his holidays, Freud had left Forsyth's address behind. Given his attitude of defiance in the face of scarcity and worsening inflation, it is hardly surprising that he should forget the address of someone who would be able to top up his depleted resources in the autumn.

It was only in early September, replying to two telegrams, that he let Forsyth know via Ernest Jones that he would be returning to Vienna in the last week of September and would then be available to begin the treatment:

> Dear Jones, . . . I am therefore only now in a position to give firm details about my plans. I also ask you to send word to Forsyth, who telegraphed me twice without my being able to reply (because I had not taken his address with me on the trip). We are leaving here on 9/September, and I go to Hamburg via Munich, from where I travel back, so that I will cross the German border on 24/9 at the latest. I shall then be in Vienna on the 26th, as there are no express trains in Austria any more.
>
> (Freud to Jones, 1/09/1919)

On receiving this confirmation, David Forsyth had been able to travel to Switzerland, where Jones had been since early July, waiting for the reopening of the borders so that he could rejoin Freud after the long separation caused by the war.

Ernest Jones will accompany us on our whole journey in his capacity as Freud's first and chief biographer – and the only official one – but also as a protagonist and witness of events. Jones crossed Forsyth's path in the summer of 1919, not for the first or the last time. We do not know if relations between the two colleagues at that time were less combative than in the past. Jones had been part of Freud's intimate circle for some while and was the undisputed leader of the young group of British analysts, whereas his former fellow student, the brilliant academic Dr David Forsyth, was still waiting to meet the professor and start a training analysis with him. It is ironic that Freud's forgetfulness made it necessary for Jones to be the intermediary with his rival, forcing him to touch the sore spot of his jealousy.

But Freud had already brought the two together in early summer when, replying to Forsyth's letter requesting an analysis, he had asked him to let Jones know his (Freud's) movements during the vacation. In effect, Freud had compelled Forsyth to make his colleague, the president of the British Society, part of his own project. So much so that Jones had immediately written to the professor:

> We shall not be allowed to go to Austria until peace with her is signed and ratified, and other formalities attended to . . . Dr F[orsyth] will also come as soon as he can. He told me that you were going to analyse him, which naturally aroused my jealousy, though do not fear that I shall not be able to control this. It may interest you to hear a little about him. He is about 42, very gentlemanly, with a fine and well-balanced mind; not brilliant, but with some originality. He has worked at Ps-A for some five years or so, has not read much of it, but has had a considerable personal experience. He would, I think, count next to me as leader in England, chiefly because of his good personality and the prestige of his position (he is physician to a medical school, equivalent to Professor in Germany and is a children's specialist; he is no neurologist or psychiatrist, but has had great experience of children and has made excellent observations on them from the psychological point of view).
>
> (1/07/1919)

Freud had obtained the information he was waiting for and had given Jones the opportunity to show esteem for the man being confirmed as his deputy.

On that morning, accompanied by this favourable – though unnecessary – introduction, the English doctor and paediatrician was preparing himself for his first encounter with Sigmund Freud. Leaving Währingerstrasse, let's follow him as he enters Berggasse, the road that slopes gently downhill from the University quarter and the elegant residential area that surrounds it, towards the Danube canal, running on into the humble and more densely populated district around the square of the *Tandelmarkt* (the flea market) as far as its boundary with the Jewish quarter of Leopoldstadt. Berggasse, "mountain alley," where Freud lived and worked, was flanked by quiet middle-class houses, abandoned shops, and a few horse chestnuts that were starting to cover the pavement with the first layer of leaves which had the colour and smell of tobacco. Halfway along, the paved alley levelled off as if coming to rest between the wings of imposing buildings. Reaching the solid apartment block which stood out from the others in its bright Renaissance-style façade, after passing the window of a kosher butcher, boarded up for the war,

Forsyth had found himself in front of the shop sign "*Siegmund*" attached to the side of the front door of number 19 and had then noticed the smaller nameplate of Prof Sigmund Freud on the other side of the entrance. With this moment of hesitation, let's leave him crossing the wide hallway lit at the back by a stained-glass window, wondering what kind of welcome the professor would give him. The fact that, back in July, Freud had forgotten to bring Forsyth's address with him did not seem like a good start . . . never mind the embarrassment of having to send him two telegrams.

Maybe, as he climbed the elegant staircase that led to the first floor, Dr Forsyth became a bit short of breath and had to pause on the landing before ringing the bell under the little ceramic plate bearing the name and visiting hour: "Prof. Dr. Freud, 3–4."

After being admitted by the maid and shown into the waiting room with its red velvet chairs and the window onto the horse chestnuts in the garden, he will have waited briefly for Freud's padded study door to open, giving a glance or two at the volumes in the library and perhaps noticing the photo of Freud's friend Ernest Jones among the portraits of the eminent colleagues hanging on the walls.

When our David Forsyth presents himself at Berggasse, like a first special package of provisions from England – Sam's consignments had not yet started to arrive – at two guineas a session for six sessions a week, he will be worth as much as all Freud's other patients put together.[33]

His first meeting with the professor will only be a few minutes long, just enough time to agree on a consultation that afternoon and to leave his visiting card. Freud will have it on the table in front of him at the start of the session with his usual 11.00 patient.

David Forsyth will be remembered for this timely arrival in Berggasse at 10.45 and for his indirect and unintentional participation in that session which will turn out to be extraordinarily "telepathic." Many years later, Freud will publish his clinical account of what will become known as the "Forsyth case."

Notes

1 Musil, 1921–1943, *II*, p. 56.
2 Gebert, 2004.
3 1942, p. 14.
4 Canetti, 1980.
5 *II*, p. 209.
6 Myers, 1915.
7 Potato pancakes.
8 Young-Bruehl, 1988, pp. 77–78.
9 The event caused an even greater number of victims and appeared some time later in a dream of jealousy that Anna Freud related to her father (07/24/1919). It had a decisive influence on the existence of Karl Popper, then a student in Vienna, who abandoned communism because he felt that Marxist intellectuals had a responsibility for the massacre of fellow workers.
10 And from little Bertha, born a few months earlier.

11 "Black devil."
12 A. Freud, 1979.
13 Using the pen name Alice Cholmondeley, Elisabeth von Arnim wrote about this in *Christine* (1917).
14 *III*, p. 4.
15 Sigmund Freud to Sam Freud, 24/11/1919, Courtesy of the Library Special Collections Division, Copyright of the University of Manchester. See all correspondence in Vincent, 1996.
16 Freud to Eitingon, 2/12/1919.
17 Gay, 1988.
18 Anna Freud to Sam Freud, 7/02/1920, Copyright of the University of Manchester, Copyright @ The Estate of Anna Freud. Published by arrangement with The Marsh Agency Ltd.
19 Sigmund Freud to Sam Freud, 7/03/1920.
20 Freud to Ferenczi, 6/11/1917.
21 Sam Freud to Sigmund Freud, 30/10/1920, Copyright of the University of Manchester.
22 15/03/1920.
23 Freud to Jones, 12/10/1920.
24 Freud to Abraham, 28/11/1920.
25 4/12/1921.
26 3/04/1922, in Roazen, 2005.
27 14/07/1922.
28 6/12/1920.
29 Freud to Anna, 17/07/1922.
30 Roazen, 1995, p. 252.
31 Sachs, 1945, p. 20.
32 Zweig, 1942, p. 282.
33 Freud to his daughter Sophie, 21/10/1919.

Chapter 3

Herr P ends his analysis with Prof Freud in a rather extraordinary way

New introductory lectures on psychoanalysis

Let's take a jump forward, over ten years, from the autumn of 1919 to the spring of 1932. Freud has just turned 76: he has been sick for some time and can hardly speak, he no longer attends conferences, and it is his daughter Anna who represents him in public. She went to Frankfurt for the award ceremony of the Goethe Prize and read his speech (1930). Again, it was Anna who went to express his thanks for the plaque placed on his birthplace in Freiburg, on the occasion of his 75th birthday (1931). The honours paid to Freud multiply: in January 1931, he is one of the first German-speaking foreigners to be invited to London to deliver the prestigious Huxley Lecture at the school of medicine. He had to decline the invitation which, let's note *en passant*, had been warmly proffered by Dr David Forsyth of the Charing Cross Hospital.

The economic and political conditions of the German world and of Austria are precarious again: in the occurrences and recurrences of history, the psychoanalytic movement is waiting for an institute to be opened in Budapest, and the publishing house is again going through a hard time. This is the context in which Freud decides to publish the *New Introductory Lectures on Psychoanalysis*: the intention is to keep interest in psychoanalysis alive and to renew the success of the publication of the first twenty-eight *Introductory Lectures* (1916–17) delivered in Vienna during the war, the aim being to fill the coffers of the *Verlag*. Freud presents these seven additional lectures as a continuation of the first series: indeed, the numbering is consecutive. In addition to this, "by an artifice of the imagination" (1933, p. 5), he decides to present them as if he were once again presenting them before an audience at the Lazarettgasse Psychiatric Clinic.

In the *New Lectures*, Freud returns to the basic concepts of his theory and proposes a summary of updates or new elements developed in the Twenties: the concept of the compulsion to repeat and the death drive, the structural organisation of the psyche (the second model, distinguishing the elements of Ego, Id, and Super-ego), the function of anxiety, the problem of female sexuality. . . . He also discusses the new perspectives offered by child psychoanalysis, as well as, more generally, the applications and possible relationships of psychoanalysis with religion, philosophy, and Marxism.

DOI: 10.4324/9781003246480-4

Freud devotes *Lecture XXX "Dreams and Occultism"* to a special subject, not included in the first *Lectures*. This is an organised and complex work whose main topic is "thought-induction," the only aspect of occultism that ever really interested him and on which he intended to shed some light using psychoanalysis. The final, and most compelling, illustration concerns a phenomenon of "apparent thought-transference" which had occurred during a psychoanalytic treatment and, as Freud clarifies, was perhaps even made possible by its influence. This was a case of thought transmission that he had experienced directly and was the one that had left the strongest impression on him. Here follows the report of that October 1919 session which, many years later, he decided to publish.

The "Forsyth case"

Let's make an initial reading of this case, keeping in mind Freud's premise:

> I shall tell it at great length and shall ask for your attention to a large number of details, though even so I shall have to suppress much that would have greatly increased the convincing force of the observation.
>
> (p. 47)

And now the *incipit:*

> Listen then:- One autumn day in the year 1919, at about 10.45 a.m., Dr David Forsyth, who had just arrived from London, sent in his card to me while I was working with a patient. . . . I only had time to greet him and to make an appointment to see him later. Dr Forsyth had a claim to my particular interest; he was the first foreigner to come to me after I had been cut off by the war-years and to bring a promise of better times.
>
> (p. 47–48)

Leaving aside Dr Forsyth, Freud moves on to describe the session with his 11:00 patient, "Herr P." Freud tells us that his analysis had already been going on for a long time: he was a man in his late 40s suffering from unspecified difficulties with women and seemed incapable of resolving them. Even though Freud had already suggested he stop the treatment, the patient had insisted on continuing "because he felt comfortable in a well-tempered father-transference." As Mr P was a pleasant and witty person, and the sessions with him were enjoyable, "in disregard of the strict rules of medical practice," Freud had agreed to continue with this analytic attempt but set the arrival of Western patients as the limit. And all of this despite the fact that the patient wasn't paying a fee, money having lost its value due to the high inflation.

As soon as the session has started, Mr P once again talks about his problems with women, mentioning the girl he had been courting, albeit very cautiously, for a long time: a beautiful, poor, and clever young woman who intimidated him also because she was still a virgin. At this point, the patient happens to mention for the first time that, when they are alone together, the girlfriend, unaware of the real reasons for his restraint, gives him the nickname "Herr von Vorsicht" (Mr *Foresight*). "I was struck by this information," Freud still remembers. "Dr Forsyth's visiting card lay beside me, and I showed it to him" (p. 48).

***

Sitting in his sturdy armchair, next to the couch where Mr P has just lain down, Freud has the newcomer, Dr Forsyth [Dr *Foresight*], still in mind, as he lets his gaze wander in the cold, dim light of the room, partly illuminated by the window overlooking the garden. The double door that is normally open onto the large and well-lit adjoining study – the second room with the desk at which he usually spends his evenings – has been blocked lately by an Egyptian stone relief, to keep the room warmer, as the tall majolica heater at the foot of the couch hasn't been used in a long while. . . . The constant creaking where the two heavy Egyptian steles rest on the oaken boards of the bookshelves seems to have stopped.

In the silence, something unusual has apparently reached Freud's trained ear. Like an oracle, the word uttered by Mr P translates into German what he's thinking in English and, as Freud bounces back and forth between his old and his new patient – from Mr *Vorsicht* to Dr *Forsyth* – emphasises its meaning of *Voraussicht* or *Vorsicht (Foresight* or *Caution!)*. The warning resounds in the presence of the ancient sculptures – Egyptian, Roman, Greek, Assyrian – which gaze fixedly from the full study's display cases and cabinets, and it echoes before the silent sphinxes and the funerary masks that peer out amongst iridescent vases, terracotta lamps, papyri, and panels depicting scenes from vanished epochs, scattered here and there on the walls, surrounded by shelves sagging with books.

The usual 11 o'clock session starts in a rather extraordinary way. What *Prophecy* is this? What should one pay *Attention* to? Has Freud, by any chance, thought about that devil, Ferenczi? About all the telepathic episodes in analysis that the Hungarian used to collect before the war? "The patient's 'thought-reading' associations always come at the beginning of the analysis," Ferenczi had written to him at the time.[1]

It seems as though the patient has already unconsciously sensed his rival's imminent appearance and the change in the attitude of the analyst towards him: through thought-induction he would have tuned in to the very same word Freud has in mind in the attempt to re-establish harmony between them.

Freud's response is a gesture: the name *Forsyth* is under his eyes. Leaning over from his armchair to the low table crammed with little statues like so many toy soldiers, he picks up the Englishman's visiting card that he had just put there and shows it to Mr P: the gesture, which relates to the concrete nature of reality, is at the same time a revelation of the "marvellous" and a chilling announcement of his dismissal, as Mr P knows that after the arrival of the new patient, Freud will no longer see him.

***

"These are the facts of the case," writes Freud (we resume reading from the *Lecture*), and immediately afterwards he warns us not to underestimate them, as there is something else hidden. With careful stage management, he builds up, but also anticipates for the reader, the session's suspense: there's more to know. He starts to explain that the combination *Forsyth-Vorsicht*, insignificant at a first glance, could not appear so to him in the light of the analytic relationship with P, as it had a close continuity with an associative chain that had already taken shape around the surname *Forsyte* in John Galsworthy's novels (1906). Freud informs us that, when he was young, Mr P had lived for some time in England, and just like him, he loved English literature: he had formed the habit of lending Freud books from his well-stocked library, thus enabling him to read works by English writers he hadn't known before. He recalls:

> One day he lent me a novel of Galsworthy's with the title *The Man of Property*, whose scene is laid in the bosom of a family invented by the author, bearing the name of "Forsyte". Galsworthy himself was evidently captivated by this creation of his, for in later volumes he repeatedly came back to the members of this family.
>
> (p. 49)

Informing us that a few days before the session, the patient had brought him a new book in the series, Freud explains that "The name 'Forsyte', and everything typical that the author had sought to embody in it" had acquired a distinctive meaning for the two of them and had become "part of *the secret language* which so easily grows up between two people who see a lot of each other" (my italics).

So there's another *Forsyte* who precedes his fellow-countryman, the doctor: in the analysis, too, a series has developed. Freud continues:

> Now the name "Forsyte" in these novels differs little from that of my visitor "Forsyth" and, as pronounced by a German, the two can scarcely be distinguished; and there is an English word with a meaning – "foresight" – which we should also pronounce in the same way and which would be translated "Voraussicht" or "Vorsicht". Thus P had in fact selected from his personal concerns the very name with which I was occupied at the same time as a result of an occurrence of which he was unaware. That begins to look better, you will agree.
>
> (p. 49)

The coincidence would seem to fit into the analytic dialogue only too well. As if P had immediately perceived the new nuance that the word "Forsyte" was taking on for Freud with the arrival of Dr Forsyth, almost anticipating his having unwittingly complained, "I'm a Forsyth too: at least, that's what my girlfriend calls me." In this statement Freud recognises both P's jealous claims and his sense of shame, because for his girlfriend, he's only a cautious "Herr von Vorsicht [gentleman of foresight]."

But the "telepathic" outburst of the patient's unconscious jealousy doesn't end here. The session goes on with two more associations that Freud, sensitised by the first coincidence, again experiences as "telepathic": not only does he consider them connected to the first association *Forsyth/Vorsicht* and produced by the same thought process, but helpful for re-evaluating and better understanding the conditions that determined it. And here he moves on to illustrate, one after the other, a slip of the tongue and a memory lapse by Mr P which had made him think of two more foreigners who could themselves be objects of jealousy.

As he shows how P, in nurturing his unconscious protest, seems to have direct access to his mind, Freud allows the reader too to take a look at the thoughts and affects he was dealing with at the time. Hence, just as in the heroic days of *The Interpretation of Dreams*, *Psychopathology of Every Day Life*, and *Jokes and Their Relation to the Unconscious*, frankly and with equal generosity, he once again opens a window onto his associations and shares with us his freely floating fantasies and memories during the session, letting us witness his creativity at work.

In the meantime, we may notice the way in which the patient picks up the "English" element introduced by Freud's gesture when he showed him the rival's name, and P consciously follows this associative thread as he goes on to ask Freud if, by any chance, Mrs Freud-Ottorego who teaches English at the People's University is his daughter. And here Freud clarifies:

> for the first time during our long period of intercourse he gave my name the distorted form to which I have indeed become habituated by functionaries, officials and compositors: instead of "Freud" he said "Freund".
>
> (p. 50)

The patient's slip of the tongue conjures up in Freud the memory of a bizarre episode.

One day in the previous week, after waiting in vain for Mr P to come for his session, he went to visit Anton von Freund, recently arrived from Hungary, and he discovered, to his great surprise, that Mr P lived on another floor of the same building that hosted his friend's *pension*. Humorously referring to this, he had then told Mr P that he had in a sense "paid him a visit," made a *house call*. He had not, however, mentioned von Freund's name.

Finally – and we're at the end of the session – he recalls that Mr P had hinted at a dream from which he'd woken "in a fright": a real nightmare, he called it. And here, he added that some time before, to someone who had asked him how to say nightmare in English, he'd wrongly replied *mare's nest*, which means "something incredible, a cock-and-bull story," forgetting the correct word *nightmare*.

Freud says nothing about the nightmare's content, nor does he analyse Mr P's memory lapse, just as he had not analysed the previous slip of the tongue, even though they are all instances that can be interpreted with psychoanalysis, breaches of the pre-conscious through which the repressed desire can find a way to express itself, overcoming censorship. Freud is only interested in explaining that for him, the direct association with the nightmare is Dr Ernest Jones, the author of a monograph on the subject,[2] and also that this last idea which had happened to surface in Mr P's mind reminds him of an episode that might have aroused his jealousy. Indeed, about a month earlier, Jones, after years of separation, had come to Vienna and – Freud emphasises this – had burst into the study right in the middle of a meeting with P. He gestured to the Englishman to move to the second room but P, having recognised him from the photo hanging in the waiting-room, had expressed the wish to be introduced to him. What Freud wonders is whether Mr P might have known about Jones's book on the nightmare, considering he didn't usually read books about psychoanalysis.

Freud proposes the interpretation that Mr P's unconscious associations, following the thread of the "English" element, had made him go back in his mind to two previous occasions which had aroused his jealousy and expressed a further protest, filled with mortification:

> A few days ago you paid a visit to my house – not, alas, to me but to a "Herr von Freund." This thought caused him to distort the name "Freud" into "Freund". The "Freud-Ottorego" from the lecture-syllabus must come in here because as a teacher of English she provided the manifest association. And now came the recollection of another visitor a few weeks before, of whom he was no doubt equally jealous, but for whom he also felt he was no match, for Dr Jones was able to write a monograph on the nightmare whereas he was at best only able to produce such dreams himself. His mention of his mistake about the meaning of "a mare's nest" comes into this connection, for it can only mean to say: "After all I'm not a genuine Englishman any more than I'm a genuine Forsyth".
>
> (p. 51)

Freud makes clear that the patient's jealous outbursts were to be considered neither inappropriate nor baffling because he'd been warned that the treatment, and their relationship, would end with the arrival of the foreign students and patients in Vienna. It's clear that he has no intention of lingering on the content of Mr P's analytic work. Freud doesn't add anything about this treatment. He's interested in discussing the issue of the transmission of thought, in distilling and clarifying the evocative impression raised in him by the three ideas emerging one after the other in his patient's associations. He works on the hypothesis that, during the session, Mr P had somehow gained unconscious access to his current thoughts and was thus able to surprise his affects more intimately and more directly than a conscious dialogue would allow. Indeed, Freud wonders if they were elements he himself was aware of (Dr Forsyth's arrival, the name of the friend-*Freund* he'd visited, the title of Jones's book): that is, a part of *his own* thoughts, which came to be integrated by way of an unconscious transmission into those of the patient, determining certain components of Mr P's associations; mentioning the nickname attributed by the girl, the Freud-Freund slip, the hint about the nightmare, and actually forgetting the word *nightmare* itself.

But could there be other ways through which the patient might know about Dr Forsyth's first visit, the name of the person he'd visited, and Jones's book on nightmares?

Freud analyses item by item the possibility that the patient could have a personal, independent knowledge of those data, and he immediately admits that – given the coincidence of the name "von Freund" with the German word "*Freund*" (friend) – that the *Freud/Freund* slip might just as easily have originated from Mr P's thoughts. Nor does he rule out the possibility of having himself inadvertently introduced the word *Freund* in his quip on the "house call," because Von Freund was actually a dear "friend" to him and the psychoanalytic movement, and his donations had made it possible to establish the publishing house. As we're in 1933, he adds a few words on the untimely death of his Hungarian friend, only a few years before Karl Abraham's: the two deaths that had, in the meantime, profoundly affected psychoanalysis.[3] He concludes:

> It is possible, therefore, that I had said to Herr P: "I visited a friend [*Freund*] in your house" and with this possibility the occult interest of his second association vanishes.
>
> (p. 52)

He then also tries to reduce the demonstrative force of the reference to the nightmare and the translation mistake – *mare's nest* instead of *nightmare* – as he doesn't feel he can exclude the possibility that Mr P may have come to know about Jones's *Nightmare* independently, from the titles of the new publications advertised on the wrappers of some of the books of the psychoanalytic publishing house that he owned.

Nevertheless, while the slip and the misremembering could also have been explained without the hypothesis of thought transference, the coincidence at the start of the session remained inexplicable. Freud dwells at length on this.

Was it possible – he wonders – that Mr P, having been informed months before about the existence of an English patient to whom he'd have to give up his place, might know his name and have found out that he'd been to see Freud on that very day, just a few minutes earlier? Could Freud himself have told him this name, a highly unlikely possibility, when at the beginning of the summer he'd told him he was waiting for a doctor from England to be instructed in analysis, "a first dove after the Deluge"? Freud is positive he has done no such thing: the hypothesis appears even more improbable to him given that mentioning the rival's name would bring up, during the session, the manifest association with the already significant "*Forsyte*," and a permanent trace would have remained in their memories. He even takes into consideration the possibility of having actually mentioned him and then erased the memory because of a resistance connected with a "secret inclination towards the miraculous" (p. 53): an inadmissible, unconscious inclination which, despite everything, he could suppose was being masked by his own declared scepticism. . . . He ends by stating that in any case, such a hypothesis would only explain why Mr P knew the Englishman's name and not that he was arriving on that very day.

At this point, in order not to neglect one last possibility, Freud considers the chance that, when P walked in, he'd noticed a particular excitement in him, of which Freud may have been unaware, and had drawn his own conclusions. Or else that he'd had the chance to bump into Dr Forsyth in Berggasse, had recognised him because of his typical English look and, jealous as he was, had immediately identified him as his dreaded antagonist.

Even though he ends his conjectures with a "*non liquet*," Freud declares his willingness to believe he has actually witnessed and participated in a phenomenon of thought transmission. He makes clear that he is not the first to have made this type of observation during an analysis: he does not mention Sàndor Ferenczi, who had never published his experiences of telepathy and from whom, in 1932, he had developed a certain emotional distance. He mentions two women instead: Helene Deutsch's work (1926) on the processes of analyst-patient "occult" transmission and on the value of intuition and empathy and, further on in the conclusion, an example taken from a recent article by Dorothy Burlingham on the "gold coin" of unconscious mother-child communication (1932).

Solve et coagula

The "Forsyth case" rightly belongs among the texts that founded the new science, those self-analytic works which the father of psychoanalysis transmitted to posterity, allowing us to participate in the intimate work of interpretation on the still raw and private material of his profound, psychic texture.[4] It is a rich and extraordinary text in which he reveals his countertransference associations, almost inadvertently, on the occasion of a session during which a potentially traumatic change is occurring: for the patient, who will have to stop his analysis, but also for the analyst, as we will understand later on.

It's a valuable opportunity for observing Freud at work. In the foreground, there is a crossroads of languages involving a constant work of translation: from English into German and vice versa, from the secret dialect of analysis into the shared language, from the gesture to the written form, and going all the way back to the original mother-child language. Different narrative forms are intertwined: the novel, the personal memoir, the clinical case study, the monograph, the theoretical dissertation, and the fiction of the university lecture which acts as the framing device.

Time expands between forecast and memory: the session in progress is filled with the expectations about the afternoon consultation and hopes for survival, while at the same time it goes back over past events, from the first intrusion by Ernest Jones, to the patient's missed appointment, to the strange home visit by the analyst. Space extends and becomes organised in order to accommodate the movements of the different subjects and of Freud himself: the consulting room with the two adjacent rooms, the two different floors of the building and the two patients' abodes . . . the comings and goings of real and imaginary characters on the scene.

In puns nouns are modified and become transformed, taking on new meanings and magical elements: surnames that are also ordinary nouns become surprisingly evocative. With the first coincidence between the twin words, *Forsyth-Vorsicht*, the nuances of meaning inscribed in the secret code of that analysis and in the still-undefined term *Forsyte*, which meant the same thing to analyst and patient, suddenly appear like a portent. Dr Forsyth separates the analyst from the patient and breaks the secret language. For Freud, he is the dove that announces the end of his adversities and allows him to look towards the future (*foresight*), for psychoanalysis but for himself as well. Mr P, who now comes with the nickname given to him by his young beloved, is left with defeat and the sense of castration (*Vorsicht*).

New and different versions of the qualities enshrined in that *Man of Property* (victory – wealth – arrogance – clout – foresight – prevention – precaution – castration – poverty – helplessness – defeat) rise up into consciousness, enabling the interpretation of this clinical case which has been presented since the very beginning not just as a likely disorder of male virility but as a place of impasse and limitation in the treatment itself.

In Vienna's emergency of extreme poverty and hunger, free treatment seems to represent Freud's generosity but also his impotence: money is short, and it has lost its significance as currency for trade, measurement, limitation, and guarantee of the sense of reality. Between a patient who will pay well, in hard currency, and a non-paying one – one who does not even satisfy a woman – between desire and need, Freud is confronted with the problem of shifting the translation from one patient to another, from the friend to the enemy, from German into English. And, like the novel's author, the analyst may have been unwittingly taken over by the *Saga* and grown fond of his old patient.

The issue here is *transference* in its full etymological sense of *transfer*, *transport*, *transmission, and translation*: from the uneasy displacement of Freud's transference from one language to another to Mr P's translation mistake.

The session is a sequence of the most diverse representations of separation: in the midst of loss, exclusion, and expectation, there is a Dr Forsyth who finally arrives, a von Vorsicht who will always be late and whom Freud gets ready to greet, a Mr P who misses the session, a Dr Anton von Freund who is about to be tragically lost – in 1933 he is counted with Abraham among the disciples who died prematurely – and finally a Dr Ernest Jones who turns up in the room like a real nightmare and is invited to leave.

The alchemy of the session, its *solve et coagula*, revolves around a play of coincidences and distinctions. The topic of English is not just a relevant associative thread for Mr P. It is becoming crucial for psychoanalysis which, by opening up to an international dimension, will have to *speak* English, which, for better or worse, is the language of the only standard translation.[5] It's crucial for Freud, who will have to analyse the new Western disciples in a foreign language and modify, with a great deal of effort and suffering, the listening act, the construction of thought and the articulation of words and accent; we also know that he will later experience serious damage to his mouth which will make it hard for him to speak and to eat, but in 1933, that will not deter him from pretending that the *New Series of Lectures* were actually delivered: "Listen then . . . ."

An associative coherence features throughout the words and actions of the characters whom Freud brings to life for us, against the background of an intense dialogue of questioning glances (*for sight*) – visiting cards, plaques, photos, book covers. . . . All of this seems to be in search of a representation for that first singular coincidence, the *mother of the entire series*, which Freud proposes as an involuntary joke, although it already contains the metaphorical sense of a deep identification with the patient: his unintentional and unexpected *home visit* to Mr P. This first construction seems to anticipate the surprise that Freud will feel on hearing his thoughts resound in the word uttered by the patient at the beginning of the session, that German term *Vorsicht*, meaning *caution, attention*! and echoing the English *Forsyth-foresight* in the sense of *forecast-prophecy*.

The *Postscript* of a *Preface*

After Freud's death, a first manuscript dating back to 1921 was found: it was untitled, bearing only the heading *Vorbericht* (Preface),[6] and it contained all the observations on the transmission of thought that he had collected up to that year and which he intended to share during a private reading with the members of the committee. The work, a sort of draft for *Lecture XXX* (1933), appears among the posthumous Freudian publications with the title *Psycho-Analysis and Telepathy* (1921 [1941]). We would seek it in vain in the original version of the "Forsyth case," the third one, which at the time was intended to close the presentation: attached to *Vorbericht* (Preface) in a separate manuscript, entitled *Nachtrag* (Postscript, 1921 [2010]), at some point it went inexplicably missing. For this reason, the version in *Lecture XXX* was, until today, the only known one.

Mr P is perhaps Freud's last great patient. He is certainly the least known: a hidden, occulted case that is missing from the famous clinical case studies.

Reading the case leads us to one of the most compelling Freudian pages, one that, like a dream, seems to open up new meanings every time in an endless series of *Chinese boxes*, with the looming risk of being dragged away by the *black tide* of occultism without being able to stop it in the interpretation. And like the dream, we will discover that the story has a "navel" which, in the linearity of the written word, filters "the remains of that big, multidimensional novel that took shape in the transference."[7]

Only a handful of authors have tackled the critical analysis of the Forsyth case: among them Servadio (1955a), Fodor (1971), Granoff and Rey (1983), Torok (1983), and Derrida, too (1981). As we engage in this endeavour, as Freud himself warns us at the beginning of the Lecture, "we will proceed along a narrow path, but one which may lead us to a wide prospect" (p. 31).

By keeping the clinical event in mind – despite its complex and enigmatic character – and most of all by maintaining Sigmund Freud's viewpoint as the narrator of that session, we will try to appreciate the greatness and the meaning of this example and find a place for the "transmission of thought" in the tradition of psychoanalytic theory.

The quintessential question of telepathy: "Whose thoughts are these that inhabit my internal world?" reveals a direct connection with psychoanalysis but also a possible competitor.[8] If, as Derrida states (1981), the most difficult truth to grasp, after Freud, would be the *non*-existence of telepathy – and a theory of the unconscious wouldn't be conceivable without a theory of telepathy – nonetheless it was and still is problematic to combine these phenomena with the defence of the *strong* theory of an individual unconscious.

And Torok writes:

> telepathy was probably the name Freud unwittingly gave to a foreign body within the corpus of psychoanalysis, . . . precursor to a type of research that dares the imagination as regards oneself and others, . . . an ongoing and groping research that – at the moment of its emergence and in the area of its relevance – had not yet grasped either the true scope of its own inquiry of the conceptual rigor necessary for its elaboration.
>
> (1983, p. 86)

It's not surprising that in October 1919, when he directly experiences it for the first time during the treatment with Mr P, Freud's attention and scientific curiosity are captured by telepathy. After that, and for over ten years, it becomes the object of private, "occult" research of his own, which only intersects with the official theory in 1932, appearing in *Lecture XXX* mentioned previously. After the first explorations on the work of fortune-tellers in the company of Ferenczi, dating back to the years 1909–1911, between 1919 and 1932, Freud's thoughts on telepathy come to consider the possibility of an unconscious psychology *à deux*. This field of exploration, the hardest, brings him once again face to face with the feminine: telepathy forces one to start over from the beginning, from the question originally asked by hysterical patients, in order to access that pre-Oedipal maternal essence in which suggestion, mystic experience, and faith in the miraculous are rooted. In the primary relationship, this is also where the sense of the reality of subject and object is based. It is in all respects a *Postscript*, a look from afar at what has passed, a retrospective thinking about origins.

Research on occultism – a necessary and valuable step for the creation of psychoanalysis – gives us the chance to retrace the great Saga of the twentieth century, the last novel that fascinated generations of historians, biographers, and writers.

The understanding of the distinctive phenomenon which Freud experiences as *direct psychical transference* requires that all the historical, affective, personal, and relational circumstances of the session be taken into consideration in order to interpret it in the light of the original context from which it was uprooted. Hence, a brief reconstruction of Sigmund Freud's history may be helpful, from his discovery to his first group of disciples.[9]

The issue of "telepathy" will lead us to acknowledge the meaning of "thought transference" at different levels: in the clinical experience of the analytic setting and in the parent-child relationship but, above all, in the specific ways that psychoanalytic knowledge was transmitted by the master to his first disciples. Those pioneers explored the boundaries of knowledge and bravely founded a discipline about man that was an alternative to suggestion and magic beliefs: this field didn't coincide with either philosophy, religion, or the materialism of scientific thought that was fast developing its techniques. Though it was a science – in having material to be observed, a method of observation to be respected, and a body of theory to be compared with the observed material and with the method[10] – from the outset, the implementation of psychoanalysis proved very different from the sciences, as it entailed an apprenticeship that passed through the personal characteristics of the living relationship with Freud. These training paths modified the discipline and made it grow, giving personal forms to the theory: the story of those first masters, as of the later ones, left its stamp on the concepts and language of psychoanalysis, which cannot be fully understood and processed if no account is taken of what was and will be, time after time, set aside in the transmission, foreclosed, denied, split, or repressed.

The events of the Forsyth case form the *fil rouge* with which to reconstruct a piece of the history of psychoanalytic theory and movement. The session takes place in a post-war period of great change involving Freud's life and the lives of the committee's members, affecting the political destiny of psychoanalysis and preparing the way for the theoretical developments of the twenties. On various levels, we are at a generational crossroads: the nucleus of knowledge that distinguished psychoanalysis from other disciplines and defined its initial international identity was no longer just a fragile achievement to be protected but a wealth of knowledge that could now be passed on.

The Forsyth case shows itself to be the turning point in this transition: between *Preface* and *Postscript*, if Freud's text has rhyme and reason, there is an *actual*[11] content that eludes discovery, an "occult" legacy with traumatic but highly valuable aspects ("foreign body"[12] and "gold coin"), of a kind that will require more than one generation of analysts and disciples to win it back. We don't find simple resistances in action, Freud's and those of the people who found themselves receiving and trying to process this legacy: Jones, to mention only one, with his chapter on *Occultism*. The postponing seems to meet the need for time to pass when faced with an experience that appears, just like telepathy, to be a short circuit, devoid of mediation and a source of amazing disquiet. Every theory is a "forecast made after the event," but in this substantial and conflicted delay, a strange mechanism of concealment, rather than occultism, seems to be at work: everything conspires to unhinge the narration from its context, but it leaves detectable traces nonetheless.

We'll pick up the repeated signals, the strange "coincidences" that crowd around this text and mark its rhythms and stages, so that we can retrace together the path that led me, as a sixth-generation psychoanalyst, to study more deeply the original roots of relational developments in contemporary psychoanalysis. And along the way, by recovering and trying to interpret the historical material available today, we'll bump into that famous manuscript which, after being many times forgotten, censored and lost, James Strachey declared irretrievably missing in the fifties. As in the "Fort-Da" game, *das Spiel von "Fortsein,"*[13] like the disappearing and returning *wooden reel*, a repeatedly intercepted letter finally reaches its destination.[14]

Notes

1 Ferenczi to Freud, 17/08/1910; see Pierri, 2022.
2 Jones, 1912.
3 Von Freund had died a few months later, at the beginning of 1920, Abraham in 1925.
4 Kamieniak, 2000.
5 Steiner, 1991.
6 I choose to translate *Vorbericht* as Preface rather than the more literal *Preliminary Report* in order to emphasize the particular meaning of the time spent waiting for the future, in the sense of avant-coup as a counterpart to the après-coup, *Nachträg(lichkeit)*, Postscript.
7 Lavaggetto, 1985, p. 250.
8 Forrester, 1990, p. 355.
9 See Pierri, 2022.
10 Riolo, 2015.
11 In the sense of time of the primeval: see Scarfone, 2014.
12 Torok, 1983 p. 86.
13 The game of "*be gone*," Freud, 1920, p. 12.
14 Derrida, 1980.

Chapter 4

The duellists*

Meeting in Zurich

Dr Ernest Jones, quoted repeatedly as a source of testimony and historical reconstructions, and cited by Freud among the characters in the Forsyth case as an object of the patient's jealousy, is not a member of the supporting cast: he was one of the story's main protagonists.

It must be admitted that, like all witnesses and biographers, he was pretty unreliable: suffice it to say that he earned the nickname of "the Welsh liar" in imitation of the more famous Lloyd George well before taking on the task of historically reconstructing Freud's work, which brought him global recognition as well as countless criticisms.

Since his narrative fictions were guided by noble and emotional motives and by his obvious personal involvement in the events as they unfolded, we intend to trust him and his subjectivity.

We will keep his version of events in mind because, while handing down institutional, formative, and official truths of psychoanalysis, it lets us intuit the censored and repressed ones between the lines.

We have just witnessed the scene in which Ernest Jones, arriving in Vienna after the long years of separation caused by the war, plunges unexpectedly into Freud's consulting room right in the middle of a session with Herr P and is asked to wait in the adjoining room.

It's like a practical joke of fate, or else of Freud's preconscious, that Jones is cited in connection with a case of thought transmission, given that he did not by any means share his teacher's interest in telepathy.

Our Jones was neither a visionary nor a dreamer. His childhood dreams were nightmares, and it is no coincidence that in 1910 he began to study mediaeval superstitions. With the aim of working through his childhood terrors of devils, vampires, werewolves, witches, and ghosts, he appropriately connected them to his oedipal images of his parents.

His monograph on the nightmare, mentioned by Freud in the Forsyth case, was written when he was living in Toronto, the time when Jung was immersing himself in astrology and Freud and Ferenczi were deep in their investigations of

DOI: 10.4324/9781003246480-5

clairvoyants and prophecies. It was as if Jones were trying to catch up with them and fight back, and he had no illusions about this: in the grip of another kind of "occultism," he was necessarily "the man of true lies and true myths," a liar who firmly believed in his own lies and eventually, as Rodrigué (1996) says, managed to make some of them true. Like Houdini, while creating his fictions, he maintained his solitary crusade against occultism as he saw it in Freud and by which he felt almost persecuted.

The irony and misfortune of the Forsyth case are accentuated by the fact that Jones figures as a walk-on in a clinical vignette centred on jealousy, where the occult protagonist and engine of the incident – the Dr Forsyth who had just arrived from England – had been a rival of his since his university days . . .

A story within a story, it is startling to discover what happens when we foreground the relationship between David Forsyth and Ernest Jones, the two Britons to whom Freud refers in recalling his own associations in the session: there are elements in the relationship that echo the fight for survival at the centre of the session to which it forms a background.

We will see how David Forsyth, this character who seems to appear quite by chance shortly before Herr P's arrival and makes only a slight contribution to the "telepathic" event before being forgotten, was far from extraneous to the profound and intense affects that were being stirred up and homing in on the Master.

In fairness to Jones, it should be remembered that he had been the first foreign visitor at the end of the war. He had managed to enter Austria and regain contact with his beloved professor just a week before the arrival of Forsyth – not a month before, as Freud recalled in *Lecture XXX* – so that on his way home at the beginning of October, he coincided with his colleague who was heading for Vienna. At least this is the version of events that Jones repeats in 1957 when, in commenting on the "Forsyth" case, he corrects a minor error in Freud's memory of the date of his own visit:

> he [Freud] had made his notes only some considerable time after the episode, and there is no guarantee against some unconscious touching up of the story. One minor error I can myself correct. Freud said I had been in Vienna a month before Forsyth's visit. In fact it was the same week, for I dined with Forsyth in Zurich when I was returning from Vienna and he on his way there.
> (*III*, p. 435)

The more substantial and incorrigible error, as Jones makes very clear to us, was his teacher's interest in occultism.

For now, let's note that – whether as a reaction to his irritation and jealousy of Forsyth, who was coming to be analysed by Freud, or as a way of circumventing his sense of exclusion by saying "I was there first" – Jones cites his having dined with his colleague in Zurich as proof for his own version of the facts.

For some, this additional note might be unseemly, inappropriate: "the imagination can indulge."[1] At the very time when Freud is trapped by his poverty in starving Vienna, waiting for foreigners to bring food, dollars, and hope for the future, the two British doctors, free, rich, and elegant, would be dining together in Zurich like gentlemen on holiday, maybe on the terrace of the luxurious restaurant of the Hotel Baur au Lac. . . . It strikes a discordant note.

There is no doubt that Zurich was a propitious venue in those days. While the war raged all around it, it had transformed itself into the most important and habitable city in Europe: a "meeting place of all intellectual trends; to be sure, it had become equally a centre for every sort of trafficker, for speculators, spies, propagandists."[2] Asylum-seekers from every nation had found shelter there: socialist and Bolshevik refugees as well as artists, writers, poets, musicians, and pacifist intellectuals in search of a new model for a homeland. In that strip of German-speaking land that had managed to stay out of the war, people seemed more inclined to communicate, even on the trams and in the streets, and all the world's languages could be heard in the restaurants and cafés. At the Cabaret Voltaire, the Dadaist group, performers with a sharply honed vitality, enlivened the evenings with noisy exhibitions of dance, music, readings, and heated discussions. And there were those who went on talking late into the night, until even the Bellevue or Odéon cafés had turned out their lights and the lake slept.

For Ernest Jones, Zurich was especially evocative because he had stayed there as a teenager during a memorable journey before his graduation, accompanied by his father.[3] He had returned to Zurich alone when he was nearly 30 to work at the Burghölzli with Carl Jung, who had put him in touch with Sigmund Freud.

Returning from Vienna in that October of 1919, Jones certainly had no intention of meeting Jung, or even Bleuler, who had both been out of the psychoanalytic movement for some time, but instead – and here we add a detail that Freud omits – he was taking on the political leadership of the movement by becoming president of the International Association, a post originally created for the Swiss.

And there was another important event awaiting him in that brief visit to Zurich: he had just enough time to marry Katherine Jokl, whom he had met at the start of the summer during his outward journey, and he set off with her to his new life in London. . . . Ernest Jones was at the high point of his existence.

Lulled by the sweet calm of the lake nestling among the mountains and the happy state of his affective and professional circumstances, he could meet his old friend Forsyth in a spirit of truce from their longstanding rivalry.

The duellists

Jones and Forsyth seemed fated to keep crossing each other's paths and renewing their private feud, since they both spent much of their lives in Freud's orbit like the duellists in Conrad's novel whose story became a legend in Napoleon's army, their duel running through the epic of the imperial wars.

Their paths had started crossing when they were both students at University College Hospital.

The Welshman, Ernest Jones, two years younger than David Forsyth, had arrived in London from Cardiff. Born in the parish of Llwchwr in Wales, an eldest child and only son, with three sisters, Jones came from a modest social background: his father was a technician in the coal mines. His mother had had to wean him prematurely, and he consequently described himself as "a puny and ailing infant, with pronounced rickets and a not very happy disposition."[4] Dark-haired, small, and stocky as a terrier, he always had delicate health and a pallid complexion, and before the age of 30, he developed a rheumatoid arthritis which flared up repeatedly throughout his life.

From his autobiography we learn about his night terrors but also about certain phobias, a fear of heights, for example (with the fear of falling or being pushed down), perhaps in reaction to his father's ambitious expectations and the intense conflict between the two of them. Born on New Year's Day, the celebration of his birthday had always been overshadowed, and – so he tells us – he never liked the names he had been given, Alfred Ernest, after Queen Victoria's second son.

He tried to live as if he were his father's younger brother, never tolerating his authoritarian behaviour or accepting the idea of following in his footsteps as a mining engineer. Instead, from childhood onwards, Ernest wanted to be a doctor. Being a dedicated student, he always achieved excellent grades at school and enrolled at Cardiff College at the age of only 16 before qualifying as a doctor in London in record time.

In 1898, before his graduation, his father had rewarded him with a journey together to Europe – France, Switzerland, and Italy – a sort of grand tour which did not prevent the final clash. Having decided to cut his ties with his father and his homeland, armed with a First Class degree and doctorate, Jones anticipated rapid progress in his career and an ascent to a higher social class. At this point, his temperament, his difficult relationship with paternal authority, and of course his Welsh origin were serious stumbling blocks for him.

Paradoxically, this ambitious Welshman's worst faults, besides his extreme efforts to defend a precarious primogeniture, were his indisputable talent, his quick Celtic intelligence, his almost ferocious stamina,[5] the fact that he was hardly ever in the wrong, and that he could always do things better than anyone else:[6] from chess to rose-growing to figure-skating [about which he even wrote a manual (1931b)], it was hard to match him. These unquestionable gifts, fed by his arrogance (the sharp tongue his mother had always scolded him for), ended up leaving him empty inside: in London, after hurting the feelings of many senior colleagues, he became *persona non grata*.

It happened that while at the North-Eastern Hospital for Children, in Bethnal Green, where he exasperated the staff with his efficiency and his incessant questions, he impudently challenged the diagnosis of none other than a director of the National Hospital in Queen's Square. He was probably correct, but he was forced to resign and, despite his gold medal and his doctorate, he failed to be appointed to the National Hospital. With his character, his gaffes, and the incidents he was starting to accumulate, Jones was not a suitable candidate.

David Forsyth, a name that seems like a destiny, could be a character in one of the "Forsyte" novels from Galsworthy's *Saga*. Were it not for Freud's *Lecture XXX*, we would not know of his existence, despite his being cited among the founders of the London and British Psychoanalytical Societies and appearing every year in the IPA Bulletin's list of the UK's analysts. Curiously, the *International Journal of Psychoanalysis* does not feature a single work by him, though there are several reviews of his articles or books on psychoanalysis – published outside the Association – signed by the editor, our Ernest Jones.

The Archives of the British Psycho-Analytical Society hold a binder containing 50 letters exchanged by Jones and Forsyth in early 1920 after they had both returned to London concerning the imminent launching of the *International Journal*: they deal with a controversy that had arisen over donations for setting up the journal and the choosing of its editors.[7]

Apart from this material and a few letters in which Freud mentions his British pupil – and discusses the withdrawal of Forsyth's support for the journal – the valuable but obscure psychoanalytic works that he was able to publish have left few traces to help us track them down.

We know that David Forsyth was born in Greenwich, London, in 1877, a few years before the calculation of the meridian and the drawing of the line through the old Observatory, a fact that fits well with our Forsyth's habitual inclination to measurement and accuracy. Coming from a more prosperous family than Jones, he was the fifth of six children (three boys and three girls). His elder brother, Cecil, was a well-known composer and musicologist who played the viola in various orchestras in London and in 1914 moved in New York. After attending the John Roan School in Greenwich, David followed the path set out for him by his father, who was a doctor, and on qualifying from Guy's Hospital, he became a fellow of the Royal College of Physicians in 1910.

He invested curiosity and expectations in the devotion to science which had found no response in his rigid Church of England education. In fact, rather than medicine, the "first love" of his youth had been biology, whose ideas were permeating and renovating medical science:

> Before my medical training, I possessed a fervent interest in natural history, and, better than any other way of spending my life, I should have liked to devote it in this direction. But like most others, I needed to earn my bread and butter.[8]

Endowed with acute, disciplined, and meticulous, perhaps even pedantic, intelligence, Forsyth was a true Englishman, "an able man," and certainly "a model of respectability,"[9] possessing that temperate humour which prevents grand gestures but can, when the occasion arises, unexpectedly catch fire.

The two were not made for mutual understanding, being so different in their origins and character and so alike in their oppositeness: Jones ambitious and defensive, Forsyth calmer, identified with his father, and always ready to wait for the right moment to come out on top in sibling conflicts.

Their friendship at university was compromised at the end of their studies by their professional examinations: Jones came first in the doctoral examination of 1903, while Forsyth had to make do with second place, but it was the Englishman who gained the post at the university hospital in 1906.

Indefatigable and tenacious, Jones's job applications were bringing a growing pile of rejections, and he also had to give up a promising betrothal (his first relationship, with a woman ten years older from an excellent family). He seemed trapped in a vicious circle dominated by what psychoanalysis is accustomed to calling a castration complex. He later tried to interpret this deeply rooted condition:

> The premature weaning and early ill-health had combined with internal factors to induce a deep feeling of insecurity and inferiority, against which the life force (for I must have had somewhere an unusual amount of vitality) had reacted by building up a defence of the opposite extreme, an unwarranted belief in the omnipotence of my wishes.
>
> (1959, p. 115)

His small stature, the fact that he seemed younger than his years, his Welsh sense of inferiority, his aspiration towards a higher social and cultural level, and finally the very common surname "Jones" (which he often thought of changing) combined to provide material for the complex that had begun to manifest itself in this young attention-seeking doctor who was also good-looking, elegant, and capable of making women fall in love with him: his lively eyes; his rapid, fluent speech; the animation of his gestures; and the elegance of his appearance made him "irresistible to women."[10]

And so, undaunted, Dr Ernest Jones had opened a private neurology clinic together with an older colleague, the neurosurgeon Wilfred Trotter (who later became his brother-in-law) and, being short of funds, tried to survive by performing every kind of medical activity. Meanwhile, despite having ruled out work in a psychiatric hospital, he began to specialise in psychopathology.

His interests turned towards psychoanalysis: he and Trotter had come across the review of Freud and Breuer's *Studies on Hysteria* in *Brain*, and they decided to take German lessons in order to begin studying the *Traumdeutung* right away.

And so Jones also started practising psychoanalysis, the first in Britain to do so, as he never failed to repeat.[11] But psychoanalysis was no help in his professional life: when one of his first patients, the sister of a colleague, was cured of hypnosis and decided on a divorce, the ex-husband, a neurologist in New York, persecuted him for years because of this unwanted consequence of the treatment. He later became responsible for a couple of unpleasant and much more embarrassing incidents while busily applying psychoanalysis to his research on sexuality by interviewing children at the School for the Mentally Handicapped and the West End Hospital for Nervous Diseases. Principally, he failed to respect the rule about visiting children in the presence of a third person.[12] This time he was accused of paedophilia and indecent behaviour, spending a day under arrest. There were no legal repercussions, and the magistrate closed the case with a letter full of cordiality – so Jones informs us – but many colleagues were inclined to believe the accusation.

This and subsequent episodes of naiveté, imprudence, or outright abuse, which cast a dark shadow over the man who was to become the world's chief exponent and ambassador of psychoanalysis, caused the decisive collapse of his reputation.

And so it was that at the age of 29, Ernest Jones was forced to emigrate to Canada.

The paths of the two old university friends seemed to have divided forever until the time came when, each unaware of the other, they both found themselves face to face with Freud.

The first training analysis in Budapest

Before leaving London for his exile, Jones decided to make a long trip to the Continent for study, visiting the best psychiatric clinics: in Paris, Munich, and lastly Zurich, at the Burghölzli, where he collaborated with Jung on organising the first psychoanalytic congress. It was in Salzburg in 1908 that he met Sigmund Freud in person.

This meeting changed the whole course of his life . . . Jones was not yet 30, and he was struck by the intellectual power of the 50-year-old Freud, who seemed such an unaffected and unassuming man and to whom Jones listened as he spoke off the cuff in his usual fascinating way for a full four hours. Freud presented the case that later became famous as *The Rat Man* (1909).

In a fit of enthusiasm, Jones decided to follow the professor to Vienna.

He arrived in Berggasse with Abraham A Brill, who, having completed his training at the Burghölzli, was about to return to New York where he had emigrated as a young child (alone, with little money in his pocket, leaving his parents in Austria along with a future as a rabbi).[13] At this first meeting with his new followers, Freud, who had an excellent though rather literary grasp of English, raised the question of translating his work, especially the problem of how to render the various technical terms, and he initially granted the rights to Brill, whom he believed to be bilingual.

The two foreigners went to lunch with Freud several times, and after a Wednesday dinner, they took part in a meeting of the "Psychological Society," which was then still held in Freud's waiting room, where Wilhelm Stekel read a paper on "The Genesis of Psychic Impotence."[14] Through the dense clouds of smoke generated by the participants on that evening of 6 May 1908, an important person momentarily appeared in the doorway of the waiting room: a pretty young girl named Anna who had been woken by the talk downstairs.[15]

Anna Freud, who was nearly 13, had already acquired the habit of attending the meetings, sitting slightly apart to listen. There was a sort of complicity with her father, and we do not know if she had had to earn this Wednesday evening privilege or if her mother's inattention had left the way clear for her. Martha later reported that, on her husband's express wishes, none of their sons had followed in his footsteps but that no one had been able to stop the youngest child from doing so.[16] On this occasion, Martha was visiting her mother in Hamburg, and Anna could not resist her curiosity about the new English-speaking guests: even in old age, she would recall the new language making such a pleasant impression on her that she decided to learn it, and remember the handsome presence of Ernest Jones, who must surely have seemed the most attractive of her father's pupils.[17]

From Vienna, Jones went on to spend some days in Budapest at the invitation of Sándor Ferenczi, whom he had just met.

Later on, once he was living in Canada, Freud's trip to America with Jung and Ferenczi gave him the chance to meet his colleagues again after two years, when they came together to attend the conference at Clark University in Worcester.[18]

In early 1911, Ernest Jones found himself involved in further career-threatening scandals in Toronto, where he had become senior physician at the new Ontario Clinic for Nervous Diseases. Not only had he been so maladroit as to insert overexplicit sexual details of his clinical cases into his publications, which had disturbed his North American colleagues, but he had been having difficulty maintaining the boundaries of the therapeutic relationship and dealing with the excesses of the transference.[19] And his professional difficulties were compounded by a crisis in his relationship with Loe Kann, the partner who had supported him since his first difficulties in London and had followed him to Canada.

Despite regaining faith in his pupil, Freud had started to worry about Jones's persistent difficulty in mastering his sexuality:[20] the news of the Canadian scandal had troubled Freud, and he was not reassured by reading the monograph on the nightmare and superstition which Jones sent him at that time,[21] in which he showed his ability to make diligent interpretations of intense, repressed incestuous desires.

After Freud had taken Loe Kann into analysis in Vienna at her request, in 1913, he persuaded Jones to go to Budapest so that he could be analysed by Sándor Ferenczi.

And so, unlike David Forsyth after the war, Jones was not analysed by Freud: even though Ferenczi could be considered the most capable and creative clinical talent of the age, it was a disappointment to be sent to someone other than Freud. Jones interpreted the professor's advice as a way of helping him with the difficult separation from his partner of so many years[22] – a break he seemed entirely unable to face – but above all as preparation for an imminent investiture. In 1912, the secret committee had been set up, and by summer 1913, relations with Jung had been completely compromised. Jones, who was about to resume practice in London, recalled, "After consultation with Ferenczi, Freud decided to recommend me – I was then thirty-four – as Jung's successor and this was perhaps the reason why he advised me that spring to undergo a didactic analysis."[23]

This was when Ernest Jones really changed, in spite of himself. It is not easy to be certain about such radical transformations, and some doubts are permissible, but there were no more scandals, or at least no obvious, gross ones. From now on, Jones was accused of excessive respectability and paying too much attention to the conformist, conservative tendency of the scientific world in his homeland. It came to the point that Freud irritably joked about Jones giving himself the airs of a diplomat from the League of Nations.[24]

Forsyth, the paediatrician "once a friend of mine"

This was the time, towards the end of Jones's stay in Budapest, that an old acquaintance, David Forsyth, reappeared in his life. The paediatrician who had stayed in London had become interested in psychology, and this had led him to discover Freud's psychoanalysis.

Since his student days, Forsyth had felt deeply dissatisfied at how medical training and the care of patients neglected the psychological aspects of illness: after qualifying, he initially gravitated towards psychiatry and planned to work in a psychiatric hospital. Like Jones, he soon gave up the idea. Many years later, recalling that brief psychiatric experience in his frank but impeccable style, after praising the administrative efficiency of the mental hospitals and deploring the absolute lack of a scientific basis to the work they were doing, he declared that for him to live in those conditions would, "psychologically speaking," mean "intellectual death" (1932).

Forsyth was certainly not an easy person, and he was searching for something to believe in, something that would really convince him. For a long time he remained interested in the incurable conflict that he felt between the demands of the religious beliefs that had sometimes made him so unhappy in his childhood and the faith and extreme freedom that he was experiencing in the increasingly assertive world of science. Psychology, and child psychology in particular, would provide him with a helpful developmental model for understanding these various expressions of the human mind, and culture more generally.

On joining the staff of Charing Cross Teaching Hospital, David Forsyth had directed his interests permanently towards medical and paediatric psychology, also starting to work at the Evelina Hospital for Sick Children and distinguishing himself among his young colleagues for his skill in clinical practice and research.[25] He won the Rogers Award for original research in medical science. Being especially passionate about understanding the importance of children's living conditions, in 1909, Forsyth had published a paediatric study which included many chapters devoted to child psychology, child-rearing, and the therapeutic relationship.

Having become familiar with the writings of Freud, he had started using psychoanalysis some time after Jones, not only with adult patients but also with children, and probably with greater care and attention than his Welsh colleague. He had presented two papers about the new discipline and his own experiences of using the treatment to the Medical Graduates' College and Polyclinic, and in 1913, these were published in the *British Medical Journal* with the title "On Psychoanalysis."

The article, one of the first on the subject to appear in the United Kingdom, summarised the theory about the aetiology of the infantile sexuality of the psychoneuroses proposed by Sigmund Freud; illustrated the method of free association together with the verbal association test devised by Jung; and gave instructions about the use of dream-interpretation, including some clinical examples. Though he expressed his puzzlement at the application of the interpretation of sexuality in all cases of psychoneurosis, Forsyth showed that he had tested the new method, had verified its scientific bases, and was keeping himself up to date.

It was this article, appearing in July, which was immediately noted by Freud, who sent a postcard to Ferenczi from Marienbad, where he was on holiday, asking him to get information about the author from Jones, who was in analysis in Budapest.

It just so happened that Ernest Jones knew this Forsyth well. What we don't know is whether Jones was aware of his colleague's commitment to psychoanalysis or that he was teaching university courses on it and had written about it in such a prestigious journal. Later on, he certainly always took care to specify his own priority in terms of British psychoanalytic publication:

> A year or two before the war an old acquaintance, Dr David Forsyth, independently became interested in psycho-analysis to the extent of practising it. A general stir of interest was beginning, but there were no other practitioners. I had already published a couple of papers in English periodicals, and these were followed by three each by Eder and Forsyth – all before the war.
>
> (1959, pp. 228–229)[26]

In Jones's reply to Freud, besides his criticisms of Jung's conferences in New York and news about the progress and imminent conclusion of his own analysis, appears the laconic comment: "The *British Medical Journal*, which you mention in your card, I have not yet seen; Forsyth is a *Kinderarzt* [paediatrician], once a friend of mine" (22/07/1913).

It cannot have been easy for him to reckon with his old rival once again.

Only two weeks later, back in London, Jones would find himself alongside Forsyth in the section devoted to psychoanalysis in the XVIIth International Congress of Medicine. On that occasion, the discussant was Pierre Janet, still a professor at the Collège de France, who unleashed a violent attack on the Freudian method, proclaiming the priority of his own psychological analysis, challenging the sexual theory and comparing the psychoanalytic organisation to a sect like Christian Science. Jung made the damage worse in his response because, after crudely accusing Janet of not knowing German and not having read Freud, he ended up agreeing with him on a tamed interpretation of the sexual theory.

In the debate that followed, Ernest Jones, *the bonny fighter*,[27] immediately hurled himself into the scrum but had to put up with David Forsyth bringing his own skill and prestige to the battle. Getting straight to the point, Forsyth stoutly defended not only the explanation of the psychoneuroses offered by psychoanalysis but also its incomparable clarifications about the affective tendencies of infantile life, a topic that Janet had merely touched on, stating that Freud had given a "unique insight into the affective attributes of children."

> The moral education of children (that moulds their deep and unrestrained desires into a form compatible with the rules of civilisation), immediately after their physical health, is the most important question of our epoch. Psychoanalysis is the best way to advance the scientific study of this.
>
> (8/08/1913)[28]

The paediatrician showed himself fully equal to the situation, an unquestionable exponent of the new discipline and promise for its future.

Admittedly, this was not the first time that Forsyth had been a spokesman for Freudian theory. Hector Cameron, the colleague with whom he had once set up the "Preposterous Club," a society dedicated to fostering cooperation between physicians involved in pre- and post-natal care of children, did not always appreciate his interest in psychoanalysis. He wrote:

> Forsyth had the misfortune to be so overcome by the persuasive force of Freud's teaching that finally, to his undergoing, it possessed him to the exclusion of all other interests.
>
> (in Craft Dodd 2017, p. 217)

Only a few months after the Congress, the *British Medical Journal* published a brief and ironic note from Forsyth under the heading "Popular Freudism":

> Sir, in your current number a nameless correspondent proclaims the need of an organized policy of ridicule and neglect in order to kill the Freudian system of psychology. Your readers will not fail to notice the implicit admission that rational argument and open discussion are not to be relied on to this end. And, incidentally, how vivid the glimpse your correspondent affords us of a mind not yet liberated from a belief in prejudice as the court of appeal in matters of science!
>
> (1914, p. 1089)

Back in London for good after an absence of five years and ready to resume his professional activities, Jones was forced against his will to team up with his old rival in the face of the British medical world's hostility and the prejudice of his fellow Londoners. They were on the same side of the barricade.

And so it was that in October 1913 he had to count Forsyth among the founding members of the London Society and to share responsibility with him for organising the London group of psychoanalysts. And in those early days, the alliance with his highly regarded university colleague was certainly very useful to him.

Notes

* Parts of this chapter summarise Chapter 15 of Pierri (2022) *Occultism and the Origins of Psychoanalysis: Freud, Ferenczi and the Challenge of Thought Transference*.
1 Granoff and Rey, 1983, p. 113.
2 Zweig, 1942, p. 272.
3 Jones, 1959.
4 *ibid.*, p. 27.
5 Winnicott, 1958b.
6 Gillespie, 1979.
7 Jones Collection, P04-C-C-05.
8 Forsyth, 1938, p. X.
9 Jones's words, 1959, p. 132.
10 Maddox, 2006, p. 4.
11 Jones, 1945.
12 Maddox, 2006.
13 Gay, 1988.
14 Stekel presented some cases of impotence that showed a marked homosexual component as an escape from incestuous fantasies (Numberg and Federn, 1962–75).
15 Brome, 1983.
16 Gay, 1988.
17 A Freud, 1979.
18 See Pierri, 2022.
19 Jones to Putnam, 13/01/1911, in Freud to Jung, 2/04/1911, note.
20 Gabbard, 1995; Appignanesi and Forrester, 1992; Paskauskas, 1993.
21 Jones, 1910; Freud to Jones, 14/01/1912.
22 Paskauskas, 1994.
23 Jones, 1959, p. 224.
24 *II*, p. 454.
25 *Science*, 4/12/1908.
26 In 1945, to correct Freud's error in this regard – in the preface to a book by Eder – Jones wrote three letters to Anna Freud complaining about this oversight by her father and a short article in the *International Journal*.
27 Gillespie, 1979.
28 In Janet, 1913, p. 115.

Chapter 5

Nachträglichkeit

Following the traces of a long deferral

Freud becomes a heretic: the debate about the "transmission of thought" within the committee

Having given a preliminary account of the Forsyth case from *Lecture XXX*, it is time to say something about the events that led to its publication. To do this, we will together retrace the steps of my work back to the point when, wondering about the meaning of this singular piece of writing by Freud, I was suddenly struck by the evident problems behind its construction.

It was a long and trouble-strewn process that, from 1919 to 1933, enabled Freud to systematise and give a finished form to that strange experience in analysis and to integrate it into his theory. In *Lecture XXX* of 1933, material which had been Freud's private research finally came into contact with public theory: it is a long and complex essay intended as his exhaustive psychoanalytic observations on the theme of thought transmission, and in it he finally gave credence to the objective possibility of thought transference and of telepathy at the same time. As he puts it,

> You will not forget that here I am only treating [these problems] in so far as it is possible to approach them from the direction of psycho-analysis. When they first came into my range of vision more than ten years ago, I too felt a dread of a threat against our scientific *Weltanschauung*, which, I feared, was bound to give place to spiritualism or mysticism if portions of occultism were proved true. To-day I think otherwise. In my opinion it shows no great confidence in science if one does not think it capable of assimilating and working over whatever may perhaps turn out to be true in the assertions of occultists. (p. 54–55)

In this context, at the end of the Forsyth case, Freud advanced the hypothesis that thought transference might constitute a primal, archaic means of communication between individuals.

It had not been an easy achievement. During the years of gestation that separated the clinical event from its public presentation, Freud tried out a series of brief papers and preparatory essays that reflect the gradual construction of his

DOI: 10.4324/9781003246480-6

thinking about a topic which had been much disputed at the time, eliciting pronouncements from the greatest figures in the scientific and cultural world.

In the meantime, not only had psychoanalytic theory changed in such a way as to accommodate this new challenging topic, but so had Freud and his relations with his pupils and the members of the secret committee.

It was the members of that very committee whom he wanted to make privy to this private research of his when, in the Hague in September 1920, at the first psychoanalytic congress after the war, they were finally able to meet again after long years of separation. On that occasion, they gave themselves a more definite organisation, deciding that they would henceforth communicate with each other in periodical circulating letters as well as in their individual private correspondence. Naturally, the contents mostly concerned the activities of the movement, psychoanalytic publications, the journals, and the publishing company. Theoretical discussion more often than not served to explore or clarify misunderstandings of an emotional kind and conflicts that often saw Rank and Ferenczi teaming up on one side, with Jones and Abraham on the other.

It should be said that, despite the inevitable internal tensions, the committee, set up in 1913 principally in response to the difficulties arising with Jung,[1] began to play a fundamental role in the psychoanalytic movement as it acquired a solid international identity.

Ernest Jones, who was elected president of the *Internationale Psychoanalytische Vereinigung*[2] at the Hague following Ferenczi's brief period in charge, often found himself isolated, and he was out of favour with Freud for a long time, above all because of his conflicts with Rank over the publishing company and the journals. Even so, Jones maintained an unconditional faith in the professor and the cause. Repeatedly pressed by both Ferenczi and Freud to resume the training analysis that he had started for a few weeks in Budapest in 1913, he always flatly refused and found himself on the brink of expulsion. Freud, disappointed, in the end declared him unsuited to the position of leader and, at Rank's instigation, the entire committee accused him not only of having unresolved problems but also of antisemitism. Sachs, who was initially very close to Jones and Eitingon, ended up disgusting Freud and being isolated because of his bachelor lifestyle and impenitent Don Juanism.

At the Berlin Congress in 1922, the last that Freud attended before becoming ill, when the famous photo of the seven members of the secret group was taken, their differences found a temporary truce. As Abraham observed, unlike in a neurotic family, the committee's conflicts became magnified in their absences and were set aside as soon as they came together.

In the end it would actually be the young favourite, Rank, not Jones, who broke with Freud and the Association, probably as a reaction to the master's illness, or maybe because he had taken on the challenge of practising as an analyst: after writing *The Development of Psychoanalysis* (1924) on psychoanalytic technique with Ferenczi, in the same year he proposed the dissolution of the committee and went public with an essay that not only questioned the Oedipal theory (anticipating later pre-oedipal developments on the process of separation from the mother) but, above all, made the somewhat unrealistic proposal to shorten the length of treatments still further (*The Trauma of Birth*). Given the threat of the committee falling apart, in place of Rank who, having taken his stand, moved to Paris and then to the United States, at Ferenczi's suggestion the Freudian *Männerbund* was joined by a woman, Anna Freud, not yet 30, who was *de facto* "the Professor's secretary."[3] In 1925, on the death of Abraham, there were no new entrants. Ferenczi maintained his close relationship with Freud, a different one from all the others, but adopted a position further and further from the centre of the movement. Freud tried to persuade him to reassume the role of president in 1932, but in vain.

In Berlin it was established that every new analyst would have to undergo their own analysis and that, to this end, each individual society would have to organise a system of training. Eitingon and Sachs had already begun working full-time as training analysts. At Bad Homburg in 1925, the International Training Commission was set up under Max Eitingon's direction and formulated the educational model that remains the model for most of the programmes across the societies of the IPA.

In 1927 at Innsbruck, it was finally made explicit that the analysis of future analysts should not simply be a way of familiarising them with the mechanisms of their own unconscious through the interpretation of dreams and the confrontation with the Oedipus complex but that it should extend to the analysis of their personality and character; that they should be more deeply analysed than their patients.[4] The IPA had now acquired a solid configuration both in reference to a distinct theoretical tradition and to its intergenerational transmission, now structured and entrusted to the training institutes. And almost all the members of the secret committee were officially in the executive.

It was at this congress that the secret committee disbanded, having fulfilled its task.

Between 1920 and 1927, they sent over 400 circular letters: in these the only common initiative for theoretical discussion was the one proposed at the start by Freud, who, in the first circular sent from Vienna in 1920, suggested a reflection on the theme of telepathy and in particular what influence it would have on the theory and practice of psychoanalysis if one accepted the possibility of the "transmission of thoughts."[5]

The question shows how committed he was to trying to integrate the two apparently incompatible spheres of experience and how, even though he might have felt that it threatened the founding elements of his theory, he had been struck by the evidence he had seen in the research on the work of clairvoyants that he had carried out with Ferenczi on their return from the trip to America[6] and by the recent "telepathic" session with Herr P in October 1919.

Within the committee, Freud now allowed himself to be a heretic: he decided to acknowledge the scientific topic of "thought-transmission" as legitimate and to assume paternity of it. We do not know when precisely he had made this decision or in what circumstances he had reappropriated the two observations of "unfulfilled" prophecies that in the winter of 1910–11 he had given to Ferenczi for his dossier, hoping that the mind-reading might become his "great discovery."[7]

For Freud, as he worked through his separation from Jung, the theme of occultism may have represented an unresolved challenge by the Swiss, a question that Freud was still pondering and no longer intended to delegate to Ferenczi.[8] And perhaps he had chosen to bring all the members of the committee into it so that he would not have to share it with Ferenczi, thus making use of this secret space as a protected area where he could keep his own emerging ideas in a state of gestation.

The question was taking on symptomatic characteristics of urgency mixed with inhibition. Further stimuli had been provided by the publication of a book by Jung on belief in spirits (1920, presented the year before to the British *Society for Psychical Research*) and even more by a monograph by Stekel on telepathic dreams (1920).

Stekel's observations, drawn from clinical experience, essentially concerned the effects of an emotional bond of particular intensity (love and jealousy) on the sensibility of the participants in the telepathic event. He took it for granted that women in love could experience intense pains or symptoms which corresponded precisely to their husbands' acts of unfaithfulness. Convinced that every individual emanated energy, he thought that the events of existence left an imprint of vibrations or rays in the surrounding environment, and he did not rule out the possibility of prophetic dreams.[9]

It certainly must have been hard for Freud to keep from intervening in a field about which he knew he had something much more significant and extraordinary to make public. In February 1921, replying to Eitingon, who had sent him some books on occultism, Freud mentioned telepathy, saying, "The thought of that sour apple makes me shudder, but there is no way to avoid biting into it."[10] A few months later, he was also mentioning the subject in his correspondence with a new acolyte, the physiatrist Georg Groddeck (1866–1934), who was trying to apply psychoanalysis to somatic illnesses: "Yet there is also the transference of thought which demands to be let in and many other things generally called occult."[11]

And also during this period, treating a couple together for the first time, the spouses James and Alix Strachey were busily investigating the possible occurrence of telepathic phenomena, though without success.[12]

A mistake by Freud

In July 1921, having gone on holiday feeling especially worn out by analytic work in English with his Anglo-American patients and pupils – "I haven't spoken a word of English since lunchtime the day before yesterday," he wrote with relief to his daughter Anna (16/07/1921) – Freud was planning a spell of complete rest: he didn't count letters and correcting proofs as work. But he had brought with him his old notes on clairvoyants and "unfulfilled prophecies," as well as his comments on the session with Herr P.[13]

The month of the holiday at Bad Gastein was filled with excursions, reading, letter-writing, and visits (the Americans S E Jelliffe and A A Brill, whom he had not seen since before the war, and Ferenczi came to say hello with Gizella, who had become his wife in 1919). Then, in the absence of mushrooms because of the early summer heat, Freud dedicated himself to writing a work on thought transmission, his first on this topic, intended for the meeting of the committee to be held in September.

To show how topical the subject was, in the circular letter of 1 August, he informed the others that he had just received the invitation to collaborate as co-editor of three different periodicals devoted to psychic research. He had declined all three requests, but, in his reply to the New Yorker Hereward Carrington, Freud had written: "If I were at the beginning rather than at the end of a scientific career, as I am today, I might possibly choose just this field of research, in spite of all difficulties."[14] Research into thought transmission seemed to reawaken in him the passion and enthusiasm of his youthful years.

So he set to work, called his text *Vorbericht* (Preface), began writing it on 2 August, and finished it on the 6th during the few days which saw the mountains around Gastein unseasonably whitened with snow and the temperature fall from 30° to 7° with a rapidity "which can only be compared with that of the crown," he commented to Anna.[15] In fact, he could not complete the article in the way he had planned because, having finished the first draft and reached the point where he wished to insert the session with Herr P, he realised to his surprise that he had not brought his notes on the case but "another sheet of indifferent memoranda on quite another topic":[16] he attributed the mistake to an unconscious resistance.

He was careful to let Ferenczi know about the new text straightaway.[17]

The Hungarian was now in a state of great distress: he had just lost his mother and, despite his recent marriage, still had Gizella's daughter Elma in his heart,[18] but she had left for America with the intention of giving her husband a second chance. Under strong pressure from Freud, Ferenczi had abandoned his own plan of moving to America, to Philadelphia where he had been given guarantees of work.[19] His psychosomatic symptoms had once again become acute – Freud regarded them as linked to Elma's departure – and while awaiting the committee's September meeting, he had decided to travel with Gizella to Baden Baden to ask Georg Groddeck for accommodation and treatment at his clinic in the hope of finding in him both a doctor and a teacher.

The memorable Harzreise

The meeting in September was a momentous event: with the aim of improving the closeness of their mutual relationships, there being no Congress scheduled for that year, the members of the committee had planned to spend ten days on vacation with Freud in the Harz Mountains of north-west Germany. In Sachs's view, this vacation was one of the best outcomes of the committee's creation.[20]

To fund it, they had drawn on the bequest from the Hungarian, von Freund. While Freud could now afford the expenditure, not all the other members were in work: Rank had never really been independent; Sachs, only recently recovered from tuberculosis, had moved to Berlin – where Abraham and Eitingon had founded an Institute and a Psychoanalytic Clinic with Ernst Simmel – and they were starting to have patients there; Ferenczi was still having serious professional problems because of the antisemitic tensions in Budapest.

The choice of location had been eagerly urged by Abraham, who wanted to make up for not having held the international congress the year before in Berlin. Under pressure from Jones, the Dutch capital had been preferred as a way to avoid the resistance of the western members: the memory of the conflict was too much alive in Anglo-American minds and their prejudice against Germany even stronger than it was after the Second World War. Berlin would have reinforced a view of psychoanalysis as a decadent German science, and it was essential to ensure its success by including the westerners who would certainly not otherwise have taken part.[21] Abraham took on the role of guide because a branch of his family came from the Harz region and he knew it well, so he drew up the programme for accommodation and travel like a military manoeuvre. Despite strikes and the various all-too-frequent but unforeseeable incidents caused by the aftermath of war, the committee members coming from all possible directions were able to reach the agreed-upon meeting place on the same Wednesday afternoon, 21 September 1921. Grosskurth[22] provides a visual representation of the various railway connections and itineraries converging on the station in the small town of Hildesheim (Hamburg-Berlin-Potsdam, Vienna-Leipzig, Hook-Leipzig, Baden Baden-Hannover-Cassel) which fits splendidly with the subject of the dense web of crossroads and coincidences in our narrative.

The pioneers of psychoanalysis descended with suitcases and knapsacks on the *Hotel d'Angleterre* – which because of the war had had to change its name to *Hotel Zur Traube* – and they stayed here for a couple of days. They moved to Goslar and then on to Halberstadt, which they made their base for their trips. Despite his 65 years, Freud showed himself to be full of energy, and the others were astonished by his speed and tirelessness on their daily excursions. Jones recalls this with a certain envy because he suffered worse than the others from the cold they all caught and from an acute return of his arthritis.

Sachs adds:

> we had a glorious time in the clear light and bracing air of those autumn days, rambling through the pinewoods along the streams and cliffs and climbing the highest peak, the Brocken, famous as the place where in the good old times the German witches held their dance on the first night in May.
>
> (1945, p. 160)

Goethe had brought Faust, led by Mephistopheles, onto the summit of the Brocken in the Walpurgisnacht scene: through the mist, with the profiles of the *Hexenaltar* (Witches' Altar) and the *Teufelskanzel* (Devil's Pulpit) on the horizon, our travellers caught a glimpse of the Brocken Spectre, a tremulous mirage emerging out of the damp fog.

Our Magnificent Seven ventured still further afield, and Freud always marched ahead of the others. Jones, who in the past had suffered from vertigo and agoraphobia, recalls a singular challenge to the void, on the platform of a tower protected by a low railing:

> Freud got us all to lean forward against the rail with our hands behind our backs and our feet well back, and then suddenly to imagine that it was not there – a quite good test for the fear of heights.
>
> (*III*, p. 85)

The group's cohesion was strengthened by the daily close contact of these days. But the tourist outings, climbs, and hearty meals were only the background to the main purpose of the occasion, the evening discussions about new theories or experiences. Ferenczi presented his theory of genital evolution that he had started to develop while on military service in Pápa but had not yet put in writing;[23] Freud discussed three works, one of which was on thought transmission.[24]

1921, an essay in two halves[25]

Vorbericht-*preface*

Today we can read this essay by Freud almost in its entirety, it having been published posthumously with the title "Psycho-Analysis and Telepathy" (1921 [1941]).

Freud began it by declaring that psychoanalysis, after surviving the attacks levelled against it by the mysticism of Jung and the will to power of Adler, could no longer put off addressing the challenge posed by occultism and that it was necessary to be prepared for a mutual sympathy to emerge between the two disciplines: "They have both experienced the same contemptuous and arrogant treatment by official science," he went on, reiterating that it would not be the first time that psychoanalysis had offered its support to "the obscure but indestructible surmises of the common people against the obscurantism of educated opinion" (p. 178).

He came to the point: "In the course of the last few years I have made a few observations which I shall not hold back – at all events from the circle that is closest to me" (p. 180). Reaffirming the genuineness of his material and the evidence for it, the indisputable demonstrative force deriving from the fact that it had only been developed and clarified during the course of analytic elaboration, he introduced three case studies. The first two, "of a similar character," were the prophecies he had given to Ferenczi. "Prophecies made by professional fortune-tellers which did not come true," as Freud put it, but which made "an extraordinary impression on the people to whom they were announced" (p. 181) irrespective of their relation to the future: the recipients had felt deeply understood and relieved. The two situations – the response of a famous court astrologer, Frau Arnold of

Munich, who had used the date of birth and a set of astrological tables to predict the death of her enquirer's brother-in-law in July or August from "crayfish- or oyster-poisoning" and the prophecy of a certain Monsieur le Professeur in Paris who, by studying a handprint in a dish full of sand, had predicted that his questioner would have "two children at the age of 32" – described in rich detail, together with the material produced in the patients' analysis.

In both cases, the analytic tool had been able to illuminate the true occult phenomenon in the work of the clairvoyant, which would otherwise have passed unobserved: being able to give a voice and fulfilment, with a surprising speed, during one brief encounter, to the questioner's unconscious desire.[26] It was the same intense desire that Freud had gradually been able to recognise in the recollections, fantasies, and free associations of the two patients during the treatment he had subsequently undertaken with them.

In the first example – a young philosophy student who had consulted Freud because of a block when facing his final examinations[27] – there was an intense incestuous bond with his newly married sister and murderous hostility towards his brother-in-law.

In the second, a woman married to a rich older relative of her mother, after discovering that her husband was infertile, had developed an anxiety hysteria followed by obsessional symptoms:[28] what was at work here was a profound infantile identification with the mother and an unconscious desire to have a baby with the father.

What was unconsciously present in the questioner as unsatisfied desire and hope was read and translated by the clairvoyant as a prophecy with a desirable outcome. As confirmation of the extraordinary "mindreading" by the fortune-tellers, in both the prophetic responses, minute details were cited relating to past circumstances, details of which were known by the enquirers and had been brought to analysis: in the first case, the patient's brother-in-law and rival had actually survived poisoning by shellfish in the August *before* the consultation with the astrologer, and in the second case it was the patient's *mother* who had given birth to two daughters in her 32nd year.

Freud proposed the conclusion that the fortune-tellers did not have the ability to read the future but that, through a series of astrological calculations or observations about the handprint (indifferent or innocuous activities intended to divert conscious attention and to keep the psychic forces occupied with automatisms, comparable to the analyst's freely floating attention), they rendered themselves unconsciously receptive and permeable to the thoughts and affects of their clients in the same way as mediums do.[29]

Psychoanalytic interpretation enabled him to make clear that the content of this thought transmission concerned the enquirer's intense desires which were not subjected to repression but simply found themselves suppressed in consciousness. In his hypothesis, the work of the fortune-teller would consist in offering a part of their own psyche in the service of the other, so as to put this desire into words. The example indicates that

> what has been communicated by this means of induction from one person to another is not merely a chance piece of indifferent knowledge. It shows that an extraordinarily powerful wish harboured by one person and standing in a special relation to his consciousness has succeeded, with the help of a second person, in finding conscious expression in a slightly disguised form – just as the invisible end of the spectrum reveals itself to the senses on a light-sensitive plate as a coloured extension.
>
> (1921 [1941], pp. 184–185)

To Freud, this distinctive feature of the fortune-teller's function – not simply reading the thought but, like a "light-sensitive plate," seeming capable of performing transformations in the visual register with an intense and barely manageable intensity which needs the other's presence so that it "reveals itself to the senses" – represents a major innovation for the reader of Freud.

It is an extremely topical intuition about the countertransference, about the developmental value of relating and of the maternal, which it was not yet possible for him to integrate with the essentially paternal function of the analyst as he had described it almost ten years before. Unlike the fortune-teller, the psychoanalyst's opacity on the visual level ("like a mirror" [1912a, p. 118] which only reflects what it is shown) and the high fidelity of his receptive and interpretative capacity on the level of speech (like "a telephone receiver" converting "the electric oscillations in the telephone line" back into sound waves, the doctor uses his unconscious to reconstruct the patient's unconscious, "the transmitting microphone": *ibid.*, p. 115–116) guaranteed the scientific nature of psychoanalysis and its emancipation from the *occult* origins of hypnotic and/or magnetic suggestion.

This innovation remained enclosed in the *Vorbericht* and was only shared on its posthumous publication. Servadio grasped its innovative significance in relation to waking dream-work:

> It was as if the seer had "lent" the defensive apparatus of his ego to the consultant, carrying out work in his stead that could have been carried out exclusively in an endopsychic way in the consultant himself, giving rise for example to a dream, or a fantasy.
>
> (1956, p. 55)

After the two prophecies, *Vorbericht* should have concluded with a third example taken from analytic work, the Forsyth case. This was the context for which it was originally destined. Though it was announced in the paper – "a third case, of another kind and open to a different assessment, is only added by way of appendix" (p. 181) – the Forsyth case does not appear in the *Vorbericht*, nor, because of the forgotten notes, was it read at the Harz gathering. "Nothing can be done against such a clear resistance. I must ask you to excuse me for omitting this case, for I cannot make the loss good from memory," (p. 190) and so Freud broke off.

In the absence of the telepathic session with Herr P, Freud concluded the *Vorbericht* with some more recent observations about a certain Rafael Schermann, a Polish graphologist and psychic who was the talk of Vienna for his alleged powers of clairvoyance and telepathy.[30] After hinting at an episode which involved him personally and which, he was careful to specify, would invalidate the fame of the fortune-teller,[31] Freud reported a third example of "unfulfilled" prophecy.

It was the case of a patient he had taken into analysis in 1920.[32] During the treatment, the man had consulted Schermann with examples of two women's handwriting: about the first, he had been warned that the person in question – his lover, one of the best-known figures in the city's *demi-monde* – would certainly kill herself. In fact, during the course of the sessions it had emerged that the patient unconsciously desired (and actively tried) to drive her to despair, as revenge against another woman who had in the past led him to make an almost successful suicide attempt. He wanted to marry a third, younger woman but was unable to leave his lover: "the miracle-man had merely revealed to my patient his own intimate wish," commented Freud (p. 192). The prophecy had not been fulfilled, the lover had not killed herself, and, during the analysis, he had been able to put an end to the relationship.[33]

This example of substitution likewise confirmed the possibility of "thought induction," the sole object of Freud's scientific interest. But in the final section of the *Vorbericht*, he did not conceal his uncertainty:

> Perhaps the problem of thought-transference may seem very trivial to you in comparison with the great magical world of the occult. But consider what a momentous step beyond what we have hitherto believed would be involved in this hypothesis alone. What the custodian of [the basilica of] Saint-Denis used to add to his account of the saint's martyrdom remains true. Saint-Denis is said, after his head was cut off, to have picked it up and to have walked quite a distance with it under his arm. But the custodian used to remark: "*Dans des cas pareils, ce n'est que le premier pas qui coûte.*" The rest is easy.
> (p. 193)

Was the hesitation in that "*premier pas*" towards the miracle of telepathy perhaps dictated by the anxiety about losing your head and having to feel your way with your head under your arm, as Derrida (1981) wonders, or by the fear that he would *déclasser* psychoanalysis, deflower it like a young woman?

Nachtrag-*postscript*

The "Forsyth" case was never read to the committee. It is possible that Freud did not yet feel able to face such a direct a confrontation between the thought transmission performed by fortune-tellers and the work of psychoanalysis.

In the light of the powerful urge to procrastinate no further in the study of telepathy, an urge which was in itself significant and symptomatic, the forgetting of the notes signals Freud's unconscious need to apply the brakes not so much on his interest in telepathy as on his observation of this phenomenon in analysis: a need to defer the moment when he shared his own personal experience. Something highly intimate must have come into play, given the surprising influence that the session clearly had on Freud, and what had particularly impressed him in the clinical event had been the striking and disturbing way that "telepathy" had cut across the theme of "prophecy" (Foresight-Forsyth) to which he had always been so sensitive.[34]

The resistance expressed itself in a slip, the displacement onto the "indifferent" alternative material, and in the presentation of a substitute case which still belonged to the group of "unfulfilled prophecies." The result was a first postponement.

On his return to Vienna, Freud made good the error and completed the text, drafting a second distinct manuscript which introduced the omitted third case, which he called *Nachtrag* (Postcript) and inserted as a supplement to the first, the *Vorbericht* (Preface). The Forsyth case, which at this point we could call *the Foresight case* (another *prophecy?* a *post-scripted prophecy?*) indeed deserved to be treated separately: the reported situation was quite different from the examples which preceded it.

The double text passed between the members of the committee, who began to refer to it as "the secret Harz essay." In a state of uncertainty, partly because of his own admitted resistances and partly because of opposition from certain colleagues – especially Jones – Freud continued to defer its publication.

In the meantime, the controversial affective significance of this "secret essay" was becoming ever clearer. The question of "thought transfer" began to take on symptomatic characteristics for Freud, and the wait was demanding a substantial exercise of self-control: between urgency and postponement, the affair suggests the need to isolate and decontextualise an experience that was felt to be explosive, to defer its working-through, challenging the impetus that was coming from within and keeping open an area of indefiniteness where he could suspend judgement.

Every act of writing is always a second time, a way of reconstructing the lived event in order to think about it. This time of latency, foretold by Freud's first defensive postponement and then by the manuscript's heading, *Nachtrag*, is a sign of how much new trauma that clinical experience had stirred up in him, requiring such a deferral-*Nachträglichkeit*.

1922, dreams and *Telepathy*

As confirmation that Freud's perplexities were not about telepathy but about telepathy in psychoanalysis (thought transference), having set aside the Harz paper, he immediately published another, written towards the end of 1921, straight after the first, on the relationship between telepathy and dream. This time, writes Jones, it was not easy to hold him back, since he evidently felt the need to speak publicly about the subject. Freud had initially thought of presenting the paper at the Wednesday meetings but then decided to send it directly to the first issue of *Imago* in January 1922 without letting the committee know about it. The journal, which from 1912 was the partner of the official organ of the Association, the *Zentralblatt für Psychoanalyse*, and a home for the applications of psychoanalysis to literature, the arts, and the social sciences, could offer a borderline space more suitable for his reflections.

Entitled "Dreams and Telepathy," this is the very first paper on the topic of occultism that Freud made public: it is a minor work, one of those "small pockets" in advance of *Lecture XXX* where he would locate his "anxiety about telepathy," a hesitant "*pas de valse*" towards its possible premonitory meaning.[35]

Let's look at its contents.

After declaring that he did not wish to take a position on the existence of telepathy, Freud claimed that he had never encountered instances of telepathic dreaming in his own patients and reiterated that he himself had never had a telepathic-prophetic dream, apart from some disagreeable dreams with premonitions that had never come true. As proof he then referred to two dreams that he had initially feared would be prophetic. The first, from 1915, concerned the death of his son Martin at the front and had coincided with a slight injury to his arm.[36] Freud set out details which he associated with an early trauma of his own:

> I saw the young soldier standing on a landing-stage, between land and water, as it were; he looked to me very pale. I spoke to him but he did not answer. There were other unmistakable indications. He was not wearing military uniform, but a skiing costume that he had worn when a serious skiing accident had happened to him several years before the war. He stood on something like a footstool with a cupboard in front of him; a situation always closely associated in my mind with the idea of "falling", through a memory of my own childhood. As a child of little more than two years old I had myself climbed on a footstool like this to get something off the top of a cupboard – probably something good to eat – and I fell down and gave myself an injury, of which I can even now show the scar.
>
> (1922b, pp. 197–199)

The second dream was about the death of an old lady, the widow of his half-brother Emanuel in Manchester, who had died at the start of the war:

> Only a short time ago, I had another dream bearing ill-tidings; it was, I think, just before I decided to put together these few remarks. This time there was not much attempt at disguise. I saw my two nieces who live in England. They were dressed in black and said to me, "We buried her on Thursday." I knew the reference was to the death of their mother, now eighty-seven years of age, the widow of my eldest brother. A time of disagreeable anticipation followed; there would of course be nothing surprising in such an old lady

> suddenly passing away, yet it would be very unpleasant for the dream to coincide exactly with the occurrence.
>
> (*ibid.*)

Freud interprets his own aggressive feelings towards his son in relation to the first dream but makes no comment on the second, which contains a recurrent fantasy (the expected death of a very old patient)[37] that could well be connected with the expectations of his own mother's death – being the same age as his English relative – a fantasy that he did not seem able to address, either in the content of slips or superstitions or in this dream.

This brief initial autobiographical part is perhaps the most authentic content of "Dreams and Telepathy," suggests Derrida (1981), and it represents Freud's renewed attempt to confront the intensity and ambivalence of the incestuous and aggressive desires concealed in his superstition.

He then moves on to investigate the relationship between the psychoanalytic interpretation of the dream and its possible telepathic elements, adopting a perspective entirely distinct from the innumerable observations about supposed telepathic dreams carried out by scholars of the period in the sphere of psychical research. To this end, he presented two dreams about which he had been consulted in letters from individuals he did not know directly and illustrated the possible interpretations of these experiences on the basis of the associations he was able to obtain from the dreamers.

The dream of twin birth. In the first dream, reported by a man of obvious intelligence who declared himself to have no inclination towards occultism, his wife appeared, having given birth to twins. However, the dreamer commented that he did not wish to have children with her, his second wife, and was not even in a position to do so, since they had stopped having sexual relations some time ago. A few days later, he received a telegram with news that his daughter (from his first marriage) had prematurely given birth, unexpectedly to twins, at the same time as his dream. In his interpretation of the coincidence, Freud identified the dream's significant element in the slight difference between what had been dreamed and the actual facts (the replacing of his *daughter* with his present *wife*), highlighting the presence of "an intimate bond of feeling existed between the father and daughter." As he made clear,

> a bond of feeling which is so usual and so natural that we ought to cease to be ashamed of it, one that in daily life merely finds expression as a tender interest and is only pushed to its logical conclusion in dreams.
>
> (p. 206)

The father's unconscious desire, reawakened by his daughter's pregnancy, had been to find a satisfaction in the dream – *I am still the father* – by means of a masking that enabled him to escape oneiric censure – *and the woman giving birth is my wife*. The coincidence of the date, three weeks earlier than forecast, and the unexpected birth of twins gave credit to a possible telepathic perception, which remained to be proven.

The vision of a brother's death. In the second case reported by Freud, the dreamer, who suffered from a neurotic condition and said she had had recurring telepathic experiences since childhood, heard her brother asking for help, calling "*Mother, Mother!*" at the same time as he actually died in the war. After subjecting this occurrence to an analytic interpretation (together with other material of a similar kind reported in the letter, which had no need of a telepathic explanation), Freud concluded with the observation that, in this second case too, intense emotions associated with the Oedipus complex appeared to be involved.

Though Freud is working with very scanty material in his brief article and skilfully declining to address the merits of telepathy's actual existence, he is able to grasp what had entirely escaped Stekel in his monograph, which is that perception, even when telepathic, cannot fail to be subjected to the same dynamic laws of distortion and unconscious resistance as those that regulate psychic processes. In both dreams, the oneiric substitution *wife-daughter* and *mother-sister* enabled him to highlight the interference of the repressed desire in both dreamers to take the place of the daughter's husband and her own mother, respectively.

Freud expressed the opinion that instances of telepathy could be encouraged by the sleeping state but that in each case the possible information thus received (the birth of twins, the brother's death) could be elaborated and transformed by the dream-work as a daytime residue with deformations, displacements, and condensations. For Freud, the apparent inexactness was the sign of the passage through the individual psyche.

He had achieved a masterstroke. In this way, what drove "psychic researchers" to despair over their material – that is to say, imprecisions, variations, everything that failed to correspond precisely and might be an error in transmission – instead revealed itself to be an integral part of the phenomenon.

At this point, just as it had succeeded in unveiling the intimate meaning of dreams, in its ability to interpret the reasons for these errors of transmission, psychoanalysis showed itself to be in a privileged position to investigate the phenomenon and even seemed able to do something with telepathy, helping it to be understood and highlighting the occult element of a quantity of material whose nature was still in doubt.

The hypothesis of telepathy showed itself to be compatible with psychoanalytic theory, but Freud was still very careful not to take a position either way: while the paper began with

> You will learn nothing from this paper of mine about the enigma of telepathy; indeed, you will not even gather whether I believe in the existence of "telepathy" or not.
>
> (p. 197)

It ended with a contorted sentence and the ambiguous assertion, "I have no opinion on the matter and know nothing about it" (p. 220).

And despite the urgency with which he had published this first brief essay, Freud suddenly seemed to have a low opinion of it, almost as if it were something to be got rid of. In fact, "Dreams and Telepathy" was the protagonist of a financial to-and-fro which Freud wrote ironically about to Anna, who was staying in Hamburg with her nephews (Sophie's orphans): he told her how he had given Martha a 50-dollar note that morning for Aunt Mitzi, who was leaving for Berlin, and by evening, the same sum had come back to him from the *Verlag* as an advance on the publication of the text in English. He explained:

> Some weeks ago an American magazine requested an article from me. I refused to write something new but said that if they wanted to translate and publish some trifle [*Dreams and Telepathy*] which is appearing in *Imago*, they could arrange it with Rank. I heard nothing further until I received half the fee, $50, from Rank yesterday for this essay. If we were paid like that for every article, we would be rich people today.
>
> (13/4/1922)

Between magic and dismissal, that strange and precious "trifle" tossed to the Americans and so well remunerated, telepathy kept entering Freud's mind even when he least expected it.

Perplexities, second thoughts, and experiments with Ferenczi and Anna

Jones was reassured at first by the professor's caution over this essay, published instead of the *Vorbericht*, but he soon had to change his mind, realising with alarm that Freud had no intention of giving up the topic of thought transmission.

A few months later, in July 1922, Freud's attention was caught by a proposal for a paper by the Russian Dr Fanja Lowtzky – a future analyst at the Berlin Institute – who, perhaps encouraged by the appearance of *Dreams and Telepathy*, took three experiences of "mediumistic" therapy reported some time previously in the *Revue Métapsychique* and interpreted them in the light of psychoanalysis and the "reading of unconscious thought." Freud asked Rank to delay its publication so that he could add an editorial comment of his own: for which purpose he began annotating Flournoy's book *Esprits et Mediums, mélanges de métapsichique et de Psychologie* (1911), which he had taken with him on holiday.[38]

This time, it would be the critical intervention of Rank and Ferenczi, even before Jones, which discouraged Freud against giving credence to experiences not observed at first hand: surprised but not convinced by these objections, the professor nevertheless thought for some time about using the material for the Berlin Congress of 1922. It should be added that this was the first congress at which Anna would participate as a member of the association, having been admitted to the Viennese Society.

Less sceptical than Jones, or rather, more aware of how attached Freud was to the subject, Eitingon was still adhering to the programme of study proposed to the committee and continued to update him about publications on the theme of telepathy. At the end of 1922, thanking him for sending Charles Richet's *Traité de métapsychique* – a summary of the principal studies on the subject of psychical research – Freud confessed to his pupil that two problems were "driving him crazy":[39] the identity of Shakespeare and occultism. He must have felt he needed to rise to a challenge set by Richet and the works of the scientists and men of culture which he cited. Since 1905, Richet had been using the term "metapsychic" instead of occult or "paranormal" (proposed by Myers) and, in trying to distinguish metapsychic phenomena from the "blind" instances studied by science, he had begun to note that the forces behind presentiments, telepathy, movement of objects without contact, apparitions, or phenomena of that kind seemed neither blind nor unconscious, lacking above all that fatal character typical of the mechanical and chemical phenomena of matter: overall, these forces seemed to contain intentions that closely resembled human motivations.

On the subject of telepathy, he was making clear his firm belief in perceptual capacities radically different from the familiar ones.

The *Traité* had cited William Crookes (the English physicist who, in addition to his "psychical research" on mediums, had made an almost ceaseless contribution to the knowledge of the effects of radiation, the invention of photography, the wireless telegraph, electricity, and the spectroscope) and William James (the Harvard psychologist whom Freud had met at Clark University and whose work had influenced the philosophy of Henri Bergson): both had served as presidents of the Society for Psychical Research in London and America, respectively.

This was a time when many illustrious contemporaries were still letting themselves be convinced by the performances of mediums, from Thomas Edison ("the Wizard of Menlo Park"), one of the most creative inventors of the age, to Thomas Mann, who called occult events "the impossible that nevertheless happens" (1924) and habitually travelled to Munich to take part in séances. After the First World War, there had been a renewal of interest in spiritualism as one of the forms of illusion available to help deal with the catastrophe. In the uncertainty of the times and the grave economic depression, it also represented a way of earning a living. This was the case with the automatic writer Emily Grant Hutchings who, in 1917, claiming to be in contact with Mark Twain (who must have been turning in his grave), published *Jap Herron*, a novel that she presented as having been dictated by the writer, risking a legal action over the copyright! (But, given the poor quality of the book, the critics hoped that in future Twain would respect the boundary with the other world.)

It is likely that the portentous demonstrations by the magician Howard Thurston – a contemporary of Houdini who levitated ethereal young women, conjured spirits, and talked with mummies – exploited the fascination of the mixture between a renewed belief in the occult and the troubling curiosity provoked by the archaeological discoveries of the early twentieth century.[40]

For others, spiritualism became a religious vocation. One of these was Sir Arthur Conan Doyle, who turned himself into a devout evangelist for spiritualism after the medium Evan Powell put him in contact with his son who had fallen in the war and who spoke to his father through Powell about the world beyond, seeming to urge him in a loud voice to "Forgive."[41] Doyle and his wife not only organised séances but held conferences in the United States to spread the word of the New Revelation.

Conan Doyle became involved in a long confrontation-clash with the magician Houdini, whom he believed against all the evidence to be endowed with supernatural powers. Houdini tried in vain to change his mind and, indeed, in the last years of his life, committed himself to unmasking the impostures of the spiritualists and revealing the false magic of the mediums who were selling immortality and claiming to speak to the dead: he proclaimed it to be trickery in the service of an unfounded hope.[42] As an illusionist, he was perfectly placed to challenge superstition and credulity. In his crusade against spiritualism, he was recruited at one point by *Scientific American*, which had offered a reward for anyone who could demonstrate telekinetic abilities under scientifically controlled conditions but was contesting its award to the famous medium Mina "Margery" Crandon.

Houdini later became a correspondent and collaborator with the Harvard Department of Psychology, and in 1924, this "arch-deceiver, the best expert on truth"[43] began to hold conferences from one side of America to the other on the methods and dangers of the spiritualists. He wrote more than one publication to expose their charlatanry and in 1926, called to testify in support of a proposed law against their practising in the future, the magician Houdini defended his own authentic talent for invention, solemnly declaring that he was no more than an illusionist, performing tricks that nobody had been able to work out but which had nothing divine or supernatural about them. He wanted to dazzle, not circumvent his audience.[44] It seems that before his death he provocatively entrusted a secret phrase to his wife, a code word that would guarantee his identity if any medium presumed to call on him . . .

Thought transmission remained a separate problem: in the twenties there was an uproar about the first large-scale experiences of telepathy organised to coincide with the start of radio broadcasting by Zenith Broadcasting in Chicago and the British Broadcasting Company (1923).[45] Experiments were also promoted by *Scientific American* and at university psychology labs in Europe and America: the experiments brought to light not only the trustworthiness of the receptive capacities of randomly selected subjects but also the distinctive characteristic of the phenomenon's instability and tendency to become less successful over time.

In this cultural climate, Freud, having become a corresponding member of the Society for Psychical Research in London from 1911 and of the American Society from 1915, also joined the Greek Society in 1923.

While Ernest Jones acted as the Houdini of the situation, other pupils shared Freud's preoccupation with telepathy and unconscious communications in analysis. In particular, his Viennese pupil Eduard Hitschmann published an article in 1924 entitled *Telepathy and Psycho-Analysis*, an amplification of a paper presented in 1921 in Vienna at the Palast Urania, in which he used the psychology of the unconscious to explain some episodes of spontaneous clairvoyance observed in analysis. In his cautious conclusions, which probably reflected Freud's thinking, such phenomena were considered as subjective mental experiences, the result of a congenital disposition reinforced by factors from childhood or particular conditions of stress:

> Forbidden wishes which have undergone repression force their way into consciousness, but reach it only in a disguised form – by which all responsibility on the part of the subject is repudiated – namely, in that of a "mystical experience" projected outwards.
>
> (1924, p. 437)

At the same time, Freud took the opportunity of a new edition of *The Psychopathology of Everyday Life* to introduce at least a hint at the phenomenon of thought transmission in that final chapter *Determinism, Belief in Chance and Superstition – Some Points of View*, which had previously been reworked several times. Where he had taken a stand against superstition, spiritualism, and any possible prediction of the future, in the 1924 insertion he made room for a bolder declaration, the fruit of his experience of cases of unfulfilled prophecies:

> I must however confess that in the last few years I have had a few remarkable experiences which might easily have been explained on the hypothesis of telepathic thought-transference.
>
> (1901, pp. 261–262)

And in early 1925, after reading "Report on Telepathy Experiments with Professor Murray" published with the signature of Oliver Lodge, Freud described it to the members of the committee as the literary work that had struck him most that month.

Murray regarded telepathy as not a merely cognitive process but one linked to the capacity for sympathy and emotional involvement in the feelings of others, and in the research that he had been conducting since 1915 with his family, he demonstrated that he was especially receptive to his daughter in recalling shared memories as he held her hand.[46]

It seems to have been at this point that Freud decided to publish his "private essay":

> I confess that the impression made by these reports was so strong that I am ready to give up my opposition to the existence of thought transference . . . I should even be prepared to lend the support of psycho-analysis to the matter of telepathy. Eitingon took with him the manuscript of the private essay in which I indicated such analytical reinforcement of the telepathic hypothesis.

> I should decide to-day to send that essay into the world, and should not flinch from the scandal it would inevitably evoke.

His greatest perplexities concerned the problems of privacy:

> But there is the insuperable obstacle of the limitation of medical discretion, which would be seriously impaired by publishing data from the life stories of two of my patients. It is the very sensation this publication would cause that imposes reserve as a duty; distortions are not permissible, nor would any sort of weakening help.

And at the end he added a troubling sentence:

> If fate brings about the death of the two people whose predictions did not come true before my own death, the obstacle would vanish.
>
> (Freud Circular, 15/02/25)

The allusion to death prompts a note on Freud's illness, which had manifested itself in 1923 and would subject him until his death in 1939 to countless painful operations and the need to use a prosthesis in order to speak and eat, with great effort and difficulty. He would live with this looming fate for years, and he no longer attended conferences or spoke in public.

In this context, it should be said that for Freud, telepathy certainly never offered the concrete illusion of life after death that it had given the first "psychic researcher," Frederic Myers, nor was it a way to avoid dealing with the bereavements he had suffered: not the greatly feared death of his sons in the war, but the unexpected deaths of his daughter Sophie and his grandson Heinele in the dreadful post-war years.

Instead, his research into telepathy developed as an indispensable distraction from death, a pastime and comfort like smoking, a puzzle to rack his brains over, a way to recover his youthful passion for exploring the mysteries of the psyche and existence, a game in which he could also involve his daughter Anna, who was now constantly at his side as secretary, assistant, deputy, and nurse. Telepathy was a private, personal, and precious area of thought which Freud now jealously defended, and, as we shall see, it led him to reflect inadvertently on the theme of motherhood.

As a reaction to his renewed proposal to publish the "secret essay," there was a great exchange of letters in this period. In his circular, Ferenczi urged Freud to release at least a summary or else try to obtain the permission of the interested parties, regretting that he had still not published anything himself on the topic of the relation between psychoanalysis and telepathy (and affirming his own interest in the matter):

> As Herr Professor knows, this problem has been occupying me for many years. I have brought together a large number of positive cases . . . [*that*] are

> not only of significance as confirmation of the actuality of thought transference, but also as a kind of objective proof of the modes of operation of the ucs. presupposed by psychoanalysis, in particular, of symbolism.
>
> (19/02/1925)

In the meantime, the article on Murry was travelling between Vienna, Budapest, and Berlin: when Ferenczi went to visit the professor in March (also to discuss the problems he was having with Rank and Rank's recent apostasy), they set up a series of experiments.

Freud wrote about this to the rest of the committee:

> Ferenczi was with us for a Sunday. We talked about many things and the three of us did experiments on thought-transference, which came out remarkably well, especially the experiment in which I myself played the medium and then analytically extended the thoughts that came to my mind. The thing is getting more and more under our skin.
>
> (Freud Circular, 15/03/1925, *b*)

Freud found that he was a medium, and we learn that he co-opted his daughter Anna into Murray's role: it is she to whom he refers in "the three of us." The same day, the Hungarian shared the experience with his colleagues, though showing less enthusiasm this time:

> It should interest you to know that we made a series of rather successful thought transference experiments in Vienna with Professor and Fräulein Anna.
>
> (Ferenczi Circular 15/03/1925)

Telepathy was becoming so important for Freud that he began to protect it from Ferenczi. It had not been enough for him to reappropriate the "unfulfilled prophecies." When the Hungarian, back in Budapest, wrote to ask him for permission to present a paper on the topic,

> What would you say if I put together my thought transference experiments of old and new for a Congress lecture and on this occasion attempted to specify the position of psychoanalysis to these events?
>
> (16/03/1925)

Freud stopped him:

> I advise you against it. Don't do it. Your experiences and experiments are certainly no more striking or unobjectionable than what has been set down about it in the literature, to which one has not wanted to grant one's faith up to now. So, the only thing new in your lecture would be the personal factor

> and the personal effect that would have to proceed from it. With it you are throwing a bomb into the psychoanalytic edifice, which will certainly not fail to explode.
>
> (20/03/1925)

Ferenczi obediently abandoned the plan but let the members of the committee know what he was giving up, making it clear that he was champing at the bit.[47]

For his part, Jones found himself not only acting as a censor but struggling to restrain his jealousy over the renewed closeness between Ferenczi and Freud. In an attempt to challenge the Hungarian's optimism, he thanked Freud for sacrificing his interest in telepathy for the sake of the cause and deprecated the idea of psychoanalysis having anything to do with it.[48] But a little later, and at odds with the prohibition imposed on Ferenczi, Freud allowed himself to publish a second work on occultism, almost as a precaution, to accompany the appearance of a revised edition of *The Interpretation of Dreams*. The topic of telepathy did not represent a wrong turning or an aberration in his work but had a precise coherence: it was becoming clear that he was taking sole responsibility for it and that he intended to manage the "bomb" personally.

1925, section C: "The Occult Significance of Dreams"

Freud had continued to embellish *The Interpretation of Dreams* with variants and additions and in October1925 prepared a brief note on the occult significance of dreams, intended for inclusion in the seventh edition, together with two other supplements from the same time. However, all three ended up in a separate text entitled *Some Additional Notes on Dream-Interpretation as a Whole (A) The Limits to the Possibility of Interpretation, B) Moral Responsibility for the Content of Dreams, C) The Occult Significance of Dreams.*

The subject of section C was prophetic and telepathic dreams. Freud declared himself firmly sceptical about the former and reiterated that he had never experienced one, while on the latter, for which evidence was accumulating rapidly, he was more inclined towards belief:

> One arrives at a provisional opinion that it may well be that telepathy really exists and that it provides the kernel of truth in many other hypotheses that would otherwise be incredible.
>
> (p. 136)

Then he digresses to introduce a brief reflection on "unfulfilled prophecies" and, despite his colleagues' obvious hesitancy, a summary of the previous case from the *Vorbericht*: the prophecy that his patient was destined to be a mother and have two children at the age of 32. He interpreted the phenomenon as the fruit of the woman's intense desire ("the strongest unconscious wish, in fact, of her whole emotional life and the motive force of her impending neurosis," p. 138) which she had presumably "directly transferred to the fortune-teller." His few pages, which extended the phenomenon of telepathy to include the transmission of *unconscious* thoughts, concluded with an explosive note – for Jones, a real volte-face. Not content merely to endorse the hypothesis of telepathy, Freud claimed to have verified its existence personally:

> I have often had an impression, in the course of experiments in my private circle, that strongly emotionally coloured recollections can be successfully transferred without much difficulty. If one has the courage to subject to an analytic examination the associations of the person to whom the thoughts are supposed to be transferred, correspondences often come to light which would otherwise have remained undiscovered. On the basis of a number of experiences I am inclined to draw the conclusion that thought-transference of this kind comes about particularly easily at the moment at which an idea emerges from the unconscious, or, in theoretical terms, as it passes over from the "primary process" to the "secondary process".
>
> (p. 138)

Jones worked hard to convince Freud that any expression of interest in telepathic phenomena would damage the dissemination and respectability of psychoanalysis. And so, despite the professor's explicit wish to include the three papers in the new edition of *The Interpretation of Dreams*, Jones was able to arrange for them to be kept in a separate volume of the *Gesammelte Schrifte* and ensure that they did not even appear in the eighth edition (1931), where all the modifications to the book were gathered in a single volume. Even in subsequent editions, and in the translated *Works of Sigmund Freud*, the three additional notes continued to be omitted because they contained section C.[49] The English version of *The Occult Significance of Dreams* had to wait to be printed in the collection edited by G Devereux in 1953. For this reason, the last sentence of the notorious section – "It would be satisfactory if with the help of psycho-analysis we could obtain further and better authenticated knowledge of telepathy" (1925c, p. 138) – written by Freud specifically to leave his most famous text open to the theme of thought transference, will never appear in the conclusion to *The Interpretation of Dreams*.[50]

This public stance in favour of telepathy stirred up quite a few diplomatic difficulties in the committee, and Freud found himself at loggerheads with the indignation of Jones, who quoted articles in the English press denouncing his "Conversion" to occultism.[51]

He justified himself like this:

> Our friend Jones seems to me to be too unhappy about the sensation that my conversion to telepathy has made in English periodicals. He will recollect how near to such a conversion I came in the communication I had the

> occasion to make during our Harz travels. Considerations of external policy since that time held me back long enough, but finally one must show one's colours and need bother about the scandal this time as little as on earlier, perhaps still more important occasions.
>
> (Circular, 18/02/1926)[52]

Not letting himself be intimidated, Jones counter-attacked

> But you are lucky to live in a country where "Christian Science", all forms of "psych. research", mingled with hocus-pocus and palmistry do not prevail as they do here to heighten opposition to all psychology. Two books were written here trying to discredit ψα on this ground alone. You also forget sometimes in what a special position you are personally. When so many things pass under the name of ψα, our great answer to inquirers is "ψα is Freud", so now the statement that ψα leads logically to telepathy etc. is more difficult to meet.
>
> (to Freud, 25/02/1926)

Losing patience with the Welshman, and sarcastic about his oversensitivity to any reason for scandal (and Jones's previous conduct had given plenty of these), Freud wrote to him personally:

> I very much regret that my views on telepathy have plunged you into new difficulties. But it really is difficult not to offend English sensibilities. I sometimes really felt I should not have written Das Ich und das Es, for das Es cannot be rendered into English. . . . [M]y personal experience through tests, which I undertook with Ferenczi and my daughter, have attained such convincing power over me that diplomatic considerations had to be relinquished. Again I was presented with an instance where, on a very much reduced scale, I had to repeat the great experiment of my life; namely, to admit to a conviction without considering the resonance of the world around me. So it was then inevitable. If anyone should bring up my Fall with you, just answer calmly that my acceptance of telepathy is my own affair, like my Judaism and my passion for smoking, etc., and that the subject of telepathy is not related to *psychoanalysis*.
>
> (07/03/1926)[53]

In Freud's indignant assertions, we can intuit the ever more intimate and private significance being assumed by telepathy, on the same level as his Jewish origin and his cigars. . . . He smoked inordinately, practically all day without stopping. In his extreme sensitivity to the psychic, characterological roots of certain gestures, Wilhelm Reich would say, "I always had the feeling he smoked . . . because he wanted to say something which never came over his lips."[54]

Freud's letter is striking because it picks up and develops the associative thread of English, the foreign language to which he had had to submit for some time and be translated into, as noted in the session of the "Forsyth" case.

Freud now blames the English language for not being in contact with the "*Es*" and for lacking words that can translate the concept without betraying its sense. He seems to be claiming his own space of idiomatic language, asserting himself in a manner that suggests acting out, but also making a vital push against every paternal castration – translation: an idiom that precedes speech, that "does not come over the lips."

For his part, Jones, eager to cleanse psychoanalysis of its popular roots and its association with hypnosis and magnetism, also used these political arguments to try and increase his own power base. During this time he regretted the appearance on cinema screens of *The Mystery of the Soul*, G W Pabst's silent film inspired by psychoanalysis which, despite the professor's disapproval, had been scripted by his Viennese pupil Siegfried Bernfeld, made use of Abraham as a consultant and was supported by Sachs after Abraham's death. Jones believed that the film was provoking a further wave of denigration against Freud in England, accusing him of trying to publicise his theory in this way since he couldn't disseminate it in scientific circles.[55]

Not all the master's pupils were so worried about his pronouncements, given that in May of that year, *Imago* published not only the paper by Lowtzky mentioned earlier but also the article by H. Deutsch on "occult processes during psychoanalysis" which Freud would cite in *Lecture XXX* and also given that in October, the German Psychoanalytic Society included a paper by Bernfeld himself, newly moved to Berlin, entitled "Some Speculations on the Subject of Telepathy."[56]

The very fine clinical paper by Deutsch, at the time director of the Training Institute in Vienna, in fact addressed the topic of empathy.[57] The hypothesis was that, observed in the continuum of the psychoanalytic process, "occult" phenomena lost their mystical character and could be understood and interpreted in the transference-countertransference relationship. She also established a kinship between the telepathic process and analytic intuition: from her perspective, by not subjecting their intense intuitive irruptions to critical elaboration, mediums would experience as clairvoyance what analysts are used to developing gradually and prudently through their art of interpreting unconscious meaning.

Deutsch was developing what came to be the main topic of reflection and teaching for Ferenczi who, unlike Deutsch, was never allowed by Freud to publish on the theme of telepathy in analysis. Later pupils, unlike the Hungarian, would not ask Freud for permission.

By the end of 1926, Freud seemed determined to return to the Harz essay with no further delays, but once again a preconscious obstacle appeared in him: when he began looking for the manuscript among his papers, he couldn't find it, and even wrote to Eitingon, believing that it must still be in his possession.[58] Eitingon assured him he had personally returned it, suggesting that it must have been misplaced, as turned out to be the case.[59] The block was enough to discourage Freud, or something else made him change his mind, since in the end he did no more about it and did not bring up the subject again for a while.

It should be added that all this was echoed in the German medical world by the psychiatrist and sexologist Albert Moll, who was anxious to defend and differentiate hypnosis from the practices of the mediums and missed no opportunity for harsh and violent denigration of anyone interested in occultism. In 1925 he had been sensationally tried for slander in a case brought by the husband of a medium whom, in his book *Spiritualism*,[60] he had accused of trickery, manipulation, and charades. After being acquitted, Moll continued his campaign, including the sexual theory of psychoanalysis in his criticism of occultism: in October 1926, during the first *International Congress for Sexual Research* in Berlin, which he chaired, during a press conference, he had used overtly inappropriate language against psychoanalysts, as a result of which some of them withdrew their support from the organising committee.[61]

This did not mean that telepathy was no longer on Freud's mind. In September 1927, when the professor, now unable to travel, was holidaying in the Villa Schüler in Semmering, he was visited by Binswanger – it was one of the last times they met – who noted in his diary a conversation in which Freud mentioned a work in progress on the meaning of religious feeling (*The Future of an Illusion*) and entertained him at length with his convictions on the topic of telepathy.[62]

Still playing for time

By the end of the twenties, experimental psychological research into telepathy had become more and more frequent: in a review for *Imago* of Carl Bruck's (1925) book on the telepathic transmission of drawings in hypnosis, which studied simultaneous processes in pairs of hypnotised people who were asked to guess the picture that was being drawn by the experimenter, Fanny Lowtzky noted the great interest of psychoanalysis in the influence which puberty, menopause, or a state of illness could exercise over the subject's telepathic ability, as well as his or her affective fixation on certain telepathic constellations (1928).

In 1930, the American writer Upton Sinclair[63] published *Mental Radio*: *Does It Work, and How?* in which he documented experiments with his second wife, Mary Craig Kimbrough, who, during a period of deep depression, had discovered that she possessed unexpected telepathic abilities. The tests involved the reproduction of nearly 300 drawings made by her husband. The book even carried a favourable preface by Albert Einstein:

> I have read the book of Upton Sinclair with great interest and am convinced that the same deserves the most earnest consideration, not only of the laity, but also of the psychologists by profession. The results of the telepathic experiments carefully and plainly set forth in this book stand surely far beyond those which a nature investigator holds to be thinkable. On the other hand, it is out of the question in the case of so conscientious an observer and writer as Upton Sinclair that he is carrying on a conscious deception of the reading world; his good faith and dependability are not to be doubted. So if somehow

> the facts here set forth rest not upon telepathy, but upon some unconscious hypnotic influence from person to person, this also would be of high psychological interest. In no case should the psychologically interested circles pass over this book heedlessly.
>
> (23/05/1930)

It is worth remembering that Einstein and many other scientists were trying to address the mysterious phenomenon of *quantum entanglement* (*the simultaneity of twin particles, spooky action at a distance*), which had an influence on the decision of the psychologist William McDougall (1871–1938), a pupil of William James and analysand of Jung, to create a laboratory of parapsychology at Duke University in the early thirties under the direction of Joseph Banks Rhine (1895–1980). It was Rhine who then systematically applied the method of experimental statistics to psychical research in the field of transmission from mind to mind, introducing the term *extra-sensory perception* (1964).

The culture of the time was permeated by the interest in occultism, which periodically came back into fashion with new critical interpretations. Thomas Mann's story "Mario and the Magician" (1930), inspired by the show of the illusionist Gabrielli, which had struck him during a stay in Tuscany because of the spell he put over an entire auditorium, could also be read as an allusion to the seductive, violent power exercised over the masses by the enchanter Mussolini, now leader of Italy.

In London during the early thirties, there was a debate in *The Times* about the news that some séances organised by the Swedish ambassador, Baron Palmstierna, had called up Robert Schumann, through whom they rediscovered his violin concerto, even receiving suggestions on interpretation and variant readings. The subject was immensely topical, and Agatha Christie published two novels in 1931, *The Sittaford Mystery* and *Peril at End House*, both centring on the revelations of a séance.

It was in this period – about 20 years after the experiences with patients about the famous unfulfilled prophecies and 10 more years after the session with Herr P – that Freud decided to publish his own long-deferred contribution on the theme of occultism. In March 1932, a few weeks after undergoing one of the numerous operations there were periodically necessary to control his cancer of the jaw, anxious once again about the fate of the psychoanalytic publishing company, Freud confided to Max Eitingon (who had lost much of his fortune) that he intended to do something to replenish the coffers of the *Verlag*, if his strength permitted, with a supplement to the first *Introductory Lectures*.[64]

Freud's project had his death looming over it, but it also offered a chance to renew the resources of the *Verlag*, of psychoanalytic theory and of Freud himself. Few other people were on the inside of the project, and Eitingon was asked to keep it secret. When in June Freud informed Ferenczi he was working on the *New Introductory Lectures*, he named the topics of some *Lectures* without mentioning the one about thought transmission, which would have been of particular interest to the Hungarian. He just complained that the work on the *Lectures* had been weighing on him for 15 years, and it seemed like rather unpleasant "ruminating."[65]

In the same month, at the Budapest Society, Istvan Hollòs, a member of the Hungarian school and a pupil of Federn as well as Freud, presented his paper "*Psychopathologie alltäglicher telepathischer Erscheinungen*" ("Psychopathology of Everyday Telepathic Phenomena"), containing an abundant body of case material that showed unconscious patient-analyst transmission in both directions along the lines of the Forsythe case, chosen during a period of over ten years.[66] Hollòs claimed that the countertransference was indeed the place for thought transference and interpreted these phenomena in the light of the theory about the induction of unconsciouses between two people learned many years before in Ferenczi's seminars. He also mentioned having the opportunity to go more deeply into the subject with Ferenczi in a long conversation during a journey from Vienna to Budapest in 1915.[67]

Unlike Hollòs, Freud would not cite the experiences of his Hungarian pupil and friend at any point. The relationship between the two men was now in a critical state.

While his own work was going into print, Freud received a letter from Edoardo Weiss consulting him on the subject of occultism.

Since the time of his training in Vienna, Weiss had been aware of Freud's stance towards the exploration of so-called occult phenomena and telepathy. He was to say to Eissler,

> Freud told everyone: Whoever feels the urge to investigate some phenomenon should go ahead and do so, whatever the subject may be. I happened to have in treatment later on, in Trieste, two patients who had been analysed previously for a short time by Freud. And through them I learned something of Freud's attitudes. In one case Freud told the patient: Suppose you have the idea that you can discover something from the lines of the hand. Don't be hindered by preconceived ideas. Go ahead and investigate! But you must consider whether your belief might be due to some unconscious motive which you don't understand, or whether the interest is genuine. At any rate, we have to feel free to investigate whatever fields interest us; there are so many things between heaven and earth (Himmel und Erde) of which we are completely ignorant.
>
> (Eissler interview in Accerboni Pavanello, 1990, p. 354)

At that time, Weiss was in Rome and had Nicola Perrotti and Emilio Servadio in training analysis with him. Together they had set up a psychoanalytic group that was still meeting at his house and had organised the *Rivista Italiana di Psicoanalisi*. Servadio had already published *La Ricerca Psichica* (1930), the first Italian treatise on parapsychology, with a preface by Charles Richet, and in 1937, he went on to found the *Società italiana di Metapsichica,* which later became the *Società italiana di parapsicologia.* As Weiss recalled:

> Dr E Servadio had let me participate in experiments with a medium, Erto, from Naples, whose telepathic and telekinetic performance amazed me. I could not verify the authenticity of his feats, of course, and I recognized that they could have been due to very clever tricks. Nor did I consider mentioning them publicly. . . . Freud was worried that I might openly express a belief in such occult phenomena, a step that would have interfered with the psychoanalytic movement in Italy.
>
> (1970, p. 66)

It was later discovered that this Pasquale Erto, who claimed to be able to emit paranormal luminous radiation, was actually a skilful trickster. In his reply to Weiss, Freud gave him advance notice about the appearance of "Dreams and Occultism":

> What you relate about your occult experiences interested me very much, but also made me a little anxious. My point of view is not of arrogant rejection *a limine*. . . . I think that so long these mediums work in the dark, in conditions which restrict so greatly the observer's capacity for judgement, they do not deserve to have any more confidence placed in them than do the conjurors. Nor do they turn out anything useful, and over again they are detected as cheats. In all probability your medium is no better. I am, it is true, prepared to believe that behind all so-called occult phenomena lies something new and important: the fact of thought-transference. i.e., the transferring of psychical processes through space to other people. *I know of proof of this observation made in daylight and am thinking of expressing my opinion publicly about it.*
>
> (24/09/1932, my italics, p. 69)

In his admonition to Weiss, Freud reiterated that what is permitted to the great is not permitted to the small: "Naturally it would be unfavorable for the part you play as the pioneer of psychoanalysis in Italy were you to proclaim yourself as the same time a partisan of occultism."

Immediately after the publication of the *New Introductory Lectures*, Ernest Jones felt it was his duty to present at the scientific meetings of the *British Psycho-Analytical Society* a seminar on the subject of occultism – "The Belief in the Occult"[68] – a counterweight to the Master's claims (not traceable in the BPS archives) which may have referred to his monograph on nightmares and mediaeval superstitions and which he would use for the chapter on "Occultism":[69] this would be his attempt to silence the embarrassing innovations proposed by Freud on the analytic relationship and the possibility of communication between two psyches which psychoanalysis, having emerged as a one-person system, was not in a position to integrate.

1933, *Lecture XXX*, "Dream and Occultism"

So we have arrived at *Lecture XXX*, where Freud publishes his observations on the topic of thought transmission adorned with an important theoretical frame: it's a work we have watched being constructed over time. In the brief introduction, he made clear his intention to proceed by applying the rigorous laws of the scientific method even in this field, without underestimating the difficulties connected to the subject: the theoretical prejudices, the general human tendency to credulity, the past joining of forces between occultism and religion in wishing to prove the existence of supernatural forces, the uncertain and improbable conditions in which this kind of "psychic" phenomena emerge and are usually observed. . . . And he likened certain incongruous occultist propositions to the thesis that the core of the Earth consists of "jam," an outlandish example to underline the implausibility of those beliefs.

After stating his hypothesis – that "there is a real core of yet unrecognized facts in occultism round which cheating and phantasy have spun a veil which it is hard to pierce" – Freud addressed the question of "telepathy," the only phenomenon that seemed to him to count for something in such "chaos," giving it a first definition:

> the alleged fact that an event which occurs at a particular time comes at about the same moment to the consciousness of someone distant in space, without the paths of communication that are familiar to us coming into question. It is implicitly presupposed that this event concerns a person in whom the other one (the receiver of the intelligence) has a strong emotional interest.
>
> (1933, p. 36)

And here he emphasises that telepathy would act almost as "a kind of psychical counterpart to wireless telegraphy": information would reach the receiver's consciousness in the form of a recognisable perception by the visual or auditory senses. Without pronouncing on the reality of such a phenomenon, he advances the hypothesis that the condition of sleep could encourage it. Beginning with the self-deprecating "Actually I have little to tell you – only a modest fact," he presents a brief summary of his observations about the telepathic dream of the "twin birth."[70]

The lecture could have been called "From Dream to Occultism," since the dream only figures in this initial example. The observation enables Freud to highlight how, after shedding light on the obscure process of dreaming, psychoanalytic interpretation could also be advantageously applied to the exploration of adjacent occult areas. So he firmly addresses the topic of "induction" or "thought-transmission" most dear to him, a phenomenon very close to telepathy, he writes, by which "mental processes in one person – ideas, emotional states, conative impulses" can be transferred to another person "through empty space without employing the familiar methods of communication by means of words and signs" (p. 39). And here he addresses the question of professional fortune-tellers, a field that had revealed itself as being particularly suited for carrying out verifiable observations of thought transmission:

> These are insignificant and even inferior people, who immerse themselves in some sort of performance – lay out cards, study writing or lines upon the palm of the hand, or make astrological calculations – and at the same time, after having shown themselves familiar with portions of their visitor's past or present circumstances, go on to prophesy their future. As a rule their clients exhibit great satisfaction over these achievements and feel no resentment if later on these prophecies are not fulfilled.
>
> (p. 40)

And so, in a much more concise manner than in the Harz essay, Freud recounted the unfulfilled prophecies he had observed in his clinical work: the prophecy of the *brother-in-law's crayfish- or oyster-poisoning* and the one about *the suicide of the lover fallen from grace*, hitherto unpublished,[71] followed by the one about *the birth of two children at the same age as the mother*.[72] In these prophecies, only seemingly erroneous, Freud emphasised how the psychoanalytic instrument could highlight the fortune-teller's ability, in a single encounter and with a speed unthinkable to the psychoanalyst, to grasp the unconscious desire of the person consulting them: jealous, rivalrous hatred; the desire for revenge; envy and competition, but especially, in all cases, the intense suppressed incestuous desires between father and daughter, brother and sister.

Mentioning that he had collected a large number of similar prophecies, Freud confirmed that he always had the impression that the fortune-teller, astrologer, graphologist, or palm-reader "had merely brought to expression the thoughts, and more especially the secret wishes, of those who were questioning him" (p. 43). He drew attention to how all these situations involved patients in treatment with him, and it was this that enabled him to interpret the prophecies received as "subjective products, phantasies or dreams of the people concerned," for the most part identifying occult facts "which would otherwise have remained unknown" (p. 47): in other words, analysis had revealed that in fact the fortune-teller had not been mistaken.

At this point, Freud moved on to the final part of the lecture and weighed the merits of the reality of thought transmission. He came to the real innovation, the example which, unlike the previous ones, he had observed first-hand during analytic treatment and, as he made clear, had perhaps been made possible by its influence; a "telepathy" *in praesentia* and not *in absentia*: the example "which has left the strongest impression behind on me" (p. 47).

And here we are at the Forsyth case that we looked at in Chapter 3.

The gold coin

In the final part of *Lecture XXX*, Freud defends the scientific nature of his observational perspective based on the psychoanalytic method against possible accusations of mysticism or occultism. He says he is in favour of research activities that do not exclude *a priori* the possibility of a transmission of thought and specifies that in the telepathic process, it would not be necessary to assume something different from natural physical forces.

> What lies between these two mental acts may easily be a physical process into which the mental one is transformed at one end and which is transformed back once more into the same mental one at the other end. The analogy with other transformations, such as occur in speaking and hearing by telephone, would then be unmistakable.
>
> (p. 55)

In his enthusiasm, Freud is willing to state that psychoanalysis and his theory of the unconscious might be able to comprehend phenomena like telepathy which "psychical research" had not been able to explain, resorting neither to physical processes nor to spiritism. It's an ambitious hypothesis but still entirely in his imagination. And even though the roots of thought transference in the pre-verbal mother-child care relationship were starting to emerge, he declines to consider the possibility of dangerous regressions in the actual reality of the analytic process. Thus, he speculates that "direct psychic transmission" could be "the original, archaic method of communication between individuals" in phylogenetic evolution (for instance, in the development of the collective will in large communities of insects) as in ontogenesis, and he wishes that one day, the analysis of the psychic life of children might bring to light the frequency of this ancient communication method, one that, pushed into the background throughout development, would return in certain circumstances, for example, in group psychology, "in passionately excited mobs" (p. 55).

After making reference to children's frequent belief that their parents know their thoughts before they are uttered, the foundation of the subsequent faith in divine omniscience, Freud cites as a decisive example Dorothy Burlingham's observation, recorded in the particular situation of a mother and a child both in analysis at the same time, a circumstance that in 1933, with the development of child psychoanalysis, was no longer unusual.

> One day the mother spoke during her analytic session of a gold coin that had played a particular part in one of the scenes of her childhood. Immediately afterwards, after she had returned home, her little boy, about ten years old, came to her room and brought her a gold coin which he asked her to keep for him. She asked him in astonishment where he had got it from. He had been given it on his birthday; but his birthday had been several months earlier and

> there was no reason why the child should have remembered the gold coin precisely then. The mother reported the occurrence to the child's analyst and asked her to find out from the child the reason for his action. But the child's analysis threw no light on the matter; the action had forced its way that day into the child's life like a foreign body. A few weeks later the mother was sitting at her writing-desk to write down, as she had been told to do, an account of the experience, when in came the boy and asked for the gold coin back, as he wanted to take it with him to show in his analytic session. Once again the child's analysis could discover no explanation of his wish. And this brings us back to psycho-analysis, which was what we started out from.
>
> (p. 56)

In the clinical vignette, the content of the thought-induction was a "gold coin" that appeared in childhood memory intensely invested with affects within the mother's analysis. Almost simultaneously it had surfaced in the child's psychic life and analysis like a concrete object, a *birthday* present which, with an inexplicable synchronicity, he had entrusted to his mother as soon as she had come back (asking her to give it back a few days later in order to show it to his analyst).

Lecture XXX leaves the reader with the idea that research on the transmission of thought could have valuable discoveries in store and widen the scientific view of psychoanalysis. The suggested hypothesis is that the "occult" treasure concerns precisely *the gold coin of the psychic birthday*, the original and generative gift of mother-child communication.[73]

This is the last word that Sigmund Freud would utter in his life about "telepathy."

This word, however, leaves an important trace in the theory, since in the next *Lecture*, "The Dissection of the Psychical Personality," in order to portray the structural relations of the personality, Freud presents a sketch (1933, p. 78) which is slightly but significantly different from the one presented in *The Ego and the Id* ten years before (1923a, p. 24). Although this new model of the psychic apparatus is described from a monistic viewpoint, the Id's border with external reality is missing: "the individual then appears to us as not only incomplete, not only fragmented or split, but also undefined."[74]

Notes

1 See Pierri, 2022.
2 I.P.V., now, I.P.A., *International Psychoanalytical Association.*
3 Circular letter, 15/12/1924.
4 See Kovács, 1936.
5 4/11/1920, in Grotjahn, 1974, p. 27.
6 See Pierri, 2022.
7 Freud to Ferenczi, 15/11/1910.
8 While it is true that, like Fliess, Jung had personified Freud's mystical elements, from now on, Freud would experience them directly (Wallace, 1980).
9 See Eisenbud, 1949 [1953].

10 4/02/1921, in Jones *III*, p. 391.
11 29/05/1921.
12 Roazen, 1995.
13 See Pierri, 2021.
14 24/07/1921. This letter is translated in Jones *III*, p. 392. "*If I had to live my life over again,* I should devote myself to psychical research, rather than psychoanalysis." Freud later denied ever having made such a statement, and N Fodor, a Hungarian student interested in psychic research, would have to retrieve the letter to remind him of it (1971, p. 84).
15 4/08/1921.
16 Freud 1921 [1941], p. 190.
17 18/08/1921.
18 See Pierri, 2022.
19 Grosskurth, 1991.
20 1945.
21 Jones to Freud, 16/01/1920. Berlin hosted the congress of 1922.
22 1991, p. 19.
23 *Thalassa: A Theory of Genitality,* 1924.
24 The second (1922b) was an intuition on the mechanism of paranoid jealousy (resulting from the study of an American patient sent to him by Jones in 1920); the last one contained some observations on the interpretation of dreams (1923d).
25 See also Pierri, 2022.
26 It was Ferenczi who proposed the hypothesis of mindreading when, on their return from the trip to America, together with Freud they went to consult a famous fortune-teller from Berlin, Frau Seidler, who claimed to be able to read the contents of a sealed envelope. blindfolded. Both had agreed that on this occasion she had read the Hungarian's thoughts on the recent trip. Freud also intervened in that case after Ferenczi had asked the questions. Freud then wrote to him: "I have now overcome the shock. . . . I subscribe to your interpretation that she guesses the thoughts, perhaps the ucs. thoughts of the experimental subject – with the corresponding misunderstandings and convergence of a kind of distortion in the transition from one psyche into another" (11/10/1909). For further detail, see Pierri, 2022.
27 Willy Haas of Nuremberg, in analysis with Freud from September 1908 to July 1909, and from October to December 1910. Philosopher of a phenomenological orientation, professor of political science and orientalist. For a while he was part of the IPV and became a founding member of the Munich Psychoanalytic Society (May, 2019).
28 Elfriede Hirschfeld, who had begun her analysis with Freud in October 1908 and continued it, with various interruptions, for many years. He shared her with several colleagues: she had been treated by Janet; had a consultation with Bleuler; and was periodically under treatment with Jung, Binswanger, and Pfister. The case appears in many of Freud's works and letters under different pseudonyms (Falzeder, 1994, Skues, 2019a).
29 Freud had already mentioned the function of this deviation or dissociation of attention: in the *Studies* (1893–95, p. 271) and in the *Project for a Scientific Psychology* (1895, pp. 240 ff.), as auxiliary techniques of the witty process in the *Jokes* (1905c, pp. 135 ff.). And again in 1921, regarding the role of hypnosis and suggestion in the formation of a collective, Freud stated that the mass (like hypnosis, a "mass of two"), could arouse in the subject something of his archaic heritage, relating to the primordial horde, restoring ancient dispositions preserved in the unconscious since the prehistoric origins of the human family. And here he also introduced the comparison with the analytic situation (*Group Psychology,* 1921, pp. 314–315).
30 In 1915 Schermann, consulted anonymously, wrote a calligraphic report on Karl Kraus which had a surprising effect and encouraged him to tackle the writing of his most

risky and combative work, *The Last Days of Mankind.* Canetti thinks that Kraus, in that particular personal and historical moment, really needed those words of recognition present in Schermann's report in order to feel seen (1974).

31 He had attributed a proof of his writing, submitted to him by Ferenczi, to "an old gentleman . . . with whom it was hard to live since he was an intolerable tyrant in his home" (1921 [1941], p. 191).

32 The young man was a partner of the famous billionaire I Kreuger, a Swedish manufacturer of matches (Roazen, 2001a). Skues later identified him as Robert Eisler (2019b).

33 Schermann advised the patient against marrying the second, younger, woman. Roazen, interviewing H Deutsch, discovered a secret connected to this case (2001a): we will return to it in Chapter 18.

34 See Pierri, 2022.

35 Derrida, 1981, pp. 210–211.

36 See also Chapter 9.

37 See Chapter 1.

38 Freud to Rank 19/07/1922. Lowtzky's paper would appear on *Imago* in 1926, without Freud's comment.

39 "*Bringen mich immer aus der Fassung,"* 13/11/1922.

40 Oatman-Stanford, 2015.

41 Phillips, 2001.

42 Houdini, 1906. See Woody Allen's movie *Magic in Moonlight.*

43 Phillips, 2001, p. 149.

44 Houdini, 1906.

45 Rhine, 1949.

46 Nestler, 1974.

47 Ferenczi to Freud, 30/03/1925 and Ferenczi Circular, 18/04/1925.

48 Jones Circular, 13/03/1925, in Jones, *III*, p. 421.

49 Grubrich Simitis, 2000.

50 See Pierri, 2016a.

51 Circular, 15/2/26.

52 Jones, *III*, p. 422.

53 My italics [German *Sündenfall*, literally, "the sinful Fall (of Man)"].

54 1952, p. 21.

55 Jones, *III*, p. 121.

56 12/190/1925 in Radó, 1927.

57 On this, see Bolognini, 2002.

58 05/11/1926.

59 Jones, *III.*

60 Moll, 1924.

61 Jones, *III*, p. 135.

62 Fichtner, 2003.

63 Sinclair would win the Pulitzer Prize in 1942.

64 20/03/1932.

65 13/06/1932. "Re-chewing, ruminating on something. Could this word suggest some remorse?" (Torok, 1983, p. 233).

66 Hollòs, 1933, quotes Freud and the Forsyth case, "which adds nothing to the lecture I gave in June 1932," he writes, "and which can only underline the similarity between the case treated (Forsyth) and those that follow" (p. 531, n. 1).

67 At the time, Ferenczi had just written the paper on the "dialogue of the unconscious" between mother and child (1915).

68 15/03/1933, in A Freud, 1933.

69 Jones, *III*, pp. 402–436.

70 Previously published in "Dreams and Telepathy," 1922b.
71 Second and third cases (substitute) in *Vorbericht*.
72 First case in *Vorbericht*, already published in "The Occult Significance of Dreams" (1925c).
73 Pierri, 2016a.
74 Semi, 2009, p. 37.

Chapter 6

The disappeared-occulted manuscript

The posthumous publication of the *Vorbericht* (1921) in "Psychoanalysis and Telepathy" (1941) and the disappearance of the *Nachtrag*

After Freud's death, the "secret Harz essay," the dual manuscript *Vorbericht-Nachtrag* (1921), was found among his papers, and in 1941, as we mentioned earlier, the editors of the posthumous writings – Anna Freud with M Bonaparte, E Bibring, W Hoffer, E Kris, and O Isakower – decided to publish only the *Vorbericht* (*Preface*) in German, in the *Gesammelte Werke*, significantly censoring it. It seems that the decision not to publish the *Nachtrag*, containing the first draft of the Forsyth case, was based on its containing an almost identical version of the "third case" already presented by Freud in *Lecture XXX* (1933).

The *Vorbericht* had to wait over ten more years to be translated into English: the first translation appeared on the initiative of G Devereux who, with support from Anna Freud, Kris, and Hoffer, made a one-volume collection in 1953 entitled *Psychoanalysis and the Occult* of all Sigmund Freud's works on the subject, along with those by other pioneers and eminent psychoanalysts from the IPA (including the essays by Deutsch and Burlingham cited by Freud in 1933).

Ernest Jones, who at the time was busily collecting documentary material for *Sigmund Freud: Life and Work*, alongside James Strachey's equally weighty work of publishing all the works in English for the *Standard Edition*, may have felt undermined by this initiative, and he made sure to criticise it harshly in his chapter on occultism (1957), claiming that (his) Freud would have been greatly distressed at the emergence of analysts ready to believe in telepathy and even to employ it during analytic treatment. In order to discredit it further, using Ferenczi as his scapegoat – even though there were none of Ferenczi's works in Devereux's book! – he added a mocking comment about the Hungarian (who, he said, claimed to have been analysed by one of his former patients in messages from across the Atlantic . . .).[1] In this indirect way, Jones was expressing his ambivalence towards Freud himself.

Meanwhile, in 1955, when James Strachey found he had to include the official English translation of the *Vorbericht* in the *Standard Edition*, he had arbitrarily

DOI: 10.4324/9781003246480-7

given it the title *Psychoanalysis and Telepathy*. Neither Devereux nor Strachey completed the *Vorbericht* by adding its *Nachtrag*. Likewise, in all subsequent editions and translations of Freud's *Works*, the *Preface* always went without its original *Postscript* and took on a life of its own as *Psychoanalysis and Telepathy*. Only the *Standard Edition* provides information about the missing "third case of another kind and open to a different assessment added by way of appendix" anticipated by Freud in the *Preface* (p, 181) and announces the disappearance of the manuscript that had originally been attached to it. Strachey refers to it in a note on the Forsyth case in *Lecture XXX*:

> This case is the one which should have been the "third case" to be included in "Psycho-Analysis and Telepathy". The circumstances of its omission were explained by Freud in the paper, *Standard Ed.*, 18, 190, and commented on in the Editor's Note, *Standard Ed.*, 175. As was indicated there, the original draft survived. It resembled the version given here so closely that it was doubtful whether it was necessary to print it separately. It should be added, however, that since that volume of the *Standard Edition* was published, in 1955, the manuscript has once again *unaccountably disappeared*.
>
> (1964, *S.E.* 22, p. 47, my italics)

And so, *Dreams and Occultism* provided the only known version of the Forsyth case.

To be absolutely precise, at some point, the "third case" had also disappeared from *Lecture XXX*, or at least from an extract of it, "*Zum Problem der Telepathie*," published in German in the *Almanach der Psychoanalyse* in 1934: in fact, only the first part had been included, with the interpretation of the "unfulfilled prophecies" and the conclusions about the primal mother-infant language.

Even so, it was this truncated article, obtained for him by Adorno's wife, which stirred the interest of Walter Benjamin: "It is wonderful if only because it places before us the never sufficiently admired *Alterstil* of the author, one of the most beautiful examples of a true universal understanding," he wrote to her enthusiastically.[2] Benjamin found Freud's conception of telepathy as a communication anticipating the formation of verbal language profoundly in tune with his own theories of mimetic identification and, more generally, on the construction of language. Unfortunately he did not read the "third case."

Hide and seek

Frequently forgotten and vanishing from Freud's desk drawers, the manuscript of the Forsyth case seemed to possess the ability to move by itself and get into the wrong place. When I started looking for it in March 2005, I had the opportunity of consulting Paul Roazen, who, despite having written a long paper on the *Vorbericht* (2001a), had no information for me about the missing "third case."

In my reluctance to take its disappearance for granted, I wanted to check directly that the manuscript was not somewhere near the *Vorbericht* in the "1941" binder of the *Sigmund Freud Archive* in the Library of Congress where it should have been filed. And here I found a trace of its presence since, attached to the holograph of the *Vorbericht*, there were some pages of an old typewritten transcription of the Forsyth case, approximate and incomplete, indicating the heading that Freud had given it: *Nachtrag*-Postscript. Armed with this information, when I went to sift through the online register of the *Sigmund Freud Collection*, it was actually quite simple for me to rediscover the notorious *Nachtrag* which, not being dated and having lost its connection to the *Vorbericht*, had ended up being archived elsewhere: in the "1934" binder, to be precise, with a hypothetical date of 1932, the annotation "Unidentified quotation" and a reference to the *Neue Vorlesungen* XXXI (sic) followed by a question mark.

I won't hide the excitement I felt when, in 2006, I finally had the manuscript in my hands. At the time I could not have imagined the long, complex, and thrilling journey I would have to commit myself to in exploring the chain of thought leading to this text, in part suggested by the autonomous situation it had attained and still has today. Located beside the obituary of Sàndor Ferenczi, the *Nachtrag* seems to indicate concretely how, for Freud, reflection on the "occult" was an element in working through his separation from the *Seher* (seer), the friend he had outlived, and how it was to him above all that it was privately addressed.

Back to Freud's secret text: *found in translation*

Let's take a first look together.

The holograph occupies six and a half pages of those characteristic large sheets, oversize, which Freud specifically commissioned and filled with his dense and distinctive handwriting: in Gothic script narrowly spaced with the lines so close together that the words nearly touched, the lines slope slightly upwards, leaving only a narrow white margin on the left side of the page. There is barely any trace of corrections. Freud "never blotted out a line" since he was not in the habit of writing down anything before the final stage: "he thought out the plan for every article or chapter thoroughly, not only the content and construction, but also the exact formulation of each sentence, before he put pen to paper."[3]

Needing an expert to transcribe the *Nachtrag*, I got in touch with Ilse Grubrich Simitis, who referred me to Ernst Falzeder. In this way, I learned that Grubrich Simitis had herself been able to examine the *Nachtrag* in the *Sigmund Freud Archives* back in 1992.[4] She told me that in *Zurück zu Freuds Texten*, after devoting a chapter to the *Vorbericht*, she had also dwelt briefly on the *Nachtrag*, quoting a few extracts from it and indicating in a note how significant it was for current psychoanalytic theory and practice.

Though it recalls the return to the mysterious untranslatability of the Freudian oeuvre that Lacan (1955) wished for in his own day, *Back to Freud's Texts* (1993b) is quite different. It is instead a demand for clarity, in the sense of clearing the field of misunderstandings (what is lost in translation), that motivates the concern of Grubrich Simitis for Freud's language as communicated in his native tongue.

With regard to the *Vorbericht*, besides its having been given a different title, Grubrich Simitis denounced the substantial modifications made to Freud's work, without any acknowledgement of the fact, by the editors of the posthumous writings: distortions and cuts which she indicates, along with their original locations.[5] She also pointed out that it was not a rough draft but a complete text, "one of rare examples of an informal, confidential, unofficial lecture text," characterised by a spontaneity appropriate to the exchange between very close colleagues (p. 205).

In relation to the *Nachtrag*, she reveals how in 1932, when he was adapting it for *Lecture XXX*, Freud had only made minor adjustments, paradoxically staying more faithful to his private text than the editors of his posthumous writings would be towards the *Vorbericht*.

Compared with the work of Grubrich Simitis, my own has a fault which is also a virtue: the fact that I have no German. This requires an interpretative view of the Freudian corpus based on a psychoanalysis *translated* by Strachey and hence filtered through the errors, distortions, and psyche of its first *English* transmission: the journey I have made takes account of time and tradition, amplifies the echo of the words, and makes me approach Freud's always *foreign* language with the same uncertainty and astonishment as a child faced with something new, with magic, and the first strangeness of verbal language. What is *found in translation* is something that readers of German, with their direct access to the original text, cannot experience.

Moreover, my interest in the *Nachtrag* obviously had nothing to do with the quality of the modifications made by Freud to the content and form of his text at the moment of making it public: I was hoping to learn about those elements that he himself regretted having to suppress and which, as he put it, would have greatly increased "the convincing force of the observation" (1933, p. 47).

On a first reading, the *Nachtrag* did not present any surprising novelties. After more analysis, a whole series of details – about the patient's symptomatology and treatment – became highly significant, and, as happens when we recount a dream for the second time, they started to indicate the specific places where Freud's resistance, which had initially manifested itself in the forgetting of his notes, must have been at work once more.

But together let's read the words with which Freud, back home in 1921 from the holiday in the Harz, and having found his notes again, turned the session into a text. First of all, let's go back with him through the series of those "telepathic" associations.[6]

Notes

1 Jones, 1957 *III*, p 436. Gay clarifies this, pointing out that Ferenczi was referring to the patient's beliefs without sharing them (1988)! See Fortune, 1993.

2 W. Benjamin to G. Adorno, 9/10/193: see Cook, 1987.
3 Sachs, 1945, p. 95.
4 1993a, 1993b.
5 In addition to the modification of some details that could make patients more identifiable, Grubrich Simitis points out the omission of two substantial paragraphs from the original *Vorbericht* manuscript. In one, Freud, referring to his resistance to following the patient of the first example (Elfriede Hirschfeld) in a treatment that had no hope of success, manifested some personal aspects of the countertransference and explained to the colleagues of the committee how, in the course of a consultation, Jung had betrayed his ambiguity towards him for the first time by criticizing his lack of empathy. In the other, the censored passage concerned the example of prophecy introduced in place of the Forsyth case and the manifest incestuous elements of the patient's story (pp. 205–215). See Chapter 18 and full publication in Freud, 2016 (in Italian).
6 Since February 2017, *Nachtrag* has been available online together with 20,000 documents relating to Freud that the Library of Congress in Washington, DC, has digitized and made available: www.loc.gov/resource/mss39990.OV1023/.

Chapter 7

Sigmund Freud

Postscript[1]

Here is the report of a case of thought induction [*Gedankeninduktion*] from analytical practice, omitted because of resistance.

On October 4, 1919, at about 10.45 a.m., Dr. David Forsyth, who had just arrived from London, sends in his card to me while I am working with a patient. I only had time to greet him and to make an appointment to see him later. Dr. F. has a claim to my particular interest; he is the first Englishman to come to me after the re-establishment of communication and to bring the promise of better times. At eleven o'clock, Herr B. arrives. He has been in treatment with me for several years. He is an intelligent man suffering from impotence, with an early fixation on the father, who has never achieved the realization of the love act. Although I had not held out the hope of success to him because of his age – he is nearer to 50 than to 40 – he insisted on trying out therapy, and has since been feeling very comfortable in his attachment to me, and is also not deterred from his continued failures with women.

Today B. talks about temptations to resume his sexual relationships, as he has abstained, for a period of 80 days, from his usual masturbatory gratification accompanied by sadistic phantasies. In this context he once again mentions the beautiful, piquante, but poor girl with whom he could succeed, but with whom he had never alone,[2] because of her virginity, risked attempting something in earnest. He has already very often talked of her, and today he tells me for the first time that, although of course she has no idea of his real impediment, she uses to call him "Herr von Vorsicht." [*Mr. Prudence, Attention*] The visiting card with the name of Dr. Forsyth on it lies before me, and I show it to him.

These are the facts. Now the following to their appraisal. When he was young, B. spent some years in England and since then has retained a permanent interest in English literature. B. possesses a rich English library. He used to bring me books from it, and I owe to him an acquaintance with such authors as Bennett, Galsworthy, and others. One day he lent me a novel of Galsworthy's with the title *The Man of Property*, whose scene is laid in the bosom of a family invented by him, bearing the name of Forsite [sic]. The writer himself has evidently been captivated by this creation of his, for in later stories he repeatedly reverts to the

DOI: 10.4324/9781003246480-8

members of this family, and just a few days ago B. again brought me such a volume. The name Forsite [sic], and everything typical that Galsworthy wanted to embody in it, had played a great part, too, in my conversations with B.; it had become part of the secret language which so easily grows up between two people who see each other on a regular basis. Now the name Forsite [sic] in the novel, as pronounced by us Germans, can hardly be distinguished from that of my visitor, Forsythe [sic]; and the meaningful English word, which we should pronounce in the same way, would be Foresight, which in German is Voraussicht or Vorsicht. Thus my patient B. had in fact come up, from his personal concerns, with the very name with which I was occupied at the same time as a result of processes within myself of which he was unaware.

I will come back again to this connection later, and will, on the one hand, present various things that may strengthen, by way of analytical reflection, the impression which this curious concurrence makes, but on the other hand I will also cite possibilities that weaken it. But before doing so I still have to deal with two of B.'s associations which came up during the same session, and which are demonstrably linked to his first feeling into my thoughts.

1) [erased: The day before] Friday last week I had waited in vain for B. to come for his session at 11 o'clock, and had then gone out to visit our dear Anton Freund in his *pension*, Atlanta. On the second floor[3] of the same house I saw the office of B. and the sign of the firm B. & R. In connection with this I had told B. one or two days before today's session that I had in a sense paid him a visit in his house, but without mentioning the person with whom I had been together in the *pension*. And today, shortly after mentioning "Herr von Vorsicht," he suddenly asks: Is Freud-Ottorego, the woman who is announcing English courses at the [erased: Urania] *Volksuniversität*,[4] your daughter? And for the first time since I have known him he mispronounces my name: instead of Freud – Freund.
2) Towards the end of the session he tells of a dream, from which he had woken in a fright; it was an "*Alptraum*", he says, and adds that not long ago he had forgotten the English word for that, and when someone had asked him said that the English for "*Alptraum*" was "a mare's nest." This would be nonsense, he goes on; "a mare's nest" means an incredible story, a cock-and-bull story, "Alptraum" is nightmare in English.

Now the only thing in common between this association and the previous one seems to be the element "English." I had to remember that he was sitting with me in the room when Jones came in, on 25th of September, after a long separation. I signed to him to go into the second room while I finished with the patient. B. recognized him at once, however, from the photograph hanging in the first room, and expressed the wish to be introduced to him. Now Jones wrote a long treatise on the "Alptraum" – nightmare – and I do not know whether it had come to B's attention, since he never used to read an analytic book.

At this point I do not want to investigate which sources B. could have used for his associations, but will rather detail what analytic understanding can be arrived at of the context of these associations and of their motives. B. was similarly attuned to the name Forsite [sic] or Forsythe [sic] as I was. In one respect it meant the same to him, and it was he to whom I owned the acquaintance with this name in the first place because he had brought me Galsworthy's novel. What seems to be the remarkable fact is that he mentioned this name spontaneously during the analysis, at the moment when it had again become significant to me in a completely different sense owing to a new event – the London doctor's arrival. But even more important than the fact itself is perhaps the form and the context in which the name appeared to him. He did not say, for instance: Now I am thinking of the name Forsite [sic], from the novel you are familiar with, but he was able, without any conscious relation to the novel, to weave the name into his own experiences and thus reproduce it again – something that could have happened long before, but had not happened till then. But then he said: I am a Forsyth too, that's what the girl calls me. The analysis – knowing that B. was at the time in a state of an intense transferential attitude – feels tempted to assume a jealous impulse in him, and to insert before his words: I am hurt that your thoughts are so much occupied with the visitor; do come back to me. To which the following is then added: After all I am a Forsyth too, a Herr von Vorsicht. Thereupon his train of thought, following the associative thread of the same element "English," reverts to two previous instances, which were able to stir up the same jealousy. "A few days ago you paid a visit to my house – not, alas, to me but to a Herr von Freund." This thought distorts – again, for the first time – the name Freud into Freund for him. The Freud-Ottorego from the university calendar has to come in, because as a teacher of English she procures the manifest association. And finally he remembers another visitor, a mere two weeks ago, of whom he was no doubt equally jealous, but in whose case he could tell himself that he was no match for him. He thinks of Ernest Jones who [erased: can] writes treatises on the nightmare whereas he at best only produces such nightmares himself. It seems that his regret because of his inferiority expresses itself in the statement that he made a mistake in the translation of the word "Alptraum," he is no genuine Englishman after all. Now I cannot call his jealous impulses either inappropriate or unintelligible. He could very well suspect that I would abandon his analysis – from which I did not expect anything – as soon as the foreigners would come to me in Vienna. I had hinted as much to him, and that was in fact what happened shortly afterwards.

The above is an analytic explanation of the three associations brought up by him in the same session and nourished by the same motive; it is rather independent of the question of whether these associations can or cannot be ascribed to thought transference. This question arises for each of the three associations and thus falls into the three following questions: Could B. have known that Dr. Forsyth had just paid me his first visit? Could he know the name of my friend in the *pension* Atlanta? Did he know that Jones had written a brochure on the nightmare? It will depend on the reply to these details whether or not my observation allows of a conclusion favorable to thought induction.

Perhaps we have to deal with another question first. I could imagine that someone disputed the justification to see a causal connection between the slip of the tongue in the second case and my visit in the *pension*, and between the mentioning of the nightmare and the thought of Jones in the third case. He would say that this is too shrewd, but after all unprovable, and that it would only show my ambition to make a connection between the three cases because the first one made such a strong impression on me. I admit that both interpretations, although plausible, are not conclusive; insofar as subjective conviction may go further than objective provability, however, I would like to argue that the analytic interpretation of all three associations is sustainable. Whatever one's inclination, the first observation does not seem to be subject to such doubts. Even seen isolated it sustains the apparent fact of thought transference.

In any case I will try to answer all three questions. 1) Could B. know that Dr. Forsyth had been with me a quarter of an hour before him? Could he have any knowledge of his existence or of his presence in Vienna? One is inclined to deny both questions flatly, but I want to make a [erased: possible] partly affirmative answer possible. I cannot rule out the possibility that some time before that I told the patient, with whom I had become quite familiar during the war years, that I was expecting an English doctor for analysis, as the first dove after the Deluge; that I may even have mentioned his name, precisely because it had that interesting connotation for both of us. This might have happened in the summer months of 1919, for Forsyth had announced his arrival for early October months before. I do not recall such a communication, and I particularly doubt that I mentioned the name, something which is out of my character, but – it may have happened nevertheless, and I may have forgotten it so completely afterwards, so that the Herr von Vorsicht struck me like a miracle in the analytic session. It is true that one regards oneself as a sceptic, but one is well-advised to also doubt one's scepticism. Perhaps the communication did take place, and forgetting it was a tendentious act in favor of the miraculous.

If we have thus got one miraculous possibility out of the way, there is a second, and more difficult one, waiting for us. Assuming that Herr B. knew that there was a Dr. F., and that he was to come to Vienna in October; how is it to be explained that he becomes receptive to him on the very day of his first visit? I think this is either not explained at all, or explained by chance, or by the assumption that he noticed a special excitement in me, of whose signs I myself was not aware, however. Or one might, not to neglect the most extreme possibility, imagine that Herr B. – who arrived only a quarter of an hour after Dr. F. – met him on the short stretch of the way both had to walk, recognized him as an Englishman and, in a state of jealous expectation, guessed: So that's F. who is to come to the Prof, for analysis. He's probably just come from him. – This is as far as I can get with this rationalistic attempt.

The conclusiveness of the second association is strongly diminished by the doubt about its interpretation. Apart from this, however, the observation is to be called a rather strong one, because I think that B. could not know the name of the person to whom I paid a visit in the *pension*. I find it impossible that he made enquiries about that person on the third floor; I believe to remember with certainty that in my short, joking reference to my visit I mentioned no name, and I think I may assume that Herr B. never became aware of the existence of that person at all. Thus this second idea would be particularly valuable as evidence for thought induction, if a chance circumstance did not reduce its value. The man whom I had visited in the *pension* was not only called Freund[5] he was also a friend to me and to my cause, and I may easily have said: I was in your house to visit a friend who lives in that *pension*.

Contrary to the other two details, the third question – could B. know that Jones had written a brochure on the nightmare – is particularly hard to answer. B. usually read more titles than books, and he could easily have read the name of Jones and the corresponding title on the covers of my books, which he owned. It cannot be proved, and it cannot be disproved.

Thus in this case, too, I am unable to reach a decision, to either dispel the glistening semblance of a thought transference, or to strengthen it and make it tangible.[6] After the fireworks have burned down, and all the pros and cons have vanished into thin air, one probably retains the impression that observations regarding associations arising in the analytic exchange, because of the incalculable possibilities and uncertainties, provide a much worse material than the prophecies in the case of a one-time concurrence as discussed above. And yet, if other experiences established thought transference as an irrefutable fact, such observations from analyses would offer a first indication of the subjective conditions and of the relations at play between the two persons, which could facilitate or bring about such an induction.

Notes

1 Sigmund Freud Archives, The Library of Congress, Washington, DC: OVERSIZE, 1859–1985, n.d. OV 10 (cont.) 5 (cont.) Writings (Container 50), "Nachtrag" [1932?], holograph manuscript [Unidentified quotation (for "Neue Vorlesungen XXXI"?)] Transcription and translation by Ernst Falzeder for Maria Pierri. First published in Pierri, 2010.
2 This word inserted later.
3 According to American usage. In British English: first floor [trans.].
4 "People's University" – adult education center [trans.].
5 Freund is the German word for "friend" [trans.].
6 One word crossed out.

Chapter 8

Manuscript details, slips, and errors

Conditions and details

Let's begin by considering the most obvious new elements. In the *Nachtrag*, Freud uses a different initial ("B") for the patient, whom we will now call "PB." Then, when he refers to the first coincidence, the "home visit" after the missed appointment, he indirectly gives us the address. In fact, he indicates the name of the hotel where von Freund was staying, the "pension Atlanta" and adds that on the second floor of the same house, he saw the sign of the firm of "B. & R." (the office of Mr PB, therefore, not his home). Having gathered these pieces of information and recovered the address of the Hotel Atlanta – which now occupies the entire historic Viennese building at Währingerstrasse 33, in district 9, not far from Berggasse – it was possible for me to search the Municipal Archive in Vienna and identify the full details of the firm "Bernfeld & Rosenberg" which was based there in 1919, to identify "PB" as Paul Bernfeld, and to track down some basic official records about him.[1] My pulse raced as I confirmed my discovery by consulting Freud's diary of the years 1918–20 where the 11.00 session is marked with the surname "Bernfeld" (with no initial or indication of Herr or Frau).[2]

Moving on to the clinical material, Freud states in the manuscript that the analysis of Paul Bernfeld lasted for several years: we learn that he was aged nearly 50 (Paul Bernfeld was then 48), that his difficulty with women was caused by symptoms of impotence, with an early fixation on the father – "he never achieved the realization of the love act" – and that he presented the usual masturbatory gratification accompanied by sadistic phantasies. We also learn that Bernfeld, who had been warned before the summer about the English patient's arrival and the likely ending of his treatment, in a renewed attempt to cure his impotence, abstained from masturbatory gratification throughout the summer break and that, for this reason, on the resumption of his analysis, he may have found himself in a state of particularly intense transferential investment. These technical characteristics of the treatment – the analyst's effort to encourage the patient's abstinence in order to prevent premature, substitute satisfactions and achieve a full development of the transference – corresponded to the model then in use and illustrated by Freud the summer before in Budapest.[3] The fact that the treatment was free of charge and that

DOI: 10.4324/9781003246480-9

its conclusion was planned – not merely as a contingent necessity but as a way to deal with the impasse in the cure – had been discussed in that session. In our case, however, Freud makes it clear that the plan to end the analysis was caused by the fact that there was no hope of success, that the therapy too was impotent.

It should be noted that the manuscript contains a number of *lapsus calami* in relation to the fateful term: sometimes Dr Forsyth becomes Dr Forsythe, and the name of the character in Galsworthy's novel is always *Forsite* instead of *Forsyte*. This last slip – quite a remarkable one given Freud's acute sensitivity for words, and the written word in particular, must be evaluated and understood within the crucial question of that session. Let's anticipate for a moment and assume that, in making room for the new patient in place of the old one, the slip seems to underline the struggle for survival and for the place (*for site*), but also raises the primal, founding question for the Jew: his being "out of place,"[4] his exile from the *Promised Land*, his displacement, and also his deportations.

In the draft, Freud calls his new pupil "the first Englishman" to arrive after the restoration of international connections, making a closer match with the subject and context of the session, instead of calling Forsyth generically "the first foreigner" (1933): the draft makes it more evident that this is the rival who has won the war and is imposing his own language.

Last, we should note a deletion concerning the place where Fräulein Freud-Ottorego is to give English courses: the "Urania" auditorium has been replaced by the "People's University." Freud's mistake might express something he has missed in his diagnosis of the patient: in fact, the German psychiatry of the time used the term "Uranism" to indicate passive male homosexuality, marked by a psychic sexuality oriented towards the feminine (from the name of the god Uranus, who, according to the legend, was affected by this anomaly).[5]

Freud's "errors" and the occulted "*dritte Fall*"[6]

The manuscript bears the date of the session, Saturday 4 October 1919, which allows us to locate it in time both within the analytic setting (treatment has just been resumed after the summer break) and in relation to the events with which Freud and the members of the committee were involved after being reunited in Vienna.

However, we should note that the holograph is full of uncertainties, mistakes, and deletions concerning references to time. In some cases, Freud contracts time, as when he initially attributes PB's missed session and his home visit to the day before, later "correcting" it as the Friday of the previous week. In other cases, he expands time, along with the affective fabric of the context: for example, placing Jones's interruption on 25 September, then putting it two weeks before the session, while in the 1932 version, he will set it even further back to the previous month.

Recently, in a book which gathers and scientifically analyses an entire collection of errors and supposed mythomanias on the part of Freud, his pupils, and heirs, with the aim of cutting the powerful, ineradicable psychoanalytic "legend" down to size, I was able to rediscover the precious transcript of a letter from James Strachey to Ernest Jones at the time when the two pupils were closely collaborating, Strachey on the *Standard Edition* and Jones on Freud's biography.

In the incriminating text, used by Borch-Jacobsen and Shamdasani (2012) to prove the unreliability of Freud (and psychoanalysis) through the testimony of his own followers – and which instead serves to help us better understand his creativity – Strachey and Jones address the chronological inconsistencies of the *Nachtrag*, sharing a less than benevolent opinion about the Master's text as a whole and not merely his oversights.

Going on to read the two British pupils' correspondence during this period, I had the impression that they were embarrassed by the scandalous subject of "telepathy" rather than Freud's supposed lack of precision.

Jones, who was then working on the chapter about "Occultism," confided that he was struck by what he considered the professor's vacillations about such phenomena (an opinion he went on to express in the biography). However, in his careful gathering of material, he wondered where the manuscript of the Forsyth case might have ended up.

> I have just written an interesting chapter on it [occultism]. It is amusing how Freud kept wobbling from belief to disbelief and back again. . . . The "dritte Fall" mentioned on p. 26, certainly refers to that silly case about the man who was jealous of Forsyth and myself (XV. 51). He had left the notes of it at home when he went to Gastein in July, 1921 (see XVII, 41). He must have written it out more fully for the Neue Vorlesungen, but only the person who went through his papers could tell you what they did with the abgesonderte Nachtrag;[7] if they destroyed it because it had been published it was not very pietatsvoll [reverent].
>
> (Jones to Strachey, 27/10/1955)[8]

> The same blurb gives an account of the "dritte Fall" mentioned in G.W. XVII, p. 26. As you will see from my remarks there (S.E. XVIII, 175), we eventually found the missing bit of MS, which I actually have before me at the moment. . . . The account of the "dritte Fall" is not identical with version of Neue Vorlesungen. It is a good deal re-drafted, with omissions and new bits. If it had been found in time, I should have included it as an Appendix in my Vol. XVIII. As it is, I wish I shall put it as an Appendix to the New Lectures (SE XXII). Of course I don't think there's any substantial difference. But I confess that I've not yet deciphered it completely.
>
> (Strachey to Jones, 6/11/1955)

> I don't think the "dritte Fall" is very reliable. For one thing he says that I was in Vienna a month before Forsyth. Actually we were there in the same week (checked by the fact that we dined together in Zurich when our journeys crossed.)
>
> (Jones to Strachey, 7/11/1955)

> I enclose two extracts from the original report of the "dritte Fall," which of course confirms what you say. It also shows how utterly incapable of accuracy over details the professor was. He'd actually got the correct facts in front of him, and simply couldn't copy them out.
>
> (Strachey to Jones, 9/11/1955)

> The facts are quite clear. Forsyth and I were in Vienna within two days of each other. My first visit to Freud was September 25, and his October 4th, an interval of nine days. In one place Freud calls this interval "a month," in another "a few weeks."
>
> (Jones to Strachey, 10/11/1955)

As we know, Jones disliked that clinical account which used him personally as evidence. Also irritated by the fact that Freud had confused the date of his arrival in Vienna, and having met Herr P, knowing David Forsyth well, and figuring in the case only fleetingly, he insisted to Strachey that Freud's chronology of the facts and the date of his first post-war visit were incorrect, citing his dinner with Forsyth in Zurich as proof.

In "Occultism," after introducing the case in this way,

> Many would consider the case the most tenuous of those related. At all events there are so many alternative explanations to telepathy that it is not surprising Freud forgot to lay it before us at our Harz meeting.
>
> (Jones, *III*, p. 435)

he went on to note that displeasing error and, as we saw in Chapter 4, would attribute it to "some unconscious touching up," trying to delegitimise the entire construction of *Lecture XXX* about the Forsyth case and the "transmission of thought."

What is of most interest in the letters is the fact that James Strachey finally came into possession of the "missing M.S." (Strachey to Jones, 6/11/1955). So it is to him, if there were any doubt, that we can attribute responsibility for its subsequent disappearance, at Ernest Jones's instigation and with his connivance. In this way, the two of them hoped that the Forsyth case would remain buried in the archives and "beyond the veil," along with the proleptic and visionary thought of Ferenczi.

Nachträglichkeit and reconstructions

The professor's chronological inconsistencies do not indicate a simple inability to be precise over "details." As we have been able to learn, "errors" are signs of the unconscious psychic content of an experience.

The more closely we observe this clinical situation, the more we witness a sort of traumatic disorientation in Freud, already suggested by the headings given to the two works: between "Preface" and "Postscript," the present, current time, and the link between past and future seem to have gone missing.

If we then consider the *Nachtrag* in its state of detachment from the *Vorbericht*, its title *Postscript* becomes especially evocative of a process of retrospective elaboration – *Nachträglichkeit* – which could only have occurred in a *second time*, ten years after the events.

As Derrida claimed in the *Scene of Writing*: "The postscript which constitutes the past present as such is not satisfied, as Plato, Hegel, and Proust perhaps thought, with reawakening or revealing the present past in its truth. It produces the present past" (1966, p. 214).

In the elaboration of the Forsyth case, it is not simple interferences and unconscious resistances that were in play: there were no thoughts available yet that would have allowed this occult and occulted letter to be integrated into the transmission of psychoanalytic knowledge. Maria Torok considers it a *crypt* (1983), Fachinelli a perinatal *claustrophilic* area, undifferentiated and potential, not yet given meaning (1983).

For Torok, the occult material concerns a type of traumatic experience not yet capable of being worked through, which remains incorporated in the Ego via a preserving repression, isolated in what she and N Abraham have called the crypt. At its origin, there would have been a libidinal wound, a disappointment connected to the sudden loss of a narcissistically indispensable object which, in the absence of the ability to put it into words (or the chance to do so), cannot be worked through in the "repressed" unconscious but would have become encysted in an "artificial" unconscious or, as we would say today, in the unrepressed unconscious.[9]

Unlike the concept of the crypt (and that of the *claustrum* developed by Meltzer, 1992), the image of the maternal *claustrum* proposed by Fachinelli refers to a psychic area which contains healthy and potentially developmental aspects: *claustrophilia* would be the tendency to withdraw into a dyadic analyst-patient unit on a perinatal level, a mode of coexistence that lives in and for itself, ignoring the passage of time and the change that would lead to separation.

In the first memory of that extraordinary session in 1919 entrusted to the manuscript we can feel Freud's anxiety directly: unlike the 1933 text, which concludes in favour of thought transmission, the last paragraph of the *Nachtrag* shows him almost blinded by the dazzling spectacle of the dream-work in the telepathic session. As in a dream, "a firework, which takes hours to prepare but goes off in a moment,"[10] he seems to observe the phenomenon in an intermediate state between dreaming and waking which he does not interrupt with a judgement about its reality since he is "unable to reach a decision." And he would rather give credit to the prodigious prophetic sleights of the fortune-tellers than have faith in the wonderful present of the analytic process.

Freud's errors, noted immediately by Jones and Strachey, have something to do with this anxiety. Strachey himself, as Winnicott notes, had learned to recognise them and tried to find their meaning:

> He [Strachey] had become vitally interested in Freud's writings and loved to speak about the links which showed the workings of Freud's mind, links that could be made because Freud reported his dreams and wrote very many letters. There were also Freud's errors of fact, reflecting feelings or conflicts that could sometimes be tracked down.
>
> (1969b, p. 130)

In his account of the session, we can see Freud passing cursorily over some significant events in his life, intertwined with the treatment of Paul B, which he struggles to locate affectively and chronologically, in a sort of defensive distillation. The chronology that can be reconstituted from the dating of the manuscript, Freud's diary, and Jones's correction sees these events taking place close together in a single week, the one before the telepathic session.

In the most reliable reconstruction, Freud returns to Austria on 24 September 1919. Jones is able to be in Vienna on Saturday the 27th, and Forsyth follows close behind on the following Saturday 4 October. Both Britons arrive by train from Zurich and visit Berggasse, each interfering in his own way with the meetings of Freud and Mr Paul Bernfeld. Ernest Jones drops right into the middle of a conversation; seven days later, Forsyth more insidiously modifies the affective context of the 11.00 session, leaving an impression on Freud's thoughts with his brief introduction a few minutes before the session begins.

So, we can affectively locate the circumstances of the clinical event and the sequence of the preceding incidents in the setting, which are cited by Freud as disconnected, random events. Jones's intrusion, Bernfeld's missed appointment, the "home visit," the gift of the book, Forsyth's arrival – all occurring in the space of a few days – come together in a significant relational coherence. We detect in them the echo of the events that become crucial in Vienna, that epoch-making disturbance which contributes from the background to preparing the form and contents of the strange session on 4 October.

During the week when the two foreigners pass the baton – when Forsyth arrives, Jones has just left – there is a turning point which brings a profound transformation for Freud and for psychoanalysis, not just for his patient.

Notes

1 See Chapter 17. Torok's (1983) suggestive but improbable interpretation, seeing the more famous S Pankeiev hidden in the role of Mr P, is categorically ruled out.
2 M Molnar, *Freud Museum*, and U May, personal communications.
3 Freud, 1919c. Freud would have recommended Weiss to make an impotent patient observe abstinence, so as not to block normal access to the woman (26/05/1922).
4 Levi Della Torre, 1995.
5 It should be noted that the term homosexual once defined the passive partner in the male homoerotic couple – in the equation of homosexuality with passivity and femininity – and did not apply to the active partner, nor did it indicate an identity of homoerotic choice (Zaretsky, 2004).
6 "Third case."

7 Separate postscript.
8 Courtesy of the archive of the British Psychoanalytical Society: Letters E Jones to J Strachey 27/10/1955, 7/11/1955 and 10/11/1955, James & Alix Strachey collection, P17-F-B-08; letters J Strachey to E Jones 6/11/1955 and 9/11/1955, Ernest Jones collection, P04-C-E-14. My grateful acknowledgements to Jackie Jones and the Society of Authors as agents of the Strachey Trust.
9 Abraham and Torok, 1987.
10 Freud, 1900, p. 576.

Chapter 9

During the Great War

Historical and personal circumstances

Let's return to the Vienna of 1919 and get back in touch with the reality that emerges from the enormous disruption that has thrown Europe into chaos, viewing it this time from the stage of Freud's inner theatre and going behind the scenes of his analytic work with Herr Paul Bernfeld.

It was a time of epoch-making change. The end of the war made history, causing an upheaval that rearranged national boundaries and changed identities (both personal and national), partitioned Europe into new areas of influence, stirring up emotions and profoundly changing modes of thought and language in groups and individuals, making them all witnesses, spectators, and protagonists of a common reality at the moment when it was taking on a new form.

With the opening of borders in September, psychoanalysis was about to undergo a further upheaval as the friends and colleagues of the committee gathered in Vienna, and after a long separation Jones, Ferenczi, and von Freund met up once again with Freud and Rank. They mourned bereavements and celebrated marriages and births in a generational transition marked for psychoanalysis by Jones's investiture and the relocating of responsibilities, money, and investment of affect from East to West. In order to survive and grow, psychoanalysis would have to translate its thoughts and learn to *speak* English, *become* English. During that week in late September, memorable changes occurred in the lives and destinies of the individual committee members and in the history of the psychoanalytic movement: a revolution which, in imitation of Austrian Chancellor Karl Renner who was negotiating the surrender, Freud summed up to Abraham on the Friday evening before the "telepathic" session as a "new orientation towards the West" (3/10/19).

For Freud, this orientation may have represented a step in that vaster movement towards the West which began in the later nineteenth century with the emigration of the Jews (and his father Jacob) from the Empire's eastern provinces, which would be completed on the threshold of the Second World War with the flight from Nazism to the United Kingdom, the United States, and South America.

But for now, let's get up to date with what had happened during the war.

DOI: 10.4324/9781003246480-10

A coming-of-age prematurely interrupted

The outbreak of the war had caught Freud unawares: only a few days before the assassination in Sarajevo, he was entirely concentrating on the "bombshell" he had thrown at Jung and Adler in his paper "On the History of the Psycho-Analytic Movement" and on the possibility of Jones and Abraham taking turns to hold the presidency of the Association.[1] The killing of Archduke Franz Ferdinand on 28 June 1914 and the international political crisis did not stop him allowing Anna to go on her promised holiday in Britain accompanied by her godmother Anna Hammerschlag Lichtheim. He himself went on holiday as usual in July, and once in Karlsbad, his greatest anxiety was about his daughter, who had sent a telegram on arrival in London: "Wonderful journey met by doctor Jones" (16/07/1914).

We do not know when Jones started eyeing Anna up, but, alerted by Loe Kann about her former lover's intentions, Freud immediately sent his daughter a series of letters to put her on guard against the Welshman's solicitations. In the case of a "declaration," he urged her to show self-possession and advised her to be vague about plans for the future.

Freud speculated that if Jones believed Loe Kann's analysis with Freud was the reason she had left him and recently got married, this might be Jones's way of taking revenge on him. He was already seeing his 18-year-old daughter in the hands of this sexually expert man, "tender and good" but, as he had learned while analysing Loe, hardly suitable for a "more refined feminine person," impulsive and himself in need of someone to guide him (16/07/1914).

He suggested that his daughter avoid being alone with Jones in a situation where he could make a definite approach. "I am sure you have the talent – after all you are a woman." But in the same letter, he asked her to give up the freedom of choice that he had granted her elder sisters and to wait for his express approval in the name of the more intimate bond that he had reserved for her: "You have turned out a little different from Math and Soph," he wrote. "You have more intellectual interests and," he insinuated, "will probably not be as happy with a purely female activity" (22/07/1914).

By contrast, she was granted full freedom of movement in the presence of Ferenczi (who was immediately alerted)[2] and the newly married Loe and Herbert Jones, who were also on their way to.

At the same time, Freud had sent Ernest Jones a letter of thanks for his attentiveness towards Anna and explicitly warned him against planning anything:

> Perhaps you know her not enough. She is the most gifted and accomplished of my children and a valuable character besides. Full of interest for learning, se[e]ing sights and getting to understand the world. She does not claim to be treated as a woman, being still far away from sexual longings and rather refusing man.
>
> (22/07/1914)

He had previously been taken by surprise when Sophie, only two and a half years older, had become engaged: married in 1913, she gave him his first grandchild in March 1914. Telling Jones about his tacit agreement with Anna that she should wait two or three years before considering marriage, Freud concluded, "I dont [sic] think she will break the treaty" (*ibid.*).

Anna must have been much struck by her father's overt reaction and, adjusting her ideas, she reassured him about her conduct, candidly confiding to him that she dreamed almost every night about her friend Loe who was about to join her: as if complying with his incestuous appeal, she declared herself more interested in women, and his female patients in particular. . . . And yet she also described an exciting Saturday spent in the Welshman's company from nine in the morning until midnight, which had stopped her replying to her father's letter straightaway. It had been a splendid excursion, first by automobile to Henley, and then on a motorboat down the Thames passing beautiful houses and palaces, which had left her hot and burnt from the wind and sun. The trusted presence of a pair of friends kept Anna safe from criticism, and some typical advice about her mother's birthday present and her father's need for rest confirmed her as a loyal and solicitous daughter (26/07/1914).

Jones was also a little late replying to Freud's letter, and he mentioned the trip with Anna:

> I had already fully appreciated what you write about her. She has a beautiful character and will surely be a remarkable woman later on, provided that her sexual repression does not injure her. She is of course tremendously bound to you, and it is one of those rare cases where the actual father corresponds to the father-imago.
>
> (27/07/1914)

Jones was trying to point out the symbolic and seductive collapse of the imago into the actual father that was implicit in the relationship Freud was nurturing with his daughter, and, to reassure Freud, he declared himself ready to resume his own analysis when Ferenczi arrived in London: however, he showed no sign of intending to give up the prospect of a few days on vacation with "so interesting a companion."

These exchanges were fated to cross with the news of a terrible turn in the international situation: the ultimatum to Serbia and Austria's bellicose utterances. Only a month after Sarajevo, the declaration of war interrupted Jones's plans and crashed onto peaceful Carlsbad in the midst of Martha's birthday celebrations, forcing Freud to return prematurely to Vienna in the confusion of the mobilisation, "with the last evening train that was even permitted to run."[3] The Dresden congress arranged for September was cancelled, and so was the planned stay in the Netherlands.

Freud's forced inactivity: the *Metapsychology* and the *Introductory Lectures*

Like many of his contemporaries, Freud expected victory to be achieved in a few months. His anxiety about the repatriation of Anna, "so-to-say a prisoner-of-war in England,"[4] from whom he heard nothing for a long time, was mitigated by the excitement of his sons Martin and Ernst, who had enlisted immediately.

This war was still an unknown entity: whole nations called up the flower of their youth, only to discover all too quickly that the cruelty of merciless modern technology in its "unleashed bestiality"[5] left no room at all for traditional heroism.

There being little freedom of movement and his usual professional activity being paralysed, in October 1914, Freud decided to offer an analysis to Sàndor Ferenczi, who had had to give up his planned visit to London with Rank. The Hungarian was too old to be called to the front, though he was required to keep himself available, and he had decided that if he couldn't spend the time and the money already withdrawn from the bank on the journey, he would invest it in analysis.[6]

By doing this, the two men seemed to be renewing their old habit of holidaying together in late summer. It was an entirely unique treatment: nobody else had as many as 18 sessions a week with Freud, but this highly intense relationship was suddenly broken off because, despite the expectations that the war would come to a speedy conclusion, a few weeks later, the Hungarian was assigned as a physician to the 7th Regiment of Hussars.

Left alone in Vienna, Freud's enthusiasm for his adopted Austro-Hungarian fatherland did not last long. In the first month of the war, the English had sunk the *Kaiser Wilhelm der Grosse*, which was no longer carrying trans-Atlantic passengers and had been employed by the Germans as a subsidiary strategic unit. And at the start of November, the adventure of the famous light cruiser *Emden* came to an end when it was forced to run aground on the Cocos Islands after tormenting the Royal Navy and firing Freud's imagination with the feats of its captain.[7] A few days later he learned about the death of his half-brother Emanuel, aged 81, in a railway accident that remains somewhat mysterious.[8] This bereavement brought with it an inward reflection about the war, and, towards the end of 1914, Freud spent several weeks once again pondering the date of his own death.

He emerged from this with a renewed investment in his theoretical work, an almost frenetic spell of productivity to which he devoted himself in the time made available by the reduction in his commitments to his patients. In October he finished writing the case study of *The Wolf Man* (whose analysis had come to an end shortly before the outbreak of war), and in the spring of 1915, he decided to dedicate himself to a major summing-up which he had been planning since 1911.[9] And so, while also writing two essays on the theme of war and death (1915b, 1916), Freud set out to undertake a general and complete treatment of the theoretical hypotheses on which psychoanalysis was founded. This material, which he called *Metapsychology* to indicate the sphere of psychic processes situated beyond consciousness and the phenomena usually recognised by psychology, was intended to fill no less than 12 *Preliminaries*.[10] In less than two months, between March 15 and May 4,[11] Freud wrote five of them and had completed work on the other seven before the summer. He was thinking of publishing these works at the end of the war, which he still believed would be very soon, but in fact, he only sent the first five to the press: *Instincts and Their Vicissitudes, Repression*, and *The Unconscious* in 1915, *Metapsychological Supplement to the Theory of Dreams* and *Mourning and Melancholia* in 1917.

Let's note *en passant* that in the essay *The Unconscious*, Freud returned to some claims on thought transmission that he had expressed at the Munich Congress.[12] While in 1913 he was speculating,

> I have had good reason for asserting that everyone possesses in his own unconscious an instrument with which he can interpret the utterances of the unconscious in other people.
>
> (1913b, p. 320)

in the chapter "Communication Between the Two Systems," Freud kept a theoretical space open for the possibility of this transmission:

> It is a very remarkable thing that the *Ucs.* of one human being can react upon that of another, without passing through the *Cs.* This deserves closer investigation, especially with a view to finding out whether preconscious activity can be excluded as playing a part in it; but, descriptively speaking, the fact is incontestable.
>
> (1915e, p. 194)

We know nothing about the other essays.[13] Despite our regret for this loss today, Freud cannot have been much satisfied with these works if he binned them: he was still unhappy about the incompleteness of his theory, especially on the topics of femininity and masochism. Just as he never wrote a *Psychology of Love Life* or a *Treatise on Psychoanalytic Technique*, so Freud never published his *Metapsychology*,[14] but the first chapters, of great conceptual value, still bear witness to the creative power he was able to display in that dark period. Jones claims without hesitation that 1915, a year so full of terrible events and emotions, was surely one of the most productive for his thought.

It must be added that during the holidays, being able to stay for some weeks with his daughter Sophie and be close to his grandson Ernst, who was then aged one and a half, Freud began to be interested in what was meant by some of the child's behaviour, his habit of throwing objects away. After the war, these reflections would lead him to develop the concept of the "compulsion to repeat" and to introduce a new theory of drives (1920b).

Not content, at the end of the summer, Freud decided to devote himself with renewed energy to his educational activities, and, as we have learned, he spent the Saturday evenings of two successive winters giving lectures at the university, the last series he gave, with the aim of summing up the fundamentals of his doctrine in an accessible manner; the first series of elementary lectures were collected under the title *Introductory Lectures on Psycho-Analysis* (1916–17).

In the meantime, while the Americans continued to stay neutral even after the dramatic sinking of the *Lusitania*, the war reached Italy in May 1915. Relations with colleagues and friends became further reduced, many Viennese analysts were called to arms, and the *Wednesday Psychological Society* meetings became fortnightly. Freud repeatedly dreamed about his sons at the front, but in the summer of 1915 (the night of 8 July), a dream of the elder son's death was so powerful and vivid that it caused him to wait in great anxiety for news from the Russian front. A few days later, a postcard and a letter from Martin informed him about a wound in the arm, already healing, and a bullet that had passed perilously through his helmet. Gripped by the idea that he had had a telepathic dream, though unable to verify the relative timings of the events, Freud confided to Ferenczi his conviction that "one can be far more sensitive at night."[15]

In 1919, he inserted a first version of the dream into *The Interpretation of Dreams*, and, attributing it to his envy of youth, he regarded it as a "punishment dream."[16] In 1922, in *Dreams and Telepathy*, as we have already seen, he would include a reworked version as an example of presentiments that did not come true.

For those left at home, it must have been very hard to bear the endless anxiety, if even the judicious and tranquil Martha took the trouble to copy out, on the back of a recipe, an astrologer's magical World War Prophecies.[17]

Freud must have found it hard to remain inactive. When at the start of 1916 the young Rank, who had until then managed not to be enlisted, was called up to edit a military newspaper in Krakow, the only member of the committee left in Vienna was Sachs, who had been exempted from military service. Even so, Abraham was still hoping to organise another psychoanalytic congress in Munich for September,[18] but the closure of the frontier with Germany during that time prevented any movement. From his posting in the Hungarian barracks at Pàpa, not too far from Vienna, Ferenczi was able to keep in touch with Freud and between June and October 1916 took advantage of spells of leave to resume his analysis with him.

In summer 1917, while the privations were beginning to be felt, the Hungarian was able to organise a holiday for the Freud family in the Tatra mountains, a Slovak region then part of Hungary, where he too could stay for two weeks and Sachs for three. They held mushroom-hunting competitions, invariably won by Freud, as he used to when collecting with his children.[19] Rank and Eitingon (the latter, a captain physician running a hospital in northeast Hungary) were also able to pay them a brief visit. And Freud told Abraham

> The Hungarians are unmannerly and noisy but obliging and hospitable; friendship and loyalty are taking the form of generosity, with the result that we are able to wallow in the abundance of bread, butter, sausages, eggs, and cigars, rather like the chief of a primitive tribe.
>
> (21/08/1917)

Back from holiday, Freud wrote the brief essay "A Childhood Recollection from *Dichtung und Wahrheit*" (1917a), in which he continued to reflect on the child's game of throwing objects away and relating it to jealousy of a new sibling; he then completed "The Taboo of Virginity" (1918b), which he had begun in January.

At this time there were insistent rumours about his being a candidate for the Nobel Prize, but, as in the previous war years, no prize was awarded. Freud said that what interested him above all was the money, which would have been most welcome.

Impotence and death anxiety. Towards the uncanny defeat

Meanwhile, there was mounting pessimism about the outcome of the war: the German submarines had not critically weakened the power of the British Navy, and, despite the revolution in Russia and the victory at Caporetto, the Allies were becoming ever more threatening now that they could count on the forces made available by Woodrow Wilson. During the summer, news came that a 20-year-old nephew of Freud's, Hermann Graf, the only son of his sister Rosa, had been killed on the Italian front.

Another painful winter was approaching, and, in an apocalyptic mood, Freud was brooding on his old superstition that he would die at the age of 61. Having survived his fateful 62nd birthday in May, he wrote to Ferenczi that there was indeed no relying on the "supernatural."[20] His ostentatious bravado was no doubt linked to the fact that only a few months earlier, because of the food shortages and his enforced abstinence from smoking, he had had to confide in Ferenczi about the appearance of a painful swelling of the gums, possibly a precancerous lesion.[21] Unfortunately, as soon as cigars were once again available, his anxiety about this evaporated.

In a letter thanking Abraham for his birthday wishes, Freud revealed his renewed anxieties about death and linked them to his seemingly immortal mother, whom he wished to spare the terrible pain of losing a son:

> My mother will be 83 this year and is now rather shaky. Sometimes I think I shall feel a little freer when she dies, because the idea of her having to be told of my death is something from which one shrinks back. So I have really reached 62. . . . My prevailing mood is powerless embitterment, or embitterment at my powerlessness.
>
> (29/05/18)

His mother would die in 1930 at the age of 95, only nine years before him: Freud wrote that he did not feel free to die, but, since childhood and the death of his little brother Julius,[22] he had in fact been struggling with maternal fragility and the fear of not being able to live his own life to the full.

With the approach of summer 1918, it began to be clear that the war undertaken by the Central Powers was turning against them: the offensives on the Marne, in Anatolia and Mesopotamia, in the Balkans, and on the Piave had failed, and the Austro-Hungarian army was in a state of psychological exhaustion.

In August, a squadron of biplanes led by Gabriele D'Annunzio flew over Vienna and, instead of bombs, dropped thousands of propaganda leaflets in the colours of the Italian flag, a legendary and romantic enterprise which took the anti-aircraft forces by surprise and caused astonished admiration in the crowds who poured into the squares and avenues, reverberating internationally but having an especially strong impact on the mood of the Austrians already prostrated by the conflict.

Freud had not witnessed the sensational Italian incursion because he had already gone on holiday. He was again vacationing in Hungary, this time as a guest with the family of Anton von Freund, who had been sent to him by Ferenczi for treatment at the start of the year and become a close friend.

It was while he was at Villa Vidor, staying with von Freund's sister, that the topic of occultism resurfaced when he received a letter from the daughter of one of his first patients, Fanny Moser.[23] During a séance, Fanny Moser Jnr, an eminent zoologist, had witnessed levitations which had convinced her about the reality of paranormal experiences.[24] In her letter, she asked a series of questions which Freud answered point by point, also mentioning the two "unfulfilled" prophecies:

> I have had little fortune in terms of personal experiences in the field of occultism, I have never undergone anything that could have withstood the most obvious criticism, with one exception. In at least two cases, by analysing "prophecies" (which in any case did not come true) I have had to acknowledge that thought-transmission probably exists by a means different from the physical [psychical].
>
> (13/7/1918)[25]

Once again, Freud said he was unhappy that he could not refer publicly to either of the two cases for reasons of professional discretion.

During that holiday in Hungary, it became clear that the long-awaited Congress planned for that September 1918 could not be held in the intended location of Breslau, and at the last minute, it was decided to rearrange it for Budapest. Thanks to the combined efforts of Ferenczi and von Freund, this improvised solution turned out to be a "superb" choice.[26] The Congress took place in an almost euphoric atmosphere of celebration shortly after the failure of the Austrian offensive on the Italian front and perhaps in the preconscious awareness of imminent defeat.

The Freuds moved from Villa Vidor to the capital. Thanks to the same favourable circumstances, various members of the professor's family were also present in Budapest: besides his wife, his son Ernst, who had recently been invalided back from the Julian Alps and received medical treatment in the Tatra region, and naturally Anna, who appeared more and more often at her father's side.

The intimacy between father and daughter had grown deeper. Being the only one of his children left in Berggasse at this time, Anna was trying to contribute to the family's income by working as a trainee schoolteacher and private tutor but had become ever more passionate about psychoanalysis. On her return from London, she had begun to translate articles for the *Zeitschrift*[27] and took the opportunity to improve her knowledge of psychoanalytic concepts, as well as asking her father, almost as a game, to interpret her dreams. A series of "examination dreams" which accompanied the awarding of her teaching diploma was interrupted by her father's ironic comment that, fortunately, in dreams, there was no fee to pay for her repeat examinations. . . .[28] In reality, Sigmund was counting on his daughter's difficulties with music to ensure that she would fail and therefore stay a little longer at home without working.[29] But uniquely among his children, Anna was more and more certain that she wanted to follow in her father's footsteps.

When she started attending his lectures at the university, she expressed the desire to study medicine like the beautiful Dr Deutsch who used to come in her white coat straight from Wagner-Jauregg's clinic, but Freud was against this. Besides, Deutsch, of whom Anna was always jealous, was only able to work as an assistant in the psychiatric clinic – where women were not yet formally admitted – because her male colleagues had been called up.

In her dreams, as in her daydreams, Anna often portrayed herself in masculine roles, and, alongside dreams about her friend Loe Kann, those featuring her father became more and more frequent: she was discussing a translation with him, she had to defend him against his enemies with a broken sabre, she was the princess and he the king. . . . To help with her translations, she had asked her father about the meaning of "transference,"[30] and it was unconsciously unfolding in their relationship. Telling him how she had woken in the posture of a soldier at attention, "with my hands down the seams of my nightdress,"[31] she addressed recurring anxieties about her sexuality with her father, completely naturally, without reservations or secrecy. It is no wonder that, after attending his lectures and taking part in the Budapest Congress, she made her official appearance as a guest at the meetings of the Viennese Psychoanalytic Society in November 1918.[32]

For his part, towards the end of the year, after the war was lost and the armistice signed by Austria and Germany, one a few days after the other, Freud, disappointed in his Hungarian hopes but continuing to work with "a few individuals on the way to extinction"[33] and with no financial security, anticipating the difficulties of that terrible post-war period, went into a new period of depression. Hunger and privations were growing alarmingly, and he wrote, "it is good that the old die, but there is as yet no new. . . . I shed no tear either for *this* Austria or for *this* Germany."[34]

In the meantime, while Sophie's second son, Heinz Rudolf, was born in December, Freud continued to be anxious about the fate of his sons, especially Martin, of whom he had no news after he had fought to the end on the Piave and been taken prisoner with his whole battalion. In February, Freud asked Binswanger to lend him 500 lire for Martin because sending money from Vienna was difficult and risky (13/02/1919).

In March 1919, Freud emerged from his writer's block: he completed a first brief essay on the origins of the sexual perversions (*A Child Is Being Beaten*) and set to work on a second paper about the compulsion to repeat. The writing of *Beyond the Pleasure Principle* took longer than he had expected,[35] and it would only be published at the end of 1920.

After writing the first draft, Freud set it aside in May so as to address the subject from a different perspective, and, returning to an idea from years earlier, he composed a valuable work of aesthetics on the sphere of the mysterious and demonic, which he called *The "Uncanny"* (1919a). Once again he was addressing coincidences, presentiments of death, and in particular the "double," in all the gradations and configurations of the identical, accentuated by the "mental processes leaping from one of these characters to another – by what we should call telepathy – so that the one possesses knowledge, feelings and experience in common with the other" (p. 234). He traced the reasons for the uncanny back to a regression "to a time when the ego had not yet marked itself off sharply from the external world and from other people" (p. 236).

Trying to locate the cause of what Nietzsche called "eternal recurrence,"[36] he connected it to a "compulsion to repeat" intrinsic to the nature of the instincts at a deep level and so powerful as to precede the pleasure principle. He considered the re-emergence of this infantile "compulsion to repeat," which is characteristic of primal narcissism and typical of children's play, the authentic uncanny ingredient of certain innocuous incidents in life which, because they are repeated beyond the simple laws of chance, could acquire the character of ineluctable fatefulness, of a destiny foretold.

This is how he rethought his own superstitions:

> we naturally attach no importance to the event when we hand in an overcoat and get a cloakroom ticket with the number, let us say, 62; or when we find that our cabin on a ship bears that number. But the impression is altered if two such events, each in itself indifferent, happen close together – if we come across the number 62 several times in a single day, or if we begin to notice that everything which has a number – addresses, hotel rooms, compartments in railway trains – invariably has the same one, or at all events one which contains the same figures. We do feel this to be uncanny. And unless a man is utterly hardened and proof against the lure of superstition, he will be tempted to ascribe a secret meaning to this obstinate recurrence of a number; he will take it, perhaps, as an indication of the span of life allotted to him.
>
> (1919b, p. 238)

That same spring, Anton von Freund was in Vienna because of one of those repeated crises which accompanied the ups and downs of his illness as it made its hidden and inexorable advance.

And Victor Tausk, who had returned psychically drained from the war (he had already been ill at the Budapest Congress), also asked the professor to take him into treatment. Freud's relationship with his acute and ambitious but deeply dependent pupil had been difficult before, when Tausk was in a relationship with Lou Andreas Salomé, who had been fully aware of his compulsion to tackle whatever Freud was engaged in, "*making himself a son* as violently as he *hates the father for it*. As if by a thought transference he will always be busy with the same thing as Freud, never taking one step aside to make room for himself."[37]

Weiss, who entered medical school in Vienna at the same time but was 11 years younger than Tausk, noted that he imitated him also in striking gestures, accents, and manners: he wore his hair in exactly the same style as Freud and in his lectures repeated almost word for word the lectures Freud had given.[38] Roazen is convinced that Freud himself was worried about "thought transference" in his dealings with Tausk.[39] He was afraid that with his lively, voracious intelligence, Tausk might use analysis and his singular capacity for attunement with Freud to appropriate his ideas as they were germinating, in the same way as he anticipated Freud's contributions to the meetings of the Wednesday Psychological Society. In a slip, making Aristotle the teacher of Plato, he had revealed his unconscious impulses, and it may have been to him that Freud was referring when he confided, "I cannot stand the parricidal look in his eyes."[40]

Freud refused Tausk's request for analysis and suggested that he ask Helene Deutsch, who had recently joined the Viennese group along with Wilhelm Reich, both coming from the Faculty of Medicine. This did not prove to be a viable solution, however, since Deutsch was in treatment with Freud and often talked to him about their colleague, so it soon became clear that there was a Tausk-Deutsch-Freud thought transmission problem (and a new triangle after the one with Salomé).[41] So Freud required Deutsch to choose between her own analysis and the one she had just started with Tausk.

Abandoned by his analyst, Tausk began a relationship with a former patient whom he decided to marry. In July, the week before his second marriage, the Viennese analysts heard the hideous, shocking news of the young pupil's suicide: he had simultaneously shot and hanged himself.

As for Freud, writing about him to Salomé, he seemed highly detached, cynical, almost relieved that Tausk's presence would no longer be a source of anxiety. Preoccupied with the thought of his own survival, he laconically attributed the Croat's action to the horrors of war and his internal battles with the paternal image.

In reality, Tausk must not only have been struggling with the oedipal conflict but with an internal breakdown linked to the demands of "primary" attachment.[42] He manifested this in his final, masterly work, "On the Origin of the 'Influencing Machine' in Schizophrenia" (1919), where he extended the field of psychoanalysis to narcissistic problems of identity and identification, trying to understand psychosis and its sufferings as a leak in the Ego's boundaries which needed to be stopped up (according to the "maternal" theory outlined by Paul Federn and before him by Ferenczi).

On the subject of "telepathy," it is interesting to recall what Tausk's article says about the schizophrenic symptom that everyone knows what the sufferer is thinking: he located it in the early situation of blurred boundaries between the baby and the mother and supported this with a note in which he quoted a comment by Freud:

> In the discussion of this paper at the Vienna Psychoanalytic Society, Freud emphasized that the infant's conception that others knew its thoughts has its source in the process of learning to speak. Having obtained its language from others, the infant has also received thoughts from them; and the child's feeling that others know his thoughts as well as that others have "made" him the language and, along with it, his thoughts, has therefore, some basis in reality.
>
> (1919, p. 193)

As often happened, the pupil had captured and given form to the ideas that the Master was still developing and would publish in 1933: when at the end of *Lecture XXX*, Freud connects thought transmission to the first communication between mother and child in infancy – also referring to "the frequent anxiety felt by children over the idea that their parents know all their thoughts without having to be told them" (p. 55) – he does not quote Tausk, but it is extraordinary how clearly Tausk had been able to understand Freud's thinking and put it into words in 1919, explaining it even better than Freud himself would later on.[43]

Having begun with Tausk's suicide, Freud's summer was coloured by death[44] and a return to the composition of *Beyond the Pleasure Principle*. Despite the precariousness of economic conditions in Austria and the impossibility of another holiday in Hungary, and though he had feared that any holiday was out of the question given Martha's struggle to recover from the chest infection caused by the flu, on 15 July, Sigmund Freud had left for Bad Gastein. The hope of visits from Jones, Ferenczi, and perhaps von Freund for a summer meeting of the committee, warmly encouraged by Jones, was dampened by the difficulty of obtaining visas. Freud was compensated by a flood of letters since the isolation of Hungary had forced him to take responsibility of managing the movement on behalf of the new president, Sándor Ferenczi.

In August, Freud moved to Badersee in the Bavarian Alps, where he was visited by Eitingon, who lent him the money that enabled him to make his usual visit to Hamburg, where his second grandson, Heinele, awaited him: this was the last time he saw Sophie. Apologising to Jones for not returning before and for making him prolong his stay in Switzerland, Freud said he planned to resume work on 26 September, asking him to inform David Forsyth, whom he had at last tracked down with his telegrams. He added, fatefully:

> I am sorry to detain you so long, but if I do not get to my children now, I do not know when I will. One should not postpone anything! And if this should result in a longer holiday for you, I can easily take the blame.
>
> (1/09/1919)

On the way home, he spent an afternoon in Berlin with Abraham and Eitingon: to the former he entrusted a copy of *The Uncanny* and to the second the first draft of *Beyond the Pleasure Principle*.

He returned to Austria on 24 September 1919.

Ernest Jones's war

The outbreak of war threw all Jones's plans into disarray. Back in June 1914, he had been disappointed to learn that Freud, Rank, and Ferenczi had been witnesses at the wedding of Loe Kann and his namesake. By a trick of fate, the woman whom he had in the past presented as his wife could now genuinely call herself Mrs Jones – Mrs Herbert Jones, to be precise. In his vexation at seeing another man win the woman who had never allowed him to possess her completely, the Welshman had for some time been considering the idea of changing his very common surname by taking his mother's.

Breaking off his relationship with Lina, Loe's governess, whom he had been relying on while Loe was in analysis in Vienna, Jones had unexpectedly discovered Freud's youngest daughter, who was about to arrive in London. Typically, he fell in love with Anna and with the idea of a closer bond between him and the Master: when the ship from the Continent docked, there he was on the quayside to welcome the young woman with a magnificent bunch of flowers, ready to drive her around England in his car and put all his seductiveness into play to win her.

To become president of the IPA, as was now the plan, and the professor's son-in-law would be the ultimate fulfilment.

Anna, however, doubting her ability to inspire love and, above all, jealous of her exclusive relationship with her father, did not trust Jones then or afterwards. Convinced he had never really cared for her, Freud's daughter was all too aware that her own prestigious position was due to her father and not her own merits, at least in the beginning,[45] and later seemed almost to enjoy the hostility with which Jones singled her out. No wonder her German shepherd dog once jumped at the poor Welshman and bit him on the thigh . . .[46]

Many years after Freud's death, after learning from the correspondence that the professor had been mistrustful of his motives, Jones wrote a letter full of remorse to Anna, claiming he had "always loved" her and "in quite an honest fashion."[47]

In her 80s, Anna wrote,

> Naturally, I was flattered and impressed, though not without a lurking suspicion that his interest was more directed to my father than to myself – a circumstance to which I had become used. However that may have been, he certainly did not show any lack of attention. He put himself out considerably to fetch me from the places where I stayed and to show me the beauties of England, which he loved. There was a never forgotten trip in a boat going up the river Thames. There was a book "The Highways and Byways of Sussex" which remained in my possession for many years.
>
> (1979, p. 285)

Still in competition with the Welshman, she added, "He also took every opportunity to correct my English."[48]

Even after all those years, when she had gained an unchallengeable place in London and Jones was long dead, the "Viennese" Anna could not forget her old fear of being overshadowed by this elder brother and especially the fact that he had used his alliance with Melanie Klein against her. In spite of Jones, in the field of psychoanalytic translation into English during the war, Freud's daughter created a space of her own, a strategic space substantial enough to ensure her future exclusive role as her father's spokeswoman.[49]

Back in 1914, after helping Anna to find a berth as part of the Austrian delegation bound for Genoa, Ernest Jones found himself dropped, cut off from the professor and all his colleagues on the enemy side. For a while, until the United States entered the war, he was able to maintain some precarious contact via American colleagues or Dutch friends, which also enabled him to obtain copies of the psychoanalytic journals. But it was a hard blow, and the rheumatoid arthritis from which he had begun to suffer when he moved to Canada developed into a more serious affliction which ruled him out of military service.

Confined to London, because of his friends "on the wrong side,"[50] disappointed about his interrupted projects and his bad health, and paying too much attention to the news of the war from which he was excluded, he found his usually frenetic scientific work completely blocked. Moreover, the Ministry of Pensions, which was setting up clinics to treat the chronic cases of these war neuroses, had decided to appoint the analyst David Forsyth as their senior physician.

Even so, he was still able to go into battle on Freud's behalf, joining the scientific discussion in *The Lancet* about "shell shock" (a syndrome which Charles Myers had described in its pages in 1915), and at the start of 1916, when an explicitly psychoanalytic article by Forsyth encountered vigorous opposition from the old guard of British psychiatrists who, having rejected Freudian theory before the war, were now worried about the newly favourable consideration it was being given by the Royal Army Medical Corps.[51]

Even though Jones was still persona non grata in the London hospital system as well as the RAMC, his psychoanalytic practice grew significantly because of his fame as the leading and most committed Freudian in Britain. Furthermore, he analysed a good many members of the recently founded London Psychoanalytical Society, perhaps with the secondary aim of keeping it more under his control.[52] Much of his energy was taken up by the attempt to heal the divergences with those who were manifesting a Jungian nostalgia, including his friend, Eder. Jones dealt with this ever more intolerantly, imposing his authority as leader, in the end even complaining about Forsyth, the oldest member, for what he considered acts of insubordination: the fact that Forsyth attended very few meetings and then found excuses for staying away. As Jones added later, "his personal jealousy of myself was already beginning to manifest itself."[53] The fact of the matter was that Forsyth had not asked him for treatment but, like Rickman, the Stracheys, and Tansley, was one of the few colleagues who instead went to Freud in Vienna.

At the start of 1919, in order to rid the London Society of its Jungian members once and for all, Jones took the drastic step of dissolving and re-founding it with his most trusted colleagues as the British Society.

There is no doubt that as the war dragged on, though psychoanalysis was beginning to meet with enthusiasm in the United Kingdom, reaching a peak of interest after the war,[54] that ultra-loyal band of Freudians felt forgotten by the analysts on the other side, especially when they learned that, in spite of everything, an *international* congress would be held in Budapest during September 1918. Jones was upset at his enforced exclusion but nonetheless prepared a paper of his own on the subject of the war neuroses and read it to the psychiatric department of the Royal Society of Medicine. It was only published after the war, alongside those of Ferenczi, Abraham, and Simmel in the Proceedings of the Congress, the first volume released by the *Verlag*. And he began to demonstrate an increasing allergy to his former analyst – some of whose work he had undertaken to translate into English – once he learned that, on Freud's suggestion, Ferenczi had become IPV president, a position which, before the war, Jones had assumed was his for the taking.

I should add that during those years, after the episode with Anna, Ernest Jones's love life had gone through several phases, first happy, then dramatic. In 1916, he had met a brilliant young Welsh pianist and composer, Morfydd Owen, falling in love with her at first sight, and three days later asked her to marry him. The marriage was happy and, given their natures, enjoyably tempestuous. Sadly, after only 18 months, Morfydd died following emergency surgery for appendicitis while the couple were visiting their families in Wales, far from Jones's surgeon brother-in-law Wilfred Trotter. It is likely that Jones had witnessed the operation: the sorrow for his wife's death, from delayed poisoning by chloroform, was complicated by regret and guilt for not being able to protect her.[55]

When the armistice was declared, Jones was still mourning this loss, his only relief coming from work and the thought of being reunited with Freud. In spring 1919, while the Versailles Peace Conference was still in progress, he obtained a travel permit and went to Switzerland for the first time to try to find out when it would be possible to enter Austria.

In Bern, he met Hanns Sachs and Otto Rank. Sachs had come to Switzerland to treat his tuberculosis and was able to extend his stay for two years thanks to generous funding by the Welshman.[56] Once he was cured, he decided to move to Berlin, where he became a full-time teacher at the Institute. Rank was in Switzerland to negotiate the publication of Freud's works: he was among the first members of the committee to return to Vienna in November 1918, immediately after the Armistice, bringing with him a small and lovely wife, the Jewish Pole Beata "Tola" Minzer. Jones found him greatly changed. Rank had suffered a period of deep depression in Cracow and may now have been in a slightly hypomanic state (these oscillations of mood accentuated the difficulties of his subsequent break with Freud). Coming from a humble background, he had met Freud when he was just 21 and was helped by him to complete his studies, graduating in philosophy and then earning a living as the salaried secretary of the Vienna Psychoanalytic Society. The professor's shadow, like a skinny teenager, "timid and deferential, much given to clicking of heels and bowing," he now seemed nervous, rigid, almost recklessly assertive. At a café one evening, Rank apparently pulled a huge revolver from his pocket and put it on the table "*für alle Fälle*" (for any eventuality), boasting to Jones that he had brought it with him from Cracow, having calmly told the border official who had noticed his bulging pocket that it was "bread." At least this is how Jones recounts it,[57] later remembering the episode when it was his own turn to try and get through Austrian customs.

Jones had gone to Zurich with Rank to check on the situation of the local analysts. In July 1914, the Zurich Society had followed Jung out of the IPA: sheltered from the war, the Jungian group had been able to continue working thanks to substantial American funding sent to Jung by a Rockefeller. The few Swiss who remained loyal to psychoanalysis were in disarray, and Jones was busily trying to contact them and establish their reliability. Meanwhile, setting aside the plan for an international congress in the autumn, he was beginning to appreciate the terrible conditions of the defeated nations, which Freud had made sure he knew about in his letters.

Undismayed by this first reconnaissance trip, Jones went back to Switzerland in early August after labouring long and hard to obtain a new permit from the Board of Trade as a publisher.

This time he set off accompanied by the young Eric Hiller, with whom he was setting up a small psychoanalytic publishing company in London, and during that month, he moved heaven and earth to reach Freud, first in Bad Gastein and then in Badersee. But entry to Austria and Germany was still impossible and, being British, he even risked being suspected of spying.

Forced to prolong his stay in Switzerland, Jones decided to take a holiday with Sachs, having become close to him when Sachs had been the only member of the committee to visit him in London just before the war. This was when Sachs introduced him to Katherine Jokl.

Having learned of Jones's publishing plans, Sachs had recommended her some months before as a translator and secretary, but after an initial exchange of letters, Jokl had declined the proposal to work for Jones.[58] This time, Sachs, who had had something quite different in mind from the start,[59] arranged a *rendez-vous* at the fateful *Hotel Baur au Lac* in Zurich, and when the two met, it was a *coup de foudre*.

It was a very warm autumn: Katherine recalled Ernest making his entrance into the magical garden café dressed in white linen and holding out his hand. They spent the afternoon chatting and dined together with friends, arranging to meet again the next day.

Early that morning, the young woman received a big basket of flowers, sweet peas, English flowers for "an English flower," as the attached card gallantly read. And on Sunday there was a walk in the Dolder woods, where Ernest wasted no time in declaring his intentions, though in a surprisingly hesitant manner: after questioning the young lady about which part of Switzerland she still wanted to see, he asked if she would like to visit it with him. And he added, "I mean as my wife of course."[60] A fortnight later Jokl became Jones's second wife (the third if we count Loe Kann): the proposal after an acquaintance of three days was followed by "36 years of happy marriage," recalled Kitty in 1979. Decisive in his amorous choices, at least when he had speedily identified and espoused a good idea, Ernest Jones proved a faithful husband and soon the father of four children.

Katherine Jokl was a Viennese Jew from a good family. Younger than Ernest – 27 to his 40 – she was as beautiful and cultivated as she was determined; having gone to Zurich to take a university course in economics because women were excluded from studying this subject in Vienna, she had just graduated with a thesis on commercial relations between Austria and Britain.

In her, Jones found all he desired: she was the Viennese girl with whom he had danced romantic waltzes in his adolescent dreams, a skilled translator and conscientious secretary who shared his passion for psychoanalysis and went on to assist him on in his editorial and political endeavours. Last but not least, though not exactly "close to Freud" (as he described her to his father), she had been at school with Sophie, and it seems that, when she heard that Jones had found a wife in Zurich, Anna Freud guessed straightaway who it might be.[61]

At this point, Jones made it an urgent priority to get to Vienna so that he could obtain the documents his fiancée needed for marriage, and during this brief separation, in a true metamorphosis, he sent her a stream of romantic, sweetly sentimental letters.[62]

It was in late September, thanks to the direct intervention of the Austrian ambassador in Bern after the Austrian provinces had declared their autonomy, that he finally obtained a pass for travel to Vienna: he and Hiller were the first foreign civilians to enter the Empire's former capital.

Ferenczi's kisses

On Saturday 27 September 1919, Ernest Jones arrived in Berggasse laden with emotions, expectations, news, plans, foodstuffs, and the famous suitcases that Anna had left with him on her hasty departure from London at the start of the war. With typical impetuosity, he plunged straight into the consulting room where Freud was in conversation with Herr Bernfeld. He had to wait in the next room for the session to end, but finally there came the reunion:

> I found Freud somewhat greyer and a good deal thinner than before the war; he never regained his former plump figure. But his mind had lost nothing of its alertness. He was as cheerful and warmly friendly as ever, so it was hard to think we had not seen each other for nearly six years.
>
> (*III*, p. 17)

And that same day, Sándor Ferenczi arrived, too:

> We had not been together long before Ferenczi burst into the room and to my astonishment effusively kissed us both on the cheeks. He had not seen Freud for more than a year.
>
> (*ibid.*)

Jones's surprise at Ferenczi's display of affection would appear to be motivated not so much by the Hungarian's lack of self-control or the latent homosexual current that he might have detected as by a stirring of jealousy at the great intimacy between Ferenczi and Freud.

If we consider the historical moment when Jones drafted his memoirs, the scandalised reference to the Hungarian's kisses should be placed in the context of the book he was writing about the Master in the Fifties as part of a more or less planned retrospective elaboration aimed at suppressing Ferenczi along with his theory and technique. Given the way Ferenczi was experimenting with modifications of the rule of abstinence (and indeed because of the kisses given to a patient), during the last year of his life, a traumatic fracture would be opened between him and the analytic community and, for the first time, between him and Freud.[63] Brief sketches scattered here and there in Jones's work would depict a Ferenczi with an insatiable need for love, a master of gaffes, a "latent psychotic," even "paranoic," capable of "homicidal outbursts," and Jones tried to write him off as seriously ill, silencing his theory by denying him an English translation of his works.[64]

Finally, without jumping ahead, we can add that Jones was embarrassed at receiving kisses and an over-warm greeting from his former analyst when Ferenczi was about to resign the post of president and hand political leadership of psychoanalysis to him.[65]

The Briton had won the war, and this precious prize, but he seemed to be wondering if he might in fact have lost something . . .

Freud and Ferenczi's friendship had just endured a whole year of being kept apart, and in conditions of privation and danger: their separation had abruptly broken into their intense mutual cathexis, which they had celebrated at the Budapest Congress, as an appropriate conclusion to the analytic treatment conducted during the war.

In reality, the two men's relationship had been affected by all this, becoming deeper but also more distant.

At the moment when the analysis was to be given its authentic shape – the analysis begun on the journey to America, continued in their constant correspondence, and periodically topped up in the holidays they took together – there had been a hesitation on both their parts. Ferenczi had been expressing his desire for a treatment with Freud since concluding Elma's therapy at the end of 1912 but did not seem fully convinced, preferring instead to benefit from a clandestine and informal "gratis analysis."[66] In May 1913, still vacillating between Gizella and Elma who, as he saw it reflected back in his narcissism, seemed to "play football" with him, he pursued Freud again in the hope of being able to work through even the old misunderstandings from Palermo: “I am convinced that my analysis could only improve relations between us.”[67]

In Freud’s opinion, Ferenczi’s analysis was really not necessary: he was anxious about tying the fate of their friendship to something different and unpredictable, alienating himself from his friend and, who knows, maybe really setting him free.[68] In 1913 the setting-up of the committee and the need to provide Jones with a training analysis had offered a good reason for postponing Ferenczi’s treatment.

Incidentally, in these formative early experiences, our pioneers obviously could not afford the luxury of safeguarding anonymity and abstinence, rules of the setting that they would have been constructing from their direct personal experience.

As we know, Freud began Ferenczi’s treatment at the end of the dizzying late summer of 1914. It consisted of three brief but highly formalised – and paid – periods of analysis:[69] the first tranche of three and a half weeks in October 1914 was carried out at a frequency of two sessions a day, including Sundays, while the subsequent spells of three and two weeks in summer 1916 consisted of three sessions a day. Ferenczi was a guest in Freud’s house, shared his family’s meagre meals, and accompanied him in his walks along the Ringstrasse on condition that he did not talk about his personal problems outside sessions.[70]

Begun under the emotional pressure of early news from the great battle in the north – the German counteroffensive on the Russian front – the first period of analysis coincided with the reopening of what Freud called Ferenczi’s “inner theater of war,”[71] in the form of Elma’s American fiancé, who was back in Budapest to marry her and take her with him to the United States. Their wedding on 16 September 1914[72] had left Ferenczi prostrated: the hope that the fait accompli might lay his fantasies to rest was very short lived.

Unlike Jones, Ferenczi was unable to choose, and would remain caught for the rest of his life between Gizella and Elma, badgering Freud endlessly for treatment. He was soon called up for military service in Hungary and, despite Freud’s opposition, set out on a self-analysis which he reported by letter and tried to reanimate on occasional visits to Vienna or by taking advantage of a visit from the Master. His brief and troubled spells of leave in Budapest, intended as tests of how strong his feelings were for Gizella, induced him to declare shamelessly, “Even the world war with its turmoil can’t bring about a decision.”[73]

His time in Pàpa, halfway between Vienna and Budapest, offers a suggestive metaphor for his divided state, the vacillation that did not allow him to make a complete investment, free of regret, in a whole woman and made him rebound into the paternal orbit. When he tried to complete his analysis with Groddeck’s help, recognising his need for a “maternal” father, Ferenczi would recall this time:

> You were right in thinking that there was something of deeper significance about the town where I was garrisoned. The place was called Pàpa (Pope); it was there that I felt uninterruptedly secure in the paternal womb.
>
> (Ferenczi to Groddeck, 27/02/1922)

Even the subsequent tranches of analysis led to no visible changes, and in January 1917, Freud wrote defeatedly to Gizella, "I have really left nothing untried and have met with no success" (23/01/1917).

When in February the Hungarian became ill with tuberculosis, Freud considered it a flight into illness, but the three-month stay at the sanatorium in Semmering achieved more than analysis had been able to, and Ferenczi asked Freud to pass on the proposal of marriage to his lover.[74] This time it was Gizella who balked, giving her daughter as the reason and fearing what would happen if Elma returned to Budapest because of the difficulties that had arisen between the young couple.

With his marriage on hold, Ferenczi also put his analysis behind him as "finished, not terminated,"[75] and tried to express his gratitude to Freud by committing himself to the movement and entering a highly fertile phase of theoretical output. It was during this time that, among the patients he sent Freud from Budapest, he put him in contact with Anton von Freund.

This friend was the son of a wealthy beer manufacturer in Budapest, a philosophy graduate who lived off his private income and devoted himself to philanthropic projects which he supported from his own fortune. After an operation for testicular cancer, in early 1918, he manifested the symptoms of a reactive psychosis, and so Ferenczi sent him to Vienna. The psychic symptomatology soon went into remission, and the physical disease seemed to have been completely overcome, a belief which Freud shared and encouraged in his patient, fortified by Binswanger's having fully recovered at a similar age from the same type of tumour.[76]

During his convalescence, von Freund began to show his gratitude to Freud with all kinds of help and provision of food, so precious in those times of privation. The professor interpreted all this as part of his complex and his fantasy of enriching his father, but even so, he allowed himself to accept this very concrete investment by his former patient.

Tony von Freund became so passionate about psychoanalysis that he decided to become its Maecenas and made a substantial donation to "the Cause." He and his family became close to the Freud family and, as we have seen, invited the Freuds to spend the summer vacation of 1918 at their villa near Budapest.

The hospitality continued in great magnificence when, for the Congress in September, the Freuds moved to the capital, where they were warmly welcomed by the mayor and the city authorities, staying at the new "Gellért-Fürdö" Thermal Baths Hotel in Buda on the left bank of the Danube, being invited to lunches and receptions, and even having a special steamer on the Danube placed at their disposal.[77] The conference took place with particular solemnity in the hall of the Hungarian Academy of Sciences, and all the participants except Freud were in uniform.[78] For the first time, official representatives of the Austrian, German, and Hungarian governments took part, and the topic of interpreting the war neuroses, about which the military experience of Simmel, Abraham, Ferenczi, and Tausk had given them a vast clinical competence, confirmed the growth of interest in psychoanalysis.

The high-ranking medical officers who were present were impressed by the varied possibilities of treatment being proposed, and there was already talk of building vast psychoanalytic clinical centres for these treatments.

There were two practitioners from neutral countries – Dutch – among the participants but no analyst from the Swiss group and obviously none from the enemy side. In 1957, Ernest Jones, the major absentee, was still grumbling about this, and about the election of Ferenczi:

> Because of the war it [the Congress] could not be truly international, but we subsequently agreed to give it this official status and to accept its decisions.
>
> (*II*, p. 222)

Anton von Freund, who had now joined the committee and supported the Congress with Ferenczi and Rank, supplying generous funding, was given the post of secretary. This Hungarian funding remained a resource for the survival and future of the movement for some time. It was hoped that Budapest would make a fitting substitute for Zurich: Rank and his wife had already planned to move to Hungary,[79] and Freud was relying on Ferenczi for this shift of the movement's centre to the east. In fact, that summer marked the Hungarian's triumph, only a brief moment of glory, since the post-war chaos brought an end to all illusions with the immediate closure of the border between Austria and Hungary.

Separated from Freud and buoyed up with enthusiasm at being president, Ferenczi actually decided to ask Gizella Pàlos to marry him, now that the new political regime meant that divorce was finally possible. This time his beloved said yes: the ceremony was held on 1 March 1919 and clouded by the death of the ex-husband, Geza Pàlos.

The fully conscious and destructive intentions in play were concealed as a heart attack, the result of chance.[80] We do not know whether Freud believed in coincidence, being so absorbed in his reflections on the power of fate in life and on the death instinct, but in a letter to the Hungarian he commented,

> The coincidence which cast a shadow on your wedding is very strange. Perhaps not something coincidental, but something demonic, in Groddeck's sense. You must certainly have taken it so as well.
>
> (4/03/1919)

1919 truly was a "demonic" year for Ferenczi, and the political upheavals convulsing Hungary shattered all his successes. While in April the ephemeral Soviet republic proclaimed by Béla Kun was still able to award him the first university chair in psychoanalysis – also signed by György Lukács, deputy minister of education[81] – the Romanian invasion in August, followed by the return to power of the conservative and monarchical forces, exposed Budapest to the bloody "white terror," an anti-communist and, above all, antisemitic regime. Its supreme commander, Admiral Miklòs Horthy, who owed his power to professional assassins and later boasted that Mussolini and Hitler had learned from him – he certainly led the way for them both[82] – installed a terrible dictatorship that lasted for over 20 years.

In these circumstances, Ferenczi not only lost his professorship but was threatened with the loss of all his professional activity. To make matters worse, given that his continuing isolation prevented him from fulfilling his role as president, in July 1919, the *Internationale Zeitschrift* had to announce that the management of the Association would be temporarily taken over by the Vienna branch, with Freud as president and Rank as secretary.

It was in these precarious conditions, and already regretting his marriage, that Ferenczi came to Vienna in the company of Anton von Freund, who was ill once again.

Notes

1 Freud to Abraham, 25/06/1914.
2 Freud to Ferenczi, 22/07/1914.
3 Freud to Abraham, 25/08/1914, Falzeder's Note.
4 Freud to Abraham, 25/08/1914.
5 Freud to Abraham, 22/09/1914.
6 Dupont, 1994.
7 Jones, *II*.
8 Freud to Ferenczi, 11/11/1914.
9 And he had already started with *Formulations on the Two Principles of Mental Functioning* (1911b), *A Note on the Unconscious in Psycho-Analysis* (1912b) and *On Narcissism: An Introduction* (1914b).
10 "*Preliminaries to a Metapsychology*" in Freud to Binswanger, 17/12/1915.
11 Freud to Abraham, 4/05/1915.
12 It is no coincidence that this work dealt with the case of Elfriede Hirschfeld, the protagonist of the second unfulfilled prophecy.
13 Five of them were about "anguish," "conscience" and "conversion hysteria," "obsessional neurosis," and "Overview of the Transference Neuroses" (Freud, 1915b): the last of these was found by Grubrich Simitis. Nothing is known about the other two, not even their titles.
14 Musatti, 1976b.
15 Freud to Ferenczi, 21 and 27/07/1915.
16 1900, the paragraph was added as a footnote in 1919, and incorporated in the text in 1930, p. 558.
17 Behling, 2002.
18 Musatti, 1976a, p. XVII.
19 Sachs, 1945, p. 108.
20 09/05/1918.
21 06/11/1917.
22 See Pierri, 2022.
23 *Emmy von N.* in *Studies*.
24 Later she would devote much of her interest and investments to the study of occultism.
25 See Bauer, 1986.
26 Freud to Andreas-Salomé, 4/10/1918.
27 Jones's reply to Janet at the London Congress of Medicine, 1913 (see Pierri, 2022) and an article by Putnam.

28 Freud to Anna, 14/07/1915.
29 Freud to Ferenczi, 08/04/1915.
30 Anna 30/07/1915. This was her father's succinct reply: "*Übertragung* is a technical term signifying the transference of the patient's latent tender or hostile feelings to the doctor" (01/08/1915).
31 27/07/1915.
32 Nunberg and Federn, 1962–75.
33 Freud to Eitingon, 29/11/1918.
34 Freud to Eitingon, 25/10/1918.
35 Freud to Andreas-Salomé 1/07/1918 and 2/04/1919; Andreas-Salomé to Freud 26/12/1920.
36 See the last part of *Thus Spoke Zarathustra* (1883–85).
37 1958, pp. 166–167.
38 In Roazen, 2005.
39 1969, p. 171.
40 Alexander, 1940, p. 136.
41 Roazen, 1969.
42 Ambrosiano, 2011.
43 The telepathic experience would be connected with the acquisition phase of verbal language, with the exit from the area of mother-child language, with the uncertainties and vicissitudes in the transition from one type of language to another.
44 Freud to Andreas-Salomé, 1/08/1919.
45 Freud to Eitingon, 5/07/27.
46 Jones, 1959.
47 "He [Freud] seems to have forgotten the existence of the sexual instinct, for I had found you (and still do) most attractive" (in Young-Bruehl, 1988, p. 68).
48 To be fair to her, she also wrote, "I only read quite recently somewhere that my father had been in the habit of correcting his German when he was in Vienna" (*ibid.*).
49 Steiner, 1991, 2017.
50 Freud to Abraham, 2/08/1914.
51 Forrester, 2008; Forsyth, 1916; Jones, 1916.
52 Forrester, 2008.
53 1959, p. 239.
54 Forrester, 2008.
55 See Jones, 1959.
56 K Jones, 1979.
57 *III*, p. 13.
58 K Jones, 1979.
59 Katherine Jokl was the sister of his then-lover, actress Grete Iml (Maddox, 2006).
60 K Jones, 1979, p. 271.
61 Maddox, 2006.
62 Brome, 1983.
63 See Freud to Ferenczi, 13/12/1931and Ferenczi to Freud, 27/12/1931.
64 Jones to Freud 3/03/1933. See Paskauskas, 1993, p. 723 note and Bonomi, 1999.
65 For Jones's analysis with Ferenczi, see Pierri, 2022.
66 Ferenczi to Freud 26/12/1912 and 29/12/1912. For more information see Pierri, 2022.
67 Ferenczi to Freud, 12/05/1913.
68 Freud to Ferenczi 4/05/1913 and 12/05/1913.
69 Ferenczi's analysis with its 13–18 hours per week was unique. No other analysand in those years received a denser analysis. See May, 2007.
70 Grosskurth, 1991.
71 Freud to Ferenczi 4/02/1916.

72 Berman, 2004.
73 Ferenczi to Freud, 18/06/1915.
74 Grosskurth, 1991, pp. 73–74.
75 "You know that I consider your attempt at analysis finished – finished, not terminated – but rather broken off because of unfavorable circumstances." And he warned Ferenczi against making the marriage decision dependent on a continuation of the analysis (Freud to Ferenczi, 16/11/1916).
76 See Freud's visit to Binswanger in Kreuzlingen in Pierri, 2022.
77 Jones, *III*.
78 Freud to Andreas-Salomé, 4/10/1918.
79 Freud to Ferenczi, 27/11/1918.
80 Roazen, 1998. For more detail, see Pierri, 2022.
81 Gutiérrez Pelàez, 2013.
82 Székely, 1949.

Chapter 10

Coincidences in Vienna

A week of fireworks in autumn 1919

The *new orientation* towards the West

"We all had endless news to exchange about what had been happening to us in all those years," recalls Jones: information and comments about the greatly changed European situation, the advent of Bolshevism, the illusory promises made by Woodrow Wilson, but also news about what they had each lived through. The next day, Sunday 28 September, was given over to celebrations. With some satisfaction, Jones describes having invited the Freud family to lunch, with Rank and his wife, at the beautiful Hotel Cobenzl on the hills overlooking Vienna where they used to gather before the war, and being moved to witness how much a proper meal seemed to mean to them.[1]

We know that this situation of extreme privation was destined to last much longer, and the next autumn in The Hague, at the first post-war Congress, Jones once again noted with satisfaction how much "the starved Central Europeans" appreciated the sumptuous concluding banquet.[2] In reality, the guests were unable to do justice to this abundance since Central European stomachs had become unused to proper food and could not tolerate it. More than 50 years later, Anna Freud, a guest at the Congress, was still regretting that desolate experience (1979).

During the lunch at the Cobenzl, greetings cards were sent to Abraham and Eitingon and to Ernst Freud, who had in the meantime recovered his health, though he was still declared unfit for active service, and had finished his architectural studies in Munich. The party continued that evening at the Freuds' house in celebration of Martin's engagement: "having returned home from his Italian imprisonment, [he] has now surrendered to another," wrote Freud to Pastor Pfister,[3] unconvinced by his son's decision.

Martin would marry on 7 December, followed in the spring of 1920 by his brother Ernst in Berlin, where Eitingon had found him a job. And in Berlin in 1923, Freud's most problematic child, Oliver, would remarry, having contracted a first unhappy marriage which had lasted less than a year during the war.

Clearly the end of the war was a moment for celebration and thoughts of marriage, for the Freud children as well as for his pupils: Rank had married in November 1918 and had a new daughter, Helene;[4] Ferenczi married in the March

DOI: 10.4324/9781003246480-11

of that year. On his return to Zurich, Jones set the date for his wedding as 9 October, and during the previous week in Vienna, he had resorted to threatening the mayor and the lieutenant governor in occupation that he would start another war if he didn't receive the dispensation for his fiancée in time.[5]

There were also bereavements to share. Jones brought news of Putnam's death in Boston in November 1918 and learned about the suicide of Tausk. But the most heartbreaking loss was the imminent death of Tony von Freund: this was not a question of hypochondria but of an almost certain relapse.

Still in the grip of the emotions and affections stirred by their coming together again, from the Monday onwards, every minute was spent in meetings for work, negotiation, and detailed planning.

It was a hectic week: the committee was without Hanns Sachs, who had stayed in Switzerland and would later be updated by Jones, and Karl Abraham, who had not left Germany but had been able to talk to the professor when Freud called in at Berlin. Freud took part as much as his newly resumed analytic work permitted. When Herr Bernfeld missed his Monday session, Freud went straight off to visit von Freund, though we should bear in mind that this was not simply a visit to a sick friend who had just arrived in Vienna but a meeting at a committee member's bedside where important decisions were to be taken, from the allocation of the Hungarian's donations to the development of the publishing wing and the management of the *Verlag*. Among these choices, given the gravity of von Freund's condition, it was necessary to replace him with Max Eitingon[6] on the committee and with Jones as director of the *Verlag* alongside Freud, Ferenczi, and Rank. After meeting him for the first time in such tragic circumstances, Ernest Jones would never forget "the mournful expression of the doomed man as he gazed at his successor."[7]

Jones would also be given the task of organising and directing the English extension of the *Verlag*, for which he had been busy seeking financial support from the British and American members for some time. In reality, this meant setting up a new publishing company since the unabated hatred of the enemy meant that London could not act as a branch of a German enterprise. The International Psychoanalytical Press would be only nominally independent of the *Verlag*, and its main activities would be the publication of the new *International Journal of Psychoanalysis* (a partner for the *Internazionale Zeitschrift für Psychoanalyse*),[8] the editing of English traditions of books published in Vienna (which would inaugurate the *International Psychoanalytical Series*),[9] and lastly the management of a bookshop in Weymouth Street, in London.[10] Jones would work closely with Rank on these editorial tasks, assisted by Hiller.

Among the various subjects under discussion during that week was the thorny question of the British and American rights for translations into English, a frequent source of misunderstandings. Freud had been convinced since the Worcester visit that Brill, having emigrated to America at an early age, was bilingual,[11] but Putnam and Jones were in agreement that his English was "atrocious."[12] What's more, Freud had never made allowances for the difficulties that Jones would face in trying to find a British publisher once the rights had been granted to the Americans.

Specifically, there was much discussion about the rights to translate the *Introductory Lectures*, which in the first instance Freud had rather hastily granted to his nephew Edward Bernays,[13] who had succeeded in sending him a precious box of Havana cigars from Paris (in Italian, we would say he had exchanged them for *una pipa di tabacco*). Still worried about the quality of the translation, but still more about his control over anglophone psychoanalysis,[14] Jones was infuriated by this. He leapt into action and sent a telegram to New York, but, to his dismay, Bernays had already taken on a team of Columbia University graduates.[15]

The committee also had to consider what to do with the funds donated by von Freund: 2 million crowns, equivalent at that time to 500,000 dollars. Unfortunately, political events in Hungary cast doubt on the possibility of accessing the money: permission had been granted to transfer a quarter of the sum to Vienna, but, despite patient and ever more relentless negotiating by Ferenczi, for some years, the bulk of the donation would only be made available in dribs and drabs by successive governments in Budapest. It became apparent that using the money there for the setting up of a Hungarian institute of psychoanalysis was not practicable. When in the spring of 1920, Ferenczi, the only designated negotiator, was expelled from the medical society,[16] all possibility of coming to an agreement was lost.

In the same week, it was nevertheless decided that half the sum available to Vienna, 250,000 crowns in cash, should be entrusted to Jones along with full executive authority. In confirmation of this, it was inevitable that Ferenczi would also have to transfer the presidency of the IPA to Jones, who wrote:

> Ferenczi agreed with a good grace, but in years to come it was a source of keen regret to him that he was never called upon to function in that position and I had good reason later for thinking that he bore me an irrational grudge for having had to supplant him.
>
> (*III*, p. 18)

By Friday 3 October, all the decisions had been taken. Ferenczi drafted the official documents which included his resignation and the official handover to Jones of the role of acting president. That same evening, Freud wrote to Abraham to inform him about the outcome of the meeting and to ask his approval for Eitingon to join the committee. The letter began by expressing the distinctive emotions of those days:

> Dear Friend, there is already something dream-like about the times behind us, when friendly solicitude kept the seriousness of life away from us. The dreadful conditions in this city, the impossibility of feeding and keeping oneself, the presence of Jones, Ferenczi, and Freund, the necessary conferences and decision-making, and the hesitant beginnings of analytic work (5 sessions = 500 crowns) result in a vivid present in the face of which memories quickly fade.
>
> (3/10/1919)

Referring to Jones's departure with Hiller and Forsyth's arrival, on Saturday, Freud confided to his daughter Sophie:

> Today, the first sigh of relief, the British took their leave yesterday. It is true that there is a new one, but this is a patient, even if it will only be for a few weeks.
>
> (4/10/1919)

On Sunday 5 October, Freud would write to Pfister and, after receiving confirmation from Abraham, to Max Eitingon on 12 October, confiding:

> Since my return a whirlwind has taken over me and sincerity forces me to say that I had to wait this Sunday afternoon to find myself in a position to do something that is not what others push me to do. Jones was here, Ferenczi and von Freund are still here, the latter is alas a man who goes out like a flame with perfect clarity and self-control. The orientation towards the West has been completed, . . . Today I hired a teacher to brush up on my English.
>
> (12/10/1919)

In all these letters, he appears to be under strain but calmer about the future of his clinical work, already augmented by the return of other patients. On 15 October, he gave Brill the news, reiterating that his daughter Anna was collaborating with him in the work of translation and the creation of the new English journal, clearly comforted by her presence in this critical period.

While Ferenczi remained in Vienna for more than a month and von Freund stayed there for treatment in a clinic where Freud would visit him every day, Jones immediately packed his bags. His mission accomplished, he went off to get married. Having arrived as a portent for Freud of better times, pupils, success, and hard currency, he left, taking with him the victor's booty and the concrete 250,000 crowns from the von Freund fund.

This was not a risk-free operation, since the cash was being smuggled out of Austria, but it succeeded with the help of Hiller:

> On crossing the Austrian frontier we were stripped naked by the Customs officials, so the manoeuvre needed some finesse. My suitcase was examined first, so I then calmly fetched the roll of notes from Hiller's case and placed it in my own, which had now passed through the Customs. Both cases were, however, to be reexamined on the following day when the train left for Switzerland, so I hired a cab the next morning and drove over the Rhine bridge separating the two countries. At its boundary we could justly claim that our luggage had been already examined and stamped.
>
> (*III*, p. 34)

The "daring enterprise," worthy of a Larry Semon, needed a cool head and a modicum of luck, but unfortunately it turned out to be pointless because, at Rank's suggestion, the money was never changed into sterling, and after a couple of years, it lost all of its value. On arriving in Zurich, Jones had time to have lunch with Forsyth, who was on his way to Vienna. He married on Thursday 9 October, and during his brief honeymoon, before returning to London, he wrote the professor a letter from Lugano full of happiness, thanks, and declarations of loyalty.[17]

The heart towards the East

We can easily imagine the upheaval and profound change that Freud lived through during that week: what was at stake was survival itself.

His Hungarian friend von Freund and his new English pupil Forsyth, whom we will meet in Freud's associations, represent two worlds, one passing the baton to the other, and Freud's two souls, the diverse and complex parts of his Self that were identified with his pupils and heirs. In the readjustments and transformations that accompanied the attainment by psychoanalysis of international development as a science and a movement, Jones's political investiture in opposition to the affective investiture of Ferenczi opened a wound which was one of the costs of progress, a maturational discontent that Freud and his theory would have to pay.

Von Freund died with a courage and dignity that honoured psychoanalysis and aroused in Freud the same heartache and admiration that he had felt in the last hours of his father Jacob ("an interesting human being, very happy within himself," a "peculiar mixture of deep wisdom and fantastic light-heartedness") whose weakness had been redeemed by the decorum with which he passed away.[18]

After his removal from the presidency, taking the side of the child and the patient, Ferenczi would continue to support the creative and troubling aspects in Freud's mind and in his private theory.

Jones, the true foreigner, vividly represents the *raisons d'état*, the normalisation of the "plague" and the guarantee of its success. He would translate psychoanalysis, giving it an English-speaking identity, and lead it into a tradition and a history recognised by the world, an evolutionary change comparable to the individual's acquisition of verbal language.

Freud soon began to feel the weight of this in the political questions that arose around the organisation of the first post-war Congress and Jones's veto of Berlin as its venue, keeping Abraham on side by repeating that "in view of our new orientation towards the West, we could not decide anything without consulting Jones."[19]

From now on, Freud would mostly have pupils in analysis and would laboriously conduct these treatments in English. Paul Bernfeld, one of the last Jewish patients he worked with in German, was the leading edge of this critical moment, which accompanied an internal fracture.

English was a foreign experience that burst into the vocalising of analytic work. Freud was compelled to give up his mother tongue, a rejection that he later described to Arnold Zweig as shedding "not an article of clothing" but his "own skin."[20] It was a change that entailed the cooling of the affective resonance in relational contact, introducing entirely new and alien accents, sonorities, melodies, and characteristics into the experience, robbing words of their poetry[21] and part of their history, altering not only the calligraphy and style of Freud's writing but even the way in which he thought – his "phonographic memory" sustained by the figurative distinctiveness of the German language: in short, modifying Freud's psyche-soma and the very fabric of his discipline. To Jones, Freud described the difficulty of abandoning gothic handwriting for Latin characters as a loss of fluency and inspiration (11/20/1926). And during his London exile, he confided to R de Saussure that among the most painful experiences there was "the loss of the language one has lived and thought in and that in spite of all efforts towards empathy one will never be able to replace by any other." He continued:

> With painful understanding I observe how otherwise familiar means of expression fail in English and how even every fibre in me wants to struggle against giving up the familiar gothic handwriting.
>
> (11/06/1938)[22]

Paradoxically, psychoanalysis returned to the language proposed at the start by Bertha Pappenheim in her "talking cure," but Freud's words changed in English, becoming more scientific: even the silences were different. . . . According to Abram Kardiner, the silent English analytic style arose from Freud's terseness with his pupils from Britain.

But what changes were in store for the theory itself? Arendt writes:

> if Freud had lived and carried on his inquiries in a country and language other than the German-Jewish milieu which supplied his patients, we might never have heard of an Oedipus complex.
>
> (1968, p. 179)

And she adds, quoting Kafka:

> "The father complex which is the intellectual nourishment of many . . . concerns the Judaism of the fathers . . . the vague consent of the fathers (this vagueness was the outrage)" to their sons' leaving of the Jewish fold: "with their hind legs they were still stuck to the Judaism of their fathers, and with the forelegs they found no new ground."
>
> (Franz Kafka *Briefe*, p. 337 – *ibid.*, footnote)

Heading off in this direction, towards the West, Freud suffered a detachment from his Jewish heritage, the contradiction and bother of "so vulgar an occupation as making money or working for it"[23] and, perhaps searching for a lost language, he felt a profound call from the East. It is also a reaction to further assimilation, a nostalgic longing not only for the mother but for his origins: *Kadimah!*[24] To Ferenczi, he confessed:

> My interest flags so easily, i.e., it likes so much to turn away from the present, wants to connect with something else, and something in me bridles against the compulsion still to earn much money, which can never be enough, and to perpetuate the same psychological skills that have maintained me for thirty years against contempt for mankind and disgust with the world. Strange secret longings rise up in me, perhaps from the legacy of my forebears, for the Orient and the Mediterranean, and for a life of a completely different kind, belated childish wishes, unfulfillable and maladapted to reality, as if to indicate a loosening of the relationship to it.
>
> (30/03/1922)

Notes

1 Jones, *III*, p. 17.
2 *ibid*., p. 29.
3 05/10/19.
4 Born on 23/08/1919, she became a psychotherapist in the United States.
5 K Jones, 1979.
6 Von Freund had arranged for his ring to pass to Eitingon, but Freud eventually gave him his own, since the widow Ròszi von Freund claimed it for herself.
7 Jones, *III*, p. 32.
8 Of which Jones was already co-editor.
9 Which in 1924 continued in association with the Hogarth Press.
10 Eric Hiller was supposed to manage this, but it very soon closed.
11 Freud to Putnam, 5/12/1909.
12 Putnam to Jones, 14/09/1910.
13 Son of Eli and Anna, a famous publicist and advertiser, he was among the first to use the psychology of the unconscious to influence public opinion in political propaganda.
14 Steiner, 2017.
15 A second and better translation by Joan Riviere then appeared in 1922.
16 Ferenczi to Freud, 30/05/1920.
17 12/10/1919.
18 Freud to Fliess, 15/07/1896 and 2/11/1896.
19 2/11/1919.
20 Freud to A Zweig, 21/02/1936.
21 Schur affirmed that translating Freud involved a commitment comparable to the experience of translating a poetic text (1972).
22 In Marinelli, 2009b.
23 Arendt, 1968, p. 179.
24 *Kadimah* was the name of the oldest Viennese Jewish Zionist guild. Freud, together with his son Martin, became an honorary member: the word *kadimah* means both forwards (*Kidmah)* and eastwards (*Kedmah*) (Freud, M 1958a, p. 164).

Chapter 11

The strange case of Dr Forsyth and Mr Vorsicht

The build-up

The "secret language"

Our path has now led us to the Forsyth case, the only one of its kind, the last one after the more famous *Case Studies*: it had no place in Freud's plans since he wanted to keep the subject of thought transmission quite separate from psychoanalysis and did not intend to analyse the example in detail but simply to use it as a starting point. Indirectly we find him getting to grips with analytic work as he had never done before: despite indicating that he would keep many things to himself, he generously reveals himself and allows a lot more to slip out inadvertently. Contents and circumstances of the treatment are revealed as being by no means tangential to understanding the "occult" phenomenon, as Deutsch wrote in the 1926 paper cited by Freud (1933):

> During psychoanalysis the psychic contact between analyst and analysand is so intimate, and the psychic processes which unfold themselves in that situation are so manifold, that the analytic situation may very well include all conditions which especially facilitate the occurrence of such phenomena. Thus, very careful observations should enable one to recognize that a given psychic process, which unfolds itself before our very eyes, is "telepathic," and should also help one to reveal its true nature by means of the methodology characteristic of psychoanalytic technique. The value of insights obtained in this manner is due principally to the fact that one is not dealing here with discrete happenings, but with psychic events which are part of a continuous process, and which can be fully understood only within the framework of that process. The same events, when torn from the contextual whole of the analytic process, would impress the outsider as typically "occult," and, because of the impossibility of interpreting them, would retain their typically "occult" character. One has the impression that only by fitting such "occult" incidents into a continuum can one deprive them of their mystical features.
>
> (p. 134)

We will proceed by reconnecting the experience of telepathy with the chain of relational events in analysis after reconstructing their sequence, trying to fill

DOI: 10.4324/9781003246480-12

in the gaps of the psychic process that had determined them, making use of help from those few writers who have attempted this before us but only had the text of *Lecture XXX* available to them.[1]

To begin with, there is a patient who has problems with women and whose analysis has run into a serious impasse. At the origin of the various forms of psychic impotence, Freud had identified the inhibitory presence of the fixation of the libido on the mother and sister and the anxiety about being castrated by the father. The additional obstacle, represented for the patient by the woman's virginity, related back to the elements of the castration complex and the difficulties in identifying and competing with the father. On a primitive level, because of fusional anxieties and the reactivation of fantasies of returning to the mother's womb, the penetration of coitus could arouse more undifferentiated tensions typical of the newborn infant's condition of helplessness. It was the need to seek support from his rival that led the patient into a complete blind alley.[2]

As in the most stubborn forms of impotence, the early fixation to the father which Herr Bernfeld manifested in the transference was probably sustained by an inverse oedipal disposition involving a retreat towards an unconscious feminine identification without a homosexual object choice and with recourse to sadistic masturbatory fantasies. Perhaps Freud's doubtful prognoses expressed during the spring of the same year in a work on the genesis of the perversions (to which we will return) were referring to the insuperable impasse in this analysis:

> We are accustomed confidently to promise recovery to psychically impotent patients who come to us for treatment; but we ought to be more guarded in making this prognosis so long as the dynamics of the disturbance are unknown to us. It comes as a disagreeable surprise if the analysis reveals the cause of the "merely psychical" impotence to be a typically masochistic attitude, perhaps deeply embedded since infancy.
>
> (1919b, p. 197)

The qualities of Paul B's transference, clearly not separate from the extraordinary nature of the external circumstances, must have influenced the special parameters of the treatment. Freud had become fond of this patient with a gift for making himself likeable, and as he tells us straightaway, the sessions were so enjoyable that they made him forget the context of the professional relationship. In those early post-war years, the general situation of helplessness and hunger made the two protagonists of the session joint participants in a common condition of need and narcissistic threat as well as a symbolic castration: and while on the one hand, the patient didn't pay his bill, the analyst for his part had no hope of success. And so, despite holding out no promise of change and being destined to end with the arrival of patients from the West, the analysis went on in an atmosphere of mutual empathy – and free of charge.[3]

It is easy to imagine how this climate of solidarity and acceptance would have been able to foster the intimate dialogue that Freud calls "the secret language which so easily grows up between two people who see each other on a regular basis." In this language, he immediately points out to us what a comforting role is played by English and the novels written in it, to which Paul B introduces him. Those books were as helpful to his survival as the foodstuffs sent by his relatives in Manchester after the borders were reopened and the hard currency arriving with his patients from the Allied countries: they contained something good which, for both of them, had roots in childhood and made them yet more familiar to each other.

Freud was polyglot, but he was especially fond of English. Partly by identification with the branch of his family that had emigrated to the United Kingdom and his desire to communicate with them in the new language, his knowledge of English had followed not far behind his German: he became acquainted with Shakespeare at the age of only eight, reading him over and over, and he was always ready with an apt quotation from his plays.[4] Sharing this foreign language accentuated the secret area of complicity with Paul B in a similar way – or so we can imagine – to the young Sigismund's experience with his schoolfriend Eduard Silberstein when they resorted to Spanish and the novels of Cervantes.[5]

Freud has nothing else to tell us about this "secret language" and that *Unspoken* that arises in habit in a relationship. He will not relate it to the phenomenon of "telepathy" even though it is via the secret term *Forsyte* that we see the *Forsyth-Vorsicht* coincidence develop at the start of the session. In his conclusions to *Lecture XXX*, he will not even link it to that "thought transference" which he hypothesises as the original, archaic method of communication between individuals, and between mother and child, and which is still able to operate under certain conditions. And yet he makes us understand clearly how he experienced such a close attunement of words, thoughts, and fantasies in the here and now of the analysis with Herr P B that the term *Forsyte* had come to "mean the same" (p. 50) for analyst and patient.

The Man of Property

At the time of the session, Galsworthy's *Forsyte Saga* had barely got going: the author would return many times to the subject in novels and stories over an arc of 15 years, building up a long cycle in instalments. The prodigious enterprise, a nineteenth-century novel sequence written well into the twentieth century, followed the lives of a wealthy bourgeois family in London in the late Victorian era and cultivated its own aesthetic of the past as a characteristically Victorian series of stories and interludes.

In autumn 1919, Herr Paul B and Freud had only read *The Man of Property* (1906): the book lent to Freud during that week, *Indian Summer of a Forsyte*, was the second in the series, appearing in 1918. By the time Freud returned from the Harz at the end of 1921, rediscovered his notes, and made the first draft of the session, *In Chancery* and *Awakening* had been published in 1920 and *To Let* in the present year, 1921. When Freud picked up the *Nachtrag* again in 1932 and inserted it into *Lecture XXX*, Galsworthy's cycle of three trilogies was complete, and he had won the Nobel Prize.[6]

When David Forsyth arrived, the term *Forsyte*, together with everything that Galsworthy had tried to embody in the character of *The Man of Property*, had become part of the "secret language" set up between Freud and Paul Bernfeld.

With the eponymous character Soames Forsyte in mind, we can form some hypotheses about how this term came to resonate with the problems being faced in the analysis. As a representative of the rich – and in this respect *provident* (*fore-sighted*) – English family, but one made antipathetic by the author, who despised the mentality of a rampant bourgeoisie, avid for possession and the cult of appearances, Soames Forsyte portrays the predatory violence of money and its acquisition which cares nothing for feelings. A collector of paintings, a meticulously calculating businessman alienated from his accumulations, he never succeeds in possessing the heart of Irene, the young and beautiful but not wealthy woman he has taken as his wife. In a ravening outbreak of jealousy, impotent in the face of her "diabolical" feminine fascination, when another man threatens his ownership by winning her love – Philip Bosinney, the "Buccaneer," one of those "poor seedy-lookin' . . . artistic chaps" – he tries in vain to reassert his dominance by possessing the woman with violence. The act does not restrain his wife and dismays his rival, leading indirectly leads to Bosinney's death. The plot is strikingly suggestive.

We do not know what the term *Forsyte* evoked in the session, what Freud and Herr Paul B said to each other or what unconscious fantasies they had so far habitually shared and nurtured. The name connoted an affective history and a secret they shared. It is likely that it conveyed fantasies about hunger, helplessness, and the wish for power, dominance over the woman, jealousy, and, last but not least, murderous sibling tensions. In the Jewish culture they had in common, the term *Forsyte* might, by contrast, evoke the *Schnorrer* and envisage an avoidance of the Oedipal conflict through helplessness. The *Schnorrer* was the poor and ingenious Jew who begs from his fellow believers, forcing them to help him, and considering this a professional activity no different from others.

Freud had experienced long-term poverty in childhood and adolescence, a vulnerability he would never forget, and every subsequent experience of this kind re-exposed him to his father's crazy recklessness and failure and his mother's outbreaks of anxiety and despair.

The humiliations of living off the generosity of relatives and friends and the cynical rage they unleashed in him were a constant and oppressive subject of Sigmund's letters to his fiancée, leading one to conclude that he resorted to the use of cocaine because of the need to "anaesthetize" himself.[7]

"I know from my youth that once the wild horses of the pampas have been lassoed, they retain a certain anxiousness for life," he wrote to Fliess on 21/09/1899. "Thus I came to know the helplessness of poverty and continually fear it." And at the start of the war he had written to Abraham, "I have always hated helplessness and penury most of all, and I am afraid we are now approaching both" (30/12/1914).

In her interpretation of the Forsyth case, Maria Torok (1983) rightly attributes certain historical determinants of the clinical event and the meaning of the term

Forsyte for Freud to the experience of poverty and hunger suffered through his father's improvidence, a father who unlike his English relatives *was not a Forsyte*. And the intense and painful affects that had come into play could have been the same as those that later bound him to the significant companions of his life.

What is certain is that Dr Forsyth's arrival sets off something unexpected in the relationship with Paul Bernfeld and signals the breaking of the system: the fantasy becomes reality, and the flesh-and-blood Englishman prepares to enter the analysis. As soon as the name of the real person takes the place of the character from the novel, the term Forsyte will revolutionise its functioning in analysis.[8] It is a disruptive, overwhelming change in the analytic link and its language: for Herr Bernfeld, a real nightmare.

Setting the scene: the preconscious at work

In the playing out of the session, Herr P B's process of association and the three *Einfälle* which repeatedly pose Freud the question of whether thought-induction exists represent the culminating expression of a real core of yet unrecognised facts, an intense desire which had until then been kept under rigid control.

For Servadio, it is a "complementarity of the analyst's emotional designs with those of the patient," a kind of "dovetailing of emotional patterns," an "unconscious dynamic configuration *à deux*," which seems to be "a very strong precondition for the occurrence of psi phenomena."[9] My hypothesis is that the *telepathic effect* is the product of a complex transferential and countertransferential construction and has its origins in the primitive elements – automatisms and unconscious identifications – experienced jointly with the patient in the rhythm of the relationship. These would be mobilised by variations in the setting and impelled to become differentiated and emerge into consciousness. In our case, the impulse would have been the imminent conclusion of the treatment as a consequence of the new English patient's arrival.[10] Though the event had been planned for some time and was announced before the summer, it catches our two protagonists unprepared and exposes them to the area of trauma, need, the struggle for survival in a *mors tua vita mea*: while Herr P B will be abandoned and betrayed, we will discover that his analyst is not as indifferent as he thinks he is at having to say goodbye to his likeable but refractory patient.

Freud did not yet have access to the affective tools and theoretical-technical knowledge he needed to address and work through the violent tensions connected to the process of separation: it was at this time that he was making his first observations on the process of the child's separation from the mother.[11] In this context, we see that sort of "Preconscious magician" being activated in the relationship, the "playwright"[12] who intervenes when there is still no capacity for reverie. We can recognise its outcome in a series of gestures, errors, slips, and enactments which disrupt the analysis as they try to find an outlet in speech. Freud refers to them without catching their coherent and orderly sequence, culminating in the "telepathic" session: here the repressed material finally succeeds in breaking through the barrier set up against it and, taking advantage of P B's word *Vorsicht*, bursts into Freud's consciousness with its surprising and demonic effect.

The psychic tools of dream-work (such as wandering attention, dissociation, negative hallucination, reversal of foreground and background, cryptomnesia, sensory hyperaesthesia, and also reconstructions of retrospective memory, etc.) all converge in a collaboration with the countless coincidences that punctuate everyday life to prepare and progressively create the "occult" event. This event makes a bonfire of all the patiently prepared and affectively determined ammunition, and its abrupt appearance in the mind brings it to the forefront with no apparent connection to the affective circumstances and context. The surprisingly "telepathic" form it assumes as a laissez-passer for emerging from the primary process into the secondary process reveals and isolates the presence of the deep nucleus of unbounded understanding with the patient but also acts as a first opening up and a developmental differentiation towards conscious awareness.

As we venture into the tangle of interconnected events, symbolic and real, which constitute the storyline of the session, we find ourselves passing step by step through the sequence of exchanges as they unfold, restoring the temporal coordinates of the facts and their affective significative congruence.

Correspondences

The event begins when Freud receives the first letter from the unknown Dr Forsyth of London, who presents himself directly as an aspiring psychoanalyst without having been introduced by his colleague Ernest Jones, as would have been expected. We are immediately in the field of sibling rivalry. But that is not all: in the multiple determinants of the "occult" effect, notes Derrida, there is the English paediatrician's surname which, *nomen omen*, inaugurates the theme of "foresight."[13] With his distinctive attention to words, Freud may have noted this, but it is not certain that he had until then associated his new patient's name with the Forsytes of the Saga and his old patient's "secret language," catching the irony of his own betrayal: Paul B would be forced to give up his place to a Forsyte, of all people!

However, something has disturbed Freud because, having given Herr B ample warning that he will have to abandon him in order to take an English pupil into treatment, he forgets to take Forsyth's address with him when he goes on holiday, and without it, he cannot make any arrangements with him.

Freud seems to have been in quite a state about this, exacerbated by the difficulties with postal communication at that time, and he clumsily exports his own conflict straightaway by creating a competition and arousing jealousy in more than one person:[14] after asking Forsyth to let Jones know about his (Freud's) plans for the summer, he then has to ask Jones to tell Forsyth the exact date of his return, forcing him to intervene in the analytic relationship he is setting up and reviving the rivalry between the "duellists."

Informed by his analyst but not prepared to give up his place to someone else so soon, we know that Paul Bernfeld set about resuming his treatment after the summer with renewed energy in a state of intense transferential investment heightened by abstinence over a "period of 80 days." But Freud's own countertransferential position must have been affectively more significant and important than he shows in his writing. The very way in which he has readied himself to bring the analysis to an end, replacing one person with another, indicates a difficulty in sustaining the vital aggression that is necessary for detaching oneself and shows him identified with a mother who finds it impossible to promote the separations of growth, conceiving one child after the other, investing massively in the last-born, tying him to her and suddenly "throwing away," affectively deleting, the eldest.

We are getting advance warning that Freud will not be rid of Paul B as quickly and easily as he imagines or intends.

The *Fortsein* game

The troublesome individual and a first repression

In the most trustworthy reconstruction, on returning to Vienna, Freud followed his custom after the annual two-month summer break and met Herr P B for an informal conversation on Saturday 27 September to arrange the timing and frequency of the analysis: in this case, it meant confirming the five weekly sessions at 11.00, with the exception of Wednesday. After the checking of diaries, it was agreed that the treatment proper would resume on Monday 29th.

Jones's bursting in during this consultation is a "primal scene," a disturbing effraction that takes the two men by surprise and arouses different emotions in them.

What a mass of emotion and excitement will have been stirred up in Freud! And what a sense of exclusion in Paul B, who recognises it instantly! Maybe he and Jones will have been introduced to each other at Herr Bernfeld's request, but Jones can never become his friend as well as Freud's: on the contrary, he announces the break-up. The Englishman is sent away: he is shown the door to the waiting room, and the disturbance is repressed. But it's only a matter of time: one week later, the real rival and the subject of the English language will occupy the thoughts of the whole "telepathic" session.

The missed appointment

The mechanism with which B reacts to the threat of abandonment introduced by Jones is active repetition of the passively suffered experience which Freud had just learned to observe in his grandson, and which he called the "*Fort-sein*" game (the game of *being gone, not being there*):[15]

> Throwing away the object so that it was "gone" might satisfy an impulse of the child's, which was suppressed in his actual life, to revenge himself on his mother for going away from him.
>
> (1920, p. 16)

It happens that when his analysis was resumed on the Monday, in an unconscious act of retaliation, B keeps Freud waiting pointlessly.[16] Since the patient was not paying, we have to wonder how such actions were managed: was it possible to interpret his disappearance and the throwing away of the session? It is possible that Paul B was repeating the childhood scene when, learning that a little brother was coming, he had thrown numerous objects out of the window.[17]

At least in his drafting of the case, Freud does not dwell on the motivations, manifest and unconscious, behind B's game of hide-and-seek and its scornful, vindictive, "All right, then, go away! I don't need you. I'm sending you away myself" (*ibid.*). He has no time to think about it and compensates himself for B's absence with apparent ease: he has someone else in mind, his former patient, now a friend and benefactor, who is causing him concern and whom he has not seen for some time. He goes to the *Pension Atlanta* where Tony von Freund has just arrived from Hungary and meets up with his colleagues on the committee who have gathered there to discuss the imminent revolution in the movement: Jones's investiture and the translation of psychoanalysis into the Western, English-speaking world.

The coincidence of the "neighbours"

Having turned his back on Paul B, Freud unexpectedly comes across him when he arrives at the *Pension* and the name plate of his office catches his eye.

> On the second floor of the same house I saw the office of B. and the sign of the firm B. & R. In connection with this I had told B. one or two days before today's session that I had in a sense paid him a visit in his house.
>
> (1921 [2010])

His attempt to distract himself from the missed appointment has not succeeded: instead, "unconsciously motivated attention of the sort that sees Helen in every woman" and the "compliance of chance" have a surprise in store for him.[18] The strange coincidence by which the name plate of the firm *B & R* catches Freud's eye, redirecting his attention to the absent patient, suggests the emergence of an unconscious identificatory link with him, as profound as it is troubled and unexpected, together with the sense of guilt.

This "house call" is almost an internal warning. The war has been lost, the treatment has not been successful and Freud – *every man for himself!* – has to try and survive by jumping on the victors' bandwagon and leaving the losers to their fate: but something is calling him back . . . "survivor's guilt"?[19]

This first remarkable coincidence, passed over in silence as pure chance, is in fact a directorial masterstroke on the part of preconscious. Not only is it not chance but, as we shall see, it corresponds to a recurring inner scene of "unconscious rendezvous" which Freud has been repeating, test-running, for years.[20] This time, it is rendered especially tragic by the fact that, as we know, the friend with whom he tries to replace Paul B and in whom he invests his affections has something in common and is just as incurable, and he will be abandoned to his fate after giving up his position to an Englishman. Von Freund will be dead even before Bernfeld's analysis is finished.

But the coincidence also entails the troubling hypothesis that the roles could be reversed. Freud is starting to feel distress, a first inner alarm: *Could I be feeling the loss of B and have I come looking for him . . . ?* or *Could the analysis end with the same pain that I am feeling for the death of Tony?* Or maybe, *Will I really save myself? These Englishmen seem to be bringing help but they are imposing their language on me and taking possession of a valuable prize. Can they be trusted?*

At the start of the war, Freud had managed to defend his daughter Anna against Jones's amorous assault, but now he was forced to hand over his other much-loved creature to him: psychoanalysis. And Forsyth himself seemed intent on mastering it after only seven weeks of sessions . . .

The joke of the "home visit"

Freud considered humour one of the most powerful means constructed by the human psyche for dealing with adversity and achieving relief from suffering. The feelings – of compassion, pity, anger, grief, sympathy – that we would expect to see in a given situation, though still they are still there in the preconscious, are viewed from a distance, and the smile of today's adult relates safely back to the intense emotions of the child.[21] Naturally there cannot fail to be a deep bitterness in this.

Showing that he has been affected by Paul B's challenge, Freud reacts with the joke of the "home visit," a house call that, while it metaphorically emphasises their intimacy (*I found you anyway*) reinforces an affective distance from B and from all that he might evoke inwardly for Freud. The joke contrasts the tendency to indulge in feelings that reveal the child (who might be protesting or despairing), puts a stop to empathy, and almost scornfully reiterates the denial of dependency. (*It's not really you I'm interested in, nor was I visiting you at home. If you leave me I won't even notice. There's someone else nearby, a brother who is now going to take your place.*)

The bitterness in the witticism and its threat of passivity and impotence might be connected to the memory of another difficult period, early in the newly married Freud's professional life, when his livelihood depended on a humiliating "home" service, sometimes without even being able to afford a cab fare: those daily visits to the "very old lady" who was not the young, wealthy patient he dreamed of welcoming into his consulting room and who might die at any moment, robbing him of an essential source of income.[22] "I was about 30, and I was very ambitious, dissatisfied with my situation. I treated only poor people at that time. No princess!" Freud told the Princess Marie Bonaparte.

Back then, too, Freud used to protect himself with irony, referring within the family to patients who did not attend as "twelve o'clock *negroes*" (from a cartoon in the *Fliegende Blätter* depicting a yawning lion muttering, "Twelve o'clock and no negro").[23]

Freud distanced himself from both the present and the earlier threat of poverty and impotence by repudiating his understanding with B, just as in the past he had despised himself and what he owed to that old and far from aristocratic lady (a hidden image of maternal incestuousness and his own helpless impotence) by hawking and spitting on the stairs in spite of the housekeeper's reproving growl.[24]

With the Englishmen's arrival, the time of hunger will pass once again.

An ambivalent gift

At this point, how should we consider Bernfeld's subsequent loan to Freud of a new volume by Galsworthy: *Indian Summer of a Forsyte*? Perhaps an attempt at a rapprochement, aimed at regaining his goodwill and reminding him of their shared passion for English, the "secret language" and complicity of their bond? The novel was the sequel to *The Man of Property* and indicated the author's intention to continue the story, showing that he was captivated by his characters. Was it an invitation to Freud to continue their relationship? Or a way for B himself to become a "Forsyte," the hero of a Saga[25]?

The novel's contents added elements to the themes of the analysis (impotence, incestuous desire, and death). It tells of the encounter between the head of the family, Jolyon Forsyte, and his nephew's ex-wife, the beautiful and lonely Irene, who is now a private tutor. The young woman is able to revive the last embers of love in the old man before his death and establishes herself as the central character of Galworthy's Saga. New shades of meaning could be entering the "secret language": a Forsyte was becoming capable of loving and dying . . .

And yet it is unlikely that Freud paid any attention to this new book during that intense week, given how busy he was dealing with quite different new questions, under the various pressures and demands imposed by his present circumstances: the "whirlwind" that had taken over his mind, "something dream-like" from which he would wake in bewilderment.[26]

Notes

1 Eisenbud, 1949 [1953]; Servadio, 1955a; Fodor, 1971; Moreau, 1976; Torok, 1983; Granoff and Rey, 1983; Derrida, 1981; Aziz, 1990; Diatkine 1992, 2013, 2020.
2 Freud, 1905b, 1912c, 1918b, 1926.
3 See Diatkine, 1992, 2013.
4 Freud spoke three ancient languages, Latin, Greek, and Hebrew, and four modern foreign languages, English, Spanish, French, and a little Italian. "He told me once that for ten years he read nothing but English books" (Jones, *I*. p. 24).
5 See Pierri, 2022.
6 Galsworthy died a few months after receiving the Nobel Prize, and Freud, who had just published *Lecture XXX*, marked it in his calendar on 01/31/1933 (Molnar, 1992).
7 Grubrich Simitis and Lortholary, 2012.
8 Granoff and Rey, 1983.

9 1955b, p. 29, 1958, p. 104.
10 On the awakening function of rhythmic variation, see Ferenczi, 1926b.
11 1920b.
12 Lopez, 1991, 2007; Grotstein, 2005.
13 Derrida, 1981, p. 228.
14 We have already learned about this defensive mode of Freud's in Pierri, 2022.
15 We note that the *Fortsein-Forsyth* association could also have been established.
16 On that date, there is a sign next to his name in the diary (Molnar, personal communication).
17 See Chapter 17.
18 Freud to Jung, 16/04/1909. Diatkine asks himself some questions about this incident (2013).
19 "the inclination to self-reproach that regularly sets in among the survivors" (Freud to Fliess, 2/11/1896). See Schur, 1972, p. 153.
20 See Chapter 17.
21 Freud, 1905a, 1927.
22 Goleman, 1985.
23 Jones, *I*, p. 166.
24 Freud, 1900, p. 239.
25 Torok, 1983, p. 229.
26 Freud to Abraham, 3/10/1919 and to Eitingon, 12/10/1919.

Chapter 12

The strange case of Dr Forsyth and Mr Vorsicht

The session

Vorsicht, forsyth, forsyte

We have reached Saturday: all the political decisions have been taken, Ernest Jones has gone again, David Forsyth has his appointment for that afternoon, and Freud's attention is finally caught by P B – in an unexpectedly lasting manner.

The whole mise-en-scène of transference and countertransference that we have seen developing takes its fully staged form at the crucial moment when Freud, ready to adjust himself to the wealthy English pupil and his foreign language, would like to say goodbye to B – who does not pay and is not powerful, not a true English Forsyte – just as if he were saying goodbye to a part of himself. It is here that the bond which is about to be definitively repressed tries to manifest itself as best it can, and does so by an apparently miraculous means.

As had been the case in Ferenczi's observations from 1910,[1] the "telepathic" jolt occurs at the start of the session.

The word *Vorsicht* spoken by Herr B, a distortion and translation into German of the name Forsyth (*Dr Foresight* or *Dr Prudence*) which Freud already has in mind, rings in his ear like a prophetic or menacing warning (*Mr Lookout!*) about the hopes of survival that he has only just had confirmed. The associative strings of the dream-work converge on this nodal point to weave the profound and embryonic threads of that "factory of thoughts" which Freud had earlier likened to the Faustian loom (1900, p. 283):

> *a thousand threads one treadle throws,*
> *Where fly the shuttles hither and thither,*
> *Unseen the threads are knit together,*
> *And an infinite combination grows.*
>
> (J W Goethe, *Faust*, Part I [Scene 4)

And maybe there's no point now in wondering which of the session's two protagonists the circulating affects and fantasies really belong to.

At this crossroads, the term *Forsyth* seems to act as a password.[2] Only now does Freud notice the coincidence between the name of the English doctor and

DOI: 10.4324/9781003246480-13

Galsworthy's character and realise how this Forsyth may be coming to break up the friendship and its secret language but may also compel him to abandon his own mother tongue. It is Bernfeld who makes him notice this. As if he had perceived that Freud is becoming estranged from him and speaking a foreign language, Bernfeld uses his *Vorsicht* first of all to ask him to return to German and not break up their "secret language" (*Your Forsyte no longer corresponds to mine*).

Like a primal word,[3] the old term *Forsyte* has revealed its ambiguity in two opposed and conflicting meanings: while in the shared secret fantasy, it could be an English friend or enemy *to them both*, the arrival of Dr Forsyth divides the analyst from his patient. For Freud, he is a forecast of salvation, for Paul B the beginning of the end: *mors tua, vita mea.*

Following the mode of interpretation that Freud has taught us,[4] the telepathic event makes itself evident precisely because of the small disturbance in "transmission" – the distortion of *Forsyth* into *Vorsicht* – which would contain the personalised psychic message added by B as he received it and his protest in conformity with his bent for wish-fulfilment (*If you want a Forsyth, a good omen, you've got one here, in truth only a poor Vorsicht, a warning, as my girlfriend calls me*).

Let's not overlook some of the hypotheses that Freud hints at but gives no credence: that at the beginning of the summer, he might have mentioned the new patient's name; that Dr David Forsyth and Paul Bernfeld might have met in Berggasse a little earlier;[5] that he himself had let slip his own emotional arousal about meeting the Englishman . . .

But also that as he lay down on the couch, Paul Bernfeld had glanced at the visiting card on the table: why not?

On the other hand, as Dorothy Burlingham claims in the very text quoted at the end of *Lecture XXX*, "The child guesses that her mother is pregnant before she is sure of it herself, or that she is in love with someone before she is aware of it herself."[6]

Maybe Freud needed Paul B's jealousy and the hypothesis of "telepathy" in order to find an external form to coincide with the internal scene he was trying to bring to light: "a powerfully constellated thought, that is to say, a thought that is highly emotionally charged."[7]

What is certain is that in the session's first exchange, the analysand is functioning as an "oracle" for the analyst, rather like a fortune-teller:[8] Freud feels he has been found out and realises the depth of the link that is about to be broken.

The visiting card

Left without words, Freud resorts to gesture and the visual register and places the visiting card with the name "Forsyth" where the patient can see it, as if completing the miracle (*for sight*). He knows B's unconscious jealousy and fears of abandonment, as well as his distinctive sensitivity to other people's unconscious psychic mechanisms,[9] but he does not interpret them as he would have done with other normal transference material.[10] Instead, he exacerbates it, confirming the imminence of the separation and adding substance to the associative threads of the "English" element.

Bernfeld does not seem to react to Freud's gesture (and *acting out*): not only is his analyst abandoning and replacing him, but he is offering him the occult as a distraction from pain and protest, seeming to say, "*You've foreseen it*" and "*I'm not responsible for it: it's been decided by destiny*." Neither of them makes any further reference to the old *Forsyte* of the analysis, which would have involved associations to the bond between them:[11] Freud's gesture is a passing of judgement announcing the end of the bond and the "secret language," cutting off any further possibility of using it.[12]

It is reasonable to think that the conflict of jealousy and separation at the centre of the session engages the analyst at a deep level, dividing him in two: on the one hand, he is identified with a wealthy, powerful matriarch who is endlessly pregnant and seduces but continually betrays and abandons; on the other hand, the one that really counts, he is identified with the infant and its desperate helplessness. The sharing and coincidence of this helplessness must have been the founding element from the start, the present traumatic element, of the unconscious complicity between analyst and patient.[13] For Freud, this involved the representation of the infantile scene shadowed by the premature death of his younger brother Julius. Paul Bernfeld, the defeated double whose fate Freud feared would be his,[14] also reflected back to him the weakness and incapacity of paternal protection: and we know how, on many occasions in the past, during the conflicted detachment from an idealised friend (Breuer and Fliess rather than Jung) he had had death fantasies or actually fainted.[15]

In the session, indulging his curiosity about the telepathic phenomenon and its magic, Freud tries to extricate himself and the patient from the affects of separation and betrayal: it is a way of enchanting, hypnotising the child, and of buying time. Telepathy is starting to look very much like a trick with smoke and mirrors: *Look how close we are!*

The Freud-Freund slip

The partiality we have for our own name suggests we've become attached to it like a part of ourselves. As Goethe put it, "We seem to have grown into them like our skin."[16]

Freud was used to putting up with slips about his own name, and we can imagine that from childhood he was amused by the assonances *Freund-Freude-Friede* (*Friend, Joy, Peace*). In the first letter of his that we know about – a note written as a schoolboy to his half-brother Emanuel in Manchester, who was helping his family with their financial difficulties[17] – it is surprising to see how he uses these puns as if trying to divert attention, to deflect his embarrassment about his father's unreliability and the fact that he was "very sorry that I did not understand any" of what young Sam had written *in English.*

Now, when poor Bernfeld in the second *Einfall* says *Freund*-Ottorego instead of *Freud*-Ottorego, asking if that English teacher is Freud's daughter, Freud is focusing on the patient's "telepathic" jealousy and reacts as if the patient was unconsciously aware of the name of another wealthy but unfortunate rival, the recipient of his "home visit."

Perhaps Herr B was simply expressing a desire for closeness, the wish to be a friend, a *Freund* as well as an Englishman and a Forsyth. But it may be the case that, in the reciprocities and symmetries deeply embedded in the session, some spitefulness, deforming Freud's surname, was making him reproduce in a striking manner the configuration of the "home visit": thus, in his slip, B could "visit" not the name Freud but a "neighbouring" one, differing only in one consonant.[18] It would seem to be a second challenge by the patient to Freud's attempt to make him accept something *un*friendly.

For Servadio, the dynamic of the "telepathic" effect would lie in the unconscious emotional premisses shared by the two protagonists and would take shape as the repeated "unmasking" of unpleasant affects that the analyst was trying to repress – his abandonment not only of Paul B but also of Anton von Freund in order to gain the support of someone more powerful – affects that he was having brought back to his attention in this indirect way, almost as a betrayal.[19]

However, Servadio is astonished at how Freud stays on a superficial, present interpretative level (the patient's paternal cathexis and the beginning of a decathexis by the analyst, who is thinking about the new arrival) and takes P B's slip as a starting point for widening the perspective to include the infantile conflicts that may have arisen in the countertransference, highlighting the theme of woman in the analytic dialogue. He writes:

> Freud (quite remarkably in my opinion) seems to attach no importance to the fact that his patient is referring to the person who mattered most to him from the parental viewpoint: that is, his favourite daughter.
>
> (1955a, p. 657)[20]

Servadio observes how the patient is manifesting the desire to occupy Anna's place, so as to arouse the same feelings as a daughter in Freud, but also how, without knowing it, he finds himself reviving the jealous conflict in the relationship with the sister who had the same name, Anna, and whom Freud would be able to outdo by means of his daughter. Servadio adds:

> From the infantile and possessive position of a son "jealous" of Anna, his rival in early childhood, Freud passed to the adult, paternal, and altruistic position towards Anna, his collaborator and supporter.
>
> (*ibid.*, pp. 657–658)

Without taking this any further, Servadio suggests that the situation may be more complex and that Freud's "countertransferential position" in relation to his client might have been much more significant and important that he was able to accept.[21]

Meanwhile we understand that at a stroke, the patient's slip had evoked in the analyst the people he most cared about at that moment and who he felt were fully dedicated to his survival, his favourite daughter and his dying rich friend, thereby completely reawakening the underlying infantile constellation.[22] "Telepathy" allows Freud to avoid direct confrontation with this traumatic nucleus, but the more he tries to deflect it away from himself, the more it reappears, as it does now in the third *Einfall*, about the nightmare.

The nightmare and Jones's monograph on the "Alptraum"

From now on, it is clear that Freud will not venture to interpret the case of Herr Paul B but will use the analytic tool only to interpret telepathic associations. Without referring to the patient's anxiety dream or trying to explain it – the greatest possible expression of his impotent passivity – he concentrates on the associations to the dream, which he only brings to our attention in order to evaluate the presence of a third "telepathic" *Einfall*.

The introduction of the word *Alptraum* (*Nightmare*) and the mistranslation, *Mare's nest*, would have fit very well with the patient's unconscious jealous protests and with his low self-esteem (*I don't know very much English and I only have nightmares when I'm with someone who can write a book in that language*) via the associative connection with a third rival, Ernest Jones, taken from the title of the monograph which P B would *read* in Freud's mind.

But then what do we say about the *mare's nest/nightmare* that bears Jones's hallmark in the week of the psychoanalytic Saga that has just passed?

Paul B's associations in the session seem to reflect the overflow of Freud's emotions connected to those recent events and not yet worked through.

Meanwhile let's have a quick look at what Jones had written in his monograph in contrast to what Jung, Freud, and Ferenczi had been exploring during this period in the field of the occult.[23] Jones's treatment began with the interpretation of the nightmare in popular beliefs and showed its influence on the creation of Mediaeval superstitions and faith in the existence of malign spirits: vampires, werewolves, devils, and witches. . . . The collective fantasy saw in the nightmare the realisation of a sexual encounter between mortals and supernatural beings who often assumed an animal form: for Jones, these unearthly powers – the visitors of women were called *Incubi*, those of men *Succubi* – concealed the images of the parents, and the nightmare itself, a sort of somatic reproduction of a sexual act, expressed an anxiety attack at the re-activation of normal incest wishes of infancy. Likening it in essence to an erotic dream that concludes with a defilement, Jones drew attention to the way the nightmare displayed every possible degree of affect, from pleasurable and voluptuous excitation to extreme terror and repulsion. Overall, from then on, he was a solo voice attributing superstitions, occultism, and even the Master's interest in thought transmission to an unresolved incestuous fixation.

Freud had not liked this essay, but he was admittedly not well disposed to Jones at that time because of the news about scandals in Toronto:

> I got no[t] the satisfaction from your nightmare, that almost all your contributions to science had given me. It is a tremendous amount of stuff, but less proof than I had expected and in some places only a translation of the known facts into the ψα dialect.
>
> (Freud to Jones, 14/01/1912)

But perhaps the theme of the nightmare was too directly connected to deep anxieties which could not be worked through. In *The Interpretation of Dreams* he had written:

> It is dozens of years since I myself had a true anxiety-dream. But I remember one from my seventh or eighth year, which I submitted to interpretation some thirty years later. It was a very vivid one, and in it I saw my beloved mother, with a peculiarly peaceful, sleeping expression on her features, being carried into the room by two (or three) people with birds' beaks and laid upon the bed. I awoke in tears and screaming, and interrupted my parents' sleep. . . . I remember that I suddenly grew calm when I saw my mother's face, as though I had needed to be reassured that she was not dead. . . . The anxiety can be traced back, when repression is taken into account, to an obscure and evidently sexual craving that had found appropriate expression in the visual content of the dream.
>
> (1900, pp. 583–584)

In the present year, 1919, while preparing *Beyond the Pleasure Principle*, Freud had returned to the question which traumatic anxiety dreams had left open. As he would anticipate at the Hague Congress (1920), he thought that nightmares could nevertheless be incorporated within the theory of dreams of desire along with the new category of "punishment dreams" that satisfy the expectations of the Ego's critical agency.[24] But the real interpretative problem was posed by the recurring anxiety dreams in traumatic or war neuroses, where he speculated that the dream-function had also been upset and "diverted from its purposes."[25]

It goes without saying that Freud did not even name Jones's "long treatise,"[26] in *Beyond the Pleasure Principle*, nor in *A Seventeenth-Century Demonological Neurosis* (1923). It is reasonable to suppose that Paul B did not know it, since Freud himself barely did: he hadn't even managed to finish reading it, as he confessed in response to Jones's protests.[27] It's a real joke on the part of the preconscious that, through his associations to the session's third *Einfall*, on this occasion, Freud cannot avoid citing him!

We understand how, at that time, the nightmare could be a good representation of the limit reached by the treatment and its impasse: a place where the patient's representational impotence (his inability to construct a dream that satisfies his desire and protects his sleep) was matched by an equally significant lacuna in the analyst's interpretative ability and his dream theory. From the perspective of present-day psychoanalysis, Paul B's nightmare, with its sensory heightening, could instead be interpreted as a sign of maturational progress, of regaining contact with the various primitive states of the Self in the profound developmental change, both internal and relational, to which the analysis was committing him. The upsurge in nocturnal anxiety caused by reduced dissociation could indicate that the transformation and readjustment of the previous identifications was reaching levels of preconscious awareness.[28]

Paul B's traumatic state of disarray in this developmental phase was also well expressed by the uproar-confusion of the term "mare's nest" that he had associated it with in the session.

The faulty translations

Freud fails to investigate Paul Bernfeld's nightmare and then does not even interpret the possible meanings of the substitution of *mare's nest* (a jumble, mess, or illusion) for *nightmare* (female demon). The writers who have got to grips with the text of the "Forsyth" case are unanimous in believing that this final passage from the session where the patient, with his attempt at translation from German into English, is creating a mirror image of the first translation (from the English *Forsyth* to the German *Vorsicht*), contains the most significant cruxes of the analysis and poses the question of what was "unanalysed" in Freud. Torok (1983) identifies *mare* as the "verbal place" that resonates in unison with the Freudian "crypt" and through which the experience of poverty suffered in childhood would come to consciousness (along with shame at his father's ineptitude and the stupidity of an uncle who was sent to prison when Sigmund was nine for distributing forged money).[29] From then on, the family needed help from their prosperous relatives in Manchester, the "English" with their greater potency, as the boy was well aware.[30]

Granoff and Rey regard *mare's nest* and the term *mare* on which the faulty translation hinges as organising elements of the whole session, signs of a shared traumatic nucleus, an *Alptraum*-nightmare "set in motion" which, in the transition from German to English, comes to resemble a mare's nest and gives a name to the trauma, becoming a "*meaningless story*," a "nest of nightmares" and lost illusions.[31]

At this point it would be natural to explore the etymology of *mare*, which in Paul B's mistake acts as the switch for inserting the binomial *mare's nest* in place of *nightmare*, and investigators would be surprised to find themselves running into Jones again (and not only because of the assonance with *Er-nest* suggested by Torok [1983]).

In 1931 *On the Nightmare*, the revised and extended English version of the 1912 German monograph *Der Alptraum*, will contain a long additional part which examines the origins of the words *nightmare* and *mare* and the root "M R." Despite the fact that the two mares (in *nightmare* and in *mare*) have different etymologies,[32] as Jones makes clear, let's follow his hypothesis which nevertheless highlights an associative continuity that helps him validate the interpretation of the sexual elements connected to the attack of nocturnal anxiety.[33]

On the other hand, the likeness between the two mares (*maere* and *meare*) was certainly present to the patient and to Freud himself, as it was in the culture of the time: "the popular confusion between the term mara that designates the demonic creature and that which designates the mare, soon established itself."[34] We need only think of the famous painting by Johann H Füssli *The Nightmare* (1781). In it the artist has developed "the complete picture of what the word *nightmare* means" and almost transposed the verbal definition into visual terms,[35] portraying together the malign spirit crouched on the voluptuous young woman and the pale mare, terrifying and terrified, lurking in the background: a Gothic parable of virginal terror. Countless reproductions of it circulated throughout Europe: Jones used it on the cover of his book (1931), and perhaps the engraving of it which appeared on the wall of the waiting room in Berggasse was a gift from him to the professor, a reminder and a warning alongside portraits of his pupils.[36]

We may think that, since "mare" is the hinge on which *nightmare* and *mare's nest* both turn – in the former, a woman exciting desire in a surprising and threatening manner (the oedipal mare of the night) who in the latter reveals her disappointing, deceptive, or unreliable maternal nature (mares do not make nests!) – Paul Bernfeld might have been unconsciously presenting Freud with the uncanny, *unheimliche* ambiguity of a primal female womb,[37] seductive and traumatic, which excites in a threatening manner or disappoints and abandons: the impenetrable and forbidden virginity of the session.

We are at the critical point of the impasse in this analysis, but Paul B must be given credit for one suggestion he gives Freud. With his mistaken translation, saying that for him "*nightmare*" (impotence in dreaming) is equivalent to a "*mare's nest*" (betrayed desire), he seems to want Freud to know the final, authentic reason for anxiety dreams and his own impotence: the betrayal and the interdiction of vital promises and expectations. He explains to Freud how, in the regression of sleep and in sexual intercourse, he is confronted with a primal female, a nest, which traps and disappoints. He invites Freud to take this encounter with the maternal into account.

Last, there is a further element in Bernfeld's erroneous translation not revealed by Freud which acts at the end of the session as a comment on the "joker" of occultism that Freud had dealt him at the start by showing him Forsyth's visiting card. Correcting himself, Paul B translates *mare's nest* (*false discovery, illusion*, or *deliberate hoax*) from English into German as "something incredible" [*unglaubliche*], "a cock-and-bull story [*Räubergeschichte*]."[38] "Why is Freud satisfied with the translation of mare's nest with Räubergeschichte?" wonders Torok (1983). Is it perhaps to avoid acknowledging what B thinks of telepathy and the use Freud makes of it in the session like a conjurer, a "Räuber-Robber," or fraudster (Freud-*Fraud*).

In the "maternal" transference, Paul Bernfeld is perhaps holding him accountable for that seductive, treacherous, and disappointing analytic containment which is destined to be suddenly broken off: the gold coin that turns out to be a forgery.

Freud seems deaf to these communications and committed to observing the "occult" phenomenon with the scientific curiosity that has always saved him in the past, while the thoughts and words of the session are isolated from their charge of pain and desire, and the preconscious coincidence with B, while recognisable, is more manageable because split off and partly estranged in the "telepathic" countertransferential effect.

But despite all this, the patient has been able to penetrate his analyst and imprint a lasting trace in him.

Notes

1 Ferenczi to Freud, 17/08/1910: see Pierri, 2022.
2 Granoff and Rey, 1983, p. 95.
3 Freud, 1910.
4 Freud, 1922a.
5 Aziz considers this explanation the most reasonable one (1990).
6 1932 [1935], p. 91.
7 Aziz, 1990, p. 118.
8 *ibid.*
9 In one of the essays read in the Harz, Freud noted in jealousy, paranoia, and homosexuality the particular sensitivity and ability to observe the unconscious of the other (1922b).
10 Eisenbud, 1949 [1953].
11 Torok, 1983.
12 Granoff and Rey, 1983.
13 Characteristic of the present traumatic element would be the propensity to take into analysis people whose history, unconsciously, resonates with one's own (Scarfone, 2014).
14 Freud to Fliess, 3/10/1897: "I greeted my one-year-younger brother (who died after a few months) with adverse wishes and genuine childhood jealousy; and that his death left the germ of [self-]reproaches in me."
15 See Pierri, 2022.
16 Freud, 1900, p. 207.
17 In Freud et al. 1976; see Goodnick, 1994.
18 As noted by Granoff and Rey, 1983.
19 1955a, 1955b, 1956.
20 Translated from French by the author.
21 1956.
22 Moreau, 1976; Pierri, 2010.
23 See Pierri, 2022. Jones published a first short article in English (1910). The monograph *Der Alptraum* appeared directly in German, in Sachs's translation, in 1912. Only in 1931 did Jones publish a book in English, after adding new chapters.
24 Frued, 1920, pp. 4–5.
25 1920, p. 13.
26 *Nachtrag*1921 [2010], see Chapter 7.
27 Jones to Freud, 5/02/1925. Freud replied, "I unfortunately neglected to check your *Nightmare*. I distinctly remember that I read only the introductory chapters," 11/02/1925.
28 Zorzi Meneguzzo, 2010.
29 Krüll, 1979; Gay, 1988.
30 Torok interprets *mare* on the basis of Freud's "verbal" association (*mare's nest-manchester*) also supported by the erroneous identification of P with Herr Pankeiev, the

"wolf man," in whose analysis the role of another "Anna," Pankeiev's sister, emerges (1983).

31 Granoff and Rey, 1983, p. 100.

32 In *Nightmare*, the term *mare* derives from *mære,* Old English for *night-goblin, incubus, female demon oppressing the sleeper's chest* (Old High German "*mara*"). In *Mare*, the term *mare* derives from *meare,* Old English for *female of the horse or any other equine animal*, also derogatory for *woman* (Old High German *meriha,* German mähre "*mare*").

33 Jones concluded that the diverse and complex roots of the "MR" group (involved in *mære* and *meare*) led back to the act of masturbation, the psychological meaning of which he considered coinciding with that of the nightmare: incestuous guilt, nocturnal experience, sadism, fear of castration or death, and so on. The fact that Jones in 1931 reworked his 1912 work – even his monograph is in two stages and moves from German to English – can still be seen in counterpoint to Freud's interest in occultism.

34 Starobinski, 1974, p. 108.

35 *ibid.*

36 It is currently in the Freud Museum in Vienna.

37 Freud, 1919a.

38 See Chapter 7.

Chapter 13

That Forsyte Woman

Return to the mothers – telepathy, "distant proximity"

The secret affective language of the relationship stays in the background of the session, along with the theme of the feminine. The communicative area of the "maternal transference" was too uncanny and was tacitly relegated by Freud to the concrete reality of the analytic setting and its distinctive circumstances: from the use of the couch to the rhythmic habits of the encounter. When he mentioned the setting in "Recommendations to Physicians . . ." (1912a), he spoke of it as one of the technical devices that he had tried out and gradually organised in partnership with his patients, something highly personal, "the only one suited to my individuality" (p. 111). We find ourselves being faced once again with the fact that Freud is putting something very precious at stake, something absolutely personal and transferential.

Freud longed for intimacy but was afraid of it. He had an arresting gaze at a first meeting, intent and penetrating, but, along with the patience and caution of maturity, it contained a child's simplicity and innocence.[1]

He admitted to finding face-to-face encounters difficult, as if he feared that eye contact meant that a boundary would be crossed. Equally, he always made clear his aversion to those suggestions of fusion with one's surroundings, typical of mystical experiences and the sacred, in which identities become labile and expansive:[2] it may be that in them he found an archaic level of affective communication related to the contagion and omnipotence characteristic of hypnosis but also of human origins in the helpless state of the *infans*.

Today it is widely agreed that the model of maternal care which characterises the analytic situation was set up as a defence against the first relationship with the object, from which Freud had averted his eyes. The decision to listen from behind the couch would have been made necessary by the affective potency that he attributed to the mutual gaze, by the need to filter the immediacy of the mimetic mother-infant mirroring. In 1933, he confided to Hilda Doolittle that he did not like to be the mother in transference: "it always surprises and shocks me a little. I feel so very masculine."[3] This constituted his real contrast with Ferenczi,

DOI: 10.4324/9781003246480-14

the fact that Freud could not conceive of a maternal analyst getting to grips with a patient who is bringing infantile elements that cannot speak.

Other peculiarities of Freud's consulting room could be symptomatic of having had to break free prematurely from the realm of the mother: its setup as a pair of adjoining spaces and the highly evocative objects with which he gradually populated it. While the photographs of his teachers and pupils on the walls supported his more mature identifications, the antiquities he had started to collect around the time when he was inventing psychoanalysis, after his father's death, and which made his consulting room look like an archaeologist's study, seem to be symbols of the rich and plastic preverbal reality abandoned too soon, "a dreamlike world" which had made a deep impact on him since he had visited the Louvre during his time in Paris.[4] Those objects were recovered childish games, fantasies surviving in stone, enigmas to be interpreted or idols for restoring a precious but fragile mother-infant scene that he preferred to situate at a distance, in a remote past. There were statuettes and vases but also masks and funerary decorations. As in his reading of Jensen's *Gradiva* and in the archaeological metaphor that he used to characterise analytic work, he may have felt that enclosed within them there was a still vital childhood which a part of him considered buried, aspects of himself and his mother that, even when he was learning to talk, had remained silently identified with the prematurely dead little brother.[5] His archaeological passion evokes "a ghostlike quality, the character of *revenants*, as it were,"[6] echo of "a status that is neither death nor life,"[7] a crypt-like and sepulchral yet embryonic dimension which Ferenczi called a "teratoma," harbouring fragments of a twin-being who has never developed.[8]

It was on these objects that Freud's gaze rested during sessions. Like Paul Klee, he also seemed to think silently:

> I cannot be grasped in the here and now. For I reside just as much with the dead as with the unborn. Somewhat closer to the heart of creation than usual. But not nearly close enough. The end has met the beginning.
>
> (Klee's epitaph, 1940)[9]

When he later invited the patient to move from the couch to the next room, he had the habit of taking one piece or another from his collection with him and examining it by sight and touch while he illustrated the topic he wanted to explore further.[10] And seized with enthusiasm for the latest addition to his collection, he would come punctually to lunch accompanied by his new find. Like a child absorbed in his game, he placed it beside him on the table to look at and touch while he ate in silence with an occasional nod to Martha, perhaps indicating the children's vacant places. These objects returned him to the sensoriality of the illusions from the preverbal period, whose uncanny "magic" they possessed. Talismans with superstitious value, Freud occasionally destroyed one with the deftness of inattention: a marble Venus, as a sacrifice to destiny for the recovery of his eldest daughter from illness, an Egyptian statuette as a propitiatory gesture to ward off the break with Fliess (in fact, the first sign of a crack in the relationship).[11]

The psychological value of archaeology for Freud also lay in its power to deal with feelings of guilt about death wishes, as Siegfried Bernfeld adds:

> Goethe reports in his autobiography that once as a boy he amused himself by throwing a considerable number of miniature dishes out of a window, and how much he enjoyed their breaking to pieces on the street. Freud analyzed this episode as a typical and healthy reaction of the child to the birth of a younger brother. In his youth Freud was tempted to such violence many times. Perhaps his carefully kept collection of glass and pottery demonstrates his mastery over such urges, and is significant for the protective and generous attitude to his whole family that he kept all through his life.
>
> (1951, p. 121)

The realm of childhood could be dangerous because it is inhabited by a damaged child and a mourning mother. Freud's sensitivity to prophecies, and "prophecies unfulfilled," relates to that potential, primitive part of the self which has been left "unfulfilled," not born, identified with a little brother who had aroused his jealousy and had not even lived long enough to learn to speak.

When he made a gift of these examples to Ferenczi, he unconsciously intended to entrust to his younger friend's "maternal womb" his own desire for illusion, his nostalgia and fear, and his regret over certain childhood promises not kept,[12] just as he had tacitly commissioned Ferenczi's exceptional clinical laboratory to conduct psychoanalytic experiments in the field of the transference-countertransference relationship and the traumatic areas of psychic life.

Research into telepathy is Freud's renewed attempt to regain intimacy with the maternal language, something he experiences as an excess of communication or a surplus of meaning,[13] that "oceanic" sensory fusionality that he fears will have more to do with death than with birth if he looks more deeply into it. In his attempt to circumvent this inner obstacle, Freud's theoretical position touches on the primitive aspects of unconscious communication and psychic continuity in certain singular, isolated but more controllable experiences, "a type of mechanistic, telepathic exchange of information between two individuals."[14]

In the session, "thought-transference" characterises a distinctive dimension of "distant proximity," "empathy at a safe distance":[15] telepathy, a kind of oxymoron, indicates both a lack of empathy and identification (a region of obtuseness towards empathy on the pattern of a negative hallucination) and the presence of the underlying unconscious identification which demands to come to consciousness[16] and is "unmasked" by means of the other.[17]

The associations experienced by Freud as telepathy seem to be precious but unexpected and dissonant fragments of a disturbed transmission sequestering his deep intimacy with B in his impotence, his jealousy, and his father-fixation, but above all his longing to return to his mother: islands in a feared "oceanic feeling," a *folie à deux*, a "contagion"[18] highlight by contrast the surrounding deficit of empathy.

We understand that the stammering B's despairing helplessness, his still-unarticulated affectivity – the wish to possess, the rage, envy, and scorn – could mirror that of Freud in his first relationship with the feminine and with the richness of its generative power, awakening the memory of the child he and of the little brother who had not survived. Bernfeld is able to reanimate Sigmund's double, Julius, perhaps reminding the analyst by his surname about the promise of a birth-nest (*Born field*) alongside the pain of a death-nest. In the end, telepathy really does show itself, metaphorically, to be a way of calling up spirits, of bringing the dead back to life and communicating with them.

Because of his violent life-impulse, Freud has to make himself resistant and emotionally obtuse to the patient but also to this part of himself; he must try to look ahead and survive, bringing with him this crypt, a past that is projected into his future like an obscure warning: *Vorsicht!*

Unconsciously capitalising on what could have been traumatic, he seems to join Goethe in proclaiming that the roots of his strength lay in the rapport he had had with his mother:

> I was a child of fortune: destiny preserved my life . . . removed my brother, so that I did not have to share my mother's love with him. . . . if a man has been his mother's undisputed darling he retains throughout life the triumphant feeling, the confidence in success, which not seldom brings actual success along with it.
>
> (Freud, 1917a, p. 156)

Along this path, the secret language's term Forsyte (every man for himself!) ends up as the Forsite that we find in the manuscript. Freud's repeated, insistent slip in writing the word expresses the longing for the mother as a place of safety (*For site*) deeply stamped in his Jewish roots, which will lead him to find in England a *Promised Land* where he can end his life in freedom.

More than the "telepathic" and oracular importance of the manifest experience, it is this profound interweaving, of which we can only recognise and follow certain cruxes and coincidences, which motivated the interest, and the associated resistances, stirred up in Freud by the Forsyth case.

In *Lecture XXX*, the enigma of telepathy remains unsolved: like Prince Hamlet, Freud asserts that "There are more things in heaven and earth, Horatio, than are dreamt of in your philosophy," but at the end, he concludes, "All this is still uncertain and full of unsolved riddles; but there is no reason to be frightened by it" (p. 55).

We can now conceive a "thought-transference" that is a whirlpool of paths of meaning into which flow intense desires that have the immediate wisdom of the heart and speak the universal language of Nature which – returning to the essay attributed to Goethe and beloved by Freud – "is ever shaping new forms . . . is incessantly speaking to us, but betrays not her secret . . . has always thought and always thinks."[19]

A ubiquitous and superior form of language, a network from which other languages are derived and propagated, "thought-transference" reflects the continuity of the transmission of psychic life, that "crossroads" and crossing over where the generations pass the baton to each other, where language renews its symbols and time renews its own dimension between prophecy of the past and memory of the future.

Don Giovanni: *Zitto, mi pare sentire odor di femmina . . .*

In the Forsyth case, there is still something to be "sniffed out" as Derrida (1981) puts it, a final context to be revealed if we are to reach the centre of the Russian doll.

Naturally we have been wondering – rightly – why on earth Freud neglects any present reference to the theme of woman, which is evident in all three of the session's *Einfälle*, and why in particular he makes no comment when Paul Bernfeld mentions his daughter. Freud leaves the traces of the woman "hidden" on the surface and uses a conjuring trick to make her disappear. As in "The Purloined Letter" by Edgar Allan Poe, the woman "escapes observation by dint of being excessively obvious."

Just as the continuum of exchanges with Paul B has lost coherence and affective significance in Freud's treatment of them, so the lineaments of the feminine image, seen too close up to be put into focus, remain disconnected and end up being blurred in the background of the session: what was manifest becomes "not seen." The long-deferred publication of the case and the uprooting of the experience from its historical, emotional, and relational circumstances complete the occultation.

Nevertheless, with the effrontery of one who is entirely above suspicion, Freud has left a clearly visible trail. Like a challenge, his *Vorsicht* is addressed to us too: *Look out!*

In 1997, having recently become a member of the Italian Psychoanalytic Society and the IPA, and reading the case for the first time, I wondered: doesn't Anna's analysis lie behind Freud's "telepathy"? Might the investment of the daughter be the incestuous-traumatic nucleus, the "present," shared by the analyst and Herr B – the hesitant courtier of the young virgin – which makes Freud unconsciously insist on *prudence*? And was his choosing her as his heir the real *foresight* into the future with which he projects himself beyond death?

After all, in the end, Freud's "crown prince" was a woman: "The grey *mare* is the better horse," writes Galsworthy in *The Man of Property* (p. 59).

As I reconstructed the session's coherence within its context, using the historical documentation that has become gradually available to us over the years, or which I myself have been able to recover, the pieces of the mosaic began to find their proper place, and Anna's face kept reappearing with all its multiple nuances.

Paul B's repeated communications all led back to this crucial presence in Freud's affections and his care of him, of which he may well have been highly jealous. Freud censors this element, excluding it from his own associations: though to what extent he is conscious of doing so, we cannot know. From the start of the session, PB's symptomatic prudence with his young virginal beloved brings the incestuous fantasy into play, the confrontation with the uncanny genital female and the limit, the taboo imposed by paternal power.[20] And it is in fact the young woman who speaks up in the first coincidence, wondering what Paul B's hesitant courtship really says about the state of his affection for her: by coining the nickname *Vorsicht*, her voice enters the secret language of the analysis like a warning to the powerful *Forsyte*.

How could we not picture this "beautiful, piquante, but poor girl" as Anny Hager Weisskopf, the same age as Anna Freud, whom Bernfeld may have been courting at the time and will marry in 1931?[21]

PB's later question – whether it is Freud's daughter who teaches at the People's University – is right on target. There actually was a young woman who was a teacher and dabbled in English: and needless to say, Freud passed onto her the novels that Bernfeld had lent him. . . .[22] The "English" associative thread of jealousy involves Anna, who was elbowing her way through the crowd of siblings, pupils, and patients (even threatening Jones). Who can say if the reference to the double-barrelled surname (Freud-Ottorego) led Freud to detect in Paul B's enquiry a question about whether his daughter was still a virgin or married, sounding out the exclusiveness of her relationship with her father?

Freud does not comment on the theme of incestuous fantasy repeatedly and insistently brought into play by the patient, including the gift of the second book by Galsworthy. In *Indian Summer of a Forsyte*, Irene, the young, beautiful, poor, and silent heroine who sparks love in Old Jolyon Forsyte and stays by him until his death, presents all too many affinities with the third and youngest daughter of destiny, Cordelia, and with what Anna had some time ago begun to represent for Freud.[23] The second novel confirms the woman's role as the Saga's real protagonist – it's not for nothing that the most famous film version of *The Man of Property* has the title *That Forsyte Woman*![24] – but we now have no doubt that the occult presence of the daughter is also playing around the session.

Freud passes too quickly over every opportunity to introduce the woman into the amorous discourse and deflects the patient's jealousy, and our attention, onto his male rivals. He does not even interpret Paul B's final association with the nightmare and the mistaken translation, which could appropriately have been connected to the contentious emergence of incestuous desires and the difficulties with the woman on both oedipal and pre-oedipal levels. Not only does he ignore Jones's tedious monograph which specifically placed repressed incestuous desires at the origin of nightmares and superstition, but he even forgets what he himself had many times reiterated, including in the first part of *Lecture XXX*: the centrality of those intense desires – for the mother, the sister, and the daughter – in the experience of "mind-reading" phenomena.

We do not know how far Paul B had actually intuited Anna's presence in his analyst's thoughts in 1919. It is understandable that Freud did not refer to her in his lecture, although doing so would certainly have strengthened the persuasive force of his argument: the omission of such an important part of the material from the session was partly motivated by discretion but also by obstacles of which he was unaware because they were traumatic and which prevented him from acknowledging the deep meaning of his relationship with Anna and the far from "prudent" analysis he had undertaken with her.

This involved a highly risky "disregard of the strict rules of medical practice" (Freud, 1933, p. 48): the warning "*Vorsicht*" could not fail to remind Freud of Breuer urging him in the past to be prudent and of Ferenczi's pertinent observations about the "present" content of "thought-transferences."[25] The ongoing treatment of young Anna and the unconscious complexes being reactivated in it constituted important elements of Freud's disturbed empathy and his resistance to the intimacy of preconscious communication with Paul Bernfeld at the base of the countertransferential "telepathic effect": that kind of "curse-blessing" at the beginning of the session.[26]

When Edoardo Weiss asked his advice in 1935 about his intention to analyse his own son, Freud did not firmly dissuade him and, confiding in the young Triestine as he had done from the start of their acquaintance (even seeking his opinion about telepathy and occultism), gave him a detailed account of his analysis with Anna. He took the opportunity to make a remarkable distinction: that that it might be simpler to analyse a daughter or a *younger brother* than a son.

> concerning the analysis of your hopeful son, that is certainly a ticklish business. With a younger, promising brother it might be done more easily. With one's own daughter I succeeded well. There are special difficulties and doubts with a son.
>
> (1/11/1935)

Freud had always maintained an idealisation of his relationship with his mother and the perennial need to deny feelings of hostility towards her, as he denied those towards his younger brother Julius (and then Alexander). In the case of Julius, he was still too young to have the words to translate his own complex feelings.[27] We understand how it was only in relation to his sister Anna that he was broadly able to manifest envy and jealousy in a genuine and vital relationship. Anna was her father's favourite, as Freud was his mother's,[28] and Roudinesco reports:

> When she was about sixteen, [Anna] was courted by an old uncle of the Nathanson family who had set out seek a new wife and claimed he would take her to Odessa. Horrified by the idea of a consanguineous union between an adolescent and an old man, Freud opposed it vigorously.
>
> (2014, p. 22)

Sigmund had woven this intensely loved and equally intensely hated sister into his life's great romantic choice, falling in love with her friend, Martha, and planning a simultaneous Freud-Bernays wedding, a kind of double pairing of brothers and sisters. Despite his protestations, it was Anna's name that he gave his youngest child.

The violation of boundaries in the analysis of his daughter, conducted without the "*special difficulties and doubts*" which would arise with a son, needs to be acknowledged as the outcome of the childhood distress that had disturbed Freud's early relationship with his mother and as an attempt at rectification.

Notes

1 Wittels, 1924; Riviere, 1939; Graf, 1942; Sachs, 1945; Jones, II; Pankeiev, in Albano, 1987.
2 Freud, 1919a.
3 Doolittle 1956, p. 147.
4 Sigmund to Martha, 19/10/1885.
5 From *Gradiva*, Freud quoted: "the female sex had been to him no more than the concept of something made of marble or bronze" (1907, p. 12).
6 Binswanger, 1957, p. 103.
7 Bernfeld, 1951, p. 119.
8 (1930) Freud's ashes would then rest in an urn from the collection (Hidas, 1993).
9 Klee F. ed. (1964) *The Diaries of Paul Klee 1898–1918* Univ. California press 1968, p. 419.
10 Sachs, 1945; Cremerius, 1985; Albano, 1987.
11 Freud, 1901, pp. 169–170.
12 Pierri, 2012, 2022.
13 Massicotte, 2014.
14 Aziz, 1990, p. 118.
15 Pierri, 2016a.
16 Bolognini states that if there is identification, there is no unconscious projective identification (2002).
17 Servadio, quoting Hollòs, says that, in the impasse the patient "carries out a sort of vicarious parapraxis, substituting himself for the analyst and 'betraying' him" (1955b, p. 29).
18 Grotstein, 2005.
19 Tobler G C (1783) "Nature: Aphorisms by Goethe" English translation by T H Huxley, *Nature*, Nov. 4, 1869.
20 Freud, 1918b.
21 See Chapter 17.
22 For instance, *Anna of the Five Towns by* Arnold Bennett (Young-Bruehl, 1988).
23 See Pierri, 2022.
24 In 1949, with Greer Garson and Errol Flynn, directed by Compton Bennett.
25 "It has already frequently occurred to me that a patient . . . sometimes includes things in his associations that occupy me with particular intensity. . . . I note that countertransference is mostly derived from the content of present or ucs.-aroused complexes (dreams, errors, unresolved matters)" Ferenczi to Freud, 17/08/1910. See Pierri, 2022.
26 See Sapisochin on countertransference, 2004.
27 Krüll, 1979.
28 Bernays Heller, 1956.

Chapter 14

Retrospective

The lost scene

Caritas Romana: "This is the place, this is the source"

There are those who have noted the indifference with which the psychoanalytic movement received Freud's writings on telepathy, all the more remarkable when we think how attentively all his other works were examined and subjected to exegetical research.[1] It is possible that the Forsyth case in particular has been neglected by the psychoanalytic literature out of reticence, a collegial protective concern for Freud, and indeed for Anna. In the past, other analysts must have made the same associations about the case as I have, despite Freud's manoeuvres of distraction and concealment: certainly Servadio did, though he makes no explicit reference to the analysis of Anna, whom he knew personally; Granoff and Rey probably did, but they choose to stop on the threshold. Peter Gay, realising that what intrigued Freud about occultism was telepathy, "inconclusive though he thought the evidence," associates this interest with Freud's relationship with his daughter and dismisses the subject with an enigmatic sentence: "When he told Abraham in 1925 that Anna possessed 'telepathic sensitivity' he was only half joking."[2]

Freud allowed himself transgressions that would be unforgivable in any analyst today but were part of the founding scene, the "origins" of psychoanalysis. He afforded himself the privileges of kings and queens, demons and gods, founding heroes.[3] Besides analysing his closest pupils and their patient-lovers,[4] Freud practised analysis on his younger brother Alexander and was unembarrassed about taking siblings into treatment (Anton von Freund and Kata Levy, Margarethe and Marianne Rie, daughters of Oscar Rie) and even spouses (James and Alix Strachey).

Jung had analysed his wife and his young daughter Agathli during the period when he was treating Spielrein; Ferenczi treated both Gizella and Elma; Groddeck and Rank analysed their wives;[5] and Abraham, Brill, and, later, Klein would subject their own children to analysis and then refer to them in scientific works. . . . There is no shortage of examples.

Britton writes that, as with all more radical discoveries, it is not the generation that makes them that fully realises their practical implications but the successors

DOI: 10.4324/9781003246480-15

(2003). Paul Roazen, who learned from Anton von Freund's sister, Kata Levy, who had been Anna Freud's analyst,[6] was the first to talk about this publicly in *Brother Animal: The Story of Freud and Tausk*, presenting it as "the most extraordinary illustration of Freud's allowing himself privileges he might have condemned in any other analyst."[7] This point was diplomatically ignored by Kurt Eissler, then director of the Sigmund Freud Archives and very close to Anna: he played it down, as something widely known, while refuting the rest of the book point by point.[8]

Few analysts have dealt with the problematic topic of Freud's relationship with his daughter, and, even after Anna's death in 1982 and the publication of her biography by Young-Bruehl in 1988, for a long time it was left to non-analysts to address this fragment of Freud's biography and this piece of psychoanalytic history.[9]

It is understandable that a certain lapse of time was necessary in order to overcome the embarrassment caused by the detailed description of Anna's analytic treatment by her father, made public by Young-Bruehl, which initially appeared to be the product of an intrusive and disrespectful curiosity. See, for example, the review by Solnit, one of Anna Freud's pupils and collaborators, written fully 8 years after the book's publication and almost 15 years after Anna's death (1996).

Among the various authors who have been interested in the identity of Freud's patients, Cremerius was the first to cite Anna, albeit fleetingly, but curiously he names her in relation to payment, wondering if the daughter had paid the father any fee (1985).

What kind of currency, what "gold or fake coin," will have passed between Sigmund and Anna?

There are those who have rightly wondered how it might be possible to learn something about this highly important chapter in the history of psychoanalysis: documents alone can tell the historian nothing about unconscious processes. What sources might there be to draw on? as Ernst Federn wondered in 1985.[10]

More recently, some female analysts have begun to reflect on how much, and in what way, that treatment influenced Anna's destiny.[11] But as Gay was already suggesting in 1988, what did it mean for Freud to analyse her; what was the cost for him personally; and how did this experience become interwoven with his own existence and the development of psychoanalytic theory, technique, and clinical practice? And also, how far can this analysis be a paradigm for the transmission of knowledge and the handing over of its intrinsic powers more generally in training analyses?[12]

My starting point in addressing what could been hastily filed away by supporters or flaunted by opponents as a false step of Freud's was the attempt to regain the burdensome but precious legacy that has been passed down to us and relates to the contradictory and transgressive essence of the unconscious,[13] to evaluate where the errors are in that series of inspired and risky explorations which accompany great discoveries and introduce the new. They are painful errors for which the protagonists paid with their own destiny: incestuous couples whom we rediscover at the origins of psychoanalysis and who functioned as "generative dyads."[14]

To which other person could Freud ever have entrusted his daughter? To whom else could Anna ever have been able to make her appeal for love? And which of his pupils would have felt able to analyse the child of such a father?[15]

The Forsyth case may provide the indirect source for learning something about the unconscious processes involved in this vitally important chapter for the history of psychoanalysis and its thought. It offers an entirely particular glimpse of the desire and traumatic necessities that were behind Freud's analysis of Anna: maybe today it is possible to talk about it and try to understand how this became part of Freud himself, inscribed in his flesh and in the theory that we try to master and convey to our pupils.[16]

In the discovery of the unconscious, Anna's symbolic destiny appears tied to the frontiers of Freud's thought. It opens with the patient Anna O, who becomes ill with day-dreaming at the bedside of her adored father (Sigmund Pappenheim); it concludes with Anna F, who, as she cares for her father (Sigmund Freud), tries to cure herself of her own daytime phantasies: the dawn and difficult sunset of the Oedipus complex. In both experiences, we can think in terms of a cure "with a defect." In their incestuous storylines, the two scenes of caring seem to combine and fold into each other: the seduction endorsed in the first scene but left in the background will be denied and enacted in the second.

Can we speak of *transference* and *countertransference* in these areas of the psyche? We are venturing into the birthplace of both subject and object, the umbilical place where maternal and foetal cells are circulating together. It is a "two-in-one psychology." It is the area outside time belonging to *in*-fancy and *pro*-phecy where the parents' visionary and oracular function can support the emergence of words that prepare the future.

In order to become master of his own destiny and free himself from fate (from *fari*, that which was announced),[17] Oedipus must be able to encounter the history and desire of Laius and Jocasta. In order to face its limitation and the impasse in treatment, the theory of *transference* must be opened up to a theory of relationship.

This is confirmation of how addressing the relationship between Freud and his daughter Anna may lead us to explore "psychic areas associated with origins": the origins of the affective relationship and the origins of psychoanalysis.[18]

In his novel, *The Retrospective* (2011), exploring the mystery of creativity, Abraham Yehoshua focuses on the representation of the *Caritas Romana*.

This is an extraordinary creation, a topic that inspired many classic paintings, originating in the legend of Pero and Cimon, written in the first century AD by Valerius Maximus in *Factorum et dictorum memorabilium libri IX* (Acts and Words to Remember): the story tells of a father condemned to die of starvation in prison but saved by the filial piety of his daughter, who offers him her milk. Portrayed by countless painters, the impact of this invention, which seems to undermine reality, provoking wonder and bewilderment, is greater in the paintings than in the story.[19] Every artist, from Guido Reni to Caravaggio, from Rubens to Murillo, tried to come up with his own version. In 1606, Caravaggio was able to insert the scene, so scandalous in its carnality, in the altarpiece for the church of

Pio Monte della Misericordia in Naples, camouflaging its sensuality among other deeds of bodily mercy.

The story of Pero saving Cimon with her milk may represent one of the varied and unexpected forms taken on by the oedipal configuration and the generous giver of love, *Caritas-Agape*, at the origin of psychic existence. The scene lost with the mother is relived with the daughter.

In 1935, quoting *Faust* [II, 7003], Freud would confide to Lou Andreas Salomé: "In the end we depend/On the creatures we made."[20]

What better image could there be than *lactatio* to portray the miraculous and perturbing relationship in which Freud and Anna found themselves united and imprisoned, attempting to reconstitute the original nutritive unity of mother and child via the incestuous fantasy of analysis?

Abraham B. Yehoshua writes:

> This is the place, this is the source. . . . The milk is warm – strong sweetish mother's milk with a mysterious taste. . . . Well, then, this is the fantasy. The inspiration I craved has returned, he muses with joy. I am drinking it straight into the chambers of my heart, against the reality that strangles us.[21]

A destiny and a choice made long ago

In the autumn of 1918, a few months after turning 62, a date which was supposed to have marked his death, at the peak of his existence but inwardly turning towards its decline, Freud had undertaken the analytic treatment of his daughter Anna, then aged 23. We have been keeping this fact in reserve.

In the critical phase of confrontation with the new upcoming generation, when the Oedipal conflict was returning with all its passionate violence, Freud had disinvested affectively from those children and pupils whom he imagined capable not only of parricide but, in particular, of not acknowledging their father: heirs who he feared were all too ready to take over and transform the tradition of knowledge they had received, denying its roots. And in his new orientation, he who had put Jung, Ferenczi, and Jones on guard against entangling their destinies with their young patients, Sabina, Elma, and Loe, and had rescued his daughter from the Welshman's amorous assault, eventually chose Anna for himself.

We cannot know if Jung had Freud's relationship with Anna in mind when in old age he finally declared his own relationship with Wolff *ethically* necessary and healthy, claiming that he had all too often noted the untold damage that fathers can do to their daughters "by not living the whole of their erotic life." When his wife was expecting their fifth child at the end of 1913, he confided to Barbara Hannah that he had spent a sleepless night before deciding to impose his lover openly on the family in the conviction that to "refuse to live the outside attraction that had come to him entirely from the unconscious against his will" would inevitably ruin the eros of his daughters.[22]

Freud did not spend sleepless nights waiting for Anna, but the choice of his "third daughter," a choice made long before, was deeply rooted in his dreams.[23]

He had not passed completely unscathed through the richness and danger of the sexual material he was exploring. The unintended and symptomatic conceiving of Anna, occurring in the context of his treatment of Emma Eckstein and the surgical operation performed by Fliess,[24] answered to his unconscious fantasies of acquiring the mother with his friend's fraternal support. In congratulating each other on the simultaneous pregnancies (for Fliess and his wife, this was their long-awaited first born, for the Freuds the last, when no further children had been planned), as if he were competing with his colleague in Berlin, Freud's associations immediately turned to his sister, Anna (born on 31 December): "*We* are prepared for December/January," he wrote to Fliess.[25]

We do not know how far Martha had already put up with Sigmund's heart problems and hypochondria, his "transferential" illness in relation to Fliess, and his cathexis to his young seductive patients and to psychoanalysis. We cannot rule out the possibility that it was she who entered the session, surprising her husband with Emma Eckstein's arms around his neck and not the "servant," as in Freud's second version of the discovery of the transference:[26]

> I had an experience which showed me in the crudest light what I had long suspected. It related to one of my most acquiescent patients, with whom hypnotism had enabled me to bring about the most marvellous results, and whom I was engaged in relieving of her suffering by tracing back her attacks of pain to their origins. As she woke up on one occasion, she threw her arms round my neck. The unexpected entrance of a servant relieved us from a painful discussion, but from that time onwards there was a tacit understanding between us that the hypnotic treatment should be discontinued. I was modest enough not to attribute the event to my own irresistible personal attraction, and I felt that I had now grasped the nature of the mysterious element that was at work behind hypnotism.
>
> (1925, p. 27)

Unlike Breuer, who had withdrawn from any affective investment in hysterical patients and stopped treating them, the pupil had made a virtue of necessity and continued along the road they had indicated, making use of his own acute intelligence as he had done in the past: dissociating himself from personal involvement, he had sublimated it into the passion for knowledge, strengthening his ardour for research, as he would say of Leonardo. With the investment in thought and verbal language which had enabled him to construct psychoanalysis, he had partly sacrificed his affects. As Wilhelm Reich would intuit before Winnicott, Freud "was caught in words."[27]

In his *Clinical Diary*, Sàndor Ferenczi expressed the conviction that, having thrown himself body and soul into treating patients, Freud had been scorched when the countertransference and the exciting, disappointing aspects of the first relationship with the mother had suddenly "opened up before him like an abyss."[28]

It must have been a challenging moment and, as we know, Freud would later confide in Jung:

> Such experiences, though painful, are necessary and hard to avoid. Without them we cannot really know life and what we are dealing with. I myself have never been taken in quite so badly, but I have come very close to it a number of times and had a narrow escape. I believe that only grim necessities weighing on my work, and the fact that I was ten years older than yourself when I came to ΨA, have saved me from similar experiences. But no lasting harm is done. They help us to develop the thick skin we need and to dominate "countertransference," which is after all a permanent problem for us; they teach us to displace our own affects to best advantage.
>
> (7/06/1909)

It had not just been good sense, modesty, fear, or pride that gave him a path to safety but age and the grim necessities weighing on his work. Freud was not someone to put his own existence at risk and to let himself be overcome by his feelings (highly reserved with his family, he rarely even kissed his children, and kissed his mother almost dutifully during his weekly visits).[29] He had the composed presence of Martha alongside him, someone quite different from Mathilde Breuer or Emma Jung, more aware of and prepared for the dangers and inevitability of hysteria, firm and severe in her ethical and familial convictions.

In this way Freud had made himself a "thick skin." A scar of insensitivity remained, comparable to that repression of the affects that he described as "the peace that has descended upon a battlefield strewn with corpses" when "no trace is left of the struggle which raged over it."[30]

In 1912, he could claim:

> I cannot advise my colleagues too urgently to model themselves during psychoanalytic treatment on the surgeon, who puts aside all his feelings, even his human sympathy, and concentrates his mental forces on the single aim of performing the operation as skilfully as possible.
>
> (p. 115)

Even his married life had to suffer this.

"Little Freud": a child is being conceived

Unlike the legend of pregnancy involving Anna O and the Breuers,[31] the Freuds' *real* pregnancy, happening in these circumstances and through an unconscious error, caused a profound marital crisis in Berggasse, enough to make us think that, paradoxically, it was just when the sexuality of the transference was being discovered that Sigmund and Martha found themselves eliminating their own.[32]

Martha was fully engrossed in her relationship with two-year-old Sophie, the "Sunday child"[33] with whom she was having a particularly rewarding experience of motherhood: she misunderstood the first signs of pregnancy and attributed them to an incipient menopause (at the age of 34!). It became a much more difficult pregnancy than her previous ones in terms of her health; she suffered from varicose veins, and yet in her sixth month, feeling unusually anxious, she insisted on travelling with her husband when he went away.[34]

Sigmund, who during his cardiac neurosis had confided to Fliess, "My libido has long been subdued,"[35] was now committed to the parallel gestation of his own scientific achievement and was testing the limits of the seduction theory: having written the *Studies*, he was beginning to analyse his dreams and to understand their meaning.

Psychoanalysis was, so to speak, born in Freud as a nostalgia for immortality in the brief space between his father's death and Anna's birth.[36] During the summer of 1895, after receiving old Jacob's gloomy diagnosis, the unconscious working-through of the conception and Martha's pregnancy took shape in the dream of Irma's injection, of which his daughter was an occult protagonist. Recalling statements made by Anna O, this dream could be given the title, "Now Dr Freud's child is coming!"[37] or "A child is being conceived,"[38] in recognition of the form which would henceforth be taken by the paternal transference towards the baby who was on the way, prefiguring the future bond between them.

In October, contemplating the possibility of a daughter – a son would certainly have been called "Wilhelm" – Freud began to fantasise about her as "Anna"[39] in honour of Anna Hammerschlag Lichtheim, the family friend and patient who had appeared in the dream as Irma, inaugurating the new method, and whom he had in mind as godmother for the baby. "Irma's name was Anna, therefore Anna," Freud explained to Marie Bonaparte.[40] He had chosen the names of his children inspired by significant figures. Gay states that he never gave family names to his children, forgetting that Anna was also his sister's name (1988).

However they might have been denied, affects and fantasies were being unconsciously directed towards his sister Anna and to the deep and intricate rapport that had bonded him with her since childhood: the figure of the dream Irma-Anna was connected to the birth of his sister and to the fears raised by his infantile sexual curiosity, and the fault of the dream would be the possessive and sadistic attack on the mother's body.[41]

In parallel, in order to perpetuate his friendship with Fliess, he hoped that meanwhile in Berlin a Pauline would be born (after his friend's sister, who had died young).[42] In December, while he was preparing to baptise his discipline and give it the name "Psycho-analysis," Freud was heartened by the vitality of its new-born "twin,"[43] and, even though she was a new mouth to feed, he considered little Anna a good omen for his work and for the arrival of patients.[44]

Martha was not so happy and did not feel up to breastfeeding the baby. This time Freud did not resort to hypnosis to help her, as he seems to have done in the past,[45] nor did they employ a wetnurse. Unlike her siblings, Anna was bottle-fed using the first artificial milk, Gärtner whole milk,[46] which could have put her life at risk in those days, and being deprived of her mother posed a serious threat to her psychic survival, leaving the trace of a lack that would accompany her throughout her life.

Even later on, Martha found it hard to look after her baby and left her in the care of a maid: she struggled to recover, developed a strange disturbance in her hand (Freud diagnosed a scribe's paresis)[47] and, when the baby was only ten months old, without thinking twice about abandoning her, went on holiday by herself for the first time since she was married. Despite her devotion to her husband and children, this time Martha left them and sought help from her mother, and perhaps also from Ida and Wilhelm Fliess: after visiting Hamburg, she stayed in Berlin to see little Robert Wilhelm, who had been born a few weeks after Anna.

After a holiday in Italy with his brother Alexander, Sigmund was in fact already detaching himself from his friend and dealing with his father's death very much on his own. The event inevitably brought him closer to his mother, who once again imposed her distress and narcissistic needs exclusively on him: from then on, she began the habit of spending most of every Sunday with her Sigmund, provoking his regressive weekend "attacks of indigestion."[48]

Shortly after her return to Vienna, Martha brought her younger sister, who had been living with their mother in Hamburg, into the house. The profound significance of this change, made possible by Freud having moved his consulting room onto the first floor of the building, is symptomatic and not easy to understand. The sister-in-law was certainly a great help with looking after the children and in general family life: but even though there were "two mothers" in the house, despite this abundance, the youngest child was entrusted to Josefine Cihlarz, the *kinderfrau* who was devoted to her and became the most important figure for Anna to identify with in childhood.[49]

Minna may have supported Martha in dealing with the increasingly demanding mother-in-law and maybe with her husband too, given the fact that Minna's room adjoined the couple's bedroom and she had to pass through theirs every time she wanted to go to her own. It is highly likely that Sigmund and Martha's relationship would not have survived without the presence of Minna,[50] which initially enabled Martha and Sigmund to take some brief holidays on their own. In August 1897, there was a first trip to Venice, Tuscany, and Umbria, but Sigmund was intolerant of his wife's ailments and the delays to their planned itinerary. The second attempt, to Italy again and then Dalmatia, ended with Martha staying in Dubrovnik while Sigmund went on alone, struggling to suppress his disappointment and aggression. The forgetting of the name Signorelli is rooted in that circumstance, the repression of the phrase "Herr, you must know, that if that comes to an end then life is of no value."[51] In 1911, he wrote to Emma Jung that his marriage had been amortised for some time now and there was nothing left but . . . to die.[52]

Apart from one last attempt in 1900, and the sacrosanct visits to spas, from then on it would be Minna who accompanied her brother-in-law on his summer travels and shared his discoveries, occupying the place previously held by his brother Alexander and Fliess. Minna developed a passion for the new discipline that Sigmund was constructing, whereas Martha preferred the tranquillity of family life and the summer break to the adventure of travelling with her husband and perhaps also welcomed the other break from his conjugal demands; besides, she was quite mistrustful of psychoanalysis, which she considered "a form of pornography" to be kept far away from her children's bedroom.[53]

Her conception of married life was quiet and rigorous. She would soon manifest that focusing of her interest in order, cleanliness, and household management that Freud would describe as a change of character typical of ageing women caused by the cooling of conjugal love.[54] There may also have been a re-emergence of Martha's old resentment at the absolute separation from her mother and her family which Sigmund had imposed, also compelling her to give up the rites of Judaism which he dismissed as "pure superstition,"[55] turning her existence upside down. It is striking that in 1939, a week after her husband's death, she resumed the habit of lighting candles to celebrate the *Shabbat*, as if more than half a century had not passed.[56]

At the height of the marital crisis, while engaged in his self-analysis and mourning his father, Sigmund had also started to treat his younger brother Alexander's symptoms of "hysteria." And while he was lamenting to Fliess that he had no choice but to conclude that his own father had been a pervert, in the same letter he was expressing the wish to make analytic incursions into the life of his growing daughter:

> Why do I not go into the nursery and experiment with Annerl? . . . the womenfolk do not support my researches.
>
> (8/02/1897)

After attacking their fathers' generation, it was only a short time, with the discovery of the transference and infantile sexual fantasy, that he was absolving his own generation, and himself, from the same errors, without ever being able to settle his account with the maternal. He realised how, in his own dreams, more and more obvious prominence was being given to his wish for possession and deeply repressed hostility towards his mother and his wife – both so idealised and loved – because of the nutritive richness and exclusive love they could deny. In early 1898 he wrote to Fliess:

> [I] had a delightful dream about it, which unfortunately cannot be published because its background, its second meaning, shifts back and forth between my nurse (my mother) and my wife and one cannot really publicly subject one's wife to reproaches of this sort [as a reward] for all her labor and toil.
>
> (09/02/1898)

It was because of this evident resentment towards Martha that he was forced to give up the idea of using that "delightful dream," "the only dream Freud ever analyzed completely,"[57] which he would have preferred as his exemplar to the earlier one about Irma's injection. He sacrificed it with great regret – we have no other mention of it – because of its irrevocable censorship by Fliess:

> Let me know at least which topic it was to which you took exception and where you feared an attack by a malicious critic. Whether it is my anxiety, or Martha, or the *Dalles* [a Yiddish word for "poverty" or "misery"], or my being without a fatherland?
>
> (Freud to Fliess, 9/06/1898)

At this point it may be right to ask ourselves once again, as many still do, what role Minna's presence may have played for Freud and for his love life, independently of the trustworthiness or otherwise of Jung's testimony, dating from 1907–1909. Starting from the mutual analysis during the American voyage and from the non-interpretation of Freud's dream about his wife and sister-in-law, could this element of his inner life have played a hidden role in the break with Jung and in the painful and inextricable bond with Ferenczi?[58] And maybe, earlier still, in the detachment from Fliess?[59]

There is no disputing that Minna was an "extremely important figure" for Freud, nor that she may have stirred "fantasies of a sexual encounter" and "pregnancy" in him, detectable in dreams or slips.[60] And yet this is the real secret before which we can do nothing but cite the formula dear to Freud, *non liquet*: the available evidence is inconclusive.

Whatever the case, it was by way of a sister (Anna-Minna) that Freud transferred his affective investment from the wife-mother to the daughter.

Me too!

The relationship with his youngest child opened up a space for Freud's hunger for life: it made possible a resumption of contact with the infantile agencies of primary need and exclusivity. The father allowed himself to seduce and be seduced by little *Annerl*, attaching himself to her with a privileged bond that excluded his wife: he loved the girl's mixture of rebellion, cheekiness, boldness, and impertinence (*Unartigkeit*), which made her his enchanting rascal, his black devil (*Schwarzer Teufel*), and he took to greeting her with a particular noise in his throat, a sound that imitated her grunt of protest.

It is likely that Anna was the daughter, "then a big schoolgirl," whom Jones recalls "cuddling on his lap in a manner that showed no doubt at all of his affection or his readiness to show it."[61] Of course, for the daughter given over so early to her father's care, this indulgence and complicity could not compensate for the lack of her mother and instead deepened the coldness of Martha, who would have preferred her to be more docile and feminine, and of Sophie who, besides being her rival, was too different in character and attitudes to understand her.

A dream of Anna's when she was little, quoted by her father together with one of her grandmother Amalia (as undeformed satisfactions of desire in reaction to somatic stimuli),[62] shows the lack of maternal containment (the gastric upset and vomiting) and the oral frustration suffered by the girl, as well as Freud's highly concentrated cathexis on his youngest child and his mother:[63]

> I have a note of a dream dreamt by a little girl of nineteen months, which consisted of a menu, to which her own name was attached: "Anna F., stwawbewwies, wild stwawbewwies, omblet, pudden!" This was a reaction to a day without food, owing to a digestive upset, which had actually been traced back to the fruit which appeared twice in the dream. The little girl's grandmother – their combined ages came to seventy years – was simultaneously obliged to go without food for a whole day on account of a disturbance due to a floating kidney. She dreamt the same night that she had been "asked out" and had been served with the most appetizing delicacies.
>
> (1916, p. 132)

Though as a child, Anna could become tiresome with her constant demands to have or do the same as her older siblings ("Me too" was her perpetual cry),[64] later on, she would display a modesty and unpretentiousness that she called "altruistic surrender"[65] as a defence against her most genuine, ambitious, and rebellious protest.

Anna grew up feeling undesired and considering herself undesirable, clumsy, and stupid . . . like a boy manqué, which was also a defence against her father's incestuous seduction. Psychoanalysis was the "soundtrack"[66] of her childhood, a dialogue with her father whom she began to accompany on his walks and in his reflections. Deeply attached to him, highly sensitive to his most elusive moods and ill disposed towards her mother, she became a bored teenager, shy at school, inclined to melancholy and feelings of abandonment, and went through a brief phase of anorexia. At the age of 13, she was taken by Martha without warning to have an appendectomy, which sharpened her resentment against her mother and probably her feelings of castration.[67]

Anna was not just unhappy but also felt inadequate or "stupid" because of her growing sense of guilt about masturbation and her intense daydreaming. She even complained about the name they had chosen for her because Anna Hammerschlag Lichtheim was not beautiful and fascinating like Sophie Schwab Paneth, her sister's godmother.[68]

She considered the name "Anna" too banal. Like her father, she always denied that it had anything to do with her aunt or any association with the pseudonym given to Breuer's first patient in the *Studies*. Freud tried to console her by pointing out that "Anna" was a palindrome, a name that could go "in both directions."[69] In fact, like her name, Anna allowed Freud to move in both directions, backwards and forwards in time: an area of ambiguity where he could seduce and be seduced, where he could illuminate or obscure parental responsibility.

Born under the star that conjoined the potentialities and damage of early life, the bond between *the father and the daughter of psychoanalysis* was not just incestuous or symbiotic but "claustrophilic,"[70] belonging to the territory of the embryonic: a place of non-life and non-death. Like a goddess of destiny and birth (one of the Fates, the Parcae, from *pario*, to give birth), for Freud, his third daughter represented the generative maternal place and the possibility of closing his own traumatic wound. She entered the self-analytic process like a "glue"[71] between the invention of psychoanalysis and the origin that was asking to be interrogated.

For the Little Freud, the bond with her father and then with psychoanalysis was her salvation, a cradle, and a prison: a heavy hereditary task of dedication and disobedience.

Notes

1 Farrel, 1983.
2 1988, pp. 442–443.
3 Argentieri, 2005.
4 See Pierri, 2022.
5 Falzeder, 1994.
6 Roazen, 1993, 1995.
7 1969, p. 100.
8 1971. Anna Freud was the first to adopt a policy of silence on the subject (Roazen, 1999).
9 Theweleit, 1990.
10 Ernst Federn, historian, son of Paul Federn, who after surviving the Buchenwald camp and spending some time in America, returned to settle in Vienna in 1972.
11 In Italy, Argentieri, 1992; Cupelloni, 1999, 2003, 2007; Braun and Polojaz, 2004; Trapanese, 2012.
12 Roazen, 2003.
13 Cupelloni, 2003.
14 Berman, 2004, p. 491.
15 According to Roazen, Freud feared that another analyst might "hurt" Anna (2003, p. 113).
16 See Pragier and Faure Pragier, 1993; Lebovici, 1995; Mahony, 1997; Modell, 1997; Spector Person, 1997; Houssier, 2009; in Italy Argentieri, 1992; Pierri, 1997a, 2001b, 2010; Balsamo and Napolitano, 1998.
17 Balsamo, 2000, p. 229.
18 Cupelloni, 2003.
19 But see the success of C. Dickens with *Little Dorrit*, 1855–57.
20 16/05/1935.
21 A. B. Yehoshua, 2011 *Hesed Sefaradi*, English translation by S. Schoffman, 2013.
22 Kress-Rosen, 1993; Hannah, 1976, in Proulx, 1994, p. 105.
23 Pierri, 2022.
24 Anzieu, 1959; Bonomi, 1994; Pierri, 2022.
25 22/06/1895.
26 The first version was the one inserted in the *Studies* 1893, p. 303. See Pierri, 2022.
27 Reich, 1952, p. 94.
28 1/05/1932.
29 H. Freud, 1956.
30 1900, p. 467.
31 Jones, *I*, p. 246–247, see Pierri, 2022.
32 Krüll, 1979.

33 *Sonntagskind,* lucky and happy; Freud's "ray of sunshine," Appignanesi and Forrester, 1992, p. 56.
34 Behling, 2002; Jones, *I*.
35 25/04/1894. See Pierri, 2022.
36 Balsamo and Napolitano, 1998.
37 See Freud to S Zweig 2/07/1932, in Freud E et al, 1976.
38 Anzieu, 1959, p. 145, by analogy with *A Child Is Being Beaten* (see Chapter 15). "The Irma dream reproduces the kind of atmosphere which surrounded the birth of Anna Freud" (*ibid.,* p. 134).
39 Freud to Fliess, 20/10/1895.
40 On 11/16/1925, See also Hartman, 1983; Fichtner, 2010.
41 Hartman, 1983; Blum, 1996.
42 Freud to Fliess, 3/12/1895.
43 Young-Bruehl, 1988.
44 Freud to Fliess, 8/12/1895.
45 see Balsamo and Napolitano, 1998.
46 Freud to Fliess, 8/12/1895.
47 Behling, 2002.
48 Roazen, 1975, p. 46.
49 Young-Bruehl, 1988.
50 Roazen suggests, p. 62.
51 1901, p. 292.
52 Theweleit, 1990.
53 Laforgue, 1956, p. 342.
54 1913b.
55 Jones I, p. 128; Gresser, 1994. Freud refused to have his children circumcised (Bonomi, 2015).
56 Gay, 1988; Behling, 2002; Steiner, 2013.
57 Masson, 1985, p. 10. See also Kris, 1950; Schur, 1966.
58 The former, convinced of the liaison, would have removed paternal authority from Freud; the latter, preconsciously aware, would on the contrary have intensely idealized him, at least up to the time of the *Clinical Diary*. For Rudnytsky, this concealment by Freud, not the fact itself, would be at the origin of the authoritarian and dogmatic drifts of psychoanalysis (2013).
59 See Pierri, 2022.
60 Kerr, 1993, pp. 138–139. See also Swales, 1982, 1998; Kuhn, 1999, quoted in Kerr, 1993, Rudnytsky, 2013.
61 Jones, *II*, p. 432.
62 Freud 1900, 1916–17.
63 It seems to me that no dream of his wife ever appears in Freud's works.
64 Sophie Freud, 1988, p. 302.
65 1936.
66 Sophie Freud, 1988, p. 299.
67 Young-Bruehl, 1988.
68 Respectively daughter and granddaughter of Freud's benefactor S Hammerschlag.
69 Anna to Lou, 12/08/1922.
70 Fachinelli, 1983.
71 Balsamo and Napolitano, 1998, p. 144.

Chapter 15

A hereditary transmission

A daughter is being analysed

During the war years, Anna had grown up. Her English adventure had jolted her out of childhood, and for the first time in her life she had felt, and been, independent. Ernest Jones noticed this immediately, while Freud was taken by surprise: as soon as his daughter had left Vienna, he discovered that he couldn't do without her and saw an unexpected threat to the tacit agreement by which he considered her bound to him. Perhaps this too had transformed Anna: having caught her father's attention and aroused his jealousy. The photograph that shows her looking thoughtful with her hat pulled down over her forehead and her long pale cheeks in the identity papers which had become essential for her departure from London after the declaration of war in August 1914, captures the extent of the change in her expression.[1] From the young girl who the previous summer had gone hesitantly for walks on her father's arm, dressed in a dirndl, Anna had blossomed, with a definite identity, more self-respect, and an almost challenging attitude: a will to be *there*. "Your daughter is frightfully brave, if you would see her you would be extremely proud of her behavior," Herbert Jones "the Second" had written to Freud at the time.[2]

Back in Vienna after her challenging adventure, *Annerl* would no longer be content with translating poetry for her father or reading the English novels he passed on to her but determinedly made clear to him that she was choosing psychoanalysis and wanted to follow him like the best of sons and to participate in his work, not just collaborating on translations for the publishing house but undertaking the prescribed analytic relationship.

Taking the form of weekly sessions on the couch, the treatment began in earnest in the summer of 1918, during the family's trip to Hungary: it stopped in 1922 and was then resumed in 1924 to 1925. These two long tranches of analysis – the second coming after the start of her father's illness – are set against the background of an analytic continuity that was "inextricably bound"[3] to their relationship through the whole of Freud's life.

It was taken for granted from the outset that the matter should be kept private, shared only with the family, Ferenczi, and the von Freunds,[4] but the secret and the emotional weight could not have been easy to bear.

DOI: 10.4324/9781003246480-16

In the beginning, Freud found the work with his daughter only too easy and, perhaps buoyed up by enthusiasm after the Budapest Congress, he incautiously confided to Ferenczi, "Annerl's analysis is getting very fine, otherwise the cases are uninteresting."[5] After four years of that apocalyptic war, when he had seen everything diminish around him and lose its value, like the defunct currency, his hopes of survival all depended on his daughter. Freud was convinced he could analyse her in a detached manner without conditioning her too much.[6]

Soon enough the countertransferential difficulties made themselves felt, affecting his mood and especially his creativity. The period of depression, mentioned earlier, that hit him at the end of the year was not only caused by the worsening conditions of life in Vienna, extreme hunger, anxieties at the lack of news from Martin about his imprisonment in Italy, or the health of von Freund who had already returned to Vienna with physical symptoms of an uncertain nature.

Freud's inhibition peaked in January 1919, when he wrote to the Hungarian that he was being "thick-headed, scientifically."[7]

A few weeks later, it was in fact the theoretical reworking of Anna's case that enabled him to renew his productivity: picking up some critical topics left in suspense by the writing of the metapsychological essays at the start of the war, he announced to Ferenczi that he had begun having some new ideas about the genesis of masochism[8] and, even as he was concluding a first essay *A Child Is Being Beaten* (1919b), he mentioned that "a second one with the mysterious heading *Beyond the Pleasure Principle*"[9] was in progress. To Ferenczi, he attributed his renewed productivity to the acute post-war shortage of heat and food and told Jones that these "two productions" were arduously "written under bodily pain caused by a bad pen":[10] Jones was the first to consider them a symptomatic pair, almost a single thought.

As for Anna, writing to her brother Ernst in early 1919, she seemed to be apologising to him for the burden she was imposing on their father – not only because his evening session with her was the tenth in his working day – and, trying to mitigate her sense of guilt, she told Ernst about her plans for the future, which she felt were finally clear (always dependent, however, on her father and his publishing house).[11] Later, during the summer which she spent with her friend Margarete Rie, who was also in treatment with Freud, Anna felt she could no longer keep the secret and confessed to her father that they had exchanged confidences about their analysis.[12]

Naturally, her constant presence could not fail to arouse curiosity and jealousy among the members of the Psychoanalytic Society, whose meetings she was still attending as a guest but without presenting a paper or taking part in the discussion.[13] Although she was carrying on with the teaching job she had begun during the war, Anna's interest in psychoanalysis was obvious to everyone, as were her commitment and increasing skill as a translator and, not least, her desire for an exclusive relationship with her father, whose favourite she clearly was and whom in her deep identification she greatly resembled. Like Freud's closest followers, she had received the gift of a ring, and in autumn 1920, during the post-war

Congress in Holland, always at her father's side, she had instantly been noticed by the highly sensitive and jealous Ernest Jones: after Freud had given his paper off the cuff in simple, perfect English, at the end of a lunch hosted by the group of British attendees, the young lady pleased her father and the English-speakers by also making a "graceful little speech" in that language.[14] At this time, Anna was already a bulwark of the English section at the publishing house and working permanently on the Western project for the survival of psychoanalysis. The following year, her father recommended her to Jones as translator of the collection of some of his minor works.[15]

Inevitably gossip started about her: her private life – will she, won't she get married? – seemed to be one of the main topics of conversation among Freud's pupils during the long hours spent in the cafés of Vienna between one session and another. . . .[16] For a time, Siegfried Bernfeld was thought to be the man in her life. Later, many analysts believed she lived in abstinence, and they regretted this.[17]

They soon began wondering about her analysis, too: there were those who said that Freud had analysed her himself, others that he had sent her to Lou Andreas Salomé, whom he was known to hold in high regard. Although there was no certainty about the identity of Anna's analyst, in fact, everyone knew the truth but tried to ignore this "public secret," which for some time they managed to keep hidden from the new generations of analysts.[18]

In spring 1921, when Groddeck invited Freud to stay at his clinic in Baden Baden before going to the Harz mountains, he had no hesitation about mentioning Anna in order to induce an acceptance: "If my information is correct, you are accustomed to having your daughter with you," he wrote.[19] And though he was unable to make the visit, Freud made it clear how tempted he was by the prospect, replying, "How clever to ask my little girl, too, to prevent me from getting homesick!"[20]

In early August, while he was finishing the *Vorbericht* at Gastein, Freud was receiving regular news from Anna, who was trying to keep her analysis going by correspondence despite the summer break.

In mid-August, when they met again in Seefeld with the rest of the family, father and daughter decided to ask Lou Andreas Salomé for help while the father was getting ready for his holiday with the members of the committee. This must also have been in Freud's mind while he was writing the *Vorbericht-Nachtrag* . . .

It is possible that Freud had been aware for some time of the inherent difficulties in the treatment. Moreover, in early 1920, a few days after receiving news of Anton von Freund's death, this reckless and complex analytic work with Anna had to deal with the sudden death of Sophie who, in that freezing January, weakened by a third, unwanted pregnancy, had died of the terrible Spanish flu after only four days.

What this loss meant for the family, for the father, the daughter, and especially Martha, it is hard to imagine. The notion of seeking help from Lou Andreas Salomé, which emerged shortly afterwards, may have its origin in this. Freud had hoped to arrange a meeting between Anna and Salomé at the Congress at the

Hague, but the Russian analyst, who was now living in Germany and had lost everything in the Revolution, had been unable to attend.

This time, Freud invited her to spend the winter in Vienna as his guest in Berggasse, even offering to pay her travel costs (he was now in a financial position to do so), and the day he left for Hildesheim and the Harz mountains, he received confirmation by post from Anna that Salomé had accepted.[21] Freud felt able to share the secret with her and entrust her with part of the analysis, which he was not even inclined to be open about with the members of the committee, apart from Ferenczi.

It must be remembered that during this period the group of the ultra-faithful around Freud was predominantly male. The vacation together cemented their friendship, and Jones recalls that Freud took the opportunity to reaffirm this: "At the end of the tour Freud said to us, 'We have lived through some experiences together, and that always binds men'."[22] But mentioning the witches in connection with the outing to the peak of the Brocken, the Welshman's aim seems to be a hint at the *demonic* feminine looming in the background. Freud's new orientation and the investiture of his daughter were coming into the open.

The resistance that had made Freud forget his notes in 1921 and stopped him inserting the Forsyth case into the paper he had planned for the Harz gathering arose not only out of the subject of the occult but indicated the impasse not yet worked through in the management of Anna's analysis, which was contemporary with and unconsciously connected to that of Paul Bernfeld. This was a time when Freud was trying to deal with the difficult question of the "early fixation on the father" in his daughter's transference.

Lou Andreas Salomé: a mother-sister

When the Russian analyst arrived in Vienna at the end of 1921, she found herself faced with the task of helping to conclude that impossible analysis and supporting Anna's official entry into the community of analysts. The initial plan, to which father and daughter were very attached, was for Anna to join the Berlin society and take part as a full member as early as the international congress of 1922.

In Berlin, Max Eitingon and his wife had begun to look after Freud's children with their generous hospitality, almost as surrogate parents. It was there that Oliver, the engineer, after the failure of his first marriage and having suffered for years from an obsessive neurosis, had been sent for an analysis with Franz Alexander – a promising Hungarian pupil of Abraham – and he would marry again in 1923. The other son, Ernst, had also been supported by the Eitingons in setting himself up as an architect, collaborating on the design of the recently opened Polyclinic building and the Psychoanalytic Institute. Led by Abraham, Eitingon, Sachs, Simmel, and Müller-Braunschweig, Berlin was becoming the most highly regarded centre of treatment and analytic training. Ferenczi's pupil Melanie Klein, among others, had just arrived there after the war. With Salomé's help, Anna Freud, on leaving the Viennese circle, would have found a fitting and worthy situation there.

Sixty years old, the same age as Martha, Lou was a completely different woman and, replying to Freud's invitation, presented herself almost as an elder sister to Anna. Though they had not yet met, Lou had understood for some time that the daughter now represented the only way into her father's heart, that she was in fact "the finest translation of her father's psycho-analysis into a feminine medium."[23]

Arriving in Vienna on the evening of Wednesday 9 November 1921, ten years after her first visit, Salomé was welcomed at the station by Anna, who had no difficulty recognising her. After stopping briefly in Berggasse, the two women braved a snowstorm and hurried to the office of the psychoanalytic society, where Freud had already started the meeting. Much had changed since the winter of 1912: the number of Viennese analysts had grown, but Salomé immediately felt the gap left by the absence of Tausk. The walk back to the house with the father and daughter was warmed for her by happy memories.[24]

Lou stayed in Vienna for a little more than a month, occupying the sitting room with the veranda and rosewood bed which had been rearranged for her. She showed herself to be a discreet and undemanding guest who fitted easily into the rhythms of family life: in the depth of the Viennese winter, she spent most of her time in long conversations with Anna sitting on the sofa, wrapped in her quilt while the younger woman tended to the stove.[25] A great admirer of Rilke, Anna had begun to cultivate a passion from poetry ever since the first month of her analysis with her father, discovering that this creative activity was a way to contain the "primitive dark forces" that she felt surging inside her, finding "that each poet sings but his own sorrow."[26] There was an immediate understanding between her and Salomé: both were passionate about literature and poetry, great dreamers and readers, and told each other their dreams and waking fantasies and shared their interpretations.

The younger woman felt that she was taking the lead in their exchanges, in a profound relationship which advanced, as Lou observed, "in I do not know what direction, but towards a common goal,"[27] using their shared relationship with Freud to guide them. Seeing his daughter's improved and sometimes radiant mood,[28] Freud thought he had found her the feminine support she was longing for, as well as further analytic experience.

Anna was loved by Lou out of devotion to her father, but she knew she was receiving authentic, personal attention: with Lou, she was experiencing something she could never have felt with her mother or her sister, discovering a more congenial model of a woman – inquisitive, cultivated, generous in her healthy narcissism, interested in her – who was helping her to get in contact with her own femininity and distinguish herself from her father. She quickly learned to recognise Lou's charisma as an inspiring muse and wrote in amazement to her father, "when you tell her something she understands it better than yourself."[29]

After Lou's departure, the two women began a rich correspondence, interspersed with brief stays by Anna at Villa Loufried, the little house where Salomé lived with her husband Andreas in the small university town of Göttingen. Her first visit was in April 1922 after stays in Berlin and Hamburg. The analysis could be considered finished, and, back in Vienna, Freud was missing his daughter badly and discovering the intensity of his primitive dependency on her, an oral craving as bad as if he had "to give up smoking!"[30]

The heartache and nostalgia for his roots and his childhood which Freud made known to Ferenczi at this time[31] can be attributed to his first separation after the analysis and Anna's plan to leave the family: she did in fact intend to consult Eitingon about joining the Berlin Society by presenting her translation of J Varendonck's *The Psychology of Day-Dreams*, newly published with an introduction by her father (1921).

On learning that this publication would not be sufficient, Anna decided to apply directly to the feared and more critical Viennese Society and prepared the necessary presentation. As part of her plan, she visited Göttingen, where she wrote the text in a few days with the full engagement of the Russian psychoanalyst, who followed her progress step by step. Anna wrote to her father:

> She says I am doing it completely on my own, but I think that she inspires me in a strange and occult fashion, because when I am alone I know nothing about these things. . . . I realize for the first time all that there is in the world.
> (30/04/1922)

At the meeting on 31 May 1922, Anna read her *Beating Fantasies and Day-dreams* (1923) to the Viennese Psychoanalytic Society, presenting it as an illustration, drawn from her own analytic practice, of Sigmund's essay *A Child Is Being Beaten* (1919b): in this autobiographical paper, she probed further into her father's version of her analysis, which she described, completing it will additional material deriving from her relationship with Lou.

The next day, Freud reassured Eitingon, informing him about Anna's success.[32] Rank then asked Jones to grant a dispensation to Lou Andreas Salomé, and so, a month later, the two women were admitted to the Viennese Society together, even though Salomé was not Austrian and had not presented a paper.

Anna's path was not smooth, however, and the development of that analysis would weigh on her for the rest of her life. The Russian analyst had often reminded Freud about the importance of the first relationship with the mother and the power of matriarchal societies which preceded patriarchy in individual and cultural history.[33] Was she able to talk to Anna about her mother (of whom there is no trace in *Beating Fantasies*),[34] her difficult relationship with Martha, and Sophie's death? Anna makes only one brief mention of her sister's illness in the correspondence they exchanged during those early years:[35] what working-through was possible for that mourning?

Despite their closeness and shared enthusiasm, Anna never felt that Salomé fully understood her need and "desire for confirmation from others and for 'something' for herself." She told Eitingon about this: "We finally both had to laugh about our mutual . . . and complete inability to understand each other."[36] Anna was never able to talk to Salomé about her friendship with Dorothy Burlingham but only confided to Eitingon about it. This was another reason their letters became less frequent after 1925.

Whatever the case, Freud was not slow to acknowledge his gratitude to Lou: "Anna is splendid and self-assured, and I often think how much she probably owes to you."[37] When, in 1925, Lou Salomé even remarked to Alix Strachey "that the parents were the only proper people to analyze the child,"[38] it was because of the exceptional experiment she had been called upon to take part in.

Thought transmission? A pair of twin papers

Authors who have reflected on Anna's analysis have chiefly focused their attention on interpreting the motivations and personal outcomes of this experience in the psychic reality of the two protagonists. Few authors have so far addressed the consequences of this unconscious analytic entanglement for Freud's thinking, how it may have been deposited in the theory and subsequent vicissitudes of the psychoanalytic movement.

Those who first considered this aspect[39] focused on its themes of perversion and masochism as they are developed in the twin texts *A Child Is Being Beaten* (S Freud, 1919a) and *Beating Fantasies and Daydreams* (A Freud, 1923).

In an IPA monograph devoted to rereading Freud's essay,[40] many contributors raised the problem of the two complementary works, openly addressing not only the treatment of his daughter Anna as an enactment of beating fantasies and the underlying incest fantasy but also emphasising its centrality in Freud's construction of his theory about masochism, the masculinity complex, and more generally about the conception of femininity and penis envy.

The father's text

Let's start by reading *A Child Is Being Beaten. A Contribution to the Study of the Origin of Sexual Perversions* (1919b). The title might lead one to think that Freud's work will be a return to the infantile aspects of seduction and abuse he had considered at the start of his career, but we quickly learn that the "child being beaten" is a representation of a fantasy, a scene that the subject experiences as a spectator and whose relationship with actual experiences of corporal punishment in a child's upbringing or at school may remain unclear or be highly tenuous. What concerns analytic investigation is the fact that this fantasy, developing from infancy in three distinct phases, accompanies and sustains masturbation: initially in accordance with the subject's wishes, then against them and coercively, reaching the point where the subject is permanently possessed by its libidinal tendency which now demonstrates a first quality of perversion. This and analogous perverse fixations which appear at the ages of five or six are regarded by Freud as sedimentations of the Oedipus complex, the product of a transformative process begun by an early incestuous choice of love object, often – he specifies – in combination with the narcissistic trauma of a younger sibling with whom to share this exclusive, privileged love.

In his short, dense essay that is not without its contradictions, Freud tries for the first time to understand the structure and phased transformations of an erotic fantasy, captures the genesis of sadomasochism and its narcissistic component, introduces the idea of guilt as a mechanism which transforms sadism into masochism, and anticipates the conception of a sadistic Superego and a masochistic Ego which he will describe in the second, structural model.[41] He also begins to clarify how perversion involves an area of non-differentiation, the negation of differences.

The eroticised fantasy of punishment, accompanied by feelings of shame, humiliation, and guilt, with the regressive copresence of previously sadistic, now masochistic elements, would express the oldest incestuous fantasy – prohibited and repressed – of being loved in an exclusive manner by the father, a fantasy containing aspects of jealousy and resentment towards possible rivals. In the girl, the unconscious representation would arise from the normal oedipal set-up and, in detaching her from incestuous love, would generally lead her to break with the feminine role (giving life to a "masculinity complex"), to flee from sexuality and amorous life in general, and to become exclusively their spectator. In the boy, it would originate from an inverted oedipal set-up and an unconscious feminine identification that takes the father as love object.

Freud left no documentation about Anna's treatment, but its dramatic quality pervades the ill-concealed incestuous seduction and sadomasochistic enactment in *A Child Is Being Beaten*: it is unanimously believed that one of the cases the essay describes concerns his daughter, and there are those who have wondered if he had her permission to write about it (highlighting a further enactment beside the treatment itself),[42] as well as those who glimpse in the title's continuous present tense and passive form the imminence of seduction and abuse, the time of the unconscious.[43]

There are references in Freud's text which support the hypothesis that the essay includes his daughter's analysis: he makes clear at the start that the fantasies portrayed in *A Child Is Being Beaten* may appear not only in neurotic individuals but "even more often among the far greater number of people who have not been obliged to come to analysis by manifest illness" (p. 179). In going on to report the diagnoses of his patients – two men and four women – "all virgins" as he later confided to Marie Bonaparte[44] – he neglects to indicate the diagnosis of the sixth. Anna could also be the patient of whom he states that she had come to be analysed merely on account of "indecisiveness in life," adding that a rough clinical diagnosis would not have classified her at all as suffering from an illness or would have dismissed her as "psychasthenic" (p. 183). Last, mentioning two female cases in whom an elaborate superstructure of day-dreams had grown up over the masochistic beating-phantasy, he states that in one case this imaginative activity almost rose to the level of a work of art (p. 191). It is quite suggestive that *A Child Is*

Being Beaten is his first and only essay based on a female model of development rather than a male one.[45]

With regard to the male, when Freud reflects on the perverse aspects of "merely psychical impotence" and indicates certain situations with a less favourable prognosis, he could be referring to Paul Bernfeld (with his father-fixation, masturbation, and sadomasochism). And indeed, in the light of *A Child Is Being Beaten*, it is hard not to think of Paul Bernfeld's case as a double of Anna Freud's. The sadism of the former's masturbatory fantasy and his inability to penetrate appear complementary to the masochistic fantasy and virginity of the other, in a coincidence of opposites, like two sides of the same coin. Today a unified and organised theory of narcissism and love would recognise in them the typical "collusion between sadism and masochism."[46] In fact, when Lou Andreas Salomé read Freud's paper, she immediately grasped the unity of the phenomenon of perversion and suggested to him that, "Both sadism and masochism in their original identity play their part in this. It is my view, in general, that as products of the *unconscious* they are in fact identical in their oppositeness."[47]

The daughter's text

What did Anna want to add to her father's essay, and what could she say about it if she secretly recognised herself among the patients he considered?

Her paper begins by citing the two female patients described by Freud in whom an elaborate superstructure of day-dreams masked a possible feeling of satisfied excitation, moving beyond the masturbatory act, and moves on to introduce the case of an unnamed patient, a 15-year-old girl whom she pretended to have in treatment (in reality, Anna Freud only treated her first case, her nephew Ernst, six months after joining the Viennese Society). She illustrates the fantasy activity that was invasively occupying the mind of this adolescent, an activity whose origin, evolution, and conclusion had been detected through analysis in antecedent autoerotic beating fantasies.

However, unlike her father, the daughter barely mentioned the beating fantasies and, instead, illustrated in detail the characteristics of the complex and elaborate activity of daydreams and poetic creations which had replaced them and which, with the giving-up of the onanistic act, represented the version with a happy ending, indirectly satisfying its exciting and threatening tensions.

As for the content of these "nice stories," which, given the recurrence of the same characters in the each of the episodes, were contributing to a narrative in instalments and, with the addition of new scenes on each repetition and the interweaving of the events of the Saga, were almost in danger of breaking through the general frame of the story, it must be said that in the end it turns out to be rather monotonous: the recurrent theme is one of rivalry between a powerful old knight and the protagonist, a poor, weak young man accused of some crime.

The storyline generally began with a first defeat of the young man who, as a result, was rendered helpless for a long time under the threat of severe punishment, and concluded with an unexpected but timely reconciliation: the older man's conduct becomes friendly and forgiving, to the satisfaction of the dreamer who starts her fantasies all over again from the beginning in order to arrive at the rewarding conclusion.

One part of the essay to which Anna was very attached concerned the written and poetic transposition of the fantasised stories which the girl had found was the way to get rid of her daydreams – as well as her masturbatory fantasies – introducing them into a communicative dialogue. In Anna's opinion, this development was an example of drives "inhibited in their aim." With the separation between the repressed sexual tendency of the beating fantasies and the manifest tendency to affection in the so-called "nice stories," the satisfaction of the pleasure could be deferred, could be invested in the act of writing and that process of sublimation previously described by Sigmund in the paper on Leonardo which, while leading to the attainment of culture, also confirmed its close connection to perversion.

We note by the way how Anna's essay is equally silent on the role of the seductive paternal appeal in the development and resolution of the incestuous fantasy, as in daydreams. Moreover, in neither work is there any trace of the mother, whether as an oedipal rival for the father's love or as a primal source of love:[48] for all that Sigmund's essay endorsed a first phase of pre-oedipal fantasies, nothing was said in it about the maternal function that is indispensable for attaining an experience of pleasure.[49]

Based on the censoring of the father's jealous and exclusive desire and the receptive maternal capacity, Freud would propose the equation between femininity, passivity, and masochism. Anna accommodates herself to this and with *Beating Fantasies and Daydreams* cements her own unconscious masculine identification with her father and brings her training analysis to completion.[50]

Naturally her application to the Viennese Society was well accepted, although a heavy-handed comment on the patient's pathology made it necessary for Freud to intervene in her defence, and his daughter's. The father immediately showed himself to be particularly touchy, even giving a cold response to Helene Deutsch's encouragement, as if in his opinion his daughter's work should be exempt from discussion.[51]

Anna was less than pleased that her listeners' interest generally turned more to the onanistic fantasies than to the daydreams or their transposition into poetry. The only one to pay attention to them was Siegfried Bernfeld, in an excellent comment on their narcissistic function. In her concluding reflections, making the most of his suggestion, Anna underlined the importance of the Ego's ambitious tendencies and the pleasure of recognising that one has found the road that leads from the fantasy life back to reality through the sublimating act of writing.

Although Anna did not turn herself into a poet, with this "rite of passage"[52] – the clinical narration of her own history – she was in a position to leave the niche where she had been shut away and protected and was initiated into her father's profession. Being recognised and admired could have temporarily replaced the realisation of her amorous life.[53] From now on, her ambitious tendencies, the narcissistic need for survival and self-affirmation, will find satisfaction in her father's light (not in his shadow, as she will often reiterate).

In these early days, during the twenties, few realised that this young girl was destined to become the leader of psychoanalysis.[54]

"Lifedeath"

Reflecting on the relationship between "gossip, telepathy and/or science" in psychoanalysis – in connection with Freud's analysis of his daughter and Klein's of her children – Forrester wonders about this sort of "analytic incest,"[55] the unelaborated roots of theory, and the conflicts that were transmitted to later generations, quoting as examples Anna's defence of her father's fame, the harsh criticism of Klein by her daughter Melitta, and then the irrelevance of the child's real relationships with its parents as maintained by the Kleinian hypotheses in contrast to those of Anna Freud.

As I pursue the theme of what cannot avoid being left unanalysed in any analysis – not only in those first pioneering ones – and is destined to be transmitted unconsciously along the analytic genealogical tree in symptoms that take the form of theorisation, I am not much interested in "gossip" or imagining – as many have tried to do – whether Anna was, or may have been, the victim in her analysis and whether Sigmund was an abusive and seductive father. Instead, I want to investigate how a father's analysis of his daughter may have been deeply inscribed in psychoanalytic thought and been transmitted as an unconscious legacy in every candidate's transference onto the theory and onto Freud himself. This may have fed, for example, the difficulties in integrating child/adolescent analysis with adult analysis, still present in the training of the IPA, or the sharpness of the contrast between the instinctual/intrapsychic model and the relational/interpsychic model.

In my opinion, the period of great creativity and change in Freud's thinking during the twenties had its roots in the need to work through the experience of analysis of and with Anna, a more bewildering process than he had been prepared for, one that wove itself deeply into the loss of his other daughter Sophie. Her death, which came in the middle of the treatment, became part of the tangle of incestuous-grieving fantasies in which Freud and his youngest child were embroiled, a bundle of such potent affects that at first they had to be denied.

Reading Freud's writings in the context of his complete oeuvre as steps, staging posts, gateways on the associative journey of his self-analytic thinking, and in the light of what he had not yet been able to think through completely,[56] we can recognise how the swirl of unconscious fantasies stirred up by the analysis with his daughter and the countertransferential tension that had led to the creation, one after the other in early 1919, of the two "symptomatic" texts (*A Child Is Being Beaten* and *Beyond the Pleasure Principle*) made him return to an old project on the theme of the occult (*The Uncanny*) in May, fine-tune a first idea about identification and *Group Psychology*,[57] and, without a break in the flow (after revising *Beyond the Pleasure Principle* over the summer), was making him approach the session with Paul Bernfeld in a state of readiness to elaborate it "telepathically."

With Sophie's death in early 1920, the denial that had accompanied the enactment of Anna's incestuous fantasy in her analysis became firmly fixed in the new and different significance taken on by the compulsion to repeat: thus, in the definitive version of *Beyond the Pleasure Principle*, Freud theorised about a "death instinct" and simultaneously reactivated his private interest in the topic of thought transmission.[58]

Although he was searching in *himself* for the mother and the lost scene with the object, in his *theory*, Freud was constructing a "solipsistic"[59] model of the isolated mind which only took account of the subject. He was using the deficiencies of his own early life to conceive the psyche's original, traumatic experiences in the lack of differentiation from the object: masochism, the death instinct, denial, ego-splitting, and so on. He describes and interprets them in a masterly way from the perspective of foreclosure, the denial of the object's presence and functions. Not only the new theory of Eros and Thanatos but also the second, structural model (divided into the agencies of Ego, Id, and Superego) are derived from this need to focus on the intrapsychic, to black out the light of the object.

Beyond the Pleasure Principle stands as the first evidence of Freud's struggle: the outcome of the incestuous crisis with Anna and the traumatic loss of Sophie, it is a controversial legacy which has the characteristics of a "crypt"[60] unconsciously transmitted between the generations.

Derrida considers this most profound and irreducible part of Freudian speculation a "Scene of writing" inseparable from a "Scene of legacy" which the psychoanalytic movement would have to face and suggestively entitles his seminar on the second chapter of *Beyond the Pleasure Principle* "life-death," as if reproducing a single and still undifferentiated primordial word.[61]

"Not to be there": the process of separation and the game of *Fortsein*

Faced with this uncomfortable legacy, many readers have reacted by rejecting *Beyond the Pleasure Principle*, considering it a false theoretical step taken by Freud.

Fritz Wittels, the Viennese pupil who took it upon himself to write the first biography of Freud, trying to reconnect psychoanalytic theory with its creator's affective roots, attributed the theorisation of the death instinct and *Beyond the Pleasure Principle*, published in December 1920, entirely to Freud's state of mind after Sophie's death in January.

Freud was far from pleased with the honour conferred on him by that biography and suggested that its author make a number of corrections. Above all, primed to defend himself and deny any such interpretation, he refuted Wittels' hypothesis, showing that the first draft of *Beyond the Pleasure Principle* had already been presented to Eitingon in the summer of 1919. Commenting on the correction, he specified:

> if I had myself been analysing another person in such circumstances, I should have presumed the existence of a connection between my daughter's death

> and the train of thought presented in *Beyond the Pleasure Principle*. But the inference that such a sequence exists would have been false. The book was written in 1919, when my daughter was still in excellent health. She died in January, 1920. In September, 1919, I had sent the manuscript of the little book to be read by some friends in Berlin [Eitingon and Abraham]. It was finished, except for the discussion concerning the mortality or immortality of the protozoa. What seems true is not always the truth.
>
> (Freud, 1924, p. 287)

With *Beyond the Pleasure Principle*, psychoanalysis, which came into being as a universal science of subjectivity based on the interpretation of its creator's personal, unique dreams, starts to renounce its private and affective origins. Freud's resistances to that biographical interpretation which *seems true* must have been strong if in summer 1920, after completing the essay, he wanted to be sure that Eitingon could testify to the fact that its contents had been thoroughly worked out in 1919 at a time when his daughter Sophie was in the best of health.

It was obviously an interpretation that had crossed his mind, and his attempt to repel it had led him to introduce a discordant tone into his reply to Wittels, almost suggesting a reversed causality, as if he were insinuating that in this case, it would have been the theory that foresaw or influenced the reality of his daughter's death, not vice versa.[62]

Unconvinced, in his own biography, Jones further refined Wittels' hypothesis about the deep link between *Beyond the Pleasure Principle* and Freud's relationship with Sophie: he especially noted how after 1915, it was by observing the behaviour of her son, his grandson Ernst, that Freud rethought the concept of the compulsion to repeat, and Jones also pointed out that the term "death instinct" had only made its appearance after his daughter's death.[63]

In fact, *Beyond the Pleasure Principle* is not a speculative essay, as Freud would have us believe. There is an extremely significant part which, as it is always possible to confirm in his writings, originates in his personal affective experience: it balances and completes *A Child Is Being Beaten*, gathering together his experiences with his other daughter, Sophie, her motherhood, and then her irreparable loss. It tells us about Freud's destiny and represents his attempt to address the theme of femininity and birth, the primal reality of the mother, and the relational foundations of the treatment itself.

Reflecting on the concept of the compulsion to repeat, in the second chapter of *Beyond the Pleasure Principle*, Freud sets out to analyse the behaviour of his grandson Ernst, a fully real child this time and one actively relating to his mother. It is the first psychoanalytic infant observation: the grandson is engaged in the phase of acquiring language, and Freud as a father and grandfather produces a highly intimate observation during his brief but repeated summer trips to Hamburg.

He notes the boy's habit of "throwing away" any small objects, accompanying the act with the emission of a long "o-o-o" (*fort* = gone) and an expression of interest and satisfaction.[64] He interprets the child's game with Sophie's help: "the only use he made of any of his toys was to play 'gone' [*fort-sein*] with them."

Over time, Freud is able to witness the development of the game as the boy learns to make skilful use of a wooden reel with a piece of string tied round it, making it appear and disappear over the edge of his curtained cot: at this point, after every "o-o-o" of farewell, there is a happy "*da*" ("there") at the reappearance. The game, now complete, was interpreted by Freud as an experience of relational learning closely connected to the acquisition of the first words, which constituted the earliest way of dealing with the mother's disappearance and her separations from him.

With the grandson's entry into the phase of oedipal rivalry, and after his father's departure for the front, the game was further transformed into an expression of the attack on his rival (the father but also the little brother born in the meantime) who, like the cotton reel, is symbolically thrown away and sent "to the Front."

Identifying with little Ernst, we see Freud himself playing *fort-da,* intent on making the other participant in the scene, the mother-daughter Sophie, appear and disappear in the background. At the start, he explains how attentively she had cared for her son, breastfeeding him herself and looking after him with no outside help; he makes us understand that from to time, it was she who patiently gave back to the boy the objects he was hurling away and especially, as if she were reading his thoughts, giving meaning to his "o-o-o" and translating it into words, "*fort*" (*gone*).

She had been able to build with him not only the game of "*Fortsein*" but also a first language.

Soon Freud begins to leave Sophie out: he claims, for example, that it is irrelevant for his treatment of the game whether the child invented it himself or took it over on some outside suggestion.[65] In the end, he makes her disappear completely, casting her aside as he relegates the news of her actual disappearance to a chilling footnote:

> When this child was five and three-quarters, his mother died. Now that she was really "gone" ("o-o-o"), the little boy showed no signs of grief. It is true that in the interval a second child had been born and had roused him to violent jealousy.
>
> (p. 16)

As was the case in *Formulations on the Two Principles of Mental Functioning*, the notes allow Freud space to contain and limit the recognition of the uncanny maternal reality. In 1911, he uses the marginal space at the foot of the page to locate the mother's indispensable function, taken for granted as a presupposition of the omnipotent infantile narcissistic organisation that he is theorising, dominated by the pleasure principle;[66] in 1920, he does it in order to mitigate and reject – just like his grandson, Ernst – the affective reality of her irreparable disappearance.

Mourning intrudes into his grandson's play and into the very process of constructing theory. In the final draft of *Beyond the Pleasure Principle*, Freud, likewise mourning, speaks about a child whose play has lost its communicative sense and can only focus on the looming experience of disappearance and on the traumatic phase of "not being there," with which he tirelessly repeats the first action of that infantile learning-game about a mutilated life. The second action, which was associated with greater pleasure and had developed when the mother was alive, could no longer follow the first, even though it was waited for time after time.[67]

Although in 1908 Freud could assert that "every child at play behaves like a creative writer" (p. 143), now all he detects in the game is the same thing vainly and monotonously repeated: instead of pondering his grandson's lost poetry and Sophie's death, he gives the name *death instinct* to still vital elements which, like a stuck record, tenaciously keep presenting themselves to the Ego once it has survived the trauma and is blindly searching for a context and an object with which to bring its destiny to completion.

The irreparable loss and the now unforgivable betrayal block the development of play and of the transference on both pre-oedipal and oedipal levels. Freud is so deeply implicated in this that, when he claims that the boy – so obedient and dutiful that he "never cried when his mother left him for a few hours" – showed no sign of grief when she died, he also seems to be observing an infantile part of himself. He rediscovers that child who had been left thunderstruck, emotionally paralysed, by the death of his little brother, deprived of the deep communication with his mother who had withdrawn into her grief: a child who is very soon seized with vengeful hostility.

In this way, Freud ventures into the exploration of the traumatic dimension and is able to describe the development of that deformation of the instinct which repeatedly renews its challenge and tests the affective links. With Heidegger, the *Dasein* of German philosophy was about to take on the characteristics of a vital "being there" (the "being in the world" that Binswanger would develop in his *Daseinanalysis*): but in the coming and going of the cotton-reel and the generations (great-grandmother, grandfather, mother, son), putting the presence-absence of a mother and an impossible mourning into the background, the *Fortsein* game enables Freud to speculate about the negative, the "not being there," that "being gone," disappearing and making disappear, which is the necessary prelude to the experience of *Dasein*, the discovery of the Self and the object as the return and recognition of existence. He will give all this the name "death instinct" and, considering it independent of the pleasure principle and more primitive, he will situate it in the deepest somatic strata of the psyche, a foundation and limit of the theoretical and interpretative system based on the Oedipus complex and speech.

In fact, it is likely that in the end, Freud was right: Wittels's and Jones's interpretations were partial and did not take into account what Anna's analysis had cost him, even before the death of Sophie. He did indeed begin his reflections on the death instinct before Sophie's death, and it was deeply entwined with the re-emergence of traumatic infantile aspects in the enactment of the incestuous fantasy with Anna: the first event, signifying the other side of mourning and death.

"Death and life stand in a mutual relationship to one another, of which the whole is inevitably concealed from us," wrote L Andreas-Salomé to Freud (26/12/1920). "Each is a half of one and the same event."

The concealment of the relationship and the collapse of the transference which accompanied the violation of boundaries in the analytic treatment of one daughter becomes firmly fixed on the death of the other. After denying paternal seduction in *A Child Is Being Beaten*, in *Beyond the Pleasure Principle* Freud represses the reality of generativity and maternal seduction, together with its function in organising the reality principle.[68]

The relationship with the object thrown away will end up in the obscure corner that is "telepathy" and thought transference: here Freud opens and defends a private field of reflection about the profound, foundational, and original bond with the mother and the unconscious communication, which, split off and repressed by the official theory, will stay there isolated but also protected.

Thanatos, the hidden hemisphere of incestuous sexuality, now occupies Freud's theoretical horizon, while Eros is defensively pushed into the background. The illness that will cause him so much long-term suffering and kill him after 16 years develops in this same period in the context of the hunger and deprivation caused by the war, his incurable dependency on smoking, his mourning for his daughter Sophie, and the impossibility of bringing Anna's analysis to a conclusion, of separating from her.

It will be left to the third generation to attempt a working-through of all this. Anna Freud will complete the work left half-finished and will maternally care for both her father and her little nephew. Ernst Wolfgang Halberstadt, Sophie's son and the protagonist of Freud's interpretations on the "death instinct," will live, unlike his little brother Heinele; he will be analysed by Anna and will become the only male descendant of his famous grandfather to become a psychoanalyst, specialising in child analysis, the early mother-child relationship, and premature births. In 1951, after his father's death, he will ask his aunt if he can take her surname and will become Ernest W Freud.[69] But on Anna's death in 1982, he will have the strength to go back and work in Germany, in the language of his childhood.[70]

Anna, Antigone

Freud was well aware that, despite Salomé's intervention, Anna was unable to form relationships with men. The problem was starting to worry him, but he was the first to dissuade her against any possible suitor. She had been fruitlessly courted by Martin's schoolfriend, the discreet Hans Lampl, with whom Anna had attended the Congress at the Hague, and gone for walks with her cousin Edward, her aunt Anna's son, who came to Europe in summer 1920. Anna had been a little bit in love with Siegfried Bernfeld, whom she met as part of the group of analysts who were beginning to work with children, and maybe also with Max Eitingon, who had the terrifying wife.[71] But she always ended up reassuring her father that she couldn't imagine any other man beside her.

Lou Salomé, who had defended and flaunted her own virginity in the past, appeared unconcerned by the young woman's asceticism when she reported with amusement to Freud how, even while Anna was with her in Göttingen, she would irritably repel any attempt at courtship. In his reply, the father expressed his fear of losing her but said he was aware of being the reason for her inhibition.[72]

While Anna was still struggling with her adolescent urge for freedom (and the plan to go and work in Berlin, encouraged by Eitingon), the early signs of Freud's cancer of the jaw doomed any possibility of bringing that already problematic analysis to a conclusion and any prospect of a separation between father and daughter. In February 1923, Freud noticed the worsening of a leucoplakia which had appeared some time earlier on his cheek and palate. Ruling out any attempt to give up smoking, and consulting no one but Felix Deutsch, in April, he had it removed by his friend the dermatologist Markus Hajek. The operation resulted in a dramatic loss of blood, caused immediate alarm in the family, and brought Martha and Anna rushing to the clinic. A second heavier and more perilous haemorrhage occurring between visits convinced the daughter not to leave her father for a moment.

During the post-operative treatment with X-rays and radium capsules – it seems that the medics had diagnosed a malignant tumour from the start, but the patient was never told this explicitly – Freud shared his convalescence with his much-loved grandson Heinele, Sophie's second child, who had had his tonsils out. Shortly before the summer, the boy's death at the age of four and a half, "the most intelligent child he had ever encountered," from a severe miliary tuberculosis, reawakened the grief for the loss of Sophie and "killed something in him for good"[73] with an even deeper pain. After this event, Freud felt inwardly removed from life, and he believed it was this indifference that gave him the strength to endure the series of operations and treatments which accompanied the long progress of his cancer.

During the vacation at Lavarone (Lafraun), where the whole committee gathered around Freud for the last time, Felix Deutsch decided that more radical surgery was necessary and recommended Professor Pichler, a new and more skilful surgeon with experience of facial reconstructions for the war-wounded. Anna now confided in Lou that she would not now be away from her father under any circumstances (29/08/1923).

During a period of remission, with the prospect of the operation ahead, Freud decided to take his daughter to Rome: it was a trip he had promised her, planned as soon as he discovered his illness, and the days were manically filled with visits to all the various, precious places he wanted her to see, a legacy before he died, together with the wealth and enjoyment he had himself found there. This two-week voyage to Italy in September, Freud's last journey, seemingly a prelude to his farewell, "unforgettable" and "wonderful" as Anna called it,[74] sealed the indissolubility of their union and their mutual dependency, both physical and psychic, for the remaining 16 years of his life and beyond.

For some, that journey was interpreted as the passing of the sceptre.[75]

On his return to Vienna, Freud underwent a massive two-stage operation, after which he required a prosthesis to separate his mouth from the nasal cavity: eating and speaking both became highly uncomfortable, as were the daily checks of the scar and the prosthesis. "From the onset of this illness to the end of his life Freud refused to have any other nurse than his daughter Anna," says Jones, adding,

> He made a pact with her at the beginning that no sentiment was to be displayed; all that was necessary had to be performed in a cool matter-of-fact fashion with the absence of emotion characteristic of a surgeon. This attitude, her courage and firmness, enabled her to adhere to the pact even in the most agonizing situations.
>
> (*III*, p. 101)

And so this was what became of the old understanding between them.

Towards the end of that demanding year, when Prof Pichler's visits to her father were less frequent and her time and thoughts were less taken up with her father's post-operative recovery, Anna was assailed by anxiety, and, on the pretext of needing supervision for the patients she had begun to treat, she resumed her analytic conversations with him. From Göttingen, Lou Salomé tried to urge her towards emancipation, offering her own personal view of the analytic process and its conclusion (18/01/1924). But the resolution of the analysis and the return to life were still more dramatic now for Anna after the deaths of her sister and nephew, and in the conditions she had been living through and her father still was. There was an immediate and intrusive re-emergence of her daydreams and masturbatory fantasies. She wrote to Salomé:

> In the last week my "nice stories" all the sudden surfaced again and rampaged for days as they have not for a long while. Now they are asleep again, but I was impressed by how unchangeable and forceful and alluring such a daydream is, even if it has been – like my poor one – pulled apart, analyzed, published, and every way mishandled and mistreated.
>
> (25/01/1924)

This was the reason for the second tranche of analysis, probably without the display of "sentiment," in which the unresolvable nature of their bond was mutually confirmed.[76] From now on Anna would be beside her father in an intimacy deepened by the need for daily physical care, taking charge of the regular medical bulletins and relations with the members of the committee, which she would also join. Completely absorbed by her father's existence, the daughter became the exclusive, jealous partner of his every activity: anyone who wanted to get in touch with Freud had to go through Anna, who screened his phone calls, made and filtered his appointments, and was sometimes present at his meetings. The denied unconscious seductiveness of this bond even came to involve itself in the experiments with telepathy and with the challenging of every psychic boundary which Freud organised with Ferenczi in this period.

Although Freud rationalised his daughter's altruism by comparing her to Antigone,[77] it is doubtful how far he was able to appreciate the Sophoclean character's tragic significance, a virgin imprisoned between life and death in a tomb-incubator:[78] he never thanked her for her sacrifice because he felt that theirs was a unique destiny which she could not have lived through differently.

The wonder was that, despite everything, Anna's theoretical and clinical work advanced rapidly. She did not devote any specific text to female sexuality[79] but in 1927 published *Introduction to the Technique of Child Analysis*, making her mark on the international scene and becoming a highly controversial figure: not only because of the then hotly debated question of psychoanalysts' medical or lay training but also because of her surname. Her professional life would never be easy.[80] It was not long before Jones at the Institute of Psychoanalysis which he had founded in London in 1924 began criticising her as part of his support for the different approach to analytic work being developed by Melanie Klein (his own children and his wife were benefiting from its efficacy). In his correspondence with Freud, he called Anna's publication premature and ventured to identify resistances incompletely analysed by her father as the reason for certain limitations in her interpretative orientation with children and for the importance she was attributing to the actual relationship with the parents.[81] Freud tried to take an impartial position and, in spite of his illness, firmly opposed Jones's campaign, which was emphasising the differences and contrasts between the two schools of child analysis and, above all, was using improper weapons to delegitimise his young rival and her nascent leadership.[82] At this point, Jones's jealousy and the old dispute over occultism had been shifted onto Anna.

After the dissolution of his committee, Freud began to form a court of women among whom to end his life, just as he had begun it in the midst of his five sisters.[83] Among these (alongside Helene Deutsch, Eva Rosenfeld, Marie Bonaparte, and Ruth Mack Brunswick), Anna certainly had a privileged place but was never able to rid herself of the jealousy she felt for these possible rivals or her daydreams – or her unflagging passion for needlework, knitting and weaving like one of the three Fates – while caring for her father and for psychoanalysis.

Life had in store a possibility of happiness just for her, when in the spring of 1925, Dorothy Burlingham made her appearance and became her beloved lifelong companion, representing the answer to that *Etwas-Haben-Wollen* (wanting-to-have-something)[84] that had always caused her so much suffering. Newly arrived in Vienna, having difficulties with her marriage, the young heiress to the American Tiffany dynasty had asked Anna to treat her children and begun an analysis of her own, first with Reik and then with Freud (from 1927 until his death).

Apparently Freud was not unduly pained by this development of Anna's life and analysis which ruled out marriage and having children (a declaration of homosexuality, probably not consummated). And yet it is in the affective context of his first awareness of his daughter's choice that he famously confided to Marie Bonaparte, whom he had just taken into analysis, that after 30 years of research into the female psyche he still did not know *Was will das Weib?* (What does a woman want?).[85]

Dorothy soon became part of the Freud family, coming to live with her children on the third floor of the Berggasse house and sharing with Anna a permanent rather than interminable analysis with her father (and together with the collusiveness of the bond). I should add that the example of thought transmission – the coincidence of the "gold coin" quoted in the conclusion to *Lecture XXX* taken from the paper with which Burlingham joined the Viennese Psychoanalytic Society (1932) – was in fact autobiographical:[86] it refers to an episode in the analysis of her son Robert (with Anna) and her own analysis (with Sigmund). We also find it mentioned in Freud's reply to Jones who had criticised the validity of the comments on the Forsyth case on the grounds of its dating.

> Regarding telepathy . . . until a few years ago I had the same thoughts as you have now. Also your argument of a delayed revision no longer holds. For instance we observed and tested again (repeated twice) the case of the gold coin.
>
> (13/01/1933)

This final element finds its place in the mosaic we have been gradually recomposing and completes the picture of the telepathic *mother-son* coin, integrating it with its hidden *father-daughter* side.

Unlike Burlingham, Anna never wrote about telepathy, but the bond which kept her tied to her father was an extreme coincidence of thoughts and affects.

> It was a deep silent understanding and sympathy that reigned between them. The mutual understanding must have been something extraordinary, a silent communication almost telepathic in quality where the deepest thoughts and feelings could be conveyed by a faint gesture.
>
> (E Jones, *III*. p. 239)

In 1929 Anna confessed to her friend Eva Rosenfeld, who was in analysis with Freud:

> You know, there is no contradiction in your undergoing analysis in a place where you would prefer to come for love's sake alone. I did the same thing, and perhaps because of it, the two things became inextricably bound together for me.
>
> (22/03/1929)[87]

The bond was sealed in London on Freud's deathbed when, in 1939, the cancer that was sharing Freud's life presented in a new and more aggressive form, and Trotter ruled out any further surgery.[88]

It was with Anna's approval that Freud reminded Schur of his promise to mitigate his final sufferings: *Caritas* had been transformed into *Pietas*, and birth and death were coming together in a woman's arms.

Like the protagonist of *The Wild Ass's Skin*, the novel by Balzac which Freud read on his deathbed, Rodrigué imagines him unconsciously taking part in a Faustian pact agreed at the time of the dream about Irma's injection and considers the disease of the mouth foretold in it as the price set by destiny for his *descent to the Mothers* and the discovery of psychoanalysis.[89]

In his biography of Freud, Jones conceals the identity of Anna's analyst but adds a message to the dedication on the title page: *To Anna Freud, true daughter of an immortal sire.*

Notes

1 Molnar, 2014.
2 Young-Bruehl, 1988, p. 69.
3 Anna Freud to E. Rosenfeld, 22/03/1929 in Houssier, 2011.
4 Anton Von Freund's sister Katà Levi was in analysis at the same time as Anna and reported it to Roazen (Albano, 1987, p. 206).
5 20/10/1918.
6 Eva Rosenfeld in Roazen, 1995.
7 06/01/1919.
8 24/01/1919.
9 17/03/1919.
10 18/04/1919.
11 In Houssier, 2011.
12 24/07/1919.
13 Kardiner in Albano, 1987.
14 Jones, *III*, p. 29.
15 6/11/1921.
16 Federn, 1985.
17 Reich, 1952.
18 Roazen, 1969, p. 100.
19 22/05/1921.
20 29/05/1921.
21 21/09/1921.
22 Jones, *III*, p. 85.
23 Andreas-Salomé to Freud, 28/08/1917.
24 Pfeiffer, 1972.
25 Andreas-Salomé to A Freud, 30/01/1922.
26 Young-Bruehl, 1988, p. 81.
27 Andreas-Salomé to A. Freud, 22/12/1921.
28 Freud to Eitingon, 11/11/21 and to E. Freud, 20/12/1921.
29 A. Freud to S. Freud, 23/03/1922.
30 Freud to Salomé, 13/03/1922.
31 30/03/1922.
32 1/06/1922.
33 "This taboo [of Virginity] may have been intensified by the fact that at one time (in a matriarchal society) the woman may have been the dominant partner. In this way, like the defeated deities, she acquired demonic properties, and was feared as an agent of

retribution. . . . which may still play its part as the earliest positive basis for the precautionary measures of the male" (Andreas-Salomé to Freud, 30/01/11919).
34 See Sayers, 1991.
35 After the flu from which Alix Strachey suffered, 26/02/1922.
36 19/02/1926, in Young-Bruehl, 1988 p. 133.
37 5/08/1923.
38 Falzeder, 2015, p. 68.
39 Pragier and Faure Pragier, 1993.
40 Spector Pearson, 1997.
41 Freud, 1922b.
42 Eifermann, 1997; Modell, 1997.
43 Mahony, 1997.
44 Quoted in Mahony, 1997, p. 50.
45 J. Novick, K. K. Novick, 1997.
46 Lopez and Zorzi, 2005.
47 20/07/1920.
48 Novick and Novick, 1997; Britton, 2003.
49 Modell hypothesizes that the sense of guilt does not come only from the incestuous fantasy but that masochistic fantasies are more complex and derive from the child's need to have permission from a damaged mother to experience pleasure (1997).
50 Eifermann, 1997.
51 Roazen, 1993.
52 Mahony, 1997, p. 49.
53 Houssier, 2009.
54 Roazen, 1975.
55 1990, p. 225.
56 Giovannetti, 1997.
57 Freud to Ferenczi, 12/05/1919; Freud, 1921a.
58 Following different paths, Torok (1983) and Semi (2009) also associate the writing of *Beyond the Pleasure Principle* with that of *Psychoanalysis and Telepathy*.
59 Roussillon, 2016.
60 Abraham and Torok, 1987.
61 1980, p. 259.
62 Balsamo and Napolitano, 1998.
63 Jones, *III*, p. 42; see Freud to Eitingon, 8/03/1920.
64 1920b, pp. 14ff.
65 This sentence will catch Winnicott's attention and stimulate his ready and exhaustive answer: on the found-created object (1963), on the function of the mother as a mirror (1967a), on the use of an object (1969a), and even more widely on the function of play (see 1971).
66 "The employment of a fiction like this is, however, justified when one considers that the infant – provided one includes with it the care it receives from its mother – does almost realize a psychical system of this kind" (Freud, 1911, p. 219, n. 4). From here, too, Winnicott, passing through Ferenczi (1913), will develop Freud's reflection in his affirmation that "there is no such thing as a baby" (Lecture to the *British Psychoanalytic Society,* 1948, p. 99).
67 In 1919, Freud added this footnote to *the Interpretation of Dreams* (Dreams of the Death of Persons of Whom the Dreamer Is Fond, p. 255): "An observation made by a parent who had a knowledge of psycho-analysis caught the actual moment at which his highly intelligent four-year-old daughter perceived the distinction between being 'gone' and being 'dead' ['*fortsein*' und '*totsein*']. The little girl had been troublesome at meal-time and noticed that one of the maids at the pension where they were staying

was looking at her askance. 'I wish Josefine was dead,' was the child's comment to her father. 'Why dead?' enquired her father soothingly, 'wouldn't it do if she went away?' 'No,' replied the child; 'then she'd come back again'."

68 Laplanche, 1997; Lopez, 2001.

69 Kamieniak, 2016; Benveniste, 2008.

70 Roudinesco, 2012.

71 Roazen, 1975, 1995; Appignanesi and Forrester, 1992.

72 Andreas-Salomé, 6/06/1922; Freud, 3/07/22.

73 Jones, *III*, pp. 96–97.

74 Rodrigué, 1996, *II*, p. 295.

75 D'angelo, 2020.

76 Also in this case, the analysis would have influenced the development of Freud's thinking about masochism (1924) and female sexuality (1925a) but also the theme of negation (1925b). It is striking that he entrusted his daughter Anna with the presentation (Homburg, 1925) of "Some Psychological Consequences of the Anatomical Distinction between the Sexes." See Argentieri (1992), Pragier and Faure Pragier (1993) and Quinodoz (1997).

77 Letter to A. Zweig 25/02/1934.

78 See Zambrano, 1967; Balsamo and Napolitano, 1998; Cupelloni, 2007.

79 Apart from *Jealousy and the Desire for Masculinity*, coeval with the second period of analysis, read in December 1925 and never published (Young-Bruehl, 1988; Stewart-Steinberg, 2011).

80 Her professional growth matured above all in London, after Freud's death, when she was able to demonstrate that she was not only "her father's daughter" (Sophie Freud, 1988, p. 298).

81 Jones to Freud, 16/05/1927.

82 See Freud to Jones: 31/05/1927; 23/09/1927; 9/10/1927; 22/02/1928.

83 Roazen, 1975.

84 Anna Freud to Eitingon 19/02/1926, in Young-Bruehl, 1988, p. 133.

85 Marie Bonaparte's journals, 8/12/1925 (Elms, 2001).

86 Hellmann, 1980.

87 Houssier, 1992, p. 144.

88 Freud to A Zweig 20/02/1939 and 5/03/1939. According to Schavelzon, it was only now that a biopsy provided a certain diagnosis of incurable and inoperable cancer (in Rodrigué, 1996).

89 1996, *II*, p. 502.

Chapter 16

1932

"Dreams and Occultism" and "Confusion of Tongues between Adults and the Child"

The "Forsyth" case has one last thing to tell us in relation to the second context, that of 1932 when Freud decided to publish it in "Dreams and Occultism": this was after his mother's death in 1930 and during the final months of Ferenczi's life.

Freud's mother had just reached the age of 95. Combative and full of vitality, she could still be demanding, vain, almost tyrannical: at 90, she could complain when buying a hat that "it makes me look old," and during her last summer, she insisted on being taken to the spa in an ambulance.[1]

As far as he could, Freud had been careful to keep the deaths in the family from her,[2] and when he became ill his first concern had been that she should not know about it; he managed to give her highly softened information about the operations that would result in a long absence. In any case, Amalia Freud had never been endowed with patience and made sure she avoided learning about other people's misfortunes or looking after them: the care she took to avoid news of this kind may have been motivated by an awareness of her inability to contain her emotions and to empathise with pain and still more by the fear of having to take responsibility for Sigmund's anxieties on top of her own.[3]

In September 1930, when Ferenczi sent him a telegram of condolences for her death, Freud replied that, unlike what he had experienced after his father's death, this great event had had a strange effect on him:

> No pain, no mourning, which can probably be explained by the secondary circumstances, the advanced age, the sympathy with her helplessness at the end. At the same time a feeling of liberation, of being set free, that I also think I understand. I was not permitted to die as long as she was alive, and now I may. Somehow, in deeper layers, the values of life will have been markedly changed.
>
> (16/09/1930)

This time, without regret, Freud did not attend the funeral and let Anna stand in for him, as she had done a month before to receive the Goethe Prize on his behalf, taking responsibility for those lively feelings that he retreated from. It is significant that in the letter I just quoted, while appreciating Ferenczi's new theoretical

DOI: 10.4324/9781003246480-17

suggestions, Freud followed this with a comment on the theme of trauma that may be applicable to his condition on "deeper layers":

> The new views about the traumatic fragmentation of mental life that you indicated seem to me to be very ingenious and have something of the great characteristic of the Theory of Genitality. I only think that one can hardly speak of trauma in the extraordinary synthetic activity of the ego without treating the reactive scar formation along with it. The latter, of course, also produces what we see; we must make the traumas accessible.
>
> (*ibid.*)

In reality, the two men were no longer so assiduously sharing their hypotheses and researches: the exchange of opinions on this occasion reveals some different but complementary points of view about the potential and the impasses of treatment.

Thanking Freud for his thoughts about his new work, Ferenczi made clear that while the "*theory of genitality*" (*Thalassa*, 1924) was the product of pure speculation, the newer views that he was preparing for the next Congress arose from his clinical practice and were being developed and modified in accordance with it, and he insisted that they were proving to be valid and usable on both the theoretical and practical levels. He had in mind concepts such as the "psychic concussion" (1934) suffered by patients with psychotic symptomatology, the fragmentation and atomisation of the personality, and the formation of psychic retreats. As he clarified:

> It goes without saying that you are completely right when you place the never resting tendency to unification in mental life alongside the trauma. . . . Only I find that the expression "scar formation," as far as my experience goes, does not characterize mastery of trauma by means of pathological reaction quite accurately, inasmuch as the mental pathological products are not so rigid and incapable of regeneration as are the scars of bodily tissues.
>
> (21/09/1930)

In the meantime, with his mind on his mother's death and the threatening scar in his mouth, Freud did not give up the cigars and nicotine that were doing him so much harm (under histological examination, further small interventions fortunately showed no signs of malignity but brought constant alarm), and he resented the fact that his friend was so absorbed in his work, got in touch less often, and did not seem interested in his health.[4] In May 1931, when the Hungarian attended the meeting of the Viennese Society in honour of his 75th birthday, Freud met him, and only him, for a few minutes, having just returned home from hospital after a new intervention to treat an enlargement of the scar.[5]

In the paper which Ferenczi had read on that occasion, *Child-Analysis in the Analysis of Adults*, he showed how he had for some time been focusing on his own psychic scars. In 1929, he had written *The Unwelcome Child and His Death-Instinct*, and now, for the IPA Congress of 1931 (which did not take place), he was preparing a further text on the compulsion to repeat in which was suggesting to Freud that dream had a "*second function*" which he called "traumatolitic," linked not to the day's residues but to the re-emergence of unresolved sense impressions, "life remains" desperate for a new and better solution.[6]

Freud no longer seemed much concerned with the new theories that Ferenczi was trying to discuss with him but instead complained that his friend was so taken up with them and could no longer spend time in Vienna, writing to him that "one shouldn't postpone anything! Everything is so uncertain."[7]

At the end of the year, Freud had a chance to call his Hungarian friend to order, taking issue with certain erotic satisfactions that he was allowing his patients. There were rumours in Vienna that Clara Thompson had boasted to other pupils and colleagues that she could "kiss Papa Ferenczi" as often as she liked.[8] Freud's letter of 13 December 1931 was resigned, ironic in tone, and sometimes cutting (perhaps because he was remembering his own experience with Eckstein or maybe in an unconscious reaction to the psychological seduction he had practised on his daughter).[9] He reprimanded Ferenczi for playing at being the tender and indulgent mother to himself, of living through a second puberty. His words strikingly recall the words he used in his youth to warn his friend Silberstein about the danger of kisses:[10] in reality, he had been upset by his friend's silence.

On 27 December, Ferenczi reassured Freud about his experiments in technique, claiming that he had taken his "youthful sins" to heart but was not repeating them.

In the *Clinical Diary* that he was starting to write at this time – "a nine-month long letter to Freud"[11] in German, as if continuing their interrupted dialogue – he showed that he had in fact been able to bring Thompson's treatment to a successful conclusion. Indeed, he had managed to interpret the deep meaning of the series of acts that he had allowed her (permitting such behaviour in sessions and the blatant, irreverent, and uninhibited showing-off that followed it), recognising in it the detailed re-enactment of the traumatic childhood scene (including the vengeful attack on her abusive father and the expiatory castration):

> As a child, had been grossly abused sexually by her father, who was out of control; later, obviously because of the father's bad conscience and social anxiety, he relived her, so to speak. The daughter had to take revenge on her father indirectly, by failing in her own life.
>
> (Ferenczi, *Clinical Diary*, 7/01/1932)

The break between Freud and Ferenczi was only apparently a disagreement about technique. There was the problem of how to work analytically on trauma, on psychically unelaborated material repressed in the unconscious but excluded from consideration because it related to experiences prior to the acquisition of language and responsible for the fragmentation of the Ego. The dispute did not arise from modifications of the setting – Freud himself often showed equally little regard for the rules[12] – but rather from the fact that Ferenczi was trying to move beyond the theoretical and therapeutic system based on the Oedipus complex in favour of a pre-oedipal system, and this meant a return to the old topic of seduction, along with that of hypnoid dissociation dear to Breuer. Moreover, because of the way he came to terms with the fascinating and "occult" aspects of the preverbal area,[13] Freud could not approve of Ferenczi increasing the patient's regression and dependency on the analyst.[14] This disturbing constellation was the Hungarian's "demonic" field of exploration as an analyst ready to listen to "the baby wailing on the couch."[15]

In his *Clinical Diary*, Ferenczi relocated traumatic dissociation in its environmental circumstances, as the effect of "an alien will," a repression "imposed" on the infant through that "hypnotic" mode of intrusion originating in the maternal abandonment or paternal terrorism that he had been describing since 1909. On these levels, the "repressed" would be "located, according to feeling and linguistic usage, 'beside itself'" (24/01/1932) and would be highlighted in a relational context through the associations which the analyst adds pre-consciously on the basis of the emotions and somatic states that come to life in the session as well as the unconscious reactions of the countertransference.

It was the transmission of thought in the present moment of the analytic process, the meeting of minds, that interested him. Reworking his concept of "dialogues of the unconscious" (1915), Ferenczi was enhancing the analyst's capacity for "relaxation" in the "free-floating attention" recommended by Freud, eventually describing certain processes of treatment as a "falling into a *trance* simultaneously."[16] This might seem like a return to somnambulism and an invitation to regression in technique and theory, but in fact, Ferenczi's methodology was using the relationship to recover the enthralling potency of the mother-infant rapport without inwardly abandoning the critical attitude and capacity for interpretation: "In time one learns to interrupt the letting oneself go on *certain signals from the preconscious*."[17]

Working on the countertransference, on the question of growth and the reciprocity and sympathy between analyst and patient, in his laboratory Ferenczi was experimenting with technical modifications that were not impulsiveness or acting out but true scientific experiments which recovered the hypnotic infantile elements set aside by Freud at the start of his discovery with the aim of bringing the trauma into analysis and reconstructing its words.

Freud could not follow him and considered him lost in "the island of dreams" with his "fantasy children."[18]

Fearful that by cultivating his new theory and technique Ferenczi would end up separating himself from the movement like Rank, but mostly as an attempt at a rapprochement, Freud tried to re-engage him in the scrummage with his colleagues by proposing him again as president of the International Association. Almost 15 years had passed since his election at the Budapest Congress and, after much hesitation, despite the prospect of Anna Freud's help as secretary and the support of two vice-presidents, in the end, Ferenczi turned down the candidature so that he could be free to pursue his research without institutional responsibilities.[19] It must have cost him a great deal to assert his autonomy in this way.

In the twists and turns of history, it was Jones who once again assumed the post of president, as he had in 1919, and this time he would keep it for many years. Thus, the Wiesbaden Congress which saw the Welshman's election also witnessed the presentation of the Hungarian's revolutionary theories.

In my opinion, when they met for the last time in Vienna just before this Congress in autumn 1932, and Ferenczi wanted to give Freud a preview of his *Confusion of the Tongues Between the Adults and the Child* in the presence of A A Brill, Freud withdrew affectively from his friend not so much because of his work's transgressiveness – which, in spite of everything Freud authorised him to read at Wiesbaden[20] – or because of possible hints at his relationship with Anna but because of the pain at acknowledging their affective differences and maybe because of his seriously deteriorating health, which was now clearly precarious. And so, when Ferenczi said goodbye, Freud refused to shake his hand.

Ferenczi already knew he was ill with pernicious anaemia, and it is possible that he was seeking a personal recognition of this but that for Freud it would have been unbearably painful to have to say goodbye to Ferenczi and then bury him.

That fact is that for both of them, teacher and pupil, the analysis was unfinished,[21] and, without knowing it, they were still thinking and writing together: it is no surprise that at the very time when Ferenczi was engaged in disentangling the unconscious Babel of the "language of tenderness" and the "language of passion" in the parent-infant dialogue, Freud was addressing the crux of telepathy and the direct unconscious communication between mother and child. When in December Freud sent Ferenczi the *New Introductory Lectures*, containing "Dreams and Occultism," as if in response to the reading of Ferenczi's paper, the old comrade of his explorations into the occult thanked him without comment. He had gone further, and in his *Clinical Diary* he had written:

> Others before me have already drawn attention to the remarkable frequency with so-called thought-transference phenomena occur between physician and patient, often in a way that goes far beyond the probability of mere chance. Should such things be confirmed some day, we analysts would probably find it plausible that the transference relationship could quite significantly promote the development of subtler manifestations of receptivity.
>
> (12/04/1932)

In the New Year wishes they exchanged at the start of 1933, Freud seemed unhappy and lightly scolded his friend for breaking the old "intimate community of life, feeling, and interest" that Ferenczi owed him (11/01/1933).

And in the end it was Ferenczi who died, in May 1933, before Freud and before the age of 60, the same age as his father.

A few years later, Freud would return to the maternal and relational element that he had sidelined, as if to reintegrate that part of the theory, the psychoanalysis that "involves two people," which he had left to the Hungarian to develop. So he set himself the task of investigating the part in the process of recollection that might be "the task performed by the analyst" which – he seems to say in self-justification – "has been pushed into the background" in order to better observe the complex dynamics in the patient's scenario.[22]

As an alternative to the mutual analysis proposed by Ferenczi, Freud makes clear from the outset that "the analyst has neither experienced nor repressed any of the material under consideration; his task cannot be to remember anything" but "to make out what has been forgotten from the traces which it has left behind or, more correctly, to construct it."[23]

The "work of construction, or, if it is preferred, of reconstruction," widens the analyst's field of action and facilitates a more unified and comprehensive intervention that supports memory and the understanding of the compulsion to repeat: he does not only interpret "some single element of the material, but "lays before the subject of the analysis a piece of his early history that he has forgotten."[24]

Reluctantly endorsing the path opened up by Ferenczi, Freud contemplates the possibility that analysis may gain access to the bit of historical truth in the traumatic area, together with the kernel of truth in delusion (p. 386): more generally, psychoanalysis shows that it is unafraid to address the reconstruction of the preverbal maternal.

Freud and Ferenczi, "the two SFs," worked together more than is thought, and Ferenczi's theories accompanied his friend's in counterpoint,[25] so in his last works Freud could not help pursuing a posthumous dialogue with Ferenczi.[26] In suppressing the value of Ferenczi's theories, including a veto on the English translation of *Confusion of Tongues*,[27] Jones was in fact censoring an occult part of Freud.

After Freud's death, the next generation of analytic practice had to navigate constantly between the styles and ideas of these two great men.[28] The first aspects of this confrontation took dialectical form in the "Controversial Discussions" (1943–44) held in London where psychoanalysts from Mitteleuropa had come to live during the build-up to the Second World War.

The debate, developing out of the experiences emerging from the technique and clinical practice of child analysis, set the theory of an early internal constitution of the Superego and unconscious phantasy – elaborated by Melanie Klein – against the theory of the Ego's development in the relationship with the parents – maintained by Anna Freud. Though very heated, the dispute did not lead to a split but instead encouraged the formation of a "middle group."

Among these analysts of "the independent group" it would be D W Winnicott, with "a look at Ferenczi" and "at a footnote by Freud,"[29] who conceived the symbolic value of that pro-phetic, pre-transferential function of the parents – "primary maternal preoccupation"[30] – which, by arousing desire, promoting "thought-transference" and the birth of language, is capable of preparing, *predicting* (etymologically, speaking before) the future.

A hundred years after the events being narrated, the gradual diminution of the need for an institutional censor or a dutiful reluctance to disseminate documents concerning the history of the pioneers, both analysts and patients, allows us to go back to the origins, making a historical recovery not only of the private and personal aspects but the of less well-known source, the "womb" in which psychoanalytic theory arose and grew, and to reformulate a history of our roots. Perhaps this work of reconstructing origins may also enable us to improve the ability of the various schools of psychoanalytic thought to converge and compare and recognise a common psychoanalytic identity and distinctiveness that go hand in hand with the realisation that theoretical models can function as expectations, defences, and predictions in relation to the analytic process itself.

Notes

1 Freud, 1957.
2 Freud to Samuel Freud, 21/08/1925.
3 See Bernays Heller, 1956.
4 Freud to Eitingon, 3/11/1930.
5 Freud to Eitingon, 7/05/1931.
6 Ferenczi to Freud, 31/05/1931 and Ferenczi, 1934.
7 Freud to Ferenczi, no date, probably 1931, p. 414.
8 See Pierri, 2022.
9 Rachman, 2003.
10 13/03/1875. See Pierri, 2022.
11 Martìn-Cabré, 1999, p. 100.
12 The so-called "Freudian" technique took shape at the Berlin institute and then in London, after his death. See Cremerius, 1985; Nissim Momigliano, 1987.
13 Roussillon, 1995.
14 Fromm, 1959.
15 *Is It an Adult or a Child Crying?* See the disagreement between Lacan and Granoff in Granoff, 2000, pp. 22–23 and 129.
16 12/04/1932.
17 1919, p. 189 (my italics).
18 Freud to Ferenczi, 12/05/1932.
19 Ferenczi to Freud, 21/08/1932.
20 Bergmann, 1997.
21 Dupont, 1985.
22 Freud, 1937, p. 258.
23 *ibid.*, pp. 258–259.
24 *ibid.*, p. 261.
25 Granoff, 2000; Haynal, 1992.
26 Press, 2006.
27 Masson deserves the credit for having first rehabilitated this essay by Ferenczi (1984).
28 Brabant, 2006.
29 Winnicott, 1967b, in 1989, p. 579.
30 1956[1958].

Chapter 17

"Herr Vorsicht," alias Paul Bernfeld

"The eldest of a family of eight or nine children"

Paul Bernfeld does not figure in any list of Freud's patients who have been so far identified. He was born in Vienna on 17/07/1871, the eldest of nine siblings,[1] and at the time of the session, he was 48 years old.

His birth was recorded in the registers of the Viennese Jewish community[2] by Adolf and Rosa Bernfeld, who were both of Czech origin. His father been in the textiles business and a distributor for Lipton's tea, and after his death in 1905, the business was taken over by the fourth son, Hans. We know that their brother Gustav was an inventor.

Paul also went into business and with Heinrich Salomon Rosenberg (born on 03/10/1871) ran a firm, *Materialwaren und Erdfarben* (Material goods and earth colours), that in the early years of the twentieth century traded in chemical and mineral products (graphite, asbestos, lime, talcum), mostly with Hungary.[3] He had been married first in 1896 to Ottilie Glogau (born on 26/11/1876) and after her death in 1926, the same year as his mother died, in 1931, at the age of 60, he married Anna Maria (Anny) Hager Weisskopf (born on 18/04/1894), a woman 23 years his junior.

We may imagine that she was "the beautiful, piquante, but poor girl" whom Paul Bernfeld, after his never-consummated first marriage, had been courting since 1919, when he was in analysis with Freud. Anny was then 25, only a year older than Anna Freud.

As we learn from the professor's diary,[4] Herr Bernfeld's analysis began on 2 April 1917, the Monday before Easter: the United States had entered the war, which was moving towards its end. It is possible that the request for treatment had been particularly motivated by his difficulties in dealing with the recent loss during that January of his brother Hans in his 30s after a long and painful illness.

There were five sessions a week, with a break on Wednesdays: after the famous session on 4 October, the treatment continued for another five months on the same pattern.

DOI: 10.4324/9781003246480-18

The last session noted by Freud is 2 April 1920, three years to the day after the first: the conclusion of the analysis coincided with Holy Week and Jones's latest visit to Vienna (during which Freud and Jones discussed *l'affaire Forsyth*).[5]

In September 1917, in "A Childhood Recollection from *Dichtung und Wahrheit*," confirming his interpretation of a scene from childhood recalled by Goethe (his pleasure in throwing dishes and plates out of the window), Freud inserted a further example of the game of "throwing objects away" as a symbolic or magical action to get rid of siblings, which is likely to refer to the recently started analysis of Paul Bernfeld.

Bernfeld seems to be the jealous patient – and the child beaten by his father – whom he uses to confirm his thesis. He writes:

> one day I had a patient who began his analysis with the following remarks, which I set down word for word: "I am the eldest of a family of eight or nine children.[1] One of my earliest recollections is of my father sitting on the bed in his night-shirt, and telling me laughingly that I had a new brother. I was then three and three-quarters years old; that is the difference in age between me and my next younger brother. I know, too, that a short time after (or was it a year before?)[2] I threw a lot of things, brushes – or was it only one brush? – shoes and other things, out of the window into the street. I have a still earlier recollection. When I was two years old, I spent a night with my parents in a hotel bedroom at Linz on the way to the Salzkammergut. I was so restless in the night and made such a noise that my father had to beat me."
>
> After hearing this statement I threw all doubts to the winds. When in analysis two things are brought out one immediately after the other, as though in one breath, we have to interpret this proximity as a connection of thought. It was, therefore, as if the patient had said, "*Because* I found that I had got a new brother, I shortly afterwards threw these things into the street." The act of flinging the brushes, shoes and so on, out of the window must be recognized as a reaction to the birth of the brother. Nor is it a matter for regret that in this instance the objects thrown out were not crockery but other things, probably anything the child could reach at the moment. – The hurling out (through the window into the street) thus proves to be the essential thing in the act, while the pleasure in the smashing and the noise, and the class of object on which "execution is done", are variable and unessential points.
>
> Naturally, the principle of there being a connection of thought must be applied as well to the patient's third childish recollection, which is the earliest, though it was put at the end of the short series. This can easily be done. Evidently the two-year-old child was so restless because he could not bear his parents being in bed together. On the journey it was no doubt impossible to avoid the child being a witness of this.
>
> [1]A momentary error of a striking character. It was probably induced by the influence of the intention, which was already showing itself, to get rid of a brother. (Cf. Ferenczi, 1912, "On Transitory Symptoms during Analysis".)

> [2]This doubt, attaching to the essential point of the communication for purposes of resistance, was shortly afterwards withdrawn by the patient of his own accord. (1917, pp. 153–154).

The concluding sentence of the example confirms the idea that the patient is Bernfeld:

> The feelings which were aroused at that time in the jealous little boy left him with an embitterment against women which persisted and permanently interfered with the development of his capacity for love.
>
> (*ibid.*)

Later, in *Beyond the Pleasure Principle*, interpreting the "*Fortsein*" game observed in his grandson Ernst, Freud refers to having known of "other children who liked to express similar hostile impulses by throwing away objects instead of persons" (1920b, p. 16).

We can very easily imagine Bernfeld's difficulties in dealing with his brother's death and also the intensity of Freud's countertransferential involvement with him.[6] It does not surprise us that, unlike what Freud might have us believe, the analysis of Paul Bernfeld may not have been broken off abruptly.

This would happen instead to Helen Deutsch in November 1919: after less than a year of treatment, at one day's notice, she had to leave her hour free for Sergei Pankeiev. Freud's former patient, made famous as the "Wolf Man," having been left penniless by the Revolution and now ill once again, arrived in Vienna from Russia after the borders reopened and was immediately taken back into analysis, this time free of charge.

We may wonder what Paul Bernfeld did to ensure that he was not abandoned and . . . did Freud in fact mean to leave him?

"Telepathy" must have counted for something: Herr Vorsicht had a much longer analysis than Dr Forsyth.

We have little other information about Paul Bernfeld's life. He died in Vienna on 30/11/1936 at the age of 65 while Europe was still at peace. He was buried beside his first wife Ottilie in Vienna's Heiligenstädter cemetery.[7] Having no children by either of his marriages, his only heirs were his second wife and his seven siblings. Of these, Otto was living in London, Sophie in Jerusalem, and the others in Vienna: before the Second World War, Juliana and Gertrude emigrated to New York and Greete to Sydney. Gustav, who stayed in Vienna, was the only victim of the Shoah.

The firm of Bernfeld & Rosenberg stayed in business until 1939, when it was shut down by the Nazis and then liquidated. In 1950, Paul Bernfeld's partner was reported missing, presumed dead: information later collected in the archive of the Shoah[8] reveals that Heinrich S Rosenberg and his wife Paula were deported to the Opole Ghetto in 1941 and Anny Bernfeld to Izbica in 1942.

None of them survived the extermination camp, most probably Belzec.[9]

The firm of Paul Bernfeld and Heinrich Rosenberg, B & R: jokes and repetitions by the preconscious

An anecdote taken from *The Psychopathology of Everyday Life* might lead us to think that Freud's relationship with Paul Bernfeld and his company went back for many years. But let's read the remarkable example taken from *Forgetting of Impressions and Knowledge*:

> I was requested by the firm of *B. and R.* to pay a professional visit to one of their staff. On my way there I was possessed by the thought that I must repeatedly have been in the building where their firm had its premises. *It was as if I had noticed their plate on a lower story while I was paying a professional visit on a higher one.* I could however recall neither what house it was nor whom I had visited there. Although the whole matter was of no importance or consequence, I nevertheless turned my mind to it and finally discovered in my usual roundabout way, by collecting the thoughts that occurred to me in connection with it, that the premises of the firm of B. and R. were on the floor below the Pension Fischer, where I have frequently visited patients. At the same time I also recalled the building that housed the offices and the pension. It was still a puzzle to me what motive was at work in this forgetting. I found nothing offensive to my memory in the firm itself or in the Pension Fischer or the patients who lived there. Moreover, I suspected that nothing very distressing could be involved; otherwise I would hardly have succeeded in recovering in a roundabout way what I had forgotten, without resorting to external assistance as I had in the previous example. It finally occurred to me that while I was actually on my way to this new patient, a gentleman whom I had difficulty in recognizing had greeted me in the street. I had seen this man some months before in an apparently grave condition and had passed sentence on him with a diagnosis of progressive paralysis; but later I heard he had recovered, so that my judgement must have been wrong. Unless, that is, there had been a remission of the type that is also found in dementia paralytica – in which case my diagnosis would be justified after all! The influence that made me forget where the offices of *B. and R.* were came from my meeting with this person, and my interest in solving the problem of what I had forgotten was transferred to it from this case of disputed diagnosis. But the associative link (for there was only a slender internal connection – the man who recovered contrary to expectation was also an official in a large firm which used to recommend patients to me) was provided by an identity of names. The physician with whom I had seen the supposed case of paralysis was also called Fischer, like the pension which was in the building and which I had forgotten.
>
> (pp. 138–139, my italics)

In fact, this is another pension, and a different company,[10] but the internal scene appears to be the same.

The example shows how in the past, far from conscious awareness, the whole coincidence of the "home visit" to Herr Paul Bernfeld had been fully prepared in Freud's psyche, confirming our hypothesis about coincidences and so-called telepathy in analysis being preconscious constructions by the analyst. In the 1901 situation, Freud is engaged in a house call and also worrying about a doubtful diagnosis, as he would be in 1919 about the fate of Anton von Freund, which is still uncertain after the initial remission of his illness.

It is hard to resist thinking that as he went to see von Freund in the Pension Atlanta, Freud knew perfectly well, preconsciously, that the building also housed Paul Bernfeld's company: his surprise and the joke that follows are a sign of something internally determined, like a scene already known and intentionally performed, in which, while playing with forgettings and negative hallucinations, the film studio of the Preconscious creates its magic. In the scheme of the unintended visit to Herr Paul B, in the disorientation as Freud looks at the panel of his office in the same building but on a different floor of the Pension Atlanta, there also seems to be a repetition of that strange case that Freud had pondered so many years before in *The Psychopathology of Everyday Life* when the cab driver had confused him by stopping at a building with the same number as the one where his very old lady patient lived, but in a parallel street.

Last, we may wonder how far the whole scene recalls Freud's visit to Kreuzlingen in 1912 and the misunderstanding (*I'm coming to your house, not actually to see you, but your neighbour Binswanger*) which made Jung jealous and hastened the break between them.[11] The similarity is accentuated by the fact that Anton von Freund was suffering from the same disease that had afflicted Binswanger at the same age: indeed, the favourable outcome for the Swiss friend prolonged Freud's hopes for his Hungarian benefactor.

It was a scene in which Freud was repeatedly confronted with the double, jealousy, and fears of death.

With Flammarion, thinking about the strange anecdote describing the cyclical return of the *plum-pudding*, quoted in our Chapter 1, we can ask ourselves, "Was it a vision? Or was it a joke?"

"All was soon explained," he concludes. "M de Fortgibu had been asked to dinner by a friend who lived in the same house, but had mistaken the door of his apartment."[12]

Notes

1 Otto, 1875; Oscar, 1878; Hans 1879; Juliana 1881; Gustav, 1882; Greete, 1883; Sophia, 1885, Gertrude, 1887 (www.geni.com/people/Paul-Bernfeld).
2 He had converted, or, at any rate, he "officially declared himself" to be of the Catholic confession.
3 Vienna city archive and Skues, 2019c.
4 Molnar, personal communication, from the *Freud Museum,* London.
5 See Chapter 19. On the internal meaning of Easter for Freud, see Bernfeld, 1951: on that date he began his private activity and also the only period of abstinence from smoking.

6 Hitschmann reported that "Goethe, too, as a little boy saw a younger brother die without regret" (Freud, 1917a, p. 151).
7 Skues, 2019c, p. 28.
8 *The Central Database of Shoah Victims' Names.*
9 In January 2016, I was able to contact two nephews of Paul Bernfeld's sister (Greete Koppstein, who died in Sydney in 1961, aged 78), who gave me some information about the family to add to what I had collected.
I thank them very much.
10 See Skues, 2019c.
11 See Pierri, 2022.
12 1900, p. 195.

Chapter 18

A secret in the "Preface"

The substitution of the third case

It must, of course, be stressed that the examples of apparently telepathic dreams and the "unfulfilled" prophecies reported by Freud in the *Vorbericht* and summarised in *Lecture XXX* may have contained an intense incestuous desire – father-daughter, mother-son, brother-sister – of which the subject had been fully aware: it was this element that had to be broadly censored when *Psychoanalysis and Telepathy* was posthumously published.[1]

As we learn from the complete version,[2] in the case of the prophecy about *crayfish- or oyster-poisoning*, Freud made it quite clear that the patient had a strong bond of love with his only sister, who was a few years younger, a love that he did not disguise: "What a pity we can't get married!" they had often said to each other.[3]

He adds that their mutual affection had never gone beyond the limits permissible between brother and sister, but when the sister became engaged, the patient caused a mountaineering accident involving his future brother-in-law which could be interpreted in analysis as an unconscious homicide-suicide attempt. Later, the Munich astrologer's extraordinary prophecy (using the date of birth to predict that "the person in question will die in July or August of this year of crayfish- or oyster-poisoning.") had caught the enquirer's persistent desire for death, as well as introducing the detail of the poisoning by prawns which had happened to his brother-in-law the previous summer.

The second prophecy, about the birth of two children by the age of 32, concerned a woman, the eldest of five sisters, whose childhood had been dominated by the unconscious desire to have a child by her father. She had consciously chosen to marry a rich cousin, Freud explains, in the fantasy of supporting her father, who used to confide in her about his difficult financial situation, as if helping her younger sisters who had no dowry.

Since she had only married her husband as a father-substitute, when she later learned that he was sterile and could therefore never become a *father*, the woman was afflicted with a severe form of neurosis. Shortly before she became ill, the prophecy of *Monsieur le professeur* (who by reading a palmprint had predicted the birth of two children at the age of 32) had amazed and satisfied her to an extraordinary degree, Freud reports, because it confirmed her identification with her mother, her being at her father's side, which had been her childhood secret.

DOI: 10.4324/9781003246480-19

And so we come to the third prophecy, the one inserted to replace the Forsyth case when Freud realised he had left his notes behind in Vienna: here the incestuous elements were concrete facts. This was the patient who had consulted the famous graphologist Schermann and received the warning that her lover "was at her last gasp, was at the point of suicide and would quite certainly kill herself."[4]

The case was complex: Freud first of all freed the patient from the compulsion that kept him tied to his lover – one of the best known demi-mondaines – in a perverse relationship where he cyclically tormented her, unconsciously trying to push her into suicide, only to make up with her and shower her with affection when he saw she had been reduced to despair. At this point, the analysis had to address the man's original relationship with another woman going back to his early youth – "a married lady in his own circle," writes Freud laconically in *Lecture XXX* – whom at the time he had only succeeded in winning over after attempting suicide. She was the one with whom he had a real bond, and it was to her that he was really aiming the love and threats of revenge being directed at the second woman. The patient was conceiving an entirely distinctive way of solving the problem with this first, older relationship. As Freud explained,

> She had a daughter, who was very fond of the young friend of the family and ostensibly knew nothing of the secret part he played. He now proposed to marry this girl.
>
> (p. 192)

The substitution of the daughter for the mother is so strikingly reminiscent of Ferenczi's painful problems with Gisela and Elma that Forrester (1997) hypothesised that the example concerned his analysis, but we have learned that the mother-daughter substitution also had to do with something intimate about Freud himself . . .

Paul Roazen was able to reconstruct the secret connected to this clinical case.[5] The young man, taken into treatment shortly after the end of the war and to whom Freud was greatly attached, was a Swedish millionaire, partner of the famous Ivar Kreuger, the "match-king."

In the long passage from *Vorbericht* that was cut but recovered by Ilse Grubrich Simitis, he is described as a man aged 35, "a person of demonic passion and energy, irresistible to women, well-liked and esteemed among men."[6] Freud goes on:

> He enjoys the reputation of a brilliant financier, and rose during the war from the position of a subordinate official to rank and fortune. The youngest child of a very ordinary family he developed an exceptionally powerful affection for his mother from infancy. His boyhood was unhappy; when he was 14 y. old, one of his much older brothers married and he transferred a passionate love to his young and beautiful sister-in-law, who at first treated him as a child. But he became more and more demanding as a lover, and, at the age of 17, unable

> to gain a hearing from his sister-in-law and having failed his examinations at business school – i. e., being spurned by both man and woman – he fired a bullet into his cardiac region and hovered for months between life and death. After this suicide attempt and the death of his mother which followed soon after he ultimately succeeded in conquering his beloved, who was 6 y older than himself. He lived in his brother's house and became the second husband of the young woman, with whom he gradually displaced the first, the father of her children. So 10 y ago when he was 25 y old, he began to chafe at the bit in this relationship, whereas she, the aging woman clung to him more and more tenderly. Characteristically, the turning point resulted from jealousy, as he watched her feed her last boy, who, incidentally, was by her account his child, because this revived in him the repressed memory of the same situation with his own mother. He now took other women as mistresses, whom he soon discarded again, until he came upon that cocotte, in whose toils he became entangled. She was, as it happens, the official sweetheart of one of his friends, whom he therefore had to deceive. The whole time he continued his intimate relations with his sister-in-law, who was also the confidant of his love affairs, which caused her great suffering.
>
> (Freud in Grubrich Simitis, 1993b, pp. 212–213)

So, the "married lady in his own circle" was his sister-in-law, and the young woman to whom the man had recently become betrothed was his brother's daughter, with whom he intended to repeat and complete the incestuous act previously consummated with his mother and wife.

Despite this, in 1921, Freud wrote, "I supported his intentions, since it offered what was a possible way out of his difficult situation even though an irregular one." He then added:

> But presently there came a dream which showed hostility to the girl; and now once more he consulted Schermann, who reported that the girl was childish and neurotic and should not be married. This time the great observer of human nature was right. The girl, who was by now regarded as the man's fiancée, behaved in a more and more contradictory manner, and it was decided that she should be analysed.
>
> (p. 192)

When he included the example in *Lecture XXX*, Freud had not mentioned the information about the family relationship, and the editors of the posthumous writings likewise decided to censor it in *Psychoanalysis and Telepathy*, together with the fact that the young woman was sent to Helene Deutsch for analysis, which had originally been reported there.[7]

Roazen's interviews with Deutsch enabled him to fill out this part of the story.[8] On reading the *Vorbericht* and recognising the case – as she had not been able to in *Lecture XXX* or in *Psychoanalysis and Telepathy* because of the cuts made by Freud and the posthumous censors – Deutsch recalled how when he recommended the patient, for whom he cared very much, Freud told her, half-joking, that there was "a secret" behind the referral, which he would leave her to find out on her own.

During a meeting some time later, Freud took Deutsch aside and "pulled over a chair for her" saying, 'So, what did you find?"[9] Deutsch told Freud that she now knew the "secret" but that there was another part to it that Freud himself did not know. During the treatment, she had found not only that the girl possessed a "preconscious perception" about the affair that had brought her mother and uncle together, a perception recorded when she was a child and which emerged in the first sessions, but that she had also built up a "family romance" in which she could imagine herself as the child of the illicit pair. It was this unconscious fantasy that was preventing the marriage while at the same time keeping her oedipally tied to her uncle.

And then Deutsch asked Freud "whether he was pleased at her solution to the mystery." She remembered that he had been "very fascinated" and had said that the marriage was "off."

Thus, once he had learned the extra secret of the affair from his pupil as it emerged in her treatment of the niece, Freud took it upon himself to urge the uncle to end that betrothal: the patient later "chose as his wife a respectable girl outside his family circle – a girl on whom Schermann has passed a favourable judgement."[10]

Notes

1 See Grubrich Simitis, 1993a; Roazen, 2001a.
2 Grubrich Simitis, 1993b; not in *SE*.
3 Freud, 1933, p. 43.
4 Freud, 1921 [1941], p. 192.
5 2001a.
6 1993b, p. 212.
7 Roazen suspects that the censoring of Deutsch, a beautiful woman who was only ten years her senior and had the credentials of a doctor and psychiatrist, was the result of Anna's jealousy.
8 2001a.
9 Roazen, 2001a, p. 805.
10 Freud, 1921 [1941], pp. 192–193.

Chapter 19

Dr David Forsyth leaves the scene and the story

Circumstances of the birth of the *International Journal of Psychoanalysis*

Seven weeks in Vienna

I hope the reader will allow some pages about the forgotten Dr David Forsyth who, it may be recalled, was the first paediatrician to try using psychoanalysis to understand the conditions of child development and the symptoms of the newborn infant (1909). This homage of ours, which is also a mark of gratitude and sympathy towards the many pioneers who, for different reasons, evade the storylines of the psychoanalytic movement, offers a chance to reflect on the importance of group dynamics and affiliations in the transmission of psychoanalysis so that we can understand how an individual's thought may enter, or depart from, the tradition.

Viewed *a posteriori*, Dr Forsyth – who will suffer the same oblivion as Paul Bernfeld – shows that he fully deserves the honour of having given his name to Freud's case study.

David Forsyth began his analysis on 6 October 1919. Freud was immediately able to appreciate the clarity and precision of his English, which made it easier for him to start his new work with foreigners, especially considering his struggle to cope with the "abominable diction" of his American patients.[1] And he was flattered by his new pupil. After a month of treatment, he confided to Abraham, "Dr Forsyth, who is still under analysis with me, turns out to be a very notable personality; he talks much about the great interest in analysis in England."[2]

Forsyth took part in Viennese social life and attended the Wednesday meetings of the Psychoanalytic Association, where he was able to meet all Freud's closest friends: Ferenczi, von Freund, and also Oskar Pfister, who had recently taken the opportunity of a humanitarian mission for Austrian children to come to Vienna and arrived in Berggasse carrying a heavy rucksack full of food. Otto and Tola Rank, despite the current privations and the small size of their apartment, generously opened their doors to hold a dinner party in honour of their British colleague.[3] Newly married, they loved hosting the members of the psychoanalytic group and, on occasion, Freud's patients and foreign visitors, rivalling the evenings organised by Helene and Felix Deutsch.

DOI: 10.4324/9781003246480-20

During his stay, David Forsyth tried in various ways to be a "prophet" bearing good tidings: he gave von Freund an encouraging prognosis – so Jones tells, missing no opportunity to cast doubt on his colleague's clinical acumen[4] – and did not hesitate to express his confidence in the prospects of the Austrian currency and the European situation. Unfortunately, his predictions, which temporarily endeared him to his hosts, all turned out to be false, not only for von Freund but also on the political front. "Our Forsyth's hopes for social progress will, I fear, not be fulfilled," wrote Ferenczi to Freud, describing the terrible conditions he found on his return to Budapest.[5]

Those seven intense weeks of analysis must have flown by for our paediatrician! On 19 November, he said goodbye to Freud and left Vienna with Pfister, who was returning to Zurich, and Rank, who should have travelled with him all the way to London (to work with Jones on the first issue of the *International Journal*) but was stopped on the Dutch border.

That same day, exhausted by all his new experiences, Freud wrote to Eitingon about Forsyth:

> a distinguished man, a little shy, reserved, senior practitioner at Guy's hospital and full Professor. He is a very good stand-in for Jones and has also been able to meet Ferenczi. And so there has been a very lively period of psychoanalysis socialising. Today silence and a hangover.
>
> (20/11/1919)

And at the end of the letter, he was careful to add: "Anna has joined the Verlag to take charge of the English correspondence and is already doing excellent work."

As for Forsyth, we know nothing about his experience of analysis and can only try to imagine the private upheavals it caused.

> Forsyth is back, deeply impressed with your technique and the excellence of your English. I am sure you found him a faithful analyst, and consolidated his devotion.
>
> (25/11/1919)

So wrote Jones to Freud, almost anticipating the clash . . .

Forsyth undoubtedly had directorial ambitions and would certainly have wanted to undermine his Welsh colleague as president of the British Society. . . . As Paul Roazen astutely observes, he was a fearsome rival for Jones: a personality of the highest intellectual attainment, he "had extensive connections with academic medicine," and, having been analysed by Freud, he could claim that "any part he played in psychoanalysis in England should be a major one."[6] What is more, before his departure, Freud himself had invited him to prepare an article for the new English-language journal.

Indeed, once he was back in Britain, Forsyth immediately showed his intolerance of Jones's pre-eminence and his inability to acknowledge his rival as Freud's representative alter Ego.

It is not out of the question that the intensity of the encounter with Freud and his fascinating yet simple personality was the reason for the violence with which hostilities were reopened, along with Forsyth's immersion in the warm welcome of his Viennese and Hungarian colleagues, which had opened up to him an unexpectedly rich cultural climate, though one fraught with conflict.

Forsyth must have begun to realise what a gold rush was in progress. Having tasted the vitality of his admittedly brief analytic experience – a direct one, rather than read, applied, or taught – and glimpsing the force of the repressed emotions and affects that were re-emerging in the transference, the fact of leaving Vienna just as things were heating up could have been unexpectedly painful for a man who had imagined he was in control of how his analysis ended, having so carefully planned it in advance. It is no coincidence that he would later write about "short analysis," cases where the patient is unable to arrange "more than perhaps a very few weeks' treatment":

> It is not only likely to result in no real benefit to the patient, but by leaving him with an erroneous opinion of the value of psycho-analysis, brings the treatment into disrepute. . . . In some cases a short treatment produces good results . . . but the selection of suitable cases as well as the conduct of the analysis require some considerable experience.
>
> (1922, pp. 21–22)

Forsyth's close acquaintance with Otto Rank did nothing to improve their collaboration with Jones on his plans for managing the funds of the *Press* and for organising the *Journal*'s first few issues. Rank, the envied pupil, had greatly changed since the early years of the war when he represented the ideal son and disciple, and Freud used to say of him, "Why is it that there can't be six such charming men in our group instead of only one?"[7] Now, alone among the pupils, he had had the privilege of appearing with two important contributions in several editions of *The Interpretation of Dreams*, even appearing on its cover as a co-author.[8] Having experienced Freud as a father-substitute (who had even funded his studies), Rank now considered himself Freud's authentic heir and was champing at the bit, even though he was still dependent on him and on the committee both for patients – he had recently begun to treat children – and for the modest salary that he was receiving as manager of the *Press*.

The fact that Jones decided to finance him personally made Rank feel patronised and gave him solid grounds for ingratitude; it was Jones he squared up to, even before he broke with Freud, in a whole series of misunderstandings and open clashes that would lead him to leave the movement within a few years.

But it was David Forsyth who stood out first against Jones, and as early as spring 1920, he was well on the way to a collision over the new psychoanalytic journal.

The Forsyth *affaire*

Let's remind ourselves that on 20 February 1919, Forsyth was one of the few analysts chosen by Ernest Jones to form the British Psychoanalytic Society, with the aim of purging its predecessor, the London Society, of members who were turning out to be compromised by the Jungian group. At that first meeting, together with the request for affiliation to the IPV and the procedures for nominating new members, approval was given to the proposed fixed annual fee of two guineas to fund the IPV and the English journal in preparation. Forsyth was more fully involved than he had been before in the new group's administrative and scientific activities, perhaps also in the light of the analysis which, unlike almost all the other members of the group, who had been analysed by Jones, he had planned with Freud in Vienna. Having joined the local executive, he had led two scientific seminars, presenting a paper in which he showed the applications of psychoanalysis to paediatrics, *The Psychology of the New-Born Infant.*[9]

In the first half of 1919, the plan for the *Journal* had been brought to the attention of the members many times by Jones in his capacity as president of the British Society and editor of the *Zeitschrift*, the official German journal which the *IJP* was to partner. They had in particular been informed[10] that the *Verlag*, the psychoanalytic publishing house which Freud had set up with Hungarian funding, would support the projected English journal, permitting translation of articles from his *Zeitschrift* provided that there was adequate support from the three Anglo-American societies (the British, American, and New York Psychoanalytic Societies).

To this end, a circular had already been sent around appealing for funds, with our Forsyth among its signatories.

On his return to London in late 1919, Jones had immediately reported to his colleagues about his visits to Switzerland and Vienna, his meeting with Freud and the members of the executive, and the agreements with Otto Rank, who would join him in managing the extension of the *Verlag* (the *International Psycho-Analytical Press*) into Britain. On 6 November, he had officially announced the publication of the *Journal*, which, after consultation with the presidents of the National Associations, the executive was proposing as the "official organ of the *International Psycho-Analytical* Association in English," specifying that under the direction of Professor Freud and on the same lines as the *Zeitschrift*, it would be entrusted provisionally to him, Jones, acting president of the Association, while waiting for his ratification at the Congress planned for September 1920.[11]

It is possible that David Forsyth, who returned to London in late November and missed the meeting, resented being kept in the dark about Jones's news and, both as a member of the local executive and as a university professor, felt high-handedly cut out of the new journal. He had put his professional credibility at risk by playing a major role in defending psychoanalysis in the medical world of London and may have felt used by his colleague.

From these beginnings develops the *affaire*, documented from the start in a frenetic series of notes and brief letters sent by Forsyth to Jones, asking to be kept better informed about the planning of the *Journal* and complaining that Jones was not reporting editorial decisions in detail to the executive of the BPS or submitting them for the approval of the members.

If we read the letters which Jones and Forsyth exchanged at this time[12] and compare them with the contemporary correspondence between Jones and Freud, we can find the tranquil Forsyth chasing after a position of eminence for himself in the prestigious sphere of scientific publications that must have been dear to his heart, with a clumsy attempt to gain it at the expense of the power he considered illicitly acquired by Jones.

Unaware of the secret executive that had been set up by the committee, Forsyth may have thought he was on the receiving end of some sharp practice on the part of his colleague: but this time it was Forsyth who made the false step, and when he realised this, he did not dare refer the matter back to Freud.

His remonstrances, which became more and more belligerent during February and March 1920, were about appointments to the editorial committee and the decision to hold their meetings in London, conditions he condemned as having been decided in advance and arbitrarily entrusted to Jones.

In the correspondence where the two competitors were trying to set out their respective positions in black and white, Forsyth moved from handwritten notes to elaborate and punctilious typewritten letters and seemed convinced that his colleague was playing a three-card trick on him. Comparing Jones to a character from Gilbert and Sullivan, he sought clarification of the puzzlement he had felt from the start about the editorial management: he advocated a more democratic and transparent awarding of responsibilities and threatened to withdraw his own support and resign from a local committee that had been reduced to a merely ornamental function, criticising its marginal role which was limited to consulting the International Assembly.

While declaring himself the spokesman for the perplexities and discontent of his British and American colleagues and their respective Societies,[13] Forsyth was really setting off on his own, impelled by an evident personal susceptibility. We may suppose that, immersed in the experience of working through the conclusion of his own analysis, he was finding a way to externalise his jealousy and resentment of the Master and reacting to his feeling of loss, threatening his abandonment and then making it a reality.

After confiding that he had agreed to contribute material to the journal only because of his regard for Freud, he was now not only refusing his financial support but actually going much further and, in a decidedly ungracious manner, declaring his intention to withdraw the two articles he had sent, even though they had been discussed, proofread, and gone to press: all this, while adding the insulting suspicion that Jones had underhandedly accepted Forsyth's work with the aim of persuading him to contribute to the journal financially.[14]

It was a low blow and quite unexpected. We know that in those days, the pupils who were able to do so vied with each other in their contributions to the funding of the movement. . . . After Anton von Freund, in May 1920, Max Eitingon provided a fund of a million crowns (5000 dollars) for the *Press*, temporarily solving the problem of publishing psychoanalysis. Jones himself had donated part of the modest inheritance from his father to the cause and to Rank's salary.

Jones's position was not easy: as both a lightning conductor for the management of the journal and acting president, in reality he was required above all to meet Freud's expectations and those of the small secret committee, which was itself divided.[15] His diplomatic response shows how much he felt he was in the spotlight and trying to control any personal animosity. In an openly friendly gesture, he challenged Forsyth to be more accommodating:

My dear Forsyth

Many thanks for the full statement of your views, which I was glad to have and which has the advantage of bringing matters to a head. I feel sure that we ought to be able to deal satisfactorily with the situation if only enough light is let in upon it. . . . Without entering into the details of your letter I should like to put the matter on another basis. Because of the great difficulty of re-establishing international contact and for other reasons especially operative in America the fortunes of psycho-analysis are just now at a very delicate, if not critical, juncture, and I am bound to regard the withdrawal of your support from our only coordinated activity as a great deal more important than your modesty would probably allow you to recognise. At a time therefore when the necessity for union is so vital, I cannot believe that you will persist in your decision so long as other courses are open to you.

I am obliged also to put forward the following personal considerations. Circumstances, including pressure from various sides, have compelled me, much against my personal inclinations, to play a prominent and active part in the ps – a movement, at the expense of much time, worry, and money. Now your letter amounts to this: that I have misused my position to such an extent as to forfeit any claim to the support of the most influential colleague in England. I have not heard a hint of similar criticism from anyone else, but it may very well be that you do not stand alone in your opinion. You must surely see that this cannot be a light matter for me, nor does the thought make it easy for me to continue my activities with the feeling that I have no confidence of these whose benefit I am working. In common fairness to myself, therefore, I feel I have the right to ask you to be willing to investigate the facts and motives more fully before taking a final decision. You will find that I am entirely open to any criticism as to the past and suggestions as to the future; fortunately, no irretrievable steps have been taken in regard to the Journal.

There are several ways in which the matter could be gone into . . .

With a good will on both sides it is unthinkable that psycho-analysts, of all people, should not be able to effect a modus vivendi, particularly in a matter so near to the cause they have at heart. (Jones to Forsyth, 8/03/1920)[16]

Jones also tried to explain himself in person, spending a long evening in discussion with his colleague to no great effect. Forsyth could not resign himself to the fact that the *Journal* was considered the sole responsibility of the international executive, and he insisted on the need to widen the organisation and management of the *Journal* more democratically to include the English-speaking societies with a view to encouraging the more vigorous growth of the movement.[17] The misunderstanding was caused by his failure to acknowledge Freud's special and personal authority at the heart of the Association (because of the need to defend his psychoanalytic copyright)[18] and his conviction that the new journal should appear as a grassroots expression of the work and power of the three English-speaking societies (the British, the New York, and the American) in alliance with the American *Psychoanalytic Review*, founded by W A White and S E Jelliffe as early as 1913 (and entirely independently of the International Association).

Instead the *Journal* came into being as an affiliate of the *Internazionale Zeitschrift für Ärztliche Psychoanalyse*, the international German-language journal founded by Freud as the official organ of the Association, managed by the central executive and under his control.[19]

When Jones returned to Vienna at Easter 1920 with his pregnant wife Kitty, among the various matters on which he consulted Freud were his difficulties with Forsyth. On his return to London, it was still his intention to win over his colleague, but in the meantime, Forsyth had gone his own way and offered the *British Journal of Psychology* a third article, "The Psychology of the New-Born Infant," which he had read and discussed with his colleagues at the British Society in spring 1919. Jones was informed about this immediately by the *BJP*'s punctilious editor and thus found himself swindled of this contribution, too, and after confirming with Forsyth that he really was determined to withdraw from the first issue of the *IJP*, so long awaited and already paginated, he referred the matter to the authority of Freud and Rank, sending them copies of the entire correspondence, commenting:

> Forsyth's resistances seem to have even increased during the interval, I am sorry to say, and I have lost all hope of his remaining with us (unless he can continue his analysis). . . . On my asking F. at the next society meeting whether this article was yet ready for press [*The Psychology of the New-Born Infant*], he became very guilty and ashamed and lied by saying "I don't know; I haven't seen it for a long time." I said no more.
>
> (24/04/1920)

This irritated Freud, and he strongly advised Jones not to indulge his colleague any further:

> As for Forsyth I regret his attitude sincerely but I have made up my mind not to address him any more unless he applies to me, which is not likely to happen. Leave him alone!
>
> (2/05/1920)

And Jones concluded:

> I am afraid I bore you with my affaire Forsyth. I will try to take your advice and leave him alone, if only he will do the same. I am now feeling distinctly hostile to him for his very scurvy behaviour.
>
> (7/05/1920)

David Forsyth finally decided to write directly to Freud, who responded with kindness and firmness in his dual authority as "teacher" and "proprietor" of the rights to psychoanalysis and made clear Forsyth's discourtesy in withdrawing his contributions to the *Journal*. He then reported to Jones: "It seemed important to me that he should not find me pliable nor think himself indispensable. It spoils a man's morals."[20] Jones was infuriated by the way his colleague was "slipping about like an eel"[21] and wanted to take the fight to Forsyth and assert the *Journal*'s rights,[22] But, after receiving Forsyth's final evasive reply, Freud repeated that it was best to proceed without him: "he must not be fortified in his disposition to think himself indispensable."[23]

Forsyth leaves the scene

By now David Forsyth had no ammunition left. The first issue of the *Journal* appeared in mid-July without his articles, and at the Hague in September the International Congress unanimously confirmed Jones's mandate. We do not know if the paediatrician was among the participants (it seems unlikely), but we learn from Freud that some time later, Forsyth got in touch again to justify his behaviour. Once again, he tried to cast Jones in a bad light (with the always valid excuse of Jones's character and his "autocratic" moods), but the Welshman's loyalty was beyond question.

Reporting this to Jones, Freud took the opportunity once again to urge transparency, inviting him to give proper consideration in the choice of co-editors and the contents of the *Journal* to the wishes of the representatives from the three English-speaking societies: "but nothing more," he stressed, insisting on the need to maintain both internal and external independence.[24] And Jones tried to rebut the accusations, claiming that he more deserved the reproach of being too democratic, diplomatic, and conciliatory.[25]

The second and subsequent volumes of the *Journal* carried the heading "Directed by Sigmund Freud" and "Edited by Ernest Jones with the assistance of D Bryan, J C Flugel, A A Brill, H W Frink, C P Oberndorf."

Forsyth lost his chance to appear among the co-editors.

The complete incompatibility between the Englishman and the Welshman, their inability to understand each other, was too deep rooted to be resolved by explanations. Although Jones was the victor, he did not win his university colleague's endorsement nor that of the always hostile London medical circle and the specialists of Harley Street and Wimpole Street (as witnessed by his indefinitely delayed election to the Royal College of Physicians, of which his paediatrician colleague had been a member since 1910).[26]

For his part, Forsyth denied Jones any recognition, keeping his distance, playing no part in the history of the movement, and never publishing a line in the *International Journal*. The already typeset article appeared in the *Proceedings of the Royal Society of Medicine* (1920), and the paper read to his colleagues but rejected by the *British Journal of Psychology* appeared in 1921 in *Psychoanalytic Review*.

From then on, "lost for the society, not for the cause,"[27] Forsyth remained on the fringes but was nevertheless able to exercise power in his own right: from his professorial chair at Charing Cross Hospital, he trained generations of students, introducing them to Freudian theory. In 1922, two years after Jones had published *Treatment of the Neuroses*, the university professor issued *The Technique of Psycho-Analysis* no less, a small volume, very clearly written and informative (it had some academic success),[28] which he sent to Jones and also to Freud.

In the introduction, he presented his book as being dictated by the need for a guide, not an alternative to analysis itself, to those who wanted to try their hand at this therapy:

> It will be my endeavour to deal from a practical standpoint with analytical procedure, to discuss the various difficulties which are likely to arise, and to show how to meet them and, better still, to forestall them.
>
> (Forsyth, 1922)

For all its skill and professionalism, this book brought no change in his dissociated position on the margins of the movement. Though the text was admirable, it omitted all analytic affiliation and reference to the movement. Jones took the opportunity to get back in touch and, not without a touch of condescension, invited his colleague to resume his membership of the Association:

Dear Forsyth,

Many thanks for getting your publishers to send me a copy of your new book. Please let me congratulate you on it for, if I may say so, I think it is very excellent, and certainly very much needed. It will of course receive a warm notice in the Journal and I wish it every success.

I do not wish to refer to past misunderstandings beyond expressing the hope that you have by now been able to deal with the conflicts they evidently provoked. But I should like to say that any time you care to rejoin the rest of us, you will be welcomed with every friendliness and respect.

(6/02/1922)[29]

Being quite capable of recognising good ideas, Jones was certainly struck by his colleague's ability and reviewed the book in the *Journal* (1922), but once again suffered feelings of inferiority and jealousy. In the letter he wrote asking Freud's opinion about the book, he mentioned his renewed intention to "amplify [his] name to Ernest Beddow-Jones," inserting one inherited by his father from his own mother, distinguishing himself from the other "half a million people called Jones."[30]

Freud's reply was comforting on all fronts: "I only know that you will continue to be Dr Ernest Jones to us," he wrote, adding, "Forsyth's little book is exceptionally good and full of sound judgement. I acknowledged it in a card to him."[31]

Forsyth's ambitious gesture fell into the void and received only this one nod from the Master, who, for his own part, had never published a book on technique, despite having frequently announced that he would do so.

Joan Riviere also wrote a review in which she astutely drew attention to certain ambivalences in the book and in its author about the centrality of free association and the analyst's place behind the couch and especially the lack of clarity about the role of the transference in treatment.[32] But to the very end, Forsyth would deny himself the satisfaction of entering into dialogue, comparing his work with others, or collaborating with them. And so, despite his unquestionable merits and his pioneering application of psychoanalysis to paediatrics, anticipating the work of D W Winnicott, he would remain a luminary unknown to most people, as would his numerous publications, certainly never adopted by psychoanalytic institutions, only read and cited by a few friendly colleagues and always benevolently reviewed in the *Journal*. He would continue to figure silently among the members of the British Society without presenting papers or joining the training committee.

From this position on the margins of the IPA but strongly placed at Charing Cross Hospital, the loyalty of the paediatrician Forsyth to Freud and to psychoanalysis remained unchanged. During the rise of Melanie Klein, who was invited to London by Ernest Jones, he found himself on the other side along with the old Freudians defending the position of Vienna and Anna Freud.[33]

As a member of the Society for the Study of Disease in Children, in 1927, he attended the lecture "The Adaptation of the Family to the Child" which Ferenczi gave to the British Psychological Society[34] during his visit to London and took a lively part in the discussion with Jones and Klein.

As we have seen, perhaps to try to counterbalance the power of the Kleinian school supported by his rival, in 1931, Forsyth used his position of authority to invite Freud to give the Huxley Memorial Lecture in London, but the professor had to decline.

In his jealousy on this occasion, too, Jones chose to remind Freud of his own loyalty and his absolute identification with "Darwin's Bulldog," T H Huxley.[35]

Time did not mitigate the intensity of the antagonism between the two duellists, who worked alongside each other for years in Harley Street, as we see from an exchange of letters in the Archives of the British Psycho-analytical Society documenting a further instance of friction in 1933, this time over the failure to pay a restaurant bill.[36]

Forsyth later devoted himself to writing more speculative works. In1935, he published *Psychology and Religion*. It was a subject that had always interested him, and in the conclusion, he compared the conflict between religion and science to an emancipatory conflict between the generations. His interpretation of the religious feeling in the light of psychology and psychoanalysis, for which he declared his debt to the writings of Freud, certainly did not go uncriticised (for example, by G K Chesterton).

In 1939, he published *How Life Began: a Speculative Study in Modern Biology* in which, seeking a general view that might include the various perspectives of the natural sciences, he brought together the topics that he had been passionate about in his youth.

About his personal life, we know only that he married and had two sons. He died in London on 10/04/1941 at the age of 64 in his house in Weymouth Street during the full fury of the Blitz: his obituary appeared in the *British Medical Journal*,[37] *Lancet*, *Nature*, and the *New York Times*, remembering him as a serious, stimulating, and highly regarded doctor and teacher and emphasised the courage with which he espoused the new psychological theories and declared his support for Freud from the earliest days without regard for the hostility this might have aroused.

There are no obituaries in the *IJP* or other psychoanalytic journals. At the first international psychoanalytic conference after the war, in Zurich in 1949, he appeared in the long list of psychoanalysts who had died since the last congress in Paris in 1938 (64 IPA members, mostly victims of Nazism) and was mentioned without further comment as being among the pioneers of psychoanalysis in England. The list, which Ernest Jones solemnly read out at the opening of the proceedings, was headed by Sigmund Freud, who had died in London in 1939, and included the last two colleagues from the committee, Max Eitingon and Hanns Sachs, so the Welshman could claim to be the only survivor of that intimate circle (forgetting Anna Freud!). The Assembly's minute's silence for the deceased members was Jones's homage and definitive farewell to his rival.

In 1986, R Horacio Etchegoyen, in the Preface to *The Fundamentals of Psychoanalytic Technique*, citing the few authors who had preceded him in the difficult task of writing a manual about technique, reported finding bibliographical references which indicated that in 1922, fully five years before the first lectures of E Glover (1927–28), another Londoner, David Forsyth, had published a work entitled *The Technique of Psychoanalysis* but that this had not had any great impact. In the preface to the 1999 edition, Etchegoyen added that when he was finally able to read it, he found it "well-written and well-thought-out, and very good for its time and place."[38]

But apart from this brief note by Etchegoyen, David Forsyth would have remained an honest and capable professor of paediatrics, an entirely anonymous English psychoanalyst, if it had not been for that session of Freud's with Herr Paul Bernfeld in 1919, which, by appropriating his name, made his seven weeks of analysis in Vienna pass into history.

Notes

1 Freud to Jones, 8/03/1920.
2 2/11/1919.
3 Roazen, 1975.
4 *III*, p. 19.
5 20/11/1919.
6 1975, p. 387.
7 Andreas-Salomé, 1958, p. 98, 12–13/02/1913; see also Marchioro, 2002–2003.

8 *Dreams and Poetry* and *Dreams and Myth* (1914) were included there for several years (eds. 4–7), see Marinelli and Mayer, 2002.
9 15/05/1919 and 12/06/1919.
10 In the meetings of 10/03/1919 and of 10/07/1919.
11 In "Reports of the I. P. A.," *Bulletin of the I.P.A.*, 1920, pp. 117–118.
12 See the archives of the British Psychoanalytical Society: E. Jones collection, P04-C-C-05.
13 He may have thought of finding an alliance in the dissatisfaction of A A Brill, initially excluded from the editorial board, or in people such as Tannenbaum who were not psychoanalysts and were not part of any company affiliated with the Association and who, together with Stekel and Silberer, released an English-language magazine, *Eros-Psyche*, which briefly rivalled the *Journal*.
14 Forsyth to Jones, 7/03/1920.
15 Also about the venue of the first post-war congress.
16 The Archives of the British Psychoanalytical Society have granted us kind permission to reproduce this unpublished letter by Ernest Jones to David Forsyth, 8/03/1920, Ernest Jones collection, P04-C-C-05. Courtesy of Jackie Jones copyright.
17 Forsyth to Jones, 21/03/1920.
18 See Kerr, 1993.
19 See Ferenczi, 1920.
20 13/05/1920.
21 Jones to Freud, 28/05/1920.
22 Jones to Freud: 18/05/1920.
23 Freud to Jones, 24/05/1920.
24 7/11/1920.
25 12/11/1920.
26 Winnicott, 1958a.
27 Freud to Jones, 7/11/1920.
28 Menninger, 1958.
29 The Archives of the British Psychoanalytical Society have granted us kind permission to reproduce this unpublished letter by Ernest Jones to David Forsyth, 06/02/1922, E. Jones collection, P04-C-C-05. Courtesy of Jackie Jones copyright.
30 16/03/1922.
31 23/03/1922.
32 1921–22.
33 Roazen, 1995.
34 Ferenczi, 1928.
35 15/01/1931.
36 Jones Collection, P04-C-C-05.
37 Which also provides the only available photo of him (1941, 1, 26 April, p. 652).
38 p. xxii. Since 1999, reprints of the Forsyth manual have appeared in London's Routledge in the *International Library of Psychology*, now also available in the internet archive.

Chapter 20

Freud's final orientation towards the West

From Vienna to London

"*Fortsein*": Professor Freud has "gone away"

Wishing to attribute a prophetic meaning to the session about the Forsyth case, based on the case's key word "foresight," one writer believed he saw in it Freud's presentiment of the illness that would strike him only a few years later, while others, looking at the case from the perspective of Jung's synchronicity theory, have seen it as a premonition of the Nazi nightmare that would fall on Vienna and force Freud into exile in England.[1]

After Hitler took power a month before his death in the spring of 1933, Ferenczi had urged Freud to leave with some of his patients and his daughter Anna and seek refuge in London while the political situation allowed him, but Freud took no notice. Most German analysts were leaving Berlin: in 1932, Sachs went to Boston, and in 1934, Eitingon decided to move to Jerusalem. Oliver and Ernst Freud also left for France and the United Kingdom.

A few years later, aged 82 and ill, Freud too would have to face the problem of emigration and the search for a safe place, and this time it was a matter of life and death allowing no further postponement.

On 12 March 1938, the Nazis invaded Austria, proclaiming its annexation to Germany: Freud noted "*Finis Austriae . . .*" in his diary.

Thomas Mann, who had moved to Switzerland in 1933 but had recently decided to seek greater safety in America, wrote in *Esquire Magazine*:

> I have a private suspicion that the élan of the march on Vienna had a secret spring: it was directed at the venerable Freud, the real and actual enemy, the philosopher and revealer of the neuroses, the great disillusioner, the seer and sayer of the laws of genius.[2]

The Führer arrived in Vienna two days after the *Anschluss*. While in nearby Schottengasse the crowd was following the line of armoured vehicles towards the Imperial Palace to acclaim Hitler's first speech, the Gestapo made an incursion into Berggasse to demand money and passports and to ransack the publishing house.

DOI: 10.4324/9781003246480-21

The efficient functionary Adolf Eichmann had also arrived in one of the columns bringing the bureaucracy of the deportations and the "final solution."[3]

Binswanger immediately wrote in alarm to Freud: "you would be welcome to come here as soon as you feel the need for a change of air."[4] And Schur recalled:

> None of us, who lived those days of gloom and horror, could ever forget them. But neither will we forget the ray of hope which was brought to us, when Jones arrived in Vienna on March 15, followed two days later by Marie Bonaparte.
>
> (1958, p. 738)

Age had done nothing to diminish Ernest Jones's courage: he flew straightaway to Prague and then took a small monoplane to Vienna, arriving in the midst of the occupying Nazi troops. He went with Anna Freud directly to the office of the *Verlag*, into the thick of the ransacking, and was immediately arrested. Since he was British, the Gestapo had to release him after an hour.[5] So Jones went to Freud's house and set about the difficult task of persuading the professor to leave.

On 20 March, in his capacity as president of the IPA, with Vice-Presidents Marie Bonaparte and Anna Freud, he attended the meeting that wound up the Viennese Psychoanalytic Society where, in the presence of the Nazi Party's Austrian Commissioner Anton Sauerwald and (representing Matthias Göring) Carl Müller-Braunschweig, Aryan member and secretary of the Berlin Psychoanalytic Society, already known as the "Göring Institute," Freud agreed that his society should be taken over by the BPS and that Jews should be excluded from it.[6]

While W C Bullit, US ambassador to France, and the consul in Vienna, Mr Wiley, alerted President Roosevelt's secretary of state and contacted the German ambassador in Paris, Count von Wilczek, with the aim of initiating all the diplomatic steps needed to obtain new emigration documents, Jones went straight back to London. There, on 21 March, a letter appeared in the *British Medical Journal* expressing alarm and solidarity with Austrian colleagues, signed by eminent clinicians, including Forsyth. With the help of his brother-in-law Trotter of the Royal Society, Jones persuaded the Home Secretary to release entry visas and UK work permits not only for Freud and those closest to him but also for his personal physician, his housekeeper, and several psychoanalysts and collaborators (Bibring, Kris, and Hoffer and their families[7]). In all, the list of those whom Jones enabled to enter the United Kingdom "clandestinely" numbered 18 adults and 6 children. The money necessary to organise this operation was found with the help of Marie Bonaparte, Dorothy Burlingham, and Bullit himself (Freud's own property had been instantly confiscated).

In Vienna, while he waited for the German documents authorising his emigration, Freud depended for his safety on Burlingham, who lived in the same apartment block and in an emergency would have been able to alert the American Embassy immediately.

For Jews, the situation was becoming more dangerous day by day; their businesses were being looted, and they were being attacked in the street even by civilians. The Gestapo had begun a terror campaign, and suicides were happening: the first convoys left for Dachau at the beginning of April, and by the middle of the month, 7500 arrested Jews were awaiting deportation.[8]

As manager of the *Verlag*, Martin Freud had been interrogated several times at Gestapo headquarters and threatened with arrest, and he was the first to leave the country. His father only agreed to his own departure on 22 March, ten days after the *Anschluss*, when the SS picked up Anna and took her in an open car to the Hotel Metropole, where she was detained for the whole day and was in danger of disappearing. This followed the intercepting of a letter that Anna had been sent by Müller-Braunschweig,[9] and she only avoided arrest thanks to a telephone call from the American ambassador, who had been promptly informed by Dorothy Burlingham. When Anna came home, she saw her father in tears for the very first time. It should be added that both she and Martin had been equipped with a lethal dose of Veronal by Max Schur.

According to Arendt, the fact that the Nazis could make exception for "special cases," individuals who were famous abroad, was part of their policy of legitimisation for their crimes (1963). But Freud's safety was partly due to the protection offered by Commissioner Anton Sauerwald, who had to oversee the liquidation of the publishing company and its financial affairs. This enigmatic Nazi seems to have started to become interested in psychoanalysis, perhaps having been struck by the old professor's personality: whether through conviction or calculation we do not know, but at risk to his own safety, he kept the audit of Freud's foreign assets hidden (which would have meant immediate arrest) and strove to facilitate Freud's emigration with his family and friends.[10] With Bonaparte's help, he took care of the collection of antiquities (2000 of the 3000 objects that Freud had collected came with him to Britain), and he was even able to arrange safe storage for many of his works in the vaults of the Austrian National Library.[11]

Less than a month before Freud's departure, the young Edmund Engelman was engaged by August Aichhorn to photograph the consulting room and the house inhabited by Sigmund Freud for over 40 years: the work was carried out over several rainy days with no artificial light or flash so as not to attract the attention of the Gestapo, who were keeping the building under surveillance.[12] Today, the black-and-white images of these interiors, observed by a visitor who had been invited to penetrate into the heart of this home under such terrible circumstances, show us the furnishings, the bookshelves, the famous couch, and the collection of antiquities but also the faces of Freud himself, Martha, and Anna in the setting that they would soon be leaving. They document a highly dramatic moment, fixing for posterity the intense atmosphere of the farewell, in which elegant, delicate arrangements of cut flowers on the tables seem to emphasise the fleeting nature of the situation.

Engelman took great risks to preserve the rolls of film until he could pass them on to Aichhorn, who was not Jewish, before escaping himself.

At the end of May, while the situation in Berggasse was still uncertain and there was no guarantee that Freud would be able to rescue his books, furniture, and the famous collection and bring them to safety, he wrote to his sister-in-law: "It is said that when a fox has a trapped leg, it cuts it with its teeth and runs off on three legs, we will follow its example."[13] The legend says that after signing the clearance form authorising his safe conduct out of the country, Freud added in his own handwriting, "I can recommend the Gestapo very much to everyone." This is in fact apocryphal, and comes from Martin Freud.[14]

On 4 June 1938, Freud boarded the Orient Express and left Vienna for ever. His apartment in Berggasse would soon be used by the Nazis as a transit station for Jews – *Sammelwohnung* – before their final deportation to death camps.[15]

August Aichhorn, a Gentile, had been one of the teachers at the psychoanalytic institute and the analyst of M Mahler, H Kohut, and K R Eissler: he managed to survive in Austria with his family throughout the war, despite his wife becoming seriously ill, one of his sons being interned in Dachau for political reasons, and his house being destroyed by bombing. He preserved as much of Freud's work as he could.[16]

There were those who could find no place on the passenger list to English safety. Of Freud's elderly sisters, Anna had been safe in the United States for years. Rosa, Maria, Pauline, all widows, and Adolfine, who had never married and always lived with her mother – "the old aunts" who made their appearance at the Sunday morning family gatherings at the Berggasse[17] – having all stayed in Vienna – received the sum of 160,000 schillings, the plan being for them to emigrate shortly afterwards since their age made it more difficult to obtain entry visas and work permits in Great Britain. The hope was that the Nazis would not be interested in such old people with neither resources nor professional activities to exploit, but this proved to be a pious illusion.[18]

Despite the efforts of Marie Bonaparte in France and Harry Freud – the son of Freud's younger brother Alexander – in New York,[19] after their money had been confiscated and especially after Sauerwald was sent to the Russian front and they lost his protection,[20] the sisters were at risk of dying from hunger even before their deportation to Theresienstadt in 1942: Adolfine died there on 5/02/1943, while Rosa, Maria, and Paula were transferred to the death camps (Rosa in Treblinka, the other two in Maly Trostinec, near Minsk) and were killed in the gas chambers between autumn 1942 and spring 1943.[21] A letter from the Red Cross informed the family in London.[22]

During the Nuremberg trials, the testimony of a Treblinka survivor, S Rajzman, enables us to reconstruct the circumstances of Rosa Freud's death at the hands of Kurt H Franz, the last commandant of the death camp:

> A train arrived from Vienna. I was standing on the platform when the people left the cars. An elderly woman came up to Kurt Franz, took out a document and said that she was the sister of Sigmund Freud. She begged him to give her light work in an office. Franz read this document through very seriously

> and said that there must be a mistake here, he led her up to the train schedule and said that in two hours a train would leave for Vienna. She should leave all her documents and valuables and then go to a bath-house; after the bath she would have her documents and ticket prepared to be sent to Vienna. Of course, the woman went to the bath-house, and never returned.
>
> (*Trial at Nuremberg 1945–1946:* Testimony of one Treblinka survivor, S Rajzman, 27/02/1946)[23]

Sigmund Freud was spared the nightmare of the Shoah, along with the pain of surviving his sisters and six million Jews: he died on 23 September 1939, a few weeks after the start of the Second World War, at home in 20 *Mares*field Gardens. This *field of mares* may also remind us of Paul Bernfeld and his translation of the German nightmare, *Alptraum* into the English illusion, *Mare's nest*.[24]

Twenty years had passed since the session in 1919, and the fantasies of reaching a promised land enshrined in the "prophetic" coincidence *Forsyth-Vorsicht* had achieved fruition and come to rest in Freud's mind. Congratulating Jones on the celebrations for the anniversary of the founding of the British Psycho-Analytical Society, he wrote in his last letter:

> It is still quite remarkable how unsuspectingly we human beings approach the future. When you told me shortly before the war about founding an analytic society in London, I could not foresee that a quarter of a century later I would be living so near to it and you.
>
> (7/03/1939)

Meanwhile in Vienna, the Nazi police, who had decreed the dissolution of the Viennese Psychoanalytic Society, tried repeatedly to arrange this through one of their representatives, unsuccessfully trying one member of the Directive Council after another.

Harald Leupold-Löwenthal, the Viennese psychoanalyst who founded the Sigmund Freud Museum in 1971 and from 1974 to 1981 was president of the Psychoanalytic Society reconstituted in Vienna after the war, reports finding some "moving notes," in the Gestapo archives, in one of which the agents had written: "According to the porter, Professor Freud has gone away. The decree could not be notified to him." And so the attempt was abandoned and, a "typically Austrian and Viennese fact," legally speaking, the dissolution of the local psychoanalytic society never took place.[25]

After Freud's death, the family's diaspora was still not left in peace.

As the war went on, in summer 1940, the males of the family who were in the United Kingdom, having been born in a country that was now the enemy, were taken into custody: Freud's son Ernst and his grandson, Sophie's son, were interned on the Isle of Man

Jean Martin spent several months in an internment camp in Liverpool before being allowed to join the Pioneer Corps and worked on clearing the rubble of the bombing, while his son Anton Walter was put on a ship to Australia. Freud's nephew, Harry, Alexander's son, reached Canada with his parents, joined the army, and then returned to fight.[26]

As for Oliver Freud, who was forced to leave Berlin after 1933, he had made his home in Nice with his second wife and his daughter, switching from engineering to photography. Following the German invasion and the installation of the Vichy government, he made several daring attempts to cross the Pyrenees. He finally succeeded in reaching Barcelona and putting himself under the protection of the committee for French Jewish Refugees, and in April 1943, he set sail with his wife for the United States. Their young daughter, who chose to stay in France with her fiancé, was able to survive the war by concealing her Jewish origin but died shortly afterwards of a mere infection.[27]

In December 2005, partly thanks to the eyewitness account given by Jones in *Sigmund Freud: Life and Work*, a tribunal in New York awarded compensation of 3 million dollars to the 23 heirs of Sigmund Freud for the losses caused by the Swiss banks handing Jewish assets over to the Nazis. Anton W Freud, eldest son of Martin Freud, born in 1921, and given the name of Sigmund's Hungarian friend, died just the year before at the age of 83.

Fort-Da. the return: story of a cap

"It is almost impossible to imagine," writes Grubrich Simitis, "the extent to which the Nazi regime succeeded in causing Freud's writings to disappear from the German book market and in banishing from the public consciousness the universe of thought he had brought into the world in his magnificent prose."[28]

In post-war Austria, there was little talk of Freud, except among specialists.

In 1950s Vienna, there was no trace of Freud at Berggasse 19, apart from a plaque placed there by the World Federation of Mental Health (1953).

Interviewed by Roazen, the widow Frau Oschner, living upstairs at the Berggasse, clearly remembered when the Freuds suddenly left, taking "all their furniture with them" she repeated, but she seemed unaware of the political events that had precipitated their flight.[29]

In 1968, the conservative Austrian government was annoyed to discover from an international survey that the best-known Austrian was neither Wolfgang Amadeus Mozart nor Franz Schubert but Sigmund Freud.[30]

This was when the *Sigmund Freud Gesellschaft* was set up: it purchased Freud's home and turned it into a museum, which had a difficult life from the outset, since it was not easy for Vienna to acknowledge the worth of their fellow citizen and even harder for them to work through their complicity with Nazism.

Freud's old home officially reopened its doors on the occasion of the 27th IPA Congress, which was held in Vienna for the first and only time in 1971: it was Anna Freud who announced it during the conference, hoping that the place which had housed the first nucleus of psychoanalysis might become a cultural institution, a base for IPA members to meet in, and a psychoanalytic library hosting research and exhibitions. . . . In these circumstances, Freud's daughter, having overcome her own grief and her rejection of all that Vienna still aroused in her, donated to the museum the furnishings of the waiting room where the Wednesday meetings had taken place, a small sample from the collection of antiquities, and some personal objects belonging to her father, which together composed the first scanty catalogue. It was in fact an empty museum made of absence, less a museum than a memorial site for what had disappeared, on whose walls there were only Engelman's large photographs of the people who had once lived there: "a space in which normality, banishment, genocide, and psychoanalytic myths of origin commingle."[31]

After Anna Freud's death, the airy spaces of 20 Maresfield Gardens were also transformed into a museum. But in this rich Freud Museum in London, the furnishings, the books, and the objects from the consulting room, including the famous couch, alienated from their original context, are displayed in a clear, cold atmosphere, just as bleak as the museum in Vienna.

The two museums, container and contained uprooted from each other, preserve the traces of the trauma that was suffered and pass on its memory. They remind the visitor of the breach with the past and the disturbing question of the "*Doppelgänger*": and so it is that the visitor to the Vienna Museum, "nothing but an address," faced with this shock, is tricked by their memory into swearing that they have seen the famous "couch" there before.[32]

But there was something to see in Berggasse: the tweed cap that Freud was wearing when he left, his walking stick, the flask he took on his walks through the woods, his suitcase, rug, and a suitcase, all in their original places in the anteroom, turned out to be particularly evocative and could make one imagine that he had come back from the exile he had been forced into, put down his suitcase, and hung his hat on the hook.

In *Danube*, C Magris describes the fascination of this hovering presence:

> The walking-stick and flask tell us everything about the greatness of Freud, his sense of the measure of things and his love of order, his simplicity as a man resolved in himself and free of manias; one who, by plunging into the abysses of human ambivalences, both learns and teaches how to love those family outings in mountains more, in greater freedom.
>
> (1986, p. 214)

A remarkable anecdote reported by Lydia Marinelli,[33] curator of the museum for over 15 years, tells us how these everyday objects of no value beyond their link with Freud the man, on display with no protective glass to distinguish them from the visitors' clothing and bags, in the end came to achieve their full symbolic value for the staff managing the *Sigmund Freud Gesellschaft*.

In the seventies, as a site of collective memory despite its humble collection of insignificant articles, Berggasse 19 succeeded in attracting a stream of visitors, mostly British and American, and one day, during the usual hurly-burly, an unobserved incident occurred: it was only after closing the museum that the custodian noticed that Freud's cap had been stolen.

That classic tweed cap had been worn over 40 years earlier and, though it was still in fashion, it had not been thought capable of attracting a thief's attention; even so, the museum's insurers paid out "12,000 [Austrian] schillings in view of the special nature of the stolen museum piece"[34] – an unhoped-for windfall into its precarious bank balance.

As for the cap, it recovered its original function in some American city and for a couple of years warmed the head of the museum's dishonest visitor who relished the fact that he was the only person who knew its special value. Marinelli comments that we might wonder, with Thomas Bernhard, if the cap had influenced the thoughts of that good-for-nothing. What is certain is that, seized with a sense of guilt or disturbed by too close a contact with Freud, and on his analyst's advice, the thief sent the cap back: at least this is the explanation given in the unsigned letter that came with it.

Since then, the cap has returned to the coatrack in the anteroom where it has the appropriate protection: as the Museum was not in a position to refund the insurance payment, in effect, it belongs to the insurance company.

Notes

1 Aziz, 1990.
2 "That Man Is My Brother" (1938), later entitled "Brother Hitler" (Boes, 2019).
3 Arendt, 1963.
4 18/03/1938.
5 Jones, *III* and K. Jones, 1979.
6 On the walls of the Göring Institute for a couple of years, the portraits of Sigmund Freud and Adolf Hitler stared at each other with mute irreducible hostility (Cocks, 1985).
7 Roudinesco, 2014.
8 *ibid.*
9 The letter had been interpreted by M Göring as sabotaging his plan to "save" the Viennese Society by incorporating it into his own (Cocks, 1985, p. 130).
10 Schur reports that Sauerwald came to England in 1939, perhaps to discuss financial matters with Freud. According to Roudinesco, the purpose of the visit was to ask for compensation (2014).
11 Cohen, 2009.
12 Engelman, 1976.
13 20/05/1938, in Molnar and Luchetti, 2009, p. 623.
14 Roazen, 2001b.
15 Sophie Freud, 2007.
16 Eissler, 1951.
17 Sophie Freud, 2007, p. XVII.
18 As part of the attempt to save them, once he was in London, Freud made available for the Nazis the contents of a Swiss bank account which had been discovered after his departure (Cohen, 2009).
19 Roudinesco, 2014.
20 Wounded and imprisoned, he was tried for war crimes but acquitted thanks to the testimony of Anna Freud and Marie Bonaparte (Schur, 1958).

21 Leupold-Löwenthal, 1989; Tögel, 1990.
22 Behling, 2002.
23 http://willzuzak.ca/lp/nuremb01.html.
24 Aziz, 1990.
25 Leupold-Löwenthal, 1985.
26 Scarpelli, 2000a.
27 Scarpelli, 2000b.
28 1993b, p. 48.
29 Roazen, 1993 p. 48.
30 Leupold-Löwenthal, 1985.
31 Marinelli, 2009b.
32 *ibid.*
33 *ibid.*
34 *ibid.*

Chapter 21

The importance of being Ernest Jones

The cycle closes

Transmission of the tradition and "crypts"

"Anyone who writes a biography is committed to lies, concealments, hypocrisy, flattery and even to hiding his own lack of understanding, for biographical truth does not exist," wrote Freud to Arnold Zweig, who had asked for permission to write his biography.[1]

Despite this, the collection of accounts, diaries, news, and biographies about Freud is inexhaustible, and from 1920 not only every manuscript, letter, or minute but also postcards, tickets, and autographs began to be regarded as precious documentary material for posterity. In 1951, the Freud Archives were set up at the Library of Congress in Washington, and Eissler, who had been appointed its director, enriched it with a long series of interviews with people who had personally met and known Freud. In some cases, this documentation could have been highly sensitive, and barriers were put up against its publication, a censorship due partly to respect for the privacy of the subjects concerned, the patients and their heirs, and partly to the immediate demands for discretion made in relation to episodes of potentially traumatic significance which the first generation of psychoanalysts had found it difficult to work through and about which it was decided to remain silent.

And so it was that certain aspects of Freud's story and the movement's, but also certain aspects of psychoanalytic theory, were kept split off or, so to speak, in a state of repression, secrets which were initially given a "cleaned up" history but were nevertheless preserved with the utmost care in the archive. This is how we should read Freud's attempt to wipe out the memory of Fliess by destroying his friend's letters and likewise the censorship applied to the first posthumous publication of their correspondence by suppressing the malpractice suffered by Emma Eckstein.[2] Even though a century has passed, a substantial quantity of documents is still unavailable for consultation, which makes the archive seem like a strongbox, or rather a "crypt" in Torok's sense: we need only think of certain binders concerning Freud's relationship with Breuer which cannot be made public until after the year 2100.[3]

On the subject of telepathy, not only was the manuscript of the *Nachtrag* made to disappear, but all Freud's works on occultism have had to wait to be translated.

DOI: 10.4324/9781003246480-22

In this respect, Freud was censored even more than Ferenczi, who almost fell into oblivion along with his theory.

In the meantime, almost every pupil, psychoanalyst, patient, acquaintance, relative (close or distant), and even the faithful housekeeper . . . in short, any person who might have had direct or indirect contact with Sigmund Freud (not David Forsyth! and not Paul Bernfeld either) has felt called upon to testify, and many of them have outdone each other in recounting that piece of their own biography which overlaps with the life of the famous genius. The historical reconstructions centred on the Freudian adventure are innumerable, as are the novels, screenplays, and cartoon strips, to say nothing of the great quantity of critical essays, scandalous compilations, or pieces of outright defamation.

The age of eyewitness accounts, of affective and mythic representation, preceded that of the more specialised and, so to speak, objective historical dimension which is linked to the interpretation of the texts and the gathering of new documents and has been enhanced over the years by the binders that have gradually become available to the public in the Freud Archives.

Paul Roazen, whom I have cited several times, belongs to the transitional phase between the heroic period and our own documentary era (from Peter Gay onwards). A historian from Boston trained in political and social sciences, Roazen began to engage with psychoanalysis in the seventies and grew so passionate about it that it became his life's work: in addition to his systematic archiving, he interviewed all the living witnesses and the sons and daughters, parents, and close friends of those who had met Freud and the psychoanalysts of the first generation, becoming the chronicler of the psychoanalytic movement's "oral memory."

One distinctive historical endeavour is naturally the kind being undertaken by many analysts from later generations who have constructed their own narrative and interpretation of Freud and the origins of psychoanalysis: that is the tradition to which this book belongs.

Ernest Jones is a phenomenon *sui generis*.[4] After long consultation, partly to silence other biographies that were considered too unreliable, he was officially asked by Anna Freud and her heirs, with the agreement of the International Association, to write a book about Freud's life and thought, specifically because he was one of the story's protagonists and a major international exponent of the psychoanalytic movement. He was the only biographer of Freud who was also an eyewitness, and he had the privilege and opportunity of access to all the material that had been collected since the fifties, before much of it was hidden away. The biography appeared in Freud's centenary year and is Jones's most important creative work: with this achievement, Ernest Jones ceases to be simply Freud's alter ego.

Free Associations: Memories of a Psycho-Analyst

Jones's narrative, though prompted by Anna Freud, started out from an internal necessity. The work of re-elaboration that he undertook in 1944, about five years after Freud's death, towards the end of the Second World War, was not the first written form in which he had tried to address this loss. He had originally begun with his own autobiography and soon completed 11 chapters about his childhood, his medical studies, the difficult and contentious start of his medical career, his encounter with psychoanalysis, and last his permanent return to London. He had brought his narrative up to the end of the First World War, to the threshold of his life's main achievement, becoming the world's chief political representative of psychoanalysis.

It was at this point that he received the request to write Freud's biography. He set aside the manuscript of his autobiography and devoted 13 years to the monumental *Sigmund Freud, Life and Work.*

It has to be acknowledged that the three volumes are exceptional in their completeness and that even with the aid of computers and the internet, we could not be more precise and detailed today in documenting events and quoting Freud: apart, obviously, from the censoring and more or less intentional distortions that he introduced. Anna Freud, who followed the growth of the work step by step, overcame her initial mistrust and was so captivated by Jones's work that she confided in him that having been convinced she knew her father better than anyone, she would now have to think again.[5]

"It was mastered by means of a system which only my parents really understood," wrote his son Mervyn Jones, "and which involved distributing papers among tall pyramids of wire baskets, of the sort you see in a supermarket."[6] Jones's wife played an important role in this work and was fully consulted before he accepted a job that would occupy them for such a long time. "It should go down to history" that Katherine Jones "typed out 1,500 personal letters of Freud all written in German script! This was done because Jones had said that he had a visual memory, and could not properly use the letters if he had to work at each one in order to understand it."[7]

Jones used all the notes collected by Max Schur about the final period of Freud's life and his illness and incorporated them in his text. He made equally expansive use, not always acknowledged, of Siegfried Bernfeld's documentation to reconstruct Freud's early childhood and youth, papers which the colleague had collected and was in a better position to understand because of certain similarities with his own personal history. Bernfeld, whom Grubrich Simitis regards as Freud's first scientific biographer,[8] was convinced that it would not be possible to enable new analysts to comprehend the distinctiveness of Freudian thought without presenting and examining the historical and biographical context. The collaboration with Jones in the fifties prompted Bernfeld and his third wife Suzanne Cassirer to resume their own researches into Freud. Like Katherine, Suzanne was also a great help to her husband in this type of investigative game. Bernfeld wrote to Jones that it was indeed "a great joy to see your book grow,"[9] and to Strachey, he confided that he had really started to enjoy "the Freud-quiz": "pure fun which takes precedence over any serious work."[10]

For Jones, the exchange of letters with his colleague brought a "pleasure that outweighed their practical value," and as the work went on, "first thing every morning he asked if there was a letter from Bernfeld."[11] Someone told Winnicott that Katherine and Ernest Jones had soaked themselves so thoroughly in Freud that "they could play games in which they would ask each other what Freud would have been doing at such and such a date at 4 o'clock in the afternoon."[12] Katherine really had become a *close friend of the Freud family*, as Jones had said she was when he introduced her to his father, making up for Anna's rejection of him at the start of the war: one of his typical lies, the kind that tend to come true over time.

Other, less plausible lies of Jones's have been condemned and had a greater historical weight: in particular, those about Sàndor Ferenczi, who had been his training analyst. Precisely because they were transferential lies connected to the psychic work of repression, which censors but also preserves in memory, they indirectly testify to the worth of the rival who was close to Freud in an entirely different way from him.

As he wrote in his autobiography, "The name Ernest seems to accord well with my serious temperament" (1959, p. 12).

It was only after the completion of his mythical work devoted to the Master – the third volume appeared in 1957 – in which he actually recounted that part of his own life which had been united with Freud and psychoanalysis that Jones could resume the autobiography of his youthful years that he had paused at the moment of his full identification with Freud and the movement. He did not live to see it printed: after his death in 1958, the book was edited and published by the son who had co-written it with him.

Mervyn Jones recalls that when his father had less than a day to live, they were still discussing the opening sentence of Chapter Eight, entitled "Approach to Psycho-Analysis," which described his first meeting with Freud. He had dictated a sentence to his wife – it would be his last – making the claim "that he was one of the first, though knowing nothing of Vienna or of the German language, to be reached by the ideas of Sigmund Freud." "A modest enough claim," comments his son, "but he was disturbed because the sentence contained no mention of an equally early follower, namely Jung." To the suggestion that Jung could be mentioned in a footnote so as not to spoil the poise of the sentence, the father replied, "'No, no. He's too important', and the last words spoken on the morning before he died were to make an improvement in the phrasing."[13]

The autobiography appeared with the title *Free Associations: Memories of a Psycho-Analyst*, which distils the positions of analyst and analysand and well expresses Jones's dual identification as teacher and pupil, witness and propagandist.

The final sentence is of particular relevance to us: here we find Jones at the end of the war, still deep in mourning for his first wife:

> Armistice night, which in happier days I had looked forward to spending with old friends, came and went. I stared at it, and at the German howitzers lining the Mall, but for me, as for so many others, it meant the end of an old world rather than the beginning of a new one.
>
> (pp. 255 and 257)

"It is certain that Chapter Twelve, had he written it," comments Mervyn Jones,[14] "would have expressed the sudden – and lasting – joy that he found in his second marriage. This took place at Zurich in October 1919, during his visit to the Continent after the war-time break."

But that is where our story begins.

Notes

1 31/05/1936.
2 See Pierri, 2022.
3 Malcolm, 1983.
4 See also Pierri, 2022.
5 In Young-Bruehl, 1994.
6 1959, p. 263.
7 Winnicott, 1958b, p. 302.
8 Grubrich Simitis, 1981.
9 14/03/1952, in Grubrich Simitis, 1981, p. 424.
10 9/06/1952, *ibid.*, p. 415.
11 18/12/1952, *ibid.*, p. 424.
12 Winnicott, 1958b, p. 306.
13 M Jones, 1958, p. 307.
14 1959, p. 259.

Epilogue

A debt to pay

To conclude, a final reference to a detail which emerged after consulting the archives of the *British Psychoanalytical Society*, which allows us to correct a minor error made by Ernest Jones.

This brings us back to the beginning of our story, to that beautiful autumn day, Saturday 4 October 1919, when, with the war over, Dr David Forsyth arrived in Vienna.

After going to Berggasse 19 and arranging the appointment with Prof Sigmund Freud for that afternoon, he went back to collect the rest of his suitcases and decided to eat at the station restaurant.

And here, just as he walked in, he bumped into. . . . Let's leave those concerned do the talking, via the last letters they exchanged in January 1933.

The first letter is from Forsyth, and it seems to start with a hint or a quip that we may assume escaped him that morning in the silent daily encounter with his colleague Ernest Jones on the doorstep of their respective offices at numbers 67 and 81 of the same Harley Street block. The cue for the conversation may have been the reading of the newly published *Lecture XXX* and the memory of that autumn in Vienna and the heroic times they'd experienced together and which Freud's text had brought back to his mind.

Perhaps Jones commented on how Freud had misremembered the facts: they both knew he hadn't arrived in Vienna a month before Forsyth but that instead they'd almost taken turns with the professor, as they'd met and had lunch together. Here Forsyth must have added something along these lines: "Talking of this, there's something you too don't remember correctly about that lunch," leaving his colleague dumbfoundedly pondering the episode alone.

10/01/1933

Dear Jones,[1]

The further particulars are these.

On my arrival in Vienna and after calling at Freud's and arranging to see him later in the day, I returned to the Bahnhof to lunch. To my surprise I found you there having just finished your lunch. You told me that Eric Hiller was travelling with you to Switzerland, and was at the moment on the train keeping your places for the journey. Saying you would be returning, you left in order to exchange places with Hiller and allow him to have his lunch. This he did at my table, found he had no cash and went out saying that you would return in a moment and settle. In point of fact I saw no more of either of you, and I had the privilege of paying for all three lunches.

I don't remember the amount of the bill, and anyway I have long since forgiven both of you landing me with "the baby" in this way. However, it does now seem as if the incident must have disturbed your sense of guilt!

Yours sincerely,
David Forsyth

In his prompt reply, Ernest Jones showed himself to be his colleague's equal in irony, even though he offered a somewhat confused series of explanations to try to justify himself and Hiller for their forgetfulness.

11/01/1933

Dear Forsyth,[2]

What a truly scandalous story! I can only admire the magnanimity and good humour with which you assimilated it. Unfortunately I can throw no further light on it, for it does not bring anything to my recollection. I do not doubt that my unconscious would be capable of such a thing on occasion, though I do not think it has ever happened in my life and it would be particularly unlikely on the occasion of meeting a friend from home in an enemy country; I remember I was very glad to see you. In this case it would have to be a conscious act, for I could have known nothing about it unless Hiller on returning to the train told me he had not paid. From all that I know of myself I should certainly have reacted by writing an apology to you at the time and settling up the next time I saw you; otherwise it would make it a duplicate imposition, which I am sure is very foreign to my nature. I should hesitate to throw the onus on Hiller did I not know from repeated experiences how prone he was to "carelessnesses" in such matters. He was acting as my secretary and courier at the time and could not have been destitute of money. It is sad to think I have lain under suspicion all these years without knowing it, but I console myself with the hope that it gave you same fresh material for starting your analysis. I know you would not like me to offer to refund the sum at this late date but shall look forward to some opportunity of restoring the balance in a more agreeable manner.

Yours sincerely
Ernest Jones

The sumptuous and convivial dinner in Zurich, which Jones had almost made us believe in,[3] had actually been a fortuitous and inconvenient encounter at the restaurant of the Franz Joseph Bahnhof in Vienna, in the mayhem of the mass attempt to board the few trains that were departing, hastily trying to occupy the seats on the carriage back to Zurich: two, possibly embarrassed, colleagues sharing a table since they couldn't avoid eating together. And maybe Forsyth had in fact eaten with Hiller.

On that occasion, the generous Jones, who liked paying for everyone, had unintentionally scrounged a meal and not just for himself but also for his young assistant, like something out of a comedy sketch: it almost seems a rehearsal for the conjuring trick performed the next day at the border when the movement's smuggled booty passed with amazing synchronisation between Jones and Hiller under the noses of the customs officers.

We will let the reader figure out why in 1957 Jones had decided to locate the meeting and the lunch in Zurich and not in Vienna, amending Freud's mistake with a lie of his own. . .

But in any case, the paediatrician was no longer there to prove him wrong.

Notes

1 The archives of the British Psychoanalytical Society have granted us kind permission to reproduce this unpublished letter by David Forsyth to Ernest Jones, 10/01/1933, Ernest Jones collection, P04-C-C-05. The author had made every effort to locate and contact David Forsyth' copyright holders. If they come forward and ask for the letters to be removed, she will be happy to do so.

2 The archives of the British Psychoanalytical Society have granted us kind permission to reproduce this unpublished letter by E. Jones to David Forsyth, 11/01/1933, Ernest Jones collection, P04-C-C-05, kind permission of Jackie Jones copyright.

3 See Chapter 4.

Bibliography

Correspondence

Andreas-Salomé L., Freud A. (2001), *À l'ombre du père. Correspondance 1919–1937*, Hachette, Paris.

Brabant E., Falzeder E., Giampieri-Deutsch P. (1993), *The Correspondence of Sigmund Freud and Sándor Ferenczi Volume 1, 1908–1914*, Belknap Press of Harvard University Press, Cambridge, MA, London.

Falzeder E. (2002), *The Complete Correspondence of Sigmund Freud and Karl Abraham 1907–1925*, Karnac, London, New York.

Falzeder E., Brabant E. (1996), *The Correspondence of Sigmund Freud and Sandor Ferenczi Volume 2, 1914–1919*, Belknap Press of Harvard University Press, Cambridge, MA, London.

Falzeder E., Brabant E. (2000), *The Correspondence of Sigmund Freud and Sándor Ferenczi, Volume 3, 1920–1933*, Belknap Press of Harvard University Press, Cambridge, MA, London.

Fichtner G. (2003), *The Sigmund Freud-Ludwig Binswanger Correspondence 1908–1938*, Open Gate Press, incorporating Centaur Press, London.

Freud E. L. (1961), *Letters of Sigmund Freud 1873–1939*, The Hogarth Press, London.

Freud E. L. (1971 [1987]), *The Letters of Sigmund Freud and Arnold Zweig*, New York University Press, New York.

Freud S. (2010 [2012]), *Lettres à ses enfants*, Aubier, Paris.

Freud S., Eitingon M. (2004 [2009]), *Correspondence 1906–1939*, Hachette, Paris.

Hale N. G. (1971), *James Jackson Putnam and Psychoanalysis: Letters between Putnam and Sigmund Freud, Ernest Jones, William James, Sandor Ferenczi, and Morton Prince, 1877–1917*, Harvard University Press, Cambridge, MA.

Masson J. M. (1985), *The Complete Letters of Sigmund Freud to Wilhelm Fliess, 1887–1904*, Belknap, Cambridge, MA, 1–13.

McGuire W. (1974), *The Freud/Jung Letters*, Princeton University Press, Princeton, NJ.

Meyer-Palmedo I. (Ed.) (2014), *Sigmund Freud, Anna Freud Correspondence 1904–1938*, Polity Press, Cambridge, UK.

Paskauskas R. A. (1993), *The Complete Correspondence of Sigmund Freud and Ernest Jones 1908–1939*, Harvard University Press, Cambridge.

Pfeiffer E. (Ed.) (1963), *Sigmund Freud and Lou Andreas-Salomé Letters*, Hogarth Press, London.

Vincent C. (Ed.) (1996), *Lettres de Famille de Sigmund Freud et des Freuds de Manchester 1911–1938*, PUF, Paris.

For the committee's circular letters, unless otherwise specified

a: Grosskurth P. (1991), *The Secret Ring*, Cape, London.
b: Freud S., Ferenczi S. (2000), *Correspondance 1920–1933*, Calmann-Levy, Paris.
The quotes from Jones E. *Sigmund Freud Life and Work* Vol *I* 1953, *II* 1955, *III* 1957, are here abbreviated to: Jones *I*, *II*, *III*.

Abraham N., Torok. M. (1986), *The Wolf Man's Magic Word: A Cryptonymy*, Minneapolis: University of Minnesota Press.

Abraham N., Torok M. (1987 [1994]), *The Shell and the Kernel*, The University of Chicago Press, Chicago.

Accerboni Pavanello A. M. (1990), Sigmund Freud as Remembered by Edoardo Weiss, the Italian Pioneer of Psychoanalysis, *Int. Rev. Psycho-Anal.*, 17:351–359.

Albano L. (Ed.) (1987), *Il divano di Freud. Memorie e ricordi dei pazienti di Sigmund Freud*, Pratiche Editrice, Parma.

Alexander F. (1940 [1973]), Recollections of Berggasse 19, in Ruitenbeek H. M. (ed.), *Freud as We Knew Him*, Wayne State University Press, Detroit.

Ambrosiano L. (2011), Maestri, *Rivista Psicoanal.*, 57:609–632.

Andreas-Salomé L. (1958), *The Freud Journal*, Quartet Books, London, New York.

Anzieu D. (1959 [1986]), *Freud's Self-Analysis*, Hogarth Press, London.

Appignanesi L., Forrester J. (1992), *Freud's Women*, Basic Books, New York.

Arendt H. (1963 [1994]), *Eichmann in Jerusalem A Report on the Banality of Evil*, Pemguin Books.

Arendt H. (1968), Walter Benjamin 1892–1940, in *Men in Dark Times*, Harcourt, Brace World, New York.

Argentieri S. (1992), Anna Freud, la figlia, in Vegetti Finzi S. (ed), *Psicoanalisi al femminile*, Laterza, Bari.

Argentieri S. (2005), Incest Yesterday and Today: From Conflict to Ambiguity, in Ambrosio G. (ed.), *On Incest Psychoanalytic Perspectives*, Karnac, New York.

Auster P. (1992), *The Red Notebook*. Faber and Faber, London.

Auster P. (ed.), (2001), *True Tales of American Life*, Faber and Faber, London.

Aziz R. (1990), *C. G. Jung's Psychology of Religion and Synchronicity*, State University of New York Press, Albany.

Backstrom L., Boldi P., Rosa M., Ugander J., Vigna S. (2011), Four degrees of Separation, *Cornell Un. Lib.*, arXv:111. 4570.

Balint M. (1968 [1984]), *The Basic Fault: Therapeutic Aspects of Regression*, Taylor Francis.

Balsamo M. (2000), *Freud et le destin*, PUF, Paris.

Balsamo M., Napolitano F. (1998), *Freud, lei e l'altro. Sulla genesi della teoria psicoanalitica*, Angeli, Milano.

Bauer E. (1986), Ein noch nicht publizierter Brief Sigmund Freuds an Fanny Moser über Okkultismus und Mesmerismus, *Freibur. Universität.*, 93:93–110.

Beckett S. (1931), *Proust*, Grove Press, New York.

Behling K. (2002 [2005]), *Martha Freud, A Biography*, Polity Press, Cambridge.

Benveniste D. (2008), Obituary: W. Ernest Freud, *Int. J. Psychoanal.*, 17:16–17.

Bergmann M. S. (1997), The Historical Roots of Psychoanalytic Orthodoxy, *Int. J. PsychoAnal*, 78:69–86.

Berman E. (2004), Sándor, Gizella, Elma: A Biographical Journey, *Int. J. Psycho-Anal.*, 85 (2):489–520.

Bernays Heller J. B. (1956), Freud's Mother and Father, *Commentary*, 21:418–421.

Bernfeld S. C. (1951), Freud and Archeology, *Am. Imago*, 8 (2):107–128.

Berti Ceroni G. (1995), Interruzioni fortuite del setting, *Rivista Psicoanal.*, 41:197–210.

Binswanger L. (1957), *Sigmund Freud Reminiscences of a Friendship*, Grune & Stratton, New York.

Bleger J. (1967a), Psycho-Analysis of the Psycho-Analytic Frame, *Int. J. Psycho-Anal.*, 48:511–519.

Bleger J. (1967b [2012]), *Symbiosis and Ambiguity*, Routledge, London.

Blum H. P. (1996), The Irma Dream, Self-Analysis, and Self-Supervision, *J. Amer. Psychoanal. Assn.*, 44:511–532.

Boes T. (2019), *Thomas Mann's War: Literature, Politics, and the World Republic of Letters*, Cornell University Press, Ithaca, New York and London.

Bolognini S. (2002), *Psychoanalytic Empathy*, Free Assn. Books, London.

Bonomi C. (1994), Sexuality and Death in Freud's Discovery of Sexual Aetiology, *Int. Forum Psychoanal.*, 3:63–86.

Bonomi C. (1999), Il giudizio di Jones sul deterioramento mentale di Ferenczi: un riesame, in Borgogno F. (ed.), *La partecipazione affettiva dell'analista*, Angeli, Milano.

Bonomi C. (2015), *The Cut and the Building of Psychoanalysis vol I Sigmund Freud and Emma Eckstein*, Routledge, New York.

Borch-Jacobsen M., Shamdasani S. (2012), *The Freud Files: An Inquiry into the History of Psychoanalysis*, Cambridge University Press, Cambridge.

Bordi S. (2001), Il trauma: una, tante memorie, in Pierri M. (ed.), *Qui e ora . . . con me*, Bollati Boringhieri, Torino.

Brabant E. (2006), Freud e Ferenczi, in Bonomi C. (ed.), *Sándor Ferenczi e la psicoanalisi contemporanea*, Borla, Roma.

Braun A., Polojaz V. (2004), Risveglio primaverile, in Esposito C. (ed.), *Adolescenza: il trauma dell'età, l'età dei traumi*, Borla, Roma.

Breuer J., Freud S. (1893–95), Studies on hysteria, *SE*, 2.

Britton R. (2003), *Sex, Death, and the Superego: Experiences in Psychoanalysis*. Abingdon, UK: Routledge.

Brome V. (1983), *Ernest Jones: A Biography*, Norton Company, London.

Bruck C. (1925), *Experimentelle Telepathie Neue Versuche zur telepathischen Übertragung von Zeichnungen*, Julius Püttmann Verlag, Stuttgart.

Bruni A. (1991 [1987]), Relazione contenitore contenuto invertita, in AA. VV. (ed.), *La cultura psicoanalitica*, Studio Tesi, Pordenone.

Burlingham D. (1932 [1935]), Kinderanalyse und Mutter, *Zeitschrift für psychoanalytische Pädagogik*, 6 (7–8):269–289; Child Analysis and the Mother, *Psychoanal. Q.*, 4:69–92.

Canetti E. (1974 [1979]), The New Karl Kraus, in *The Conscience of Words*, Seabury Press, New York.

Canetti E. (1980 [1982]), *The Torch in My Ear*, Farrar, Straus and Giroux, New York.

Christie A. (1931a), *The Sittaford Mystery*, Harper, London, 2017.

Christie A. (1931b), *Peril at End House*, HarperCollins, London, 2007.

Chused J. F., Raphling D. L. (1992), The analyst's mistakes, *J.A.P.A.*, 40:89–116.

Cocks G. (1985 [1988]), *Psicoterapia nel Terzo Reich*, Bollati Boringhieri, Torino.

Cohen D. (2009), *The escape of Sigmund Freud*, Peach Publishing, North Aston.

Cook D. (1987), Psychoanalysis and Telepathy, *Intern. Review Psychoanal.*, 14:419–420.

Craft A., Dodd K. (Eds.) (2017), *From an Association to a Royal College: 1988–2016*, Springer, New York.

Cremerius J. (1985), *Il mestiere dell'analista*, Bollati Boringhieri, Torino.

Cupelloni P. (1999), Anna e il padre, *Psicoter. Psicoanal.*, 4, 2 luglio-dicembre, www.psychomedia.it.

Cupelloni P. (2003), Sigmund analista di Anna. Le origini della psicoanalisi tra Edipo e Antigone, *Annual Conference*, FEP, Sorrento.

Cupelloni P. (2007), Sigmund Freud: padre di Anna e padre della psicoanalisi, in *Genealogia e formazione dell'apparato psichico*, Franco Angeli, Milano.

D'Angelo M. (2020), *So will ich mir entfliehen*, Psychosozial-verlag.

Derrida J. (1966 [2017]), Freud and the Scene of Writing, in *Writing and Difference*, University of Chicago Press, Chicago.

Derrida J. (1980 [1987]), *The Post Card: From Socrates to Freud and Beyond*, University of Chicago Press, Chicago.

Derrida J. (1981 [1983]), Télépathie, *Cahiers Confrontation*, 10:201–230.

De Toffoli C. (1996), Origine intersoggettiva ed inconscia dell'esperienza di sé come individuo, *Rivista Psicoanal.*, 42:79–93.

Deutsch H. (1926 [1953]), Occult Processes Occurring during Psychoanalysis, in Devereux G. (ed.), *Psychoanalysis and the Occult*, International University Press, New York.

Devereux G. (Ed.) (1953), *Psychoanalysis and the Occult*, International University Press, New York.

Diatkine G. (1992), Dites-le avec des feuilles, *Revue française de psychanalyse*, 56:547–559.

Diatkine G. (2013), La gratuité de la cure analytique pour le patient et pour l'analyste, *Revue française de psychanalyse*, 77:36–45.

Diatkine G. (2020), L'auto-analyse et les très longues cures, *Revue française de psychanalyse*, 84:641–651.

Doolittle H. (1956), *Tribute to Freud*, A New Direction Books, New York.

Dupont J. (1985/1988 [1932]), Introduzione, in Ferenczi S. (ed.), *Diario clinico*, Milano, Cortina.

Dupont J. (1994), Freud's Analysis of Ferenczi as Revealed by Their Correspondence, *Int. J. Psycho-Anal.*, 75:301–320.

Eifermann R. R. (1997), The Exceptional Position of "A Child Is Being Beaten," in Learning and Teaching of Freud, in Spector Person E. (ed.), *On Freud's "A Child Is Being Beaten,"* Yale University Press, New Haven and London.

Einstein A. (1930), Preface to Sinclair U. (1930 [2001]), in *Mental Radio: Does It Work, and How?* Hampton Road, Charlottesville.

Eisenbud J. (1949 [1953]), Psychiatric Contributions to Parapsychology: A Review, in Devereux G. (ed.), *Psychoanalysis and the Occult*, International University Press, New York.

Eissler K. R. (1951), Biographical Outline of August Aichhorn, in Aichhorn A. (ed.), *Wayward Youth*, Imago Publishing Co., London.

Eissler K. R. (1971), *Talent and Genius: A Psychoanalytic Reply to a Defamation of Freud*, Grove Press Inc., New York.

Ellenberger H. (1970), *The Discovery of the Unconscious; the History and Evolution of Dynamic Psychiatry*, Basic Books, New York.

Elms A. C. (2001), Apocryphal Freud, *Ann. Psychoanal.*, 29:83–104.

Engelman E. (1976), *Berggasse 19: Sigmund Freud's Home and Offices, Vienna 1938*, Basic Books, New York.

Etchegoyen R. H. (1986), *The Fundamentals of Psychoanalytic Technique*, Karnac Books, London, 1991.

Fachinelli E. (1983), *Claustrofilia: saggio sull'orologio telepatico in analisi*, Adelphi, Milano.

Faimberg H. (2000), Ascolto psicoanalitico e costruzione delle teorie *Lecture* at Centro Milanese di Psicoanalisi (SPI) 21/01/2000.

Falzeder E. (1994), My Grand-Patient, My Chief Tormentor: A Hitherto Unnoticed Case of Freud's and the Consequences, *Psychoanal Q.*, 63:297–331.

Falzeder E. (2015), *Psychoanalytic Filiations*, Karnac, London.

Farrel D. (1983), Freud's "Thought-Transference," Repression, and the Future of Psycho-Analysis, *Int. J. Psycho-Anal*, 64:71–81.

Federn E. (1985 [1987]), É possibile scrivere una storia della psicoanalisi?, in AA. VV. (ed.), *La cultura psicoanalitica*, Studio Tesi, Pordenone.

Ferenczi S. (1909), *Introjection and Transference First Contributions to Psycho-Analysis*, Karnac, London, 35–93.

Ferenczi S. (1913), Stages in the Development of the Sense of Reality, *First Contributions*, 213–239.

Ferenczi S. (1915), Psychogenic Anomalies of Voice Production, in *Further Contributions to the Theory and Technique of Psycho-Analysis*, Karnac Books, London, 105–109.

Ferenczi S. (1919), On the Technique of Psychoanalysis, *Further Contributions*, 177–189.

Ferenczi, S. (1920), Open Letter. *Int. J. Psychoanal.*, 1:1–2.

Ferenczi S. (1924 [1989]), *Thalassa: A Theory of Genitality*, Karnac Books, London.

Ferenczi S. (1926b), The Problem of the Acceptance of Unpleasant Ideas: Advances in Knowledge of the Sense of Reality, *Further Contributions*, 366–379.

Ferenczi S. (1928), The Adaptation of the Family to the Child, in *Final Contributions to the Problems and Methods of Psycho-Analysis*, Karnac, London, 61–76.

Ferenczi S. (1929), The Unwelcome Child and His Death Instinct, *Final Contributions*, 102–107.

Ferenczi S. (1930), The Principle of Relaxation and Neocatharsis, *Final Contributions*, 108–125.

Ferenczi S. (1931), Child-Analysis in the Analysis of Adults, *Final Contributions*, 126–142.

Ferenczi S. (1932 [1995]), *The Clinical Diary*, J. Dupont (ed.), Harvard University Press, Cambridge, MA.

Ferenczi S. (1933), Confusion of Tongues between Adults and the Child, *Final Contributions*, 156–167.

Ferenczi S. (1934), Some Thoughts on Trauma. *Final Contributions*, 216–279.

Ferenczi, S., Rank, O. (1924), *The Development of Psychoanalysis*. Dover, New York, 1956.

Fichtner G. (2003), Reciprocal Visits between Binswanger and Freud, in *The Sigmund Freud-Ludwig Binswanger Correspondence 1908–1938*, Open Gate Press, incorporating Centaur Press, London.

Fichtner G. (2010), Freud and the Hammerschlag Family: A Formative Relationship, *Int. J. Psycho-Anal.*, 91:1137–1156.

Flammarion C. (1900), *L'Inconnu et les problèmes psychiques*, http://gallica.bnf.fr/ark:/.

Flournoy T. (1899), *Des Indes à la Planète Mars, étude sur un cas de somnambulisme avec glossolalie*, http://gallica.bnf.fr/ark:/.

Flournoy T. (1911), *Esprits et Mediums, mélanges de metapsichique et de Psychologie*, http://gallica.bnf.fr/ark:/.

Fodor N. (1971), *Freud, Jung and Occultism*, Univ. Books, New York.
Forrester J. (1990), *The Seductions of Psychoanalysis: Freud, Lacan, Derrida*, Cambridge University Press, Cambridge.
Forrester J. (1997), *Dispatches from the Freud Wars*, Harvard University, Cambridge.
Forrester J. (2008), 1919: Psychology and Psychoanalysis, Cambridge and London, Myers, Jones and Maccurdy, *Psychoanal. Hist.*, 10:37–94.
Forsyth D. (1909), *Children in Health and Disease*, John Murray, London.
Forsyth D. (1913), On Psychoanalysis, *BMJ*, 2:13–17.
Forsyth D. (1914), Popular Freudism Letter, *BMJ*, Dec. 19; 2 (2816):1089.
Forsyth D. (1916), Functional Nervous Disease, *Lancet*, 187 (4825):430.
Forsyth D. (1920), Psycho-Analysis of a Case of Early Paranoid Dementia, *Proceedings of the RSM, Psychiatry Section*, 13 (3):65–81.
Forsyth D. (1921), The Rudiments of Character: A Study of Infant Behavior, *Psychoanal. Rev.*, 8 (2):117–143.
Forsyth D. (1922), *The Technique of Psycho-Analysis*, Kegan Paul, Trench, Trubner & Co., London.
Forsyth D. (1932), The Place of Psychology in the Medical Curriculum, *Proceedings of the R S M, Psychiatry Section*, 25:1200–1212.
Forsyth D. (1935), *Psychology and Religion*, https://archive.org/.
Forsyth D. (1938), *How Life Began: A Speculative Study in Modern Biology*, William Heinemann, London.
Freud A. (1923), The Relation of Beating-Phantasies to a Day-Dream, *Int. J. Psychoanal.*, 4:89–102.
Freud A. (1933), I. Reports of Proceedings of Societies, *Bul. Int. Psychoanal. Assn.*, 14:453–459.
Freud A. (1936 [1966]), The Ego and the Mechanisms of Defense, in *The Writings of Anna Freud II*, International University Press, New York.
Freud A. (1979), Personal Memories of Ernest Jones, *Int. J. of Psycho-Anal.*, 60:285–287.
Freud E., Freud L., Grubrich Simitis I. (Eds.) (1976), *Sigmund Freud: His Life in Pictures and Words*, André Deutsch, London.
Freud H. (1956 [1973]), My Uncle Sigmund, in Ruitenbeek H. M. (ed.), *Freud as We Knew Him*, Wayne State University Press, Detroit.
Freud M. (1957), *Glory Reflected: Sigmund Freud–Man and Father*, Angus Robertson, London.
Freud M. (1958a), *Sigmund Freud - Man and Father*, J. Aronson, New York.
Freud M. (1958b), Freud: My father, in Ruitenbeek H. M., ed. (1973), *Freud as we knew him*, Wayne State Univ. Press, Detroit.
Freud S. (1893), The Psychotherapy of Hysteria from Studies on Hysteria, *The Standard Edition of the Complete Psychological Works of Sigmund Freud*, 2:253–305.
Freud S. (1895 [1950]), Project for a Scientific Psychology, *SE*, 1:281–391.
Freud S. (1899 [1941]), Appendix A Premonitory Dream Fulfilled, *SE*, 4:623–625.
Freud S. (1900), The Interpretation of Dreams, *SE*, 4:ix–627.
Freud S. (1901), The Psychopathology of Everyday Life, *SE*, 6:vii–296.
Freud S. (1905a), Fragment of an Analysis of a Case of Hysteria, *SE*, 7:1–122.
Freud S. (1905b), Three Essays on the Theory of Sexuality, *SE*, 7:123–246.
Freud S. (1905c), Jokes and Their Relation to the Unconscious, *SE*, 8:1–247.
Freud S. (1907), Delusions and Dreams in Jensen's Gradiva, *SE*, 9:1–96.
Freud S. (1908), Creative Writers and Day-Dreaming, *SE*, 9:141–154.

Freud S. (1909), Notes upon a Case of Obsessional Neurosis, *SE*, 10:151–318.

Freud S. (1910), The Antithetical Meaning of Primal Words, *SE*, 11:153–162.

Freud S. (1911), Formulations on the Two Principles of Mental Functioning, *SE*, 12:213–226.

Freud S. (1912a), Recommendations to Physicians Practising Psycho-Analysis, *SE*, 12:109–120.

Freud S. (1912b), A Note on the Unconscious in Psycho-Analysis, *SE*, 12:255–266.

Freud S. (1912c), On the Universal Tendency to Debasement in the Sphere of Love, *SE*, 11:177–190.

Freud S. (1913a), On Beginning the Treatment, *SE*, 12:121–144.

Freud S. (1913b), The Disposition to Obsessional Neurosis, *SE*, 12:311–326.

Freud S. (1914b), On Narcissism: An Introduction, *SE*, 14:67–102.

Freud S. (1915a), Instincts and Their Vicissitudes, *SE*, 14:109–140.

Freud S. (1915b), *A Phylogenetic Fantasy: An Overview of the Transference Neuroses*, Grubrich-Simitis I. (ed.). Harvard University Press, Cambridge.

Freud S. (1915c), Repression, *SE*, 14:141–158.

Freud S. (1915d), Thoughts for the Times on War and Death, *SE*, 14:273–300.

Freud S. (1915e), The Unconscious, *SE*, 14:159–215.

Freud S. (1916), On Transience, *SE*, 14:303–307.

Freud S. (1916–17), Introductory Lectures on Psycho-Analysis, *SE*, 15:1–463.

Freud S. (1917a), A Childhood Recollection from Dichtung Und Wahrheit, *SE*, 17:145–156.

Freud S. (1917b), A Metapsychological Supplement to the Theory of Dreams, *SE*, 14:217–235.

Freud S. (1917c), Mourning and Melancholia, *SE*, 14:237–258.

Freud S. (1918a), From the History of an Infantile Neurosis, *SE*, 17:1–124.

Freud S. (1918b), The Taboo of Virginity, *SE*, 11:191–208.

Freud S. (1919a), The "Uncanny," *SE*, 17:217–256.

Freud S. (1919b), A Child Is Being Beaten, *SE*, 17:175–204.

Freud S. (1919c), Lines of Advance in Psycho-Analytic Therapy, *SE*, 17:157–168.

Freud S. (1920), Beyond the Pleasure Principle, *SE*, 18:1–64.

Freud S. (1921a), Group Psychology and the Analysis of the Ego, *SE*, 18:65–144.

Freud S. (1921 [1941]), Psycho-Analysis and Telepathy, (*Vorbericht*) *SE*, 18:173–194.

Freud S. (1921 [2010]), *Nachtrag*, in Pierri M. (2010), Coincidences in Analysis: Sigmund Freud and the Strange Case of Dr. Forsyth and Herr von Vorsicht, *Int. J. Psycho-Anal.*, 91:745–772.

Freud S. (1922a), Dreams and Telepathy, *S.E.*, 18:195–220.

Freud S. (1922b), Some Neurotic Mechanisms in Jealousy, Paranoia and Homosexuality, *SE*, 18:221–232.

Freud S. (1923a), The Ego and the Id, *SE*, 19:1–66.

Freud S. (1923b), A Seventeenth-Century Demonological Neurosis, *SE*, 19:67–106.

Freud S. (1923d), Remarks on the Theory and Practice of Dream Interpretation', *SE*, 19:107–122.

Freud S. (1924), Letter to Fritz Wittels, *SE*, 19:286–288.

Freud S. (1925a), Some Additional Notes on Dream-Interpretation as a Whole, *SE*, 19:123–138.

Freud S. (1925b), Negation, *SE*, 19:233–240.

Freud S. (1925c), Some Additional Notes on Dream-Interpretation as a Whole, *SE*, 19:123–138.

Freud S. (1926), Inhibitions, Symptoms and Anxiety, *SE*, 20:75–176.

Freud S. (1927), The Future of an Illusion, *SE*, 21:1–56.

Freud S. (1933), New Introductory Lectures on Psycho-Analysis, *SE*, 22:1–182.

Freud S. (1934), Zum Problem der Telepatie, *Almanach der Psychoanalyse*, 9–34. https://archive.org/.

Freud S. (1937), Constructions in Analysis, *SE*, 23:255–270.

Freud S. (1988), *My Three Mothers and Other Passions*, Univ. Press, New York, London.

Freud S. (2007), *Living in the Shadow of the Freud Family*, Praeger, Westport, CT.

Freud S. (2016), *Telepatia*, Luchetti A. (ed.), BUR Rizzoli, Milano.

Fromm E. (1959), *Sigmund Freud's Mission*, Peter Smith, New York.

Gabbard G. O. (1995), The Early History of Boundary Violations in Psychoanalysis, *J.A.P.A.*, 43, 1115–1136.

Gaddini E. (1962), Sui fenomeni costitutivi del contro-transfert, *Riv. Psicoanal.*, 2:97–118.

Galsworthy J. (1906 [1994]), *The Forsyte Saga the Man of Property*, Wordsworth Classics, Knoxville.

Gay P. (1988), *Freud: A Life for Our Time*, Anchor Book, New York, London.

Gebert K. (2004 [2011]), *Un secolo in dieci giorni*, Feltrinelli, Milano.

Gillespie W. (1979), Ernest Jones: The Bonny Fighter, *Int. J. Psycho-Anal.*, 60:273–279.

Giovannetti M. de F. (1997), The Scene and Its Reverse: Considerations on a Chain of Associations in Freud, in Spector Person E. (ed.), *On Freud's A Child Is Being Beaten*, Yale University Press, New Haven and London.

Glover E. (1927–28), Lectures on Technique in Psycho-Analysis, *Int. J. Psycho-Anal.*, 8:311–338, 486–520; 9:7–46, 181–218.

Goleman D. (1985), Freud's Mind: New Details Revealed in Documents, *New York Times*, 12 November, pp. C1, C3.

Goodnick B. (1994), A Childhood Letter of Sigmund Freud, *Psychoanal. Psychology*, 11 (4):537–543.

Graf M. (1942), Reminiscences of Professor Sigmund Freud, *Psychoanal. Q.*, 11:465–476.

Granoff W. (2000), *Lacan, Ferenczi et Freud*, Gallimard, Paris.

Granoff W., Rey J. M. (1983), *L'occulte, objet de la pensée freudienne*, PUF, Paris.

Gresser M. (1994), *Dual Allegiance: Freud as a Modern Jew*, State University of New York Press, New York.

Grosskurth P. (1991), *The Secret Ring: Freud's Inner Circle and the Politics of Psycho-analysis*, Cape, London.

Grotjahn M. (1974), The Rundbriefe between Sigmund Freud and the Committee during the Years 1920–1924, *Annual of Psychoanal*, 2:24–39.

Grotstein J. S. (2005), "Projective Transidentification": An Extension of the Concept of Projective Identification, *Int. J. Psycho-Anal.*, 86:1051–1069.

Grubrich Simitis I. (1981), Siegfried Bernfeld: Historiker der Psychoanalyse und Freud-Biograph, *Psyche – Z Psychoanal*, 35 (5):397–434.

Grubrich Simitis I. (1993a), Einblicke in Sigmund Freuds Manuskripte; Das Kapitel Psychoanalyse und Telepathie, *Bull. Wiener Psychoanal. Verein.*, 1:25–47 (*Anna Freud lecture*, Wien 1992).

Grubrich Simitis I. (1993b [1996]), *Back to Freud's Texts*, Yale University Press, New Haven and London.

Grubrich Simitis I. (2000), Metamorphoses of the Interpretation of Dreams: Freud's Conflicted Relations with His Book of the Century, *Int. J. Psycho-Anal.*, 81:1155–1183.

Grubrich Simitis I., Lortholary B. (2012), Germes de concepts psychanalytiques fondamentaux. À propos des lettres de fiancés de Sigmund Freud et Martha Bernays, *Revue franç. Psychanal.*, 3 (76):779–795.

Gutiérrez Pelàez M. (2013), Sàndor Ferenczi y la intelectualidad hùngara del siglo XX, *Affectio Societatis*, 10 (18/junio).

Hannah B. (1976), *Jung: His Life and Work (A Biographical Memoir)*. Michael Joseph, London.

Hartman F. R. (1983), A Reappraisal of the Emma Episode and the Specimen Dream, *J. Amer. Psychoanal. Assn.*, 31:555–585.

Haynal A. (1992 [1993]), Introduzione, in *Freud S. e Ferenczi S. (1908–1914). Lettere*, Vol. I., Cortina, Milano.

Hellmann I. (1980), Contribution Read during the Memorial Meeting at The Hampstead Clinic, *Bulletin Anna Freud Centre*, 3:79–83.

Hidas G. (1993 [1998]), Fluttuazione: Transfert, Controtransfert, Telepatia, in Aron L., Harris H. (eds.), *L'eredità di Sándor Ferenczi*, Borla, Roma.

Hitschmann E. (1924), Telepathy and Psycho-Analysis, *Int. J. Psycho-Anal.*, 5:425–438.

Hollòs I. (1933), Psychopathologie alltäglicher telepathischer Erscheinungen1, *Imago*, 19 (4):529–546.

Houdini H. (1906 [2020]), *The Right Way to Do Wrong: An Exposé of Successful Criminals*, Nabu Press.

Houssier F. (1992), *Anna Freud, Lettres à Eva Rosenfeld (1919–1937)*, Hachette, Paris.

Houssier F. (2009), À partir de l'analyse d'Anna Freud par son père: reflets théoriques dans la construction d'une théorie psychanalytique de l'adolescence, *Recherche en psychanalyse*, 8:253–264.

Houssier F. (2011), S. Freud et son Antigone: adolescence et liens de mutualité théoriques, *Topique*, 2:17–32.

Hutchings E. G. (1917), *Jap Herron: A Novel Written from the Ouija Board*, by M. Twain (Spirit), Mitchell Kennerley, New York, https://archive.org/.

Janet P. (1913 [2004]), *La psychanalyse de Freud*, L'Harmattan, Paris.

Jones E. (1910), On the Nightmare, *Am. J. Insanity*, 66:383–417.

Jones E. (1912), *Der Alptraum in Seiner Beziehung zu Gewissen Formen des Mittelälterlichen Aberglaubens*, Hanse, Leipzig, Vienna.

Jones E. (1916), Functional Nervous Disease, *Lancet*, 187 (4828):588–589.

Jones E. (1922), The Technique of Psycho-Analysis: By David Forsyth, *Int. J. Psycho-Anal.*, 3:224–227.

Jones E. (1931a), *On the Nightmare*, Grove Press Inc., London, New York.

Jones E. (1931b), *The Elements of Figure Skating*, Methuen, London.

Jones E. (1945), Reminiscent Notes on the Early History of Psycho-Analysis in English-Speaking Countries, *Int. J. Psycho-Anal.*, 26:8–10.

Jones E. (1953), *Sigmund Freud Life and Work I*, Hogarth Press, London.

Jones E. (1955), *Sigmund Freud Life and Work II*, Hogarth Press, London.

Jones E. (1956), Our Attitude Toward Greatness, *J. Amer. Psychoanal. Assn.*, 4:626–643.

Jones E. (1957), *Sigmund Freud Life and Work III*, Hogarth Press, London.

Jones E. (1959), *Free Associations Memories of a Psycho-Analyst*, Basic Books, New York.

Jones K. (1979), A Sketch of E. J.'s Personality, *Int. J. Psycho-Anal.*, 60:271–273.

Jones M. (1958), Ernest Jones: Funeral Addresses, *Int. J. Psycho-Anal.*, 39:304–307.

Jones M. (1959), Epilogue, in Jones E. (ed.), *Free Associations Memories of a Psycho-Analyst*, Basic Books, New York.

Jung C. G. (1920), The Psychological Foundations of Belief in Spirits, in *The Collected Works of C. G. Jung*, 8. Princeton University Press, Princeton.

Jung C. G. (1952), Synchronicity: An Acasual Connecting Principle, in *The Collected Works of C. G. Jung*, 8. Princeton University Press, Princeton.

Kamieniak J. P. (2000), Freud: un enfant de l'humour? Delachaux Lausanne.

Kamieniak J. P. (2016), My Name Is Sigmund Freud. Freud, le nom et l'identité, *Le Coq-Héron*, 224:138–150.

Karinthy F. (1929), *Chain-Links*, https://djjr-courses.wdfiles.com/local-files/soc180%3Akarinthy-chain-links/Karinthy-Chain-Links_1929.pdf.

Kerr J. (1993), *A Most Dangerous Method: The Story of Jung, Freud, and Sabina Spielrein* Random House, New York.

Kluzer Usuelli A. (1999), Dall'analisi reciproca di Ferenczi all'analisi interattiva, in Borgogno F. (ed.), *La partecipazione affettiva dell'analista*, Angeli, Milano.

Kovács V. (1936), Training- and Control-Analysis, *Int. J. Psycho-Anal.*, 17:346–354.

Kress-Rosen, N. (1993), *Trois figures de la passion*, Springer/Arcanes, Paris.

Kris E. (1950), Introduction, to Freud S. (1950) *The Origins of Psychoanalysis: Letters to Wilhelm Fliess, Drafts and Notes from the Years 1887–1902*, in Bonaparte M., Freud A., Kris E. (eds.), London: Imago Publishing Co.

Krüll M. (1979 [1986]), *Freud and His Father*, W W Norton & Co Inc.

Kuhn P. (1999), A Professor Through the Looking-Glass: Contending Narratives of Freud's Relationships with the Sisters Bernays, *Int. J. Psychoanal.*, 80:943–959.

Lacan J. (1955), La chose freudienne ou sens du retour à Freud en psychanalyse, *Évol. Psychiatrique*, 1956:225–252.

Laforgue R. (1956 [1973]), Personal Memories of Freud, in Ruitenbeek H. M. (ed.), *Freud as We Knew Him*, Wayne State University Press, Detroit.

Laplanche J. (1997), The Theory of Seduction and the Problem of the Other, *Int. J. Psycho-Anal.*, 78:643–666.

Lavaggetto M. (1985 [2001]), *Freud, la letteratura e altro*, Einaudi, Torino.

Lebovici S. (1995), Quelques Propos D'un Psychanalyste Sur Les Controverses Concernant Les Découvertes Freudiennes Sur L'inceste et L'oedipe, in Gabel M., Lebovici S., Mazet P. (eds.), *Le Traumatisme de L'inceste*, Presses Universitaires de France, Paris.

Leupold-Löwenthal H. (1985), La psicoanalisi a Vienna, in AA. VV. (ed.), *La cultura psicoanalitica*, Studio Tesi, Pordenone.

Leupold-Löwenthal H. (1989), Die Vertreibung der Familie Freud 1938, *Psyche–Z Psychoanal.*, 43:918–928.

Levi Della Torre S. (1995), *Essere fuori luogo*, Donzelli, Roma.

Lodge O. (1924), Report on Telepathy Experiments with Professor Murray, *Proceedings of the Society for Psychical Research*, December.

Lopez D. (1991), *Il mondo della persona*, Cortina, Milano.

Lopez D. (2001), Thanatos/Eros, Sé Luciferino/volontà consapevole, in Pierri M. (ed.), *Qui e ora . . . con me*, Bollati Boringhieri, Torino.

Lopez D. (2007), *Schegge di sapienza, frammenti di saggezza, e un po' di follia*, Angelo Colla, Vicenza.

Lopez D., Zorzi L. (2005), *Narcisismo e amore*, Angelo Colla, Vicenza.

Lowtzky F. (1926), Eine okkultistische Bestätigung der Psychoanalyse, *Imago*, 12 (1):70–87.

Lowtzky F. (1928), Zur Psychologie des Okkultismus: Bruck C.: Experimentelle Telepathie Neue Versuche zur telepathischen Übertragung von Zeichnungen, *Imago*, 14:536–537.

Maddox B. (2006), *Freud's Wizard: Ernest Jones and the Transformation of Psychoanalysis*, Da Capo Press, Cambridge.

Magris C. (1986 [2001]), *Danube*, The Harvill Press, London.

Mahony P. J. (1997), A Child Is Being Beaten: A Clinical History, and Textual Study, in Spector Person E. (ed.), *On Freud's A Child Is Being Beaten*, Yale University Press, New Haven and London.

Malcolm J. (1983), *In the Freud Archives*, Review Books, New York.

Mann T. (1924 [1929]), An Experience in the Occult, in *Three Essays*, Knopf, New York.

Mann T. (1930 [1996]), *Mario and the Magician: & Other Stories*, Vintage, London.

Marchioro F. (2002–2003), Sigmund Freud – Otto (Rosenfeld) Rank. Un'amicizia del tutto particolare, 2010, www.psychomedia.it/.

Marinelli L. (2009a), Fort, DA: The Cap in the Museum, *Psychoanal. Hist.*, 11:116–120.

Marinelli L. (2009b), Body Missing at Berggasse 19, *Amer. Imago*, 66:161–167.

Marinelli L., Mayer A. (2002), *Dreaming By the Book*, Other Press, New York, 2003.

Martín-Cabré L. (1999), Il contributo di Ferenczi al concetto di controtransfert, in Borgogno F. (ed.), *La partecipazione affettiva dell'analista*, Franco Angeli, Milan.

Massicotte C. (2014), Psychical Transmissions: Freud, Spiritualism, and the Occult, *Psychoanal. Dial.*, 24:88–102.

Masson J. M. (1984), *The Assault on Truth: Freud's Suppression of Seduction Theory*, Farrar, Strauss & Giroux, New York.

Masson J. M. (1985a), *The Complete Letters of Sigmund Freud to Wilhelm Fliess, 1887–1904*, Belknap, Cambridge, MA, 1–13.

Masson J. M. (1985b), Introduction to *The Complete Letters of Sigmund Freud to Wilhelm Fliess, 1887–1904*, Belknap, Cambridge, MA, 1–13.

May U. (2007), Freud's Patient Calendars: 17 Analysts in Analysis with Freud (1910–1920), *Psychoanal. Hist.*, 9 (2):153–200.

May U. (2019), Willy Haas: Ein junger Münchner Philosoph in Analyse bei Freud, *Luzifer-Amor: Zeitschrift zur Geschichte der Psychoanalyse*, 32:35–57.

McDougall J. (1989), *Theaters of the Body*, Free Association Books, London.

Meltzer D. (1992 [2008]), *The Claustrum*, Karnac Books, London.

Menninger K. A. (1958), *Theory of Psychoanalytic Technique*, Basic Books, New York, https://archive.org/details/theoryofpsychoan00menn.

Milgram S. (1967), The Small-World Problem, *Psychology Today*, 1:61–67.

Miller A. I. (2009), *Jung, Pauli, and the Pursuit of a Scientific Obsession*, W. W. Norton & Company, New York.

Modell A. H. (1990), *Other Times, Other Realities: Toward a Theory of Psychoanalytic Treatment*, Harvard University Press, Cambridge, MA.

Modell A. H. (1997), Humiliating Fantasies and the Pursuit of Unpleasure, in Spector Person E. (ed.), *On Freud's a Child Is Being Beaten*, Yale University Press, New Haven and London.

Moll A. (1924), *Der Spiritismus*, Franckh'sche Verlagshandlung, Stuttgart.

Molnar M. (1992), *Sigmund Freud, Chronique la plus brève. Carnets intimes 1929–1939*, Albin Michel, Paris.

Molnar M. (2014), *Looking through Freud's Photos*, Karnac Books, London.

Molnar M., Luchetti A. (2009), Note alla "Cronaca minima" del 1938, *Rivista Psicoanal.*, 55 (3):623–662.

Moreau C. (1976), *Freud et l'occultisme: l'approche freudienne du spiritisme, de la divination, de la magie et de la telepathie*, Edouard Privat, Toulouse.

Musatti C. (1976a), Introduzione, *OSF*, 8:IX–XVIII.

Musatti C. (1976b), Avvertenza editoriale, *OSF*, 8:3–12.

Musil R. (1921–43 [1966]), *The Man without Qualities*, Coward – McCann.

Myers C. S. (1915), Contribution to the Study of Shell Shock, *The Lancet*, 185:316–330.

Nestler V. (1974), *La Telepatia. Fenomenologia, ipotesi*, Ed. Mediterranee, Roma.

Nietzsche F. (1883–85 [2006]), *Thus Spoke Zarathustra*, Cambridge University Press, Cambridge.

Nissim Momigliano L. (1987), A Spell in Vienna–But Was Freud a Freudian?, *Int. R. Psycho-Anal.*, 14:373–389.

Novick J., Novick K. K. (1997), Not for Barbarians: An Appreciation on Freud's a Child Is Being Beaten, in Spector Person E. (ed.), *On Freud's A Child Is Being Beaten*, Yale University Press, New Haven and London.

Nunberg H., Federn E. (Eds.) (1962–75), *Minutes of Vienna Psychoanalytic Society*, 4 vols, International University Press, Madison, CT.

Oatman-Stanford H. (2015), The Magician Who Astounded the World by Conjuring Spirits and Talking with Mummies, *Collectors Weekly* 5/05/15, www.collectorsweekly.com/.

Ogden T. H. (1993), *Projective Identification and Psychotherapeutic Technique*, Jason Aronson, North-vale, NJ.

Paskauskas R. A. (1993), Notes to Letter from Ernest Jones to Sigmund Freud, October 12, 1919, in *The Complete Correspondence of Sigmund Freud and Ernest Jones 1908–1939*, Harvard University Press, Cambridge, MA.

Paskauskas R. A. (1994), Ferenczi's Analysis of Jones in Relation to Jones' Self-Analysis, *Cahiers Psychiatriques Genevois*, Special Issue:225–255.

Pfeiffer E. (1972), Notes to Letter from Lou Andreas-Salomé to Freud, January 12, 1922, *Int. Psycho-Anal. Lib.*, 89:110–111.

Phillips A. (2001), *Houdini's Box: The Art of Escape*, Pantheon, New York.

Pierri M. (1994), Spazio e percorsi dell'esperienza, *Gli Argonauti*, 61:137–145.

Pierri M. (1997a), Coincidenza e fraintendimento: alle soglie della relazione, seminari del Centro Veneto e *XXX Seminari Multipli SPI*, Bologna.

Pierri M. (1997b), Coincidenza e fraintendimento: alle soglie della relazione, *Gli Argonauti*, 72:43–72.

Pierri M. (1998), "Un fil di fumo": l'impasse come sfida per la sopravvivenza, in Racalbuto A. (ed.), *Impasse e patologie narcisistiche*, Dunod-Masson, Milano.

Pierri M. (2001a), Trasmissione e generazione del sapere: le *tre scimmiette*, in Pierri M., Racalbuto A. (eds.), *Maestri e allievi. Trasmissione del sapere in psicoanalisi*, Angeli, Milano.

Pierri M. (2001b), Eredità e creatività nella tradizione, in Pierri M., Racalbuto A. (ed.), *Maestri e allievi. Trasmissione del sapere in psicoanalisi*, Angeli, Milano.

Pierri M. (2002), Coincidenze in analisi: il linguaggio segreto del setting e la sua psicopatologia quotidiana, *Incontro Italo Argentino*, S.P.I., A.P.A, Bologna.

Pierri M. (2006), Destino, transfert ed emancipazione, *Gli Argonauti*, 111:299–305.

Pierri M. (2008), Kairòs, il tempo propizio dell'incontro: coincidenze in psicoanalisi, *Gli Argonauti*, 118:229–237.

Pierri M. (2010), Coincidences in Analysis: Sigmund Freud and the Strange Case of Dr. Forsyth and Herr von Vorsicht, *Int. J. Psychoanal.*, 91:745–772.

Pierri M. (2012), Freud e le due profezie non avverate, *Gli Argonauti*, 135:305–320.

Pierri M. (2014), Freud al lavoro: rileggendo il caso del sig. Paul B. dalla Lezione XXX "Sogno e Occultismo," Incontro Veneto Emiliano S.P.I.

Pierri M. (2016a), Una lontana vicinanza, ovvero la moneta d'oro della telepatia, introduzione a S. Freud (2016), *Telepatia*, BUR Rizzoli, Milano.

Pierri M. (2016b [2020]), Costruzioni vive: il compiersi dell'evento in analisi, *VII Colloquio* del C.V.P., Venezia, in Pierri M., Costantini M. V. (eds.), *Transfert di vita*, Angeli, Milano.

Pierri M. (2021), 1921, un anniversario freudiano poco conosciuto: Vorbericht-Nachtrag, il "saggio segreto" dello Harz sul transfert del pensiero, *Riv Psicoanalisi*, LXVII (3):597–616.

Pierri M. (2022), *Occultism and the Origins of Psychoanalysis: Freud, Ferenczi and he Challenge of Thought transference*.

Pragier G., Faure Pragier S. (1993), Une fille est analisée: Anna Freud, *Rev. franç. Psychoanal.*, 2:447–457.

Press J. (2006), Constructing the Truth, *Int. J. Psycho-Anal.*, 87 (2):519–536.

Proulx C. (1994), On Jung's Theory of Ethics, *J. Anal. Psychol.*, 39 (1):101–119.

Quinodoz J. M. (1997), *A Child Is Being Beaten* A Seminar with Candidates from Perspective of Contemporary Psychoanalysis, in Spector Person E. (ed.), *On Freud's "A Child Is Being Beaten,"* Yale University Press, New Haven and London.

Rachman A. Wm. (2003), Freud's Analysis of His Daughter Anna: A Confusion of Tongues, in Roland A., Ulanov B., Babre C. (eds.), *Creative Dissident: Psychoanalysis in Evolution*, Praeger, Westport, CT, 59–71.

Radó S. (1927), German Psycho-Analytical Society, *Int. J. Psycho-Anal.*, 8:305–307.

Rank O. (1924 [1993]), *The Trauma of Birth*, Dover Publications, New York.

Reich W. (1952 [1970]), *Reich speaks of Freud parla di Freud*, Sugarco, Milano.

Rhine J. B. (1949 [1972]), Storia delle prime ricerche, in Guarino S. (ed.), *Telepatia di ieri, di oggi, di domani*, IEM, Napoli.

Rhine J. B. (1964), Extra-Sensory Perception. Branden pub.

Richet C. (1922), *Thirty Years of Psychical Research: A Treatise on Metapsychics 1923*, The Macmillan Company, New York, https://archive.org/details/30YearsRichet.

Riolo F. (2015), Teoria delle trasformazioni: un modello di campo, 12 dicembre, Centro Veneto Psicoanalisi.

Riviere J. (1921–22), Book review: D. Forsyth, *The Technique of Psychoanalysis, BJM*, 2:325–329.

Riviere J. (1939 [1973]), An Intimate Impression, in Ruitenbeek H. M. (ed.), *Freud as We Knew Him*, Wayne State University Press, Detroit.

Roazen P. (1969), *Brother Animal: The Story of Freud and Tausk*, Knopf, NewYork.

Roazen P. (1975), *Freud and His Followers*, Knopf, NewYork.

Roazen P. (1993), *Meeting Freud's Family*, University of Massachusetts Press, Amherst.

Roazen P. (1995), *How Freud Worked: First-Hand Accounts of Patients*, J. Aronson, Northvale, NJ.

Roazen P. (1998), Elma Laurvik, Ferenczi's Stepdaughter, *Am. J. Psychoanal.*, 5:271–286.

Roazen P. (1999), Freud's Analysis of Anna, in Prince R. M. (ed.), *The Death of Psychoanalysis*, Aronson, London.

Roazen P. (2001a), Using Oral History about Freud: A Case in His "Secret Essay", *American Imago*, 58:793–812.

Roazen P. (2001b), *The Historiography of Psychoanalysis*, Transaction Pub., New Brunswick, London.

Roazen P. (2003), *On the Freud Watch: Public Memories*, F.A.b., London.

Roazen P. (2005), *Edoardo Weiss, the House That Freud Built*, Taylor & Francis, Lewes.

Rodrigué E. (1996), *Sigmund Freud: El Siglo Del Psicoanalisis*, Vol. 2, Editorial Sudamericana, Buenos Aires.

Rosenfeld H. A. (1987), *Impasse and Interpretation*, Routledge, London.

Roudinesco E. (2012 [2006]), Préface a *Sigmund Freud et Anna Freud Correspondance 1904–1938*, Fayard, Paris.

Roudinesco E. (2014 [2016]), *Freud in His Time and Ours*, Harvard University Press, Cambridge, MA.

Roussillon R. (1995 [1997]), *Il setting psicoanalitico*, Borla, Roma.

Roussillon R. (2016 [2020]), Ripetere per il piacere o ripetere per integrare, in Pierri M., Costantini M. V. (eds.), *Transfert di vita*, Angeli, Milano.

Rudnytsky P. L. (2013), Freud, Ferenczi, and Rosmersholm: Incestuous Triangles and Analytic Thirds, *Am. J. Psychoanal.*, 73:323–338.

Sachs H. (1945), *Freud: Master and Friend*, Imago Pub., London.

Sapisochin G. (2004), Dos tópicas, dos modelos freudianos de la escucha: ¿maldición o bendición?, *Revista de Psicoanálisis*, 41:77–94.

Sayers J. (1991), *Mothers of Psychoanalysis*, Norton Company, NewYork, London.

Scarfone D. (2014), *L'impassé, actualité de l'inconscient*, C.P.L.F., Montréal.

Scarpelli G. (2000a), "Raccomando a tutti la Gestapo." I destini della famiglia F., *Aperture*, 9:47–50.

Scarpelli G. (2000b), La lunga fuga di Oliver Freud, *Aperture*, 9:41–46.

Schur M. (1958), Ernest Jones 1879–1958, *Bull. Am. Psychoanal. Assn.*, 14:736–739.

Schur M. (1966), Some Additional 'Day Residues' of the Specimen Dream of Psychoanalysis, in Loewenstein R. M. et al. (eds.), *Psychoanalysis – A General Psychology*, International Universities Press, New York.

Schur M. (1972), *Freud: Living and Dying*, Hogarth Press and the Institute of Psycho-Analysis, London.

Semi A. A. (2009 [2010]), The Unconscious and the Limits of the Individual, *The Italian Psychoanalytic Annual*, 4:23–38.

Servadio E. (1930), *La Ricerca Psichica*, Cremonese, Roma.

Servadio E. (1955a), Le conditionnement transférentiel et contre-transférentiel des événements "psi" au cours de l'analyse, *Acta Psychother. Psychosom. et Orthopaedagogica*, 3 (S):656–661.

Servadio E. (1955b), A Presumptively Telepathic-Precognitive Dream During Analysis, *Int. J. Psycho-Anal.*, 36:27–30.

Servadio E. (1956), Freud et la parapsychologie, *Revue française de psychanalyse*, 20:432–438.

Servadio E. (1958 [1972]), Telepatia e psicoanalisi, in Guarino S. (ed.), *Telepatia di ieri, oggi domani*, I.E.M., Napoli.

Sinclair U. (1930 [2001]), *Mental Radio: Does It Work, and How?*, Hampton Road, Charlottesville.

Skues R. (2019a), Elfriede Hirschfeld: Freuds Großpatientin und Hauptplage neu betrachtet, *Luzifer-Amor*, 32:58–69.

Skues R. (2019b), Robert Eisler: Freuds Patient in seinen familiären Verstrickungen, *Luzifer-Amor*, 63:70–89.

Skues R. (2019c), Freuds Entzauberung der Telepathie. Analyse der Gedankenübertragung und die Geschichte eines unveröffentlichten Aufsatzes, *Luzifer-Amor*, 63:7–34.

Solnit A. J. (1996), Biography, *J. Amer. Psychoanal. Assn.*, 44:13–25.

Spector Person E. (1997), Introduction, in Spector Person E. (ed.), *On Freud's a Child Is Being Beaten*, Yale University Press, New Haven, London.

Spector Person E. S. (Ed.) (1997), *On Freud's a Child Is Being Beaten*, Yale University Press, New Haven, London.

Starobinski J. (1974), *Trois fureurs*, Gallimard, Paris.

Steiner R. (1991), To Explain Our Point of View to English Readers in English Words, *Int. Rev. Psycho-Anal.*, 18:351–392.

Steiner R. (2013), *Die Brautbriefe*: The Freud and Martha Correspondence, *Int. J. Psycho-Anal.*, 94 (5):863–936.

Steiner R. (2017), La haute mer ouverte, *L'alto mare aperto* – psychanalyse et traduction, *Psychanalyse en Europe, Bulletin FEP*, 71:45–74.

Stekel W. (1920), *Der Telepatiche Traum*, Johannes Baum, Berlin.

Stewart-Steinberg S. (2011), *Impious Fidelity: Anna Freud, Psychoanalysis, Politics*, Cornell University Press, Ithaca.

Strachey J. (1964), *The Standard Edition of the Complete Psychological Works of Sigmund Freud*, Vol. XXII (1932–1936), The Hogarth Press and the Institute of Psycho-Analysis, London.

Swales P. (1982 [1989]), Freud, Fliess, and Fratricide: The Role of Fliess in Freud's Conception of Paranoia. In Spurling L. (ed.), *Sigmund Freud: Critical Assessments, vol. 1*, Routledge, London, New York.

Swales P. (1998), In Statu Nascendi: Freud, Minna Bernays and the Creation of Herr Aliquis. *Lecture* for the History of Psychiatry Section, Cornell University Medical Center, New York Hospital, New York, 7 January, *Psicoterapia e Scienze Umane*, 31:67–101.

Székely J. (1949 [2020]), *Temptation*, New York Review of Books, New York.

Tausk V. (1919 [2017]), On the Origin of Influencing Machine in Schizophrenia, in *Sexuality, War, and Schizophrenia: Collected Psychoanalytic Papers*, Routledge, Abingdon, UK.

Theweleit K. (1990 [1994]), *Objet Choise: All You Need Is Love*, Verso, London, NY.

Tögel C. (1990), Bahnstation Treblinka. Zum Schicksal von Sigmund Freuds Schwester Rosa Graf, *Psyche – Z Psychoanal.*, 44:1019–1025.

Torok M. (1983 [1986]), What Is Occult in Occultism?, in Abraham N., Torok M. (eds.), *The Wolf Man's Magic Word: A Cryptonimy*, University of Minnesota Press, Minneapolis.

Trapanese G. (2012), Anna: "figlia d'oro," in A. A. (ed.), *Psicoanaliste il piacere di pensare*, Angeli, Milano.

Tustin F. (1981), *Autistic States in Children*, Routledge, London.

Varendonck J. (1921 [1922]), *The Psychology of Day-Dreams*, London, A. Freud trans., https://archive.org/.

Von Arnim E. (1917), *Christine (1917) By Alice Colmondeley* CreateSpace Independent Publishing Platform November 19, 2016.

Wallace E. R. (1980), A Commentary on the Freud-Jung Letters, *Psychoanalytic Review*, 67:111–137.

Weiss E. (1970), Sigmund Freud as a Consultant: Recollections of a Pioneer in Psychoanalysis.

Winnicott D. W. (1948), Reparation in Respect of Mother's Organized Defence against Depression, in (1975) *Through Paediatrics to Psycho-Analysis*, Tavistock, London.

Winnicott D. W. (1956), On Transference, *Int. J. Psycho-anal.*, 37:386–388.

Winnicott D. W. (1958 [1956]), Primary Maternal Preoccupation, in (1975) *Through Paediatrics to Psychoanalysis*, Tavistock, London.

Winnicott D. W. (1958a), Ernest Jones, *Int. J. Psycho-Anal.*, 39:298–304.

Winnicott D. W. (1958b), Ernest Jones: Funeral Addresses, *Int. J. Psycho-Anal.*, 39:304–307.

Winnicott D. W. (1963), Communicating and Not Communicating Leading to a Study of Certain Opposites, in (1965) *The Maturational Processes and the Facilitating Environment*, Hogarth Press, London, 64:1–276.

Winnicott D. W. (1964), Memories, Dreams, Reflections: By C. G. Jung, *Int. J. Psycho-Anal.*, 45:450–455.

Winnicott D. W. (1967a), Mirror-Role of Mother and Family in Child Development, in (1971) *Playing and Reality*, Tavistock, London.

Winnicott D. W. (1967b), Postscript: D.W.W. on D.W.W., in (1989), *Psycho-Analytic Explorations*, Karnac Books, London.

Winnicott D. W. (1969a), The Use of an Object, *I. J. Psychoanal*, 50:711–716.

Winnicott D. W. (1969b), James Strachey–1887–1967, *Int. J. Psycho-Anal.*, 50:129–131.

Winnicott D. W. (1971), *Playing and Reality*, Tavistock, London.

Winnicott D. W. (1989), *Psycho-Analytic Explorations*, Karnac, London.

Wittels F. (1924), *Sigmund Freud: Der Mann, die Lehre, die Schule*, Tal, Leipzig.

Yehoshua A. (2011 [2013]), *The Retrospective*, Houghton Mifflin Harcourt, Boston.

Young-Bruehl E. (1988), *Anna Freud: A Biography*, Yale University Press, New Haven, CT.

Young-Bruehl E. (1994), A History of Freud Biography, in Micale M. S., Porter R. (eds.), *Discovering the History of Psychiatry*, Univ. Press, Oxford.

Zambrano M. (1967), *La tumba de Antigona*, Alianza Editorial, Madrid, 2019.

Zaretsky E. (2004), *Secrets of the soul*, Alfred A. Knopf, New York.

Zorzi Meneguzzo L. (2010), Intermittenze dissociative: l'incubo, *Gli Argonauti*, 127:353–359.

Zweig S. (1942), *The World of Yesterday: Memories of a European*, Hallam Ed., London, 1953, http://archiv.org.

Index

For Product Safety Concerns and Information please contact our EU representative GPSR@taylorandfrancis.com
Taylor & Francis Verlag GmbH, Kaufingerstraße 24, 80331 München, Germany

www.ingramcontent.com/pod-product-compliance
Lightning Source LLC
Chambersburg PA
CBHW050631280326
41932CB00015B/2604

* 9 7 8 1 0 3 2 1 5 9 5 8 4 *